Clio in the Classroom

Clio in the Classroom

A Guide for Teaching U.S. Women's History

Edited by

CAROL BERKIN

MARGARET S. CROCCO

BARBARA WINSLOW

OXFORD
UNIVERSITY PRESS
2009

OXFORD
UNIVERSITY PRESS

Oxford University Press, Inc., publishes works that further
Oxford University's objective of excellence
in research, scholarship, and education.

Oxford   New York
Auckland   Cape Town   Dar es Salaam   Hong Kong   Karachi
Kuala Lumpur   Madrid   Melbourne   Mexico City   Nairobi
New Delhi   Shanghai   Taipei   Toronto

With offices in
Argentina   Austria   Brazil   Chile   Czech Republic   France   Greece
Guatemala   Hungary   Italy   Japan   Poland   Portugal   Singapore
South Korea   Switzerland   Thailand   Turkey   Ukraine   Vietnam

Copyright © 2009 by Oxford University Press, Inc.

Published by Oxford University Press, Inc.
198 Madison Avenue, New York, New York 10016

www.oup.com

Oxford is a registered trademark of Oxford University Press

Library of Congress Cataloging-in-Publication Data
Clio in the classroom : a guide for teaching U.S. women's history /
edited by Carol Berkin, Margaret S. Crocco, and Barbara Winslow.
   p. cm.
Includes bibliographical references and index.
ISBN 978-0-19-532012-1; 978-0-19-532013-8 (pbk.)
1. Women's studies—United States.   2. Women—History—Study
and teaching (secondary)—United States.   3. Women—History—
Study and teaching (higher)—United States.
I. Berkin, Carol.   II. Crocco, Margaret.   III. Winslow, Barbara, 1945–
HQ1181.U5C49 2009
305.4071'073—dc22   2008019389

Printed in the United States of America
on acid-free paper

To the women who made history
and
the teachers who bring it into the classroom every day

Acknowledgments

We would like to thank our agent, Dan Green, who helped bring the concept into reality as a book; Susan Ferber, our editor at Oxford University Press, who recognized the importance of both women in history and the history of women; and Jennifer Cutsforth, who provided exemplary assistance in bringing the project to completion.

Contents

Contributors

Erica L. Ball is an Assistant Professor in the American Studies Department at California State University, Fullerton. She teaches a variety of courses on race in American culture and is currently working on a book manuscript titled *Mothers and Fathers of the Race: The Cultural Origins of the Black Middle Class.*

Carol Berkin is Presidential Professor of History at Baruch College and the Graduate Center of the City University of New York. She is the author of several books on the Revolution and the Early Republic, including *First Generations: Women in Colonial America; A Brilliant Solution: Inventing the American Constitution;* and *Revolutionary Mothers: Women in the Struggle for America's Independence,* and coeditor of *Looking Forward/Looking Back: A Women's Studies Reader.* She is currently working on a book on women in the Civil War. She has appeared in numerous history documentaries on PBS, The History Channel, A&E, and the Discovery Channel. She serves on the boards of the National Council for History Education, The Brooklyn Historical Society, and the Gilder Lehrman Institute of American History.

Christine L. Compston has written a young adult biography of Chief Justice Earl Warren and coedited *Holmes & Frankfurter: Their Correspondence, 1912–1934.* She is currently serving as Special Assistant for Undergraduate Initiatives at Western Washington University.

MARGARET S. CROCCO is Professor and Coordinator of the Program in Social Studies at Teachers College, Columbia University. She is coauthor of *Pedagogies of Resistance: Women Educator Activists, 1880–1960* and *Learning to Teach in an Age of Accountability* and coeditor of *"Bending the Future to Their Will": Civic Women, Social Education, and Democracy* and *Social Education in the Twentieth Century: Curriculum and Context for Citizenship*. She taught American history and women's studies at the high school and college levels before coming to Teachers College.

ANNE M. DEROUSIE and VIVIEN E. ROSE are the Historian and Chief of Cultural Resources, respectively, at the Women's Rights National Historical Park in Seneca Falls and Waterloo, New York. The park preserves the homes of the organizers of the 1848 First Women's Rights Convention and the Wesleyan Chapel in which it was held. Rose and Derousie have forty years of experience in teaching history through artifacts, historic structures, and cultural landscapes.

VIRGINIA G. DRACHMAN is the Arthur and Lenore Stern Professor of American History at Tufts University. She is the author of *Enterprising Women: 250 Years of American Business; Sisters in Law: Women Lawyers in Modern American History; Women Lawyers and the Origins of Professional Identity in America: The Letters of the Equity Club, 1887–1890*; and *Hospital with a Heart: Women Doctors and the Paradox of Separatism at the New England Hospital, 1862–1969*.

MARY E. FREDERICKSON is Professor in History and Women's Studies at Miami University of Ohio. She has published on women's workplace activism and resistance in the United States. A specialist in oral history and memory, her current research is on "Memory and Desire in the Lives of American Women Abroad."

MICHAEL LEWIS GOLDBERG is Associate Professor in the Interdisciplinary Arts and Sciences program at the University of Washington, Bothell. He is the author of *An Army of Women: Gender and Politics in Gilded Age Kansas* and *Breaking New Ground: American Women, 1800–1848*. His current research focuses on the scholarship of teaching and learning in history, composition, and film studies.

LINDA LEVSTIK is Professor in the Department of Curriculum and Instruction at the University of Kentucky, Lexington. Her primary research interests focus on the development of children's and adolescents' historical understanding, nationally and internationally. She is coauthor with Keith C. Barton of *Doing*

History, Teaching History for the Common Good, and *Researching History Teaching and Learning* and coeditor with Cynthia Tyson of *Handbook of Research in Social Studies Education*.

CINDY R. LOBEL is Assistant Professor of History at Lehman College, City University of New York. Her research interests include nineteenth-century U.S. history, urban history, consumer culture, and gender. She is currently completing a manuscript about food and the rise of a consumer culture in nineteenth-century New York City.

CHRISTY REGENHARDT is Assistant Editor on the Eleanor Roosevelt Papers Project at George Washington University. She received her PhD in history from the University of Maryland, College Park, in 2006.

JENNIFER SCANLON is Professor and Director of the Gender and Women's Studies Program at Bowdoin College in Maine. She teaches and writes on women's history and popular and consumer culture. Her most recent work, a biography of Helen Gurley Brown, is forthcoming with Oxford University Press.

NICHOLAS L. SYRETT is Assistant Professor of History at the University of Northern Colorado and author of the forthcoming *The Company He Keeps: A History of White College Fraternities, Masculinity, and Power*.

REBECCA TANNENBAUM is Lecturer in the History Department, Women's, Gender, and Sexuality Studies Department, and History of Science and Medicine Department at Yale University. She is the author of *The Healer's Calling: Women and Medicine in Early New England*.

RONALD G. WALTERS is Professor of History at Johns Hopkins University. His teaching and research focus primarily on the history of nineteenth- and twentieth-century reform movements and on commercial popular culture.

TRACEY WEIS is Associate Professor in the Department of History at Millersville University. She also coordinates the university's Women's Studies Program.

BARBARA WELTER has a PhD in history from the University of Wisconsin and is Professor of History at Hunter College and the Graduate Center, City University of New York. She has written on the history of women and religion in the United States and edited *The Woman's Bible*. She is working on a book on the concept of "mission" in nineteenth-century America.

BARBARA WINSLOW, former Coordinator of the Women's Studies Program at Brooklyn College, City University of New York, is Associate Professor in the School of Education there. She is the author of *Sylvia Pankhurst: Sexual Politics and Political Activism,* plus a number of memoirs, articles, and book chapters on women's suffrage and the women's liberation movement. She is currently writing a book about the women's movement in Seattle, Washington, and compiling the Shirley Chisholm Archive of Brooklyn Women's Activism to be housed at Brooklyn College.

Clio in the Classroom

Introduction

Over the last thirty years, women's history has experienced great growth within the academy. Countless books, journal articles, and conferences on women's history in the United States and around the world have accompanied measurable progress in women's rights, visibility, and educational and professional achievement, both in the United States and elsewhere. A solid preparation in women's history is now critical for history teachers and professors to enable them to present an accurate and inclusive version of American history.[1]

Our major goal in this book is to offer history instructors at the high school and college levels the key content, concepts, and teaching strategies that have proven successful in teaching this subject to students. *Clio in the Classroom: A Guide to Teaching U.S. Women's History* is intended as an introduction to contemporary themes, issues, questions, debates, strategies, and resources for instructors teaching survey courses in U.S. history and U.S. women's history or electives dealing with related topics.

The essays in this book move beyond the notion of women's history as a compendium of "firsts," with an emphasis on chronicling women's entry into male fields. Women's history presented in terms of women's "contributions" is still found in many textbooks. "Contribution history" has an understandable appeal and has produced some positive results: Most schoolchildren now recognize the names of women like Abigail Adams, Susan B. Anthony, and Rosa Parks. This way of doing women's history, however, misses much: how women lived their lives, how their activities were—or were not—shaped by expectations about what a woman should be, do, and become, and how ideas about what it means to be a man or a woman circulated, were enforced, and were resisted during each historical period. Women's history should do more than add women to traditional male stories. Ultimately, it changes the story of the American past, challenging facile conclusions reached by leaving out half the population.

Invoking the notion of gender, which gets at the social construction of men's and women's identities and their relatedness to each other, signals one of the ways in which the field of women's history has changed over the last twenty years. Certain periods of American history have been notable for magnifying the differences between men and women and for producing change in gender prescriptions. Studying gender in history, however, is not the same as studying women's history, although the two are clearly related. Although we recognize the contributions made by gender studies—an interdisciplinary field—to women's history, we limit our scope in this book to women's history, providing readers with an overview of American women's history at the beginning of the book and, in subsequent sections, more innovative ways of conceptualizing and teaching it at secondary and college levels.

Women's history is firmly established at the college level today; nevertheless, it has made fewer inroads into the K-12 curriculum. Various reasons account for this situation, too numerous to mention here. It is the editors' hope that *Clio in the Classroom* will assist teachers who recognize the importance of women's history and want to find ways to get it into the curriculum, despite the challenges, chief among them being the startling lack of coverage of women's history in many high school American history textbooks.[2] Individuals committed to telling a story of this nation's past that includes both women and men often find ways to introduce the subject into their curriculum, not only in women's history month.

This book was born out of collaboration, as are many achievements associated with women's history. Collaborations across difference can be particularly productive. As editors, we come from distinct yet complementary places in the academy: Carol Berkin is a historian of the eighteenth century and women's history who teaches at a public university. Margaret Crocco is a professor of social studies education teaching at a private graduate school of education, who spent eight years in a secondary classroom teaching women's history. Barbara Winslow is a former coordinator of the Women's Studies Program at a public institution, with responsibilities for social studies education and a personal history of involvement in the radical women's movement. From the start, our motivation has been to provide a forum for showcasing both how to conceptualize and how to teach women's history. We conceived of our primary audience as instructors at the secondary and college levels who were not specialists in women's history but were interested in incorporating the subject into their courses, as well as their students and anyone else interested in women's history.

The book does not aim at presenting up-to-date research or a comprehensive historiography concerning topics in women's history; other works do that admirably well. We asked contributors, all of whom are experts on their chapters' topics, to consider how the addition of women's history would alter and enrich the teaching of U.S. history. It is this sort of integration of women's history into the traditional American history narrative that provides, in our judgment, an exciting way to move beyond the "contributions" approach. This is not to say that teachers of women's history as a stand-alone course will not benefit from this book. We simply recognized that more people teach the U.S. history survey course than teach specialized courses on women, and we wanted to accommodate both audiences simultaneously.

We tried to keep in mind the needs of teachers and their students, especially the different contexts in which readers might be situated. For new teachers and individuals preparing to teach, this book serves as an introduction to teaching women's history. For experienced teachers at the college and university levels, the ideas proposed here offer new ways of thinking about familiar topics. For instructors and students in social studies courses in schools of education, the book provides needed content, along with pedagogical approaches that can be incorporated into methods courses or tried out in student teaching placements. For high school teachers, the book offers a solid synthesis of U.S. women's history that has utility for an American history survey, elective, or advanced placement course.

Clio in the Classroom begins with three chapters in part I that provide a comprehensive review of U.S. women's history since the nation's founding. Part II comprises nine chapters analyze important concepts and themes related to teaching U.S. women's history. Part III provides five pedagogically oriented chapters, and Part IV, a chapter outlining what educational and psychological researchers have learned about how students learn history and applying these findings to teaching and learning women's history. The book concludes with a list of recommended resources.

Because we envision our readership to include students and teachers new to women's history, we have tried to keep the material presented in part I as foundational and informative as possible. Carol Berkin provides an overview of the colonial era; Cindy Lobel, the nineteenth century; and Barbara Winslow, the twentieth century. For readers familiar with women's history, part I effectively synthesizes important topics, themes, and events for each era, with an emphasis on presenting an engaging narrative in a reasonably compact form.

Part II shifts the focus to consideration of "big ideas" related to teaching U.S. women's history. Over the last thirty years, numerous concepts and themes have emerged within the field—and been hotly debated. We do not attempt to be comprehensive in tackling all the current concepts, themes, issues, and questions in women's history; there are simply too many. However, we have made an effort to highlight as broad a range as possible.

We asked authors of chapters in Part II to prioritize depth over breadth. In response, several of them provide "case studies" of how concepts such as radicalism, consumerism, or transnationalism have worked in women's history during particular periods. As a result, the chapters are not comprehensive in treating a concept across the centuries; rather, they suggest models that can be applied to other times and places. Also, the organization of part II reflects a decision not to isolate categories of difference shaping women's identity. In other words, we chose not to include separate chapters on particular ethnic groups of women. Instead, we offer a chapter on "intersectionality" that explores the ways in which race and gender—in this case, dealing chiefly with African American women—come together. We also asked authors to weave race, class, region, age, sexuality, and other dimensions of difference into each chapter. To the extent that individual chapters are not successful in providing more diverse examples, the problem may reflect gaps in the historical research, which proceeds unevenly across topics.

Rebecca Tannenbaum and Christy Regenhardt open part II with chapters dealing with women's bodies and medicine and with women and sexuality, respectively. In these two chapters, issues of definition and changing attitudes toward women, bodies, and sexuality are important in understanding historical change. Both authors make the point that themes associated with these topics in women's history are closely related to larger issues of economic, political, and cultural change.

Christine Compston looks at the evolving status of women's citizenship in the United States. Although most students today know something about the Nineteenth Amendment providing suffrage to women, many students and adults are unaware of the many aspects of citizenship, such as jury duty, that women have been prohibited from in many states until well into the twentieth century.

The notions of citizenship and consumerism, especially in regard to women, have been closely intertwined, as have economics and politics more broadly since the nation's inception. In recent years, consumerism has emerged as an important issue within women's history, with women sometimes being portrayed as victims of a consumer culture. Jennifer Scanlon argues instead for considering women's agency as consumers, finding opportunities in their role as the family's chief purchasing agent for shaping a sense of authority and autonomy. Virginia Drachman takes a look at another aspect of women's agency—the success they have achieved as they have entered male bastions such as medicine, law, and business.

Next, Erica Ball examines the ways in which the intersectionality of race, class, and gender has shaped women's experiences in the United States. Ball demonstrates the powerful consequences such an approach provides, not only in highlighting the differences between African American and other women's experiences in U.S. history but also in contributing new analytical tools to the conventional American history narrative. Barbara Welter's and Ronald G. Walters's chapters provide an interesting counterpoint. Welter writes about women and religion, Walters about women and radicalism. In different ways, the problems associated with "presentism" as it relates to radicalism and religion create challenges for instructors trying to bring these important topics into their classrooms.

Mary Frederickson concludes part II with a chapter that examines the concept of transnationalism for teaching U.S. women's history, which, like American history in general, has focused on the "exceptionalism" of the American experience. Frederickson offers readers a set of considerations about why it is important to put U.S. women's history into a global context and how one might go about doing so.

Part III offers strategies for teaching U.S. women's history that are neither narrowly prescriptive nor exhaustive of the range of possibilities. Those who teach women's history often make effective use of what have been called student-centered approaches to teaching their subject matter. Part III offers an array of such approaches nicely integrated with U.S. women's history content that can complement the traditional lecture format of most history classrooms.

Michael Lewis Goldberg begins part III with a big topic: how to redesign a women's history course in light of feminist pedagogy, new scholarship on learning, and technology. Much of what Goldberg has to say is applicable to contexts other than the women's history survey course, especially other history and/or women's studies courses.

Tracy Weis then considers visual resources, widely available on the Internet today, and their utility for women's history. Making effective use of online materials—texts as well as visual materials and objects—requires retooling some instructors' skill sets, not just technical but also pedagogical. Not every instructor is conversant with the best ways of exploiting primary sources in high school and college classrooms; visual resources provide an often unfamiliar type of primary source, which, like artifacts, presents teachers and students with new ways of thinking about and interpreting historical evidence. Anne Derousie and Vivien Rose's chapter on "history you can touch" suggests useful considerations for bringing material objects and the built environment more generally into classrooms effectively.

One well-known adage of the "third-wave" feminist movement of the 1960s and 1970s holds that, when it comes to women, "the personal is the political." Margaret S. Crocco's chapter on oral history takes this notion as a first premise. In this age of celebrity culture, where boundaries between public and private seem to have dissolved, resources providing glimpses into the lived experiences of women, as retold in the first person, can enliven a class. As much as social history has opened up new vistas for historical exploration, sometimes personal stories get overlooked in the attention to social, political, and economic movements. In the same vein, part III concludes with a personal story by Nicholas Syrett about his own experiences—as a man—teaching women's history. A reflective and intriguing chapter, Syrett offers a "lesson," if you will, for the entire book: Women's history is for everyone.

In part IV, we asked Linda Levstik to review the growing body of empirical research on historical thinking, much of it dealing with developmental issues related to cognition, and consider whether and how it could be applied to teaching and learning women's history. Levstik finds little research directly related to women's history, but she does suggest how what we know about students' learning history might be applied to women's history.

The book wraps up with a brief list of recommended resources for teaching women's history organized according to category: books, articles and chapters, audiovisual, and digital resources. Although not comprehensive, these suggestions, in conjunction with the notes at the end of each chapter, offer a solid foundation of resources appropriate for teaching about U.S. women's history.

NOTES

1. Organizations such as the National Women's History Project, the Berkshire Conference, and the National Women's Studies Association have enhanced knowledge of women's history.

2. Roger Clark, J. Allard, and Timothy Mahoney. "How Much of the Sky? Women in American High School History Textbooks from the 1960s, 1980s, and 1990s." *Social Education*, 69, 41–47.

PART I

Three Eras of U.S. Women's History

I

Women in Colonial and Revolutionary America

Carol Berkin

The modern field of women's history did not grow in a linear fashion. The first area of interest for the women scholars who turned to study their own lost past was not colonial society but the era of industrialization. These scholars, often motivated by their own participation in the radical politics or reform movements of the 1960s, were sharp critics of a modern America that they believed had its roots in the isms and izations of the nineteenth century. Social relations had gone terribly wrong, they argued, when capitalism took productive labor out of the household, defined "paid" labor as the only legitimate labor, and sharpened the separation between women's confined sphere and men's broader domain. They began a close examination of these developments—and produced, in the process, many insightful and analytically powerful studies. Meanwhile, modern study of the colonial and early national eras and the twentieth century lagged behind; nineteenth-century women's history was like an alpine peak, its two sloping sides of past and future buried in shadow.

These nineteenth-century scholars dramatized the subordination and confinement of women within a domestic sphere by accepting the idea of a golden age for women before industrialization. The developments of the nineteenth century became, in effect, a fall from grace at worst and a declension at best. For them, just as for many labor historians and political historians, the seventeenth and eighteenth centuries were romanticized as the era before paradise was lost. Because capitalism was so bad, anything that preceded it was, ipso facto, better. It was sometimes an unconscious and most often an implicit use of a golden age before the rise of industrial America; it served a purpose but did not attract their scholarly interrogation.[1]

The idea of the golden age was conveniently present in the limited existing literature on colonial women.[2] For scholars such as Julia Cherry Spruill and Elisabeth Anthony Dexter, several factors created this golden age for white women. First, there was an imbalance in the sex ratio among white colonists that these scholars assumed worked to women's advantage. They were not alone in this assumption, for as a seventeenth-century wag observed, the great number of men and the scarcity of women made Maryland "a paradise for women." The competition for a wife, it was assumed, gave women a power they would lose in later centuries. Second, women made vital economic contributions that were acknowledged by their husbands and by the wider male community. Their labor was both productive—from candle making to soap making to churning butter—and reproductive, generating the labor force that would assist in sustaining the family in agriculture. As a result, a "rough equality" existed between husband and wife. The nineteenth century's sharp divisions between paid and unpaid, between visible and invisible labor, lay in the future; on the family farm of the colonial centuries, women's obvious contributions earned them a voice in decision making within their families. Third, the boundaries between male and female spheres were porous and flexible, and thus colonial society boasted female blacksmiths and newspaper editors, women tavern keepers and doctors. The rigid divisions that separated the parlor and the shop, that defined women's domain as the "haven" and men's as the "heartless world," did not exist in this understanding of the colonial era.

This golden age theory was among the first casualties as historians of the colonial era turned their attention to women's experiences and to gender ideologies. First, they challenged the conclusions drawn from the evidence: Scarcity, for example, can lead as easily to rigid control as to empowerment; productivity can be exploited as well as rewarded. Every slave learned this lesson well in the years before emancipation. But the challenges were not made to interpretation alone. For the past three decades, colonial women's historians have sought and uncovered new evidence about women's lives that complicates the story. But the model of a golden age, which rests on comparison, never entirely vanished. As the literature developed, a regional comparison between New England and the Chesapeake, especially during the seventeenth century, often emerged to replace the older chronological one. This contest of regions spurred much research, but it also rested on shaky assumptions about the implications of conditions. For example, in the Chesapeake, the disease environment and work conditions produced a high mortality rate. Parents had often died before a marriage-age girl selected a husband. In New England, on the other hand, a healthier climate aided longevity, and few girls entered marriage without their parents present. Which condition was preferable? Chesapeake girls had more autonomy in their choice of a mate, but would they have preferred parental advice and protection in making arguably the most important decision of their lives? Did New England girls view their parents' active advisory role as a benefit or a hindrance? Unless the historian holds in her hand letters or personal papers that indicate the young woman's attitude, there can be no answer. Differences are worth discovering, but on the whole, the better/worse paradigm has proved less valuable.

Historians of the era now work with a far more complex understanding of the category "women" than in the past, considering issues of gender alongside race, religion, region, class, and age. Yet women's stories are not equally available: It is possible to examine the emotional lives of white women of Massachusetts but not those of enslaved black women of the South Carolina rice paddies. Even within white society, the nature of the sources varies greatly by region and class. The lives of seventeenth-century Chesapeake women are still more likely to be reconstructed collectively, through demographic data, than their Puritan counterparts in New England, whose diaries and daybooks are windows into individual lives. There is also recognition that there was no single, static "colonial era," but decade after decade of changes in law, economic activities, settlement patterns, and cultural assumptions. Current research is expanding the arena of our research, as scholars seek to understand the social construction of masculinity as well as femininity and as they look for clues in the language and material culture of these centuries.[3]

As in most cultures, Anglo-American colonists had a firm understanding of gender roles and gender differences. The ideology they inherited and sustained was legitimated by God, Nature, and custom, a triumvirate of authorities few dared to challenge. The Genesis story of the Bible, which both Protestant and Catholic colonists accepted, explained woman's purpose on earth: to serve as "helpmate" or, as colonists would put it, "helpmeet" to man. And because of Eve's role in the disobedience to God's law that led to the expulsion from the Garden, it was clear that women were more susceptible to temptation, weaker in resisting sin—and thus in need of guidance if society was to function properly. Women, then, were to be both helpful and subordinate to men.

Nature also made evident the need for women to be guided and restrained by men. Anglo-American society in the seventeenth and early eighteenth centuries focused on mental differences between the sexes. Women, it was said, were endowed with weaker brains than men, brains so weak that women were incapable of rational—and therefore moral—thought. Unable to judge right from wrong in many important areas, the unsupervised woman was a danger to society. Civilization required that she be held in check by a father, brother, or husband.

Finally, law and custom confirmed what God and Nature decreed, shaping women's legal status and social choices accordingly. Legal writers waxed lyrical over the relationship between husband and wife, comparing her loss of legal identity to a stream losing itself in a mighty river. But the truth was more prosaic: A wife was *feme covert*, translated as "woman covered." In exchange for her marriage vows, she gave up her right to sue or be sued, keep any wages she earned, and alienate or purchase property. All that she owned became her husband's, even the clothes on her back and her body. Unless she or her father had the foresight to arrange a prenuptial agreement, a woman suffered this restriction of her legal identity—and sealed her subordination and dependency. Only an adult woman who remained single could retain her full legal identity; she was, in the language of the courts, *feme sole*, or woman alone.[4]

If the terminology of women's legal status suggests the greater desirability of marriage—a protected woman as opposed to a woman without companionship or assistance—social customs reinforced this view. A woman's destiny was to marry and have children; Anglo-American Protestant society offered few if any alternatives. There was no convent to which a woman could retreat; professions such as the ministry were closed to women; education on any but the most rudimentary level (and limited largely to the New England colonies) was unavailable; most crafts were, by law or custom, exclusively male. A woman who did not become head of her own household through marriage was likely to spend her adult years as a dependent in a brother or sister's home.

More subtle but equally powerful social pressures channeled a woman into marriage. For example, there were few markers along the route to adulthood and community respect for a female except marriage and motherhood. Men could become members of the militia, elders in the church, voters, and office holders—all public acknowledgments of maturity or success. A woman could hope to earn the accolade of "notable housewife"—a recognition that required husband and family.

But the ideal of womanhood conveyed from the pulpit, judge's bench, and academy—obedient, fertile, skilled in household crafts and duties, busy, and productive—was just that, an ideal. Colonial court records and newspapers reveal that women attacked their mates with pots and pans; mothers committed infanticide; wives ran away, alone or with other men; housewives proved to be slovenly or lazy or unskilled at vital tasks; and on occasion, women spoke out publicly to challenge the restraints of the gender ideology their community embraced. The ideal is important not because it is entirely synonymous with reality but because it defined the acceptable and desired parameters of Anglo-American colonial women's lives.

White women in Virginia were as subject to the ideology as their counter-parts in Massachusetts, but conditions in the Chesapeake and New England produced striking variations in the lived lives of these two groups. The diseases that ravaged the colonial populations of Virginia and Maryland did not strike New Englanders. High mortality rates in the south meant early death for the young and a short adulthood for those who survived infancy. A woman's life expectancy was thirty-nine; a man's forty. This, combined with a skewed sex ratio because of the preference for male field workers on the tobacco planta-tion, produced a relatively unique family structure. Creole, or American-born, girls married young, often to older husbands, and produced children. Wife, or more likely older husband, died; a new spouse was immediately available, per-haps a widower himself. Families blended—and new children were born. This process has been tracked through multiple serial marriages, resulting in chil-dren living in a household in which neither parent is a blood relative. The lan-guage of the era reflects the normality of these repeatedly constructed households: Men referred to their "now-wives" and parents to their "sons in law." In New England's benign disease environment, parents lived long enough to see their children married and their grandchildren born. As one scholar put it, New England invented grandparents. And because family units were typical among the earliest immigrants to the region, the sex ratio was relatively even. Thus, female marriage age was older, and the pressure to marry young lower.[5]

No matter what age they married, most colonial women did so. What was expected of her once she was married? While New England ministers were more likely to spell out a wife's duties and responsibilities, women in every col-ony knew they were to be industrious, economical, fertile, and obedient. The gendered division of labor among white colonists ensured that the fields and livestock were a male domain; the household, the dairy, the garden, and the orchard were a female domain. While access to imported manufactured goods varied, and few farm households were entirely self-sufficient, in the majority of cases women were expected to engage in vital household manufacturing. Women were the family's skilled craftspeople, trained to transform a variety of raw materials into usable goods and supplies: changing wheat into bread, tal-low into candles, fruit into preserves, lye and other ingredients into soaps, and threads into cloth. In addition, women performed maintenance tasks: washing clothing, ironing, baking bread, slaughtering animals and preparing meat, cooking—and only occasionally cleaning the home. In addition, women might serve their communities as midwives. The range of skills and activities expected of the housewife led in many instances to collective cooperation: Women in towns specialized in certain crafts, exchanging their products for the products of neighbors.

Women were also the producers of the family labor force. While not all women fit the pattern, most women bore a child—or lost one through miscarriage or stillbirth—every two and a half years until menopause or death. It was not childbirth itself that led to a mother's demise but the exhaustion and decline in resistance to infection that resulted from the repeated pregnancies. Primary sources have shown that mothers and their adult daughters could be pregnant or nursing children at the same time. If one of these women had trouble nursing, was sick, or had infected nipples, the other would engage in the "courtesy nursing" of her grandchild or sibling. Some women undoubtedly used herbal abortifacients and other means to induce miscarriages, but most sought to space their pregnancies through delayed weaning of their infants. The statistics suggest that most white women were either pregnant, nursing infants, or tending small children through most of their fertile years of marriage.

Marriage, motherhood, household production—these formed the central realities in a colonial white woman's life. Yet if these forces tied her to the domestic sphere, there were forces pulling her outside as well: church and markets, and those moments when war, business, or family crisis drew husbands away from their traditional tasks and required wives to step in. As historian Laurel Ulrich has noted, women served as "surrogate" or "deputy" husbands, managing the farm or shop for the family. The gender ideology of the era was flexible enough to allow women to define these actions that carried them out of the domestic sphere as part of their "helpmeet" duties.[6]

Native American women, primarily members of the Algonquin and Cherokee cultures, experienced a gender ideology and a gendered division of labor that stood in sharp contrast to their English counterparts.[7] Private property, and its passage from fathers to sons, played no role in Indian society. Many Indian groups were both matrilineal—tracing their children through the mother rather than the father—and matrilocal, with a couple and their offspring housed with the clan or family of a wife's mother rather than in a household set up by the husband. Male and female roles, duties, and privileges were distinct within these Indian communities, but the division of labor was surprising to the early white colonists. In European cultures, men labored in the fields and women in the household; in the communities of these eastern woodland Indians, women were the agriculturalists. While men often assisted in the planting or harvesting, their primary obligations were hunting, fishing, warfare, and protection of the community. Women's control of the basic food supply gave them considerable influence in determining the community's diplomacy: Men could decide to go to war, but women could decide not to pro-vision them from their silos and storehouses. Women's councils functioned as both advisory groups and pressure groups upon the men who led their com-munity, and although the information is incomplete, women warriors appeared among Cherokees and Iroquois.

Although white observers, both male and female, often spoke negatively of Indian society, describing it as heathen, savage, and "unnatural" because of gender roles and sexual practices that seemed a mirror opposite of their own culture, there were white women who found Indian culture preferable to their own. Captives like Mary Jemison resisted any efforts to return them to their colonial towns or villages, citing the pleasures of collective female work in the fields and the personal autonomy within a society with few patriarchal tendencies.[8]

By the mid-seventeenth century, colonial America was not simply bira-cial, but triracial. Although Africans were relatively rare in the Chesapeake during the 1630s or 1640s, the shift from indentured servants to enslaved Africans and African Americans was virtually complete by the early eigh-teenth century. Brought to the tobacco and rice fields of the Chesapeake and the Low Country and to the northern colonies as well, these bound laborers usually ended their horrendous middle passage across the Atlantic in the Caribbean, where they were "seasoned" and then sold to the mainland. The increase in the black population was striking: In 1680, Maryland had only 1,611 Africans; by 1720, the number had risen to more than 12,000; Virginia's black population went from 3,000 to more than 26,000 over the same period. In South Carolina, where planters coming from Barbados arrived in the early eighteenth century with their slaves, the black population was almost 12,000, and by mid-century, blacks constituted a majority of the population in the colony. Black slaves labored in the fields, households, and shops and on the ships and docks of the northern colonies as well: There were more than 14,000 women and men of African descent in New Hampshire, Vermont, Massachusetts, Connecticut, Rhode Island, New York, New Jersey, and Pennsylvania by 1720.

If the Indians shocked white settlers with their gendered division of labor, slave masters did not honor their own traditions when they assigned work to male and female slaves. Black women as well as men labored in the fields and rice paddies, and in fact, as activities such as plowing, brick making, and barrel making took men out of the fields, women remained to do such backbreaking tasks as weeding, draining swamps, and deworming the tobacco. By the eigh-teenth century, women on Chesapeake plantations were regularly assigned the least desirable tasks, including building fences, cleaning seed out of winnowed grain, cleaning stables, and spreading manure. Few women worked in the plantation household until the nineteenth century. The servants who waited on the master's family were often children, too young to pull their weight in the fields.

If white society channeled women into marriage and motherhood, slavery made the creation of a family far more difficult. Formal, or legal, marriage was not allowed, but slave women and men nonetheless established sexual and familial loyalties. Historians have focused a great deal of attention on the conditions necessary for the development of a slave culture, at the heart of which was the family. The demographic preconditions were critical: Was the sex ratio favorable, and was the concentration of slaves sufficient for couples to establish relationships, produce families, and pass on religious, cultural, and ethnic traditions? Raw figures have sometimes proven deceptive: A tobacco plantation might have a balanced sex ratio among its slave labor force, but the composition of the small gangs into which slaves were divided might militate against relationships. In many instances, women were paired with children, while all-male gangs cultivated distant areas of the plantation. As a county or parish's black population grew in density, contact was certainly more likely, and visits from one plantation to another were not necessarily accomplished with ease or regularity. In addition, the periodic arrival of "saltwater" or newly imported slaves into a native-born or acculturated community of slaves was disruptive of community life.

Enslaved couples did not control their personal or familial lives. Indeed, black women did not have authority over their own bodies. Children, usually maturing sons, were frequently sold; wives or husbands or children could be given as wedding presents to the master's children; the death of a planter could lead to the sale of his slaves. The continuous search for new tobacco lands meant that younger men and women could be forced to relocate to western lands, where they would have to begin the process of creating a community anew.

Although black women delivered their children in the company of other women just as white women did, African nursing practices widened the interval between pregnancies. On average, slave women bore nine children, spaced at twenty-seven- to twenty-nine-month intervals. Gaps occurred, of course, if masters separated husbands and wives. While white southern women usually delivered their children in the fall and early winter, black babies in the Chesapeake were born between February and July. This meant that the later stages of pregnancy coincided with the laborious tasks of spring planting. As a result, childbirth was riskier for black mothers, and rates of infant mortality higher.

Black women in the Lower South—the Carolinas and Georgia—worked under a task system rather than in gang labor. This allowed them, and their male counterparts, to control the pace of their workday, but the labor itself—cultivating rice—was far more taxing and dangerous to their health. Women faced the most grueling of these tasks, pounding the grain with mortar and pestle, and their mortality rates reflected the burdens imposed upon them. But the task system appears to have allowed for the development of entrepreneurial activity and an internal market. When not working for masters or overseers, Low Country slaves cultivated their own gardens, raising corn, potatoes, peanuts, melons, and pumpkins. These crops—as well as catfish, handmade baskets, eggs, and poultry—were sold by slave women, often to their own masters. In the city of Charleston, slave women paid their masters a fee for the right to sell pies, cakes, produce, and handmade items. In these activities, slave women drew on the West African tradition of female traders.

Slave women in the northern cities were more likely to work in the households of their masters and mistresses. Their days were spent cooking, cleaning, washing and ironing, tending fires and gardens, and caring for the children of the household. On farms that produced wheat for the market, female slaves labored in the fields. On family farms, they tended large gardens, milked cows, and raised poultry. They might also be called upon to spin cloth in areas where imported British cloth was scarce or expensive.

Were Northern slave women better off than their counterparts in the rice paddies or the tobacco fields? Household chores might be less onerous than work on the plantations, but the personal life of the northern household slave might be lonelier and a family less likely. Isolated in a white home, the household slave had limited contact with enslaved or even free black males. She also lacked the emotional renewal or companionship of the slave quarter. An urban slave woman's loneliness worked to the advantage of her master; slave offspring might be welcomed on a plantation, but in a Philadelphia townhouse, infants and young children only threatened diminished productivity from their mother. A master might solve the problem of an unwanted pregnancy by selling his household slave or, in at least one case, giving the baby away. Even if a woman managed to keep a child, its life was likely to be abbreviated because disease and cramped quarters took their toll in infant mortality.

Resistance to slavery knew no regional or gender boundaries. There are instances of plantation slave women who poisoned their mistresses and set fire to their master's homes, yet they were less likely than enslaved men to run away because they were less willing to abandon children and aging parents or other relatives. The likelihood of success for runaways was lower for women than for men because few occupations other than prostitution were open to them. The life of a sailor, a black man's best hope of success as a runaway, was not available to women. In northern cities, enslaved women joined the rare, violent group revolts such as the 1712 slave revolt in New York City.⁹

The "colonial period" was not, of course, one long static era. The early days of settlement in Jamestown or Plymouth bear as little resemblance to the eighteenth-century world of Abigail Adams as the world of Elizabeth Cady Stanton resembles that of Hillary Clinton. By the 1720s, for example, a consumer revolution was altering white women's domestic duties. Prosperous urban women and wealthy planters' wives benefited most from the availability of manufactured goods, but all white women were affected. For example, few eighteenth-century women with access to imported goods markets were seen sitting at their spinning wheels. Especially in colonial cities, housewives purchased the food and clothing whose production was once the core of housewifery. Servants and slaves took over other tedious but necessary chores, leaving wealthier women and their daughters with something new in colonial America: leisure time. A new attention to luxuries emerged, increasing the distinctions between the colonial elite and their less prosperous neighbors. Where once, in the seventeenth century, the rich simply had more of the same things the poor had, by the eighteenth century, the material and social lives of the wealthy were noticeably different. The signs were everywhere: from the tea services and the rituals of the tea table that genteel women relished to the popularity of cookbooks and the desire to follow the latest London fashions in clothing and manners. In short, the domestic sphere was changing: The emphasis for genteel women was on childrearing and creating an attractive home rather than on housewifery. By 1763, political circumstances would lead to even more radical changes.¹⁰

Boycotts of British imported goods that followed the Stamp Act and the Townshend Acts were effective, in large part, because white women participated. From boycotts of merchants' shops that offered imported items to the organization of spinning bees to produce homespun, "Daughters of Liberty" were active participants in the protests of the new English policies after the French and Indian War. Both the boycotts and the making and wearing of homespun politicized women's domestic world; for the fourteen years between the end of the French and Indian War and the beginning of the war for independence, what women bought and what they wore, even whether they drank tea or not, became a statement of political loyalties. Men who had once enjoined women to be silent both in church and in the political sphere now sang the praises of women who printed pledges not to drink English tea in the newspapers or penned poetry that chided men to be more radical in their response to British policy. In diaries and letters, women acknowledged that they had "commenced perfect statesmen," avidly following political news, debating the constitutionality of the new taxes, and vowing support for further acts of resistance.

Once the war began in earnest, women quickly mobilized. In the long home front war that followed the Declaration of Independence, women took over the management of farms and shops, devised ingenious substitutes for vital supplies cut off by Britain, raised funds for the army, allowed soldiers and their officers to transform those homes into barracks, nursed the sick and wounded, spied for both the patriots and the Crown, served as messengers and couriers, and on occasion disguised themselves as men and enlisted in the army. Women left to fend for themselves and their families while their husbands went off to war struggled to fulfill unfamiliar male duties and their own household tasks in the face of scarcity, inflation, and danger. For some, the burdens of the deputy husband role in times of crisis proved too much. For others, like the wealthy Loyalist's wife whose reports to her absent husband referred first to "your" farm, later to "our" farm, and finally to "my" farm, the experience of male duties and prerogatives was exhilarating. But rich or poor, women were vulnerable to the abuses of war: rape and theft. Thousands of women chose to follow their husbands into the army camps, where they earned their half-rations by cooking, cleaning, washing clothes, and nursing the soldiers. These "camp followers" often traveled with the army, and many risked their lives on the battlefield as they scavenged for weapons, ammunition, and clothing from the wounded and the dead. Camp followers in the forts frequently took their husbands' place at the cannon when the men fell; these "Molly Pitchers" were sometimes wounded as well.

Although revolutionary women rallied to the principle of no taxation without representation, the war meant something very different to Indian, African American, and Loyalist women. For most Indian groups, freedom and liberty meant opposing the revolutionaries. They understood that their lands were at risk if the always land-hungry Americans were released from the restrictions placed on their westward movement by the British government. The British appreciated the power and influence that a woman like Molly Brant, widow of Sir William Johnson and sister of Joseph Brant, wielded among the Mohawks and their Iroquois allies and were grateful that she chose to remain loyal to the Crown.

For African American women, the warnings of a British conspiracy to enslave the colonists and the rallying cries of liberty and freedom must have seemed ironic. Many thousands of enslaved blacks used the war between two white societies to make a bid for their own freedom. As the British army marched across the south, women and children flocked to their camps, risking death or recapture, and seeking their own release from slavery. Many died from the diseases that spread through the camps; others were returned to their former masters or reenslaved by greedy British soldiers and officers. Women lucky enough to survive these disasters joined other African Americans who relocated to Canada at war's end. Other slaves chose to support the revolutionaries, hoping that the commitment to liberty would be contagious. Northern states did indeed put a slow end to slavery, but in the south, the restrictions that shaped black life grew more stringent. The women of the communities of free blacks that grew in cities like Philadelphia devoted their energies to creating new institutions such as churches.

A sizable number of colonists refused to support independence. These loyalists denied that the British government had proven itself tyrannical; they were unwilling to abandon their connection to the mother country. Loyalist women participated in the revolutionary struggle in much the same way as patriot women: running farms and shops, spying, supplying loyalist and British troops, and caring for the sick and wounded. When the war ended, most made their way to Canada with their families. Here, in what many called "Nova Scarcity," they began their lives anew.

But if women played key roles in the success of the Revolution, did the Revolution play a significant role in improving or changing women's roles in American society? Some scholars argue that the Revolution had limited if any impact on gender ideology, on women's work roles, or on women's access to legal and political rights. Indeed, some have argued that changes after the Revolution—such as changes in property law—actually operated against white women's interests. Others argue that the changes begun in the 1720s and 1730s—for example, the consumer revolution and the adoption among the elite of Enlightenment notions—were more important factors in women's lives than war. Still others see positive changes in the postwar era. The articulation of a new gender ideology, "Republican Motherhood," gave women higher status within the family and opened the way to the growth of women's formal education in the young ladies' academy movement. How many women this affected and what its lasting impact was remain uncertain, as does whether women initiated and shaped the new ideology or men imposed it upon them. Nevertheless, reformers, political leaders, and a number of articulate women, such as Judith Sargent Murray, debated women's role in the new republic— and this alone might be seen as a radical step.[11]

Many strands of thought and practice came together in this debate. Enlightenment ideas that all people, including women, were capable of rational and therefore moral thought were reinforced by the political activism and patriotic loyalties of women during the long war. The consumer revolution and the presence of servants and slaves had freed middle-class and elite white women from many of the time-consuming activities of housewifery; the revolution had channeled what women did with that time into a single civic obligation: educating or socializing sons and daughters as patriotic republicans. Men like Benjamin Rush of Pennsylvania argued persuasively that the survival of the republic depended upon the ability of the revolutionary generation to instill patriotism and a readiness to sacrifice personal interests in the next generation. This solemn duty, he and others insisted, rested on the shoulders of white mothers. Thus, if before the revolution what a woman did with her "spare" time was a personal choice, after the war, it became a political choice. Mothering had, in effect, become a civic act.

While this elevated the status of women, it also relegated them to the domestic sphere by endowing that sphere with a quasi-public role. Republican Motherhood demanded that women sacrifice the development of their own individuality for the good of the state; such private pleasures or intellectual pursuits as novel reading were condemned as a distraction from a mother's civic duties. As the liberal capitalism of the nineteenth century encouraged white men to pursue their own selfish interests without guilt, Republican Motherhood demanded self-abnegation and sacrifice from wives and mothers. And as the anxiety over the survival of the new nation diminished, as its institutions acquired greater legitimacy, and as the new belief in the value of self-interest rather than self-sacrifice to the prosperity and growth of the nation took root, the idea that women were to instill civic virtues in their sons lost its power. By the 1820s, women's work was to produce and educate sons to compete in the marketplace, not sustain a national experiment.

NOTES

1. See Mary Beth Norton, "The Paradox of 'Women's Sphere,'" in Carol R. Berkin and Mary Beth Norton, eds., *Women of America: A History* (Boston: Houghton Mifflin, 1979), pp. 139–149; Carol Berkin, "'What an Alarming Crisis Is This': Early American Women and Their Histories," in Michael V. Kennedy and William S. Shade, eds., *The World Turned Upside Down: The State of Eighteenth-Century American Studies at the Beginning of the Twenty-First Century* (Bethlehem, PA: Lehigh University Press, 2001), pp. 254–267.

2. See, for example, Elisabeth A. Dexter, *Colonial Women of Affairs* (Boston: Houghton Mifflin, 1931), and Julia Cherry Spruill, *Women's Life and Work in the Southern Colonies* (1938; repr., New York: Norton, 1998).

3. See, for example, Merrill D. Smith, ed., *Sex and Sexuality in Early America* (New York: New York University Press, 1998); Larry D. Eldridge, ed., *Women and Freedom in Early America* (New York: New York University Press, 1997); Jane

Kamensky, *Governing the Tongue: The Politics of Speech in Early New England* (New York: Oxford University Press, 1997); Kathleen M. Brown, *Good Wives, Nasty Wenches, and Anxious Patriarchs: Gender, Race and Power in Colonia Virginia* (Chapel Hill: University of North Carolina Press, 1996).

4. See Carol Berkin, *First Generations: Women in Colonial America* (New York: Hill and Wang, 1996); Marylynn Salmon, *Women and the Law of Property in Early America* (Chapel Hill: University of North Carolina Press, 1986); Marylynn Salmon, "Equality or Submersion? Feme Covert Status in Early Pennsylvania," in Berkin and Norton, eds., *Women of America*, pp. 92–113.

5. See the following essays in Thad Tate and David Ammerman, eds., *The Chesapeake in the Seventeenth Century: Essays on Anglo-American Society* (Chapel Hill: University of North Carolina Press, 1979): Carville V. Earle, "Environment, Disease, and Mortality in Early Virginia," pp. 96–125; Lorena S. Walsh, " 'Till Death Us Do Part': Marriage and Family in Seventeenth Century Maryland," pp. 126–152; and Darrett B. Rutman and Anita H. Rutman, " 'Now-Wives and Sons-in-Law': Parental Death in a Seventeenth Century Virginia County," pp. 153–182. See also Lorena S. Walsh and Lois G. Carr, "The Planter's Wife: The Experience of White Women in Seventeenth Century Maryland," *William and Mary Quarterly*, 3d. series, 34 (1977), and Berkin, *First Generations*.

6. Laurel Ulrich, *Good Wives: Image and Reality in the Lives of Women in Northern New England, 1650–1750* (New York: Knopf, 1982); Mary Beth Norton, *Liberty's Daughters: The Revolutionary Experience of American Women, 1750–1800* (Glenview, IL: Scott, Foresman, 1980).

7. See Theda Perdue, *Cherokee Women: Gender and Cultural Change, 1700–1835* (Lincoln: University of Nebraska Press, 1999); James Merrell, *The Indians' New World: Catawbas and Their Neighbors from European Contact through the Era of Removal* (Chapel Hill: University of North Carolina Press, 1989); Daniel Richter, *The Ordeal of the Longhouse: The Peoples of the Iroquois League in the Era of European Colonization* (Chapel Hill: University of North Carolina Press, 1992); Gretchen L. Green, "Gender and the Longhouse: Iroquois Women in a Changing Culture," in Eldridge, *Women and Freedom*, pp. 7–25; and Eirlys M. Barker, "Princesses, Wives and Wenches: White Perception of Southeastern Indian Women to 1770," in Eldridge, *Women and Freedom*, pp. 44–61.

8. Kathryn Zabelle Derounian-Stodola and James Arthur Levernier, *The Indian Captivity Narrative, 1550–1900* (New York: Twayne, 1993).

9. See Ira Berlin, *Generations of Captivity: A History of African American Slaves* (Cambridge: Harvard University Press, 2004); Allan Kulikoff, *Tobacco and Slaves: The Development of Southern Cultures in the Chesapeake, 1680–1800* (Chapel Hill: University of North Carolina Press, 1986); Phillip Morgan, *Slave Counterpoint: Black Culture in the Eighteenth Century Chesapeake and Low Country* (Chapel Hill: University of North Carolina Press, 1998); Berkin, *First Generations*; Gerald Mullin, *Flight and Rebellion: Slave Resistance in Eighteenth Century Virginia* (New York: Oxford University Press, 1974); Sylvia Frey, *Water from the Rock: Black Resistance in a Revolutionary Age* (Princeton, NJ: Princeton University Press, 1991).

10. Berkin, *First Generations*.

11. Carol Berkin, *Revolutionary Mothers: Women in the Struggle for America's Independence* (New York: Knopf, 2005); Mary Beth Norton, *Liberty's Daughters;* Linda Kerber, *Women of the Republic: Intellect and Ideology in Revolutionary America* (Chapel Hill: University of North Carolina Press, 1980); Carol R. Berkin and Clara M. Lovett, eds., *Women, War and Revolution* (New York: Holmes and Meier, 1980); Nancy Cott, *The Bonds of Womanhood: 'Women's Sphere' in New England, 1780–1835* (New Haven, CT: Yale University Press, 1977).

2

Women in Nineteenth-Century America

Cindy R. Lobel

The early historians of colonial era women thought that they had discovered a golden age for women, one in which women's productive contributions to the family created a "rough equality" between husband and wife. This model lost its potency as scholars learned more about the ideological, legal, and customary patterns that ensured women's subordinate status. Early studies of women in the nineteenth century relied on a different paradigm or model— "separate spheres"—and it, too, has lost its interpretive power as new research has followed.

Separate spheres for men and women seemed to result from the great changes taking place in American society in the nineteenth century, chief among them industrialization and the rise of a market-driven capitalist economy. As men and work left the home, women remained in a domestic, or private, sphere that took on an important symbolic function. The ideal home was no longer just a structure; rather, it was a place of refuge, a moral and spiritual shelter from the heartless world of commerce and politics, and women played a crucial role in the development and maintenance of this domestic haven. It was up to them to foster an environment of morality and comfort to fortify their family members and protect them from the evils of the public sphere.

Women needed to be careful to protect themselves from the public sphere as well. Women in public were women in danger—

both physical and symbolic—and thus a series of strong cultural strictures emerged to limit women's public role. Woman's productive role disappeared as well, as the household goods and services provided by her foremothers now were available as manufactured goods or through hiring domestic servants. Women increasingly served a primarily reproductive role, both of children and of the cultural values that helped to maintain the status and reputation of their families.[1]

For more than a generation, this separate spheres paradigm dominated historians' understanding of the nineteenth century. But before long, scholars found this model far too limiting. First and foremost, it described the experience of a very specific group—white, native-born, middle-class, and elite women of the Northeast. Seeking to chronicle and analyze the lives of working-class, African American, Native American, immigrant, Southern, and Western women, women's historians found that the one-size model of separate spheres simply did not fit the experience of all or even most women. Before long, even those who studied white, middle-class women of the Northeast found separate spheres too constricting. They found ample evidence of a public role for middle-class women in voluntary associations, commerce, political culture, and consumer society.[2]

By the late 1980s, scholars were publishing scores of studies that complicated the model to such an extent that it had lost its use as an organizing principle. In recent years, women's historians have abandoned the very notion of dichotomized public and private spheres and showed the various ways in which public concerns crossed into domestic life and vice versa. Thanks to these studies, we now have a far more balanced and nuanced understanding of the variety of experience of nineteenth-century American women.

The idea of separate spheres has not entirely disappeared. We cannot ignore its presence in the prescriptive literature—sermons, domestic manuals, women's magazines, and sentimental novels—of the nineteenth century. Scholars agree that the convention, while an ideal, did not adhere to the *lived* experience of nineteenth-century women. Yet, in some important ways it shaped the discourse of middle-class gender norms and thus influenced some of the cultural and legal *expectations* of women, if not their actual behavior.

We also now understand that gender is not necessarily the primary category influencing women's social experience. In many cases, social class, race, or ethnicity cut across gender lines to separate rather than unite women and to shape their daily lives and practices. For this reason, the scholarship on nineteenth-century women tends to focus on particular groups of women rather than attempting a synthetic overview of the whole. Despite the variety of experience, however, the history of American women in the nineteenth century, like that of the United States at large, is a story of modernization: of the move from a preindustrial, agrarian nation to a modern, industrial one. How women experienced that shift and contributed to it was shaped by race, economic status, ethnicity, region, and, of course, gender.

Early National and Antebellum Women

As Carol Berkin shows in the preceding chapter, women emerged from the American Revolution with a dubious political and social position. As is often the case with wars, the economic and political roles they had assumed during the conflict were resumed by the men returning from the front. Political and social theorists posited a role for women in the polity—as wives and mothers, responsible for educating future generations of virtuous citizens. But in law, women remained subject to their male relatives in *feme covert* status, much as their mothers, grandmothers, and great-grandmothers had been. Indeed, the only state to grant women political power in its constitution—New Jersey— seems to have done so as an oversight, a mistake it corrected in 1807, when its legislature amended its constitution to specify that voting privileges extended only to propertied *males* and not their female counterparts. Enslaved women maintained their status as chattel. Even the Northern states that abolished slavery in their constitutions did so gradually. So most enslaved Northerners remained so for decades after the Revolution ended.

As the nineteenth century began, the United States was overwhelmingly rural and so, too, the lifestyle of its citizenry. Living and working on family farms in the Northeast, on farms and plantations in the South and Southwest, and in households in the burgeoning seaports of the Atlantic coast, early national women experienced work and patterns of daily life that were similar to their colonial counterparts. White farm women carried the skills of housewifery into the nineteenth century. Like their mothers, they tended gardens, slaughtered animals, made candles and soap, and spun wool and flax, in addition to doing laundry, cooking, and laying up foods for the winter months.

In the South, the plantation system was in transition in the early nineteenth century, between the waning tobacco farms of the colonial period and the soon-to-be-booming cotton plantations of the antebellum era. Southern cotton society was just emerging, and slavery was becoming an increasingly entrenched institution. Within the plantation household, enslaved women performed tasks similar to white farm women's, including weaving, cooking, cleaning, and household production. They also worked in the fields alongside men, picking the crop, whether tobacco or the increasingly important cotton.

Industrialization changed these patterns significantly. Manufactured items replaced domestically produced goods in both the cities and the increasingly market-oriented countryside. This situation particularly prevailed in the North, where family farms were quickly giving way to commercial farms and the tentacles of the market were reaching farther into the rural hinterlands. Wealthy and middle-class women increasingly relied on the market for household goods like soap, candles, clothing, and food. They hired servants to cook, clean, and care for their children. And the number of children they bore diminished, as the family resources were geared toward educating children and preparing them to replicate the family's—in some cases, recently achieved—middle-class status. The time middle-class women had previously spent completing household chores was now directed toward household management, childrearing, voluntary activities, visiting, and shopping. Indeed, middle-class urban women became central figures in the burgeoning consumer society of the nineteenth century. By the end of the century, a host of new institutions had emerged to accommodate them, from ladies' restaurants to family-friendly theater matinees to department stores with services for ladies, including hair salons, restrooms, and home delivery.

Middle-class women expanded their domestic role through their involvement in reform movements and political culture. Women were particularly receptive to the perfectionist message of the Second Great Awakening of the early nineteenth century and were on the front lines of both the religious revivals that characterized it and the reform movements that grew out of it. Protestant women were drawn to causes such as diet reform, dress reform, temperance, moral reform (antiprostitution), and abolitionism, a movement that included African American women as well as white. While barred by and large from leadership positions in these movements, women played an important role in spreading the message of reform, getting their sons and husbands involved, hosting bazaars, forwarding petitions, and in some cases, speaking in public forums to spread the word to other women, as well as mixed audiences. Their involvement in reform movements gave middle-class women valuable experience in fund-raising and political organization. It also served—in the parlance of a later generation of women activists—to raise their consciousness of their own subordination.

Indeed, the nineteenth-century women's rights and suffrage movement grew directly out of women's experience in agitating against slavery. Some abolitionist women, barred from leadership or public positions in abolitionist organizations, chafed at the limitations placed on them because of their gender. When the first World's Anti-Slavery Convention, held in London in 1840, refused to seat the female delegates of the American Anti-Slavery Society, the delegation withdrew. Two of the female delegates, Lucretia Mott and Elizabeth Cady Stanton, began discussions about holding a convention to address the question of American women's rights. In 1848, their plans reached fruition with the first national convention for women's rights in Seneca Falls, New York. Their manifesto, the Declaration of Sentiments, was modeled on the Declaration of Independence. Among its demands were education and property rights, more equitable divorce laws, entry into the professions, and most radically, the extension of suffrage to women.

As the nineteenth century progressed, differences of opinion, goals, and approach emerged within the women's movement over questions of equality versus difference. Some female activists demanded full equality with men; others focused on gender differences and protections for women based on the particular needs of their sex. Women activists also disagreed on the question of suffrage and how (or whether) to achieve it. In the 1860s, the splits within the women's rights movement came to a head over the issue of support for voting rights for African Americans.

The proposed Fourteenth and Fifteenth Amendments to the Constitution enumerated citizenship rights and extended the suffrage to African American males. Some woman suffragists refused to support the amendment unless it included women and, in fact, evinced a willingness to fight for the vote for white women at the expense of black women and men. Others argued that African American enfranchisement was a more pressing need, even if it excluded the female half of the African American population. The first group, led by Susan B. Anthony and Elizabeth Cady Stanton, formed the National Woman Suffrage Association, demanding a constitutional amendment providing for woman's suffrage. The other wing, led by Henry Blackwell and Lucy Stone, organized the competing American Woman Suffrage Association. They pledged to work for woman suffrage at the state level while supporting the Fifteenth Amendment's provision for universal male suffrage. The organized struggle for woman's rights and particularly suffrage was thus split until 1890, when suffrage became a more mainstream movement. At this point, the two organizations merged into the National American Woman Suffrage Association (NAWSA). While the suffrage movement did achieve some successes on the state level in the nineteenth century, a federal suffrage law would await passage until the Nineteenth Amendment to the Constitution was ratified in 1920.

Women's rights activists made strides in other areas, though, most notably changes to women's property laws. In a series of acts passed in the 1840s, state legislatures began to overturn the laws of coverture that had governed women's property rights since the colonial period. These laws granted a woman the right to hold onto the property she brought into a marriage and to manage her own property within the marriage; a later set of laws granted married women control over their own earnings. By the 1870s, coverture had been abandoned in most states, and many states, especially in the North, had passed earnings acts as well. The loosening of laws governing women's property was not necessarily a feminist victory. For the most part, the male legislators who passed these laws were interested in protecting commerce and property from the poor management of husbands, rather than extending more rights to women. Nonetheless, the result of these laws was that married women were being redefined under the law, casting off their centuries-long status as the property of their husbands.

While the industrial economy encouraged new patterns of associational and recreational life for middle-class women, it fostered new patterns of work for laboring women. Other than teaching, there was virtually no white-collar work available to women in the early nineteenth century. Work tended not to be a choice, as it would be for some American women of later generations, but rather a necessity for women without adequate male support. Some women—widows especially—kept boarding houses or taverns, extending their domestic role beyond the traditional household. Others opened businesses catering to women, such as millinery shops. But the vast majority of working women had to choose from a limited number of options, which were exploitive or back-breaking or worse. They included laundry, factory work, and prostitution. Women swelled the ranks of the urban poor and were dominant in some of the most degraded occupations, including streetwalking, scavenging, ragpicking, and huckstering—selling second-rate market produce on the streets.

Indeed, poor and working-class urban women experienced the street in a host of ways unknown to their wealthier counterparts. Increasingly crowded into rented tenement apartments, these women experienced little in the way of the domestic privacy that was a growing expectation for middle-class and elite women who were ensconced in comfortable homes. Much of the social and economic life of these tenement-dwelling women thus took place in the streets of their neighborhoods, where they worked, shopped, and socialized.[3]

Industrial jobs became available to women as American industry began to take off in the first decades of the nineteenth century. The young government enacted favorable tax and legal policies for industry and encouraged technological and transportation developments that allowed for the emergence of a full-fledged market economy. In the Northeast especially, investors and entrepreneurs like Samuel Slater of Pawtucket, Rhode Island, and the Boston Associates in Lowell, Massachusetts, harnessed steam power, mass production techniques, and a growing labor force to create the American system of manufacturing. Manufacturers sought a cheap, dutiful labor force, and in these early years, they found it in white, native-born girls. These young women took the productive work that generations of women had done in the home— spinning, weaving, and sewing—to the new factories that were replacing their hand labor and changing their position within the home.

While the Lowell mill girls—the young, native-born women who worked in the mills of the paternalistic company town—have garnered much attention from historians and contemporaries, they represent only a small percentage of early nineteenth-century working women. In the industrial sector, women worked in a variety of manufacturing jobs. Although textiles led the field, women were employed in more than a hundred antebellum industries, including manufacturing gunpowder, nails, and shoes, even processing lumber. Outwork—industrial finishing completed in the home—was a crucial piece of women's industrial employment. Almost half of women wage earners in Massachusetts in 1837 were employed in finishing straw hats and bonnets by the piece in their homes. Such piecework was arduous and hardly lucrative and highlights the wage differentials between working-class men and women that prevailed throughout the nineteenth century. A woman performing sewing work from her tenement apartment in the 1840s might earn $2 a week; an unskilled male factory worker stood to earn a still scant $10 to $15 per week.

Most of the women who made up the workforce during the antebellum period were drawn from the flood of immigrants streaming into the United States at this time. Between 1820 and 1860, almost 5 million immigrants entered the United States, more than 4 million of them coming in the decades between 1840 and 1860. Hailing from Northern European nations, especially Ireland, Germany, and England, these newcomers settled largely in cities, swelling the population of these urban areas and contributing to the growth of many American cities from large towns to metropolises. New York City, the largest American city, saw its population increase from about 120,000 in 1820 to more than 800,000 in 1860; half of these residents were foreign born. In addition to the immigrant women who sought jobs in the burgeoning cities were the native-born black and white women whose circumstances required them to seek remunerative work.

Irish women dominated domestic service, in some cases sharing and in others wresting these positions from the African American women who had previously held them. By maintaining the appearance of the household and attending to the needs of its members, domestic servants left time for the mistress of the household and her daughters to engage in the consumer and educational activities central to replicating their middle-class status. A shift in domestic service in the early nineteenth century changed the relationship between female heads of household and their domestic help. Antebellum servants' relationship with their employers was far more formal and characterized by class distinction than that of earlier generations of hired help, who were generally drawn from neighboring families and were not necessarily considered members of a different class from the families they served.[4]

Domestic service came with certain drawbacks that made these jobs untenable for many women. For example, domestics lived under the roof of their employers and were, in many cases, expected to be at their beck and call, with little free time of their own. Employers often tried to influence how their servants dressed, ate, and worshipped, an issue that Irish Catholic servants particularly resented. Female domestics also faced frequent sexual exploitation on the part of their male employers. And unlike factory girls, they had few opportunities for socialization on the job, since they were isolated within the middle-class household.

While industrialization was taking hold in the North, the South saw the rapid development of a cotton society. The invention of the cotton gin in 1793 and the extension of the national domain with the Louisiana Purchase of 1803 made short-staple cotton a viable cash crop. The potential of cotton spurred a land boom in the soil-rich territories of the Southwest such as Mississippi, Louisiana, western Georgia, Arkansas, and Alabama, the area that came to be known as the cotton belt. Slavery might have died out in the South as the staple economies that depended on it in the eighteenth century—tobacco farming in the Chesapeake, rice and indigo cultivation in the Carolinas and Georgia—began to diversify, the soil depleted from decades of overuse. But the lure of cotton was irresistible to many people: Southern planters, Northern manufacturers, merchants in both regions and in England, as well as the many consumers in the United States and Europe who clamored for the manufactured cloth being produced in the mills and factories of New and Old England. Cotton was not the South's sole agricultural product; indeed, only half of Southern plantations produced this staple. Tobacco, rice, and sugar remained important crops. But cotton was so profitable that it overrode all other crops in importance and helped to shape a distinctive culture in the Deep South.

A central part of this culture was the explosive growth of slavery and its entrenchment as the South's "peculiar institution." Slavery's centrality to antebellum Southern society and culture belies the fact that only a quarter of white Southern families actually owned slaves. Designation as a "planter" required ownership of twenty slaves or more; about 40,000 Southern families fulfilled this requirement, and a mere 2,000 families owned more than 100 slaves. The vast majority of slave-owning families owned five slaves or fewer and worked alongside them in the fields and farms. And most white Southern women were part of the three-quarters of Southern families who owned no slaves at all. They lived on small family farms on the edges of the cotton belt, the farm-rich low country, and the remote hills of the Appalachian region. Farmers in these areas followed a subsistence-plus lifestyle that was reminiscent of the eighteenth-century model.

Despite their small numbers, the planter ethos and example dominated white Southern culture. Central to this ethos was the myth of the plantation mistress. The "Southern Lady" of prescription was a model of grace, piety, and charm. She was also considered a weak, dependent being, like her children reliant upon her husband in matters economic and political. While the myth elevated her on a pedestal, it gave her a largely ceremonial and decorative position in the family. In reality, the myth of Southern ladyhood worked to confine Southern planter wives to the home to a much greater extent than their Northern counterparts.

While few white Southerners owned slaves, most supported the system of slavery. The opulent lifestyle and extraordinary wealth of the tiny planter elite animated the dreams of many a white yeoman farmer and small slaveholder. Nonslaveholding whites were also tied into the system of slavery through family connections and employment. Plantation overseers, drivers, and hired laborers were drawn from the local, nonslaveholding white population. Racism also served as a powerful justification for nonslaveholding whites' support of slavery.

Wealthy or poor, white women of the South did share some common experiences that distinguished them from their Northern counterparts. One such commonality was their relative isolation. Southern transportation and communication networks remained rudimentary throughout the period. The spread-out nature of the Southern plantations and farms denied Southern white women the opportunities for daily visiting and socializing enjoyed by women in Northern towns and cities. Furthermore, the rich associational life of the North was virtually absent in the South, with the important exception of the church.

The reform movements that swept the North in the antebellum period made few inroads into the South. This situation was due in part to the strong links—perceived and actual—between reform movements and the abolitionist cause. In addition, these movements were inextricably tied to the burgeoning market culture of the North, to which the South remained largely aloof until after the Civil War. Thus, with few exceptions, Southern women were not involved in the areas of political life that consumed many of their Northern counterparts. And the bourgeois gender ideology that gave Northern middle-class women more say in the affairs of their households did not adhere in the households of the South.

Furthermore, both the Southern plantation and yeoman households remained largely self-sufficient in the antebellum period, although for different reasons. On the plantation, enslaved and free laborers produced the clothing, foodstuffs, and household goods that Northerners were increasingly purchasing ready-made. In the farms, hills, and backcountry, the market economy and technological advances such as transportation and communication developments took hold far later than in the North. Yeoman and poor farm families who lived in these areas still relied largely on women's household labor for their food, clothing, and other daily necessities. Even on small plantations and large farms with a few slaves, white women were responsible for much of the production of the household while the enslaved laborers worked mainly in the fields. Thus, the areas of consumer culture that claimed the attention of middle-class and elite Northern women and brought them into the streets of the antebellum cities and towns were not as available to Southern women.

Despite their isolation and the myth that represented them, planter wives did not lead idle lives. Plantation mistresses oversaw and to some extent managed extremely large, complex households. They were responsible for the care of sick children and slaves, for managing domestic affairs including the legions of domestic servants, and, when their husbands were away from the plantation, for overseeing its smooth running.

Perhaps nowhere else were the limits of gender solidarity—and of a monolithic approach to women—more evident than in the antebellum South. Gender was always trumped by race in the Southern social hierarchy. White women had more privileges by nature of their race than African American women and men. Thanks to an entrenched system of white supremacy, racism, and gender subjugation, plantation mistresses, as well as poor white women, were unlikely to feel common cause with their enslaved counterparts.

Women under slavery experienced a variety of working and living conditions. Some lived on large cotton plantations, others on small farms that grew corn and wheat, and others still in Southern cities. Each of these groups was distinguished by the kind of work they did, the number of whites and other enslaved blacks with whom they interacted, their living arrangements, and a host of other particulars. However, 75 percent of the antebellum slave population lived on large plantations and shared some common experiences.

First, the gender mores that applied to the white plantation mistress did not extend to enslaved women. Labor was hardly gender-segregated in the rice, tobacco, and especially cotton fields of the plantation South. Female and male field slaves did similar jobs, although the gangs in which they worked might be separated by gender. Enslaved women's work extended beyond the fields as well, to plowing, fence building, and some processing industries such as cotton mills, sugar refineries, and tobacco plants, which hired them out from their masters. Within the slave owner's household, enslaved domestics performed gender-defined tasks: Women worked as cooks, nurses, and maids, and men served as man-servants, butlers, and waiters.

Although they performed many of the same jobs as men, gender shaped the lives of enslaved women in very particular ways. Perhaps most important, women represented reproductive in addition to productive value to the slave owner. Their ability to bear children became even more important as the international slave trade was abolished in 1808 and the domestic slave trade came to rely on natural increase to fulfill the increasing demand for slaves. Fertile enslaved women were considered more valuable in terms of trade than were their less fecund sisters. But this situation did not bring them more power within the plantation structure. To the contrary, by marking them as "breeders," it made them vulnerable to rape and sexual exploitation. The prevalence of rape of enslaved women by their white overseers and owners was less common in reality than the abolitionist literature suggested. In general, racism and slave resistance militated against overwhelming sexual abuse of enslaved women. Nonetheless, rape of a slave woman was not illegal under Southern law, and the possibility of sexual exploitation was pervasive, highlighting the limits enslaved blacks had over their own lives.

Some of these limits related to the slave family. Marriages among enslaved people were not sanctioned by law. In the case of "broad" marriages—those between slaves from different plantations—they required the cooperation of slave owners. And despite the value placed on the fertility of enslaved women, an owner invested in slaves for productive work. Encouraging family life was secondary at best. Families could be separated because of the whim, death, or poor financial decisions of the slave owner.

Despite these constraints, enslaved Southerners did manage to establish and maintain strong family ties. On large plantations, a measure of autonomy adhered after hours in the slave quarters. A mix of family patterns could be found there, including nuclear families, female-headed households, polygyny, extended family households, matrifocality, and fictive kin. Given the precariousness of slave family life, a combination of these situations might apply to the same family over time. Women were at the center of most of these arrangements, and evidence suggests that slave families—and the women who often headed them—did not adhere to the domestic conventions that shaped family life for white Southerners and Northerners during this period. Enslaved women often lived on different plantations from their husbands and, in cases where family members were sold off to other plantations, lost touch with their husbands altogether. The net result of these factors was a strong, female-centered focus of slave family life and strong ties among enslaved women.[5]

Regardless of its shape, the slave family was a source of continuity, fostering the transmission of language, songs, dance, religion, history, and tradition and contributing to the vitality of the culture enslaved African Americans created. Fear of family separation worked to discourage flight, especially among slave women. Separation could be used by the slave owner as a threat to encourage docility and obedience. Evidence suggests that these efforts were only marginally successful. Although enslaved women *were* far less likely than men to attempt escape, they participated equally in daily acts of rebellion on the plantation, from theft to work slowdowns. The importance of family ties became especially evident following emancipation, when reuniting families became a first priority of many former slaves.

While prevalent, slavery certainly did not delimit the lives of all black women in the nineteenth-century United States. On the eve of the Civil War, about 500,000 free blacks lived in the United States, most in the Upper South. Spared many of the legal restraints of slavery—property ownership, marriage, control over their own comings and goings—free blacks nonetheless faced significant limits on their freedom, including restrictions on movement, voting, gun ownership, testifying in court, and serving on a jury. Most free black women worked for wages, largely in menial jobs like domestic work, laundry, and farm labor. A small but significant African American middle class formed in the antebellum period. Middle-class black women participated in reform activities like temperance and abolitionism, as well as other efforts to elevate the status of African Americans.

The Civil War

The increasingly divergent cultures of North and South came into armed conflict in the 1860s. Few American women escaped the effects of the Civil War. Families were ripped apart as husbands, sons, and fathers on both sides went off to fight and, in a huge number of cases, never returned. As in previous wars, women stepped into roles previously closed to them and ran businesses, farms, and plantations. The war also opened up opportunities to women that were closed to them in peacetime. Women worked in government jobs in both the Union and Confederate bureaucracies. In the Confederacy, women gained equal pay to men for government jobs over the course of the war. They also worked in factory jobs in the growing industrial economy of both regions, including munitions factories, which, in the Confederacy, had a majority-female workforce.

As they had in the American Revolution, a number of women disguised themselves as men and served in both the Union and Confederate Armies. A more common military contribution was working as nurses in army hospitals on both sides. Many male doctors and military leaders looked askance upon women witnessing some of the horrors of the military hospitals. On the Union side, reformer and overseer of army nurses Dorothea Dix worked to gain acceptance for female nurses by insisting on high standards of dress, conduct, and morality from the women who worked under her charge. Women also could be found in the Union and Confederate army camps, serving as cooks, laundresses, and camp followers. Some of these women were married to soldiers and officers. Others were former slaves, hundreds of thousands of whom fled their plantations and escaped to Union lines. While some freedmen served in the black-only regiments the Union Army established after 1863, most contrabands—and all women refugees—worked for the Union Army in roles similar to those they had performed during slavery: cooking, laundry, chopping wood, and tending fields belonging to planters loyal to the Union cause.

Seeking protection and work from the Army, they received a mixed reception from Union soldiers, many of whom shared the white supremacist views of the soldiers on the other side. Freedmen and women suffered deprivation and sometimes death in makeshift refugee camps. But most enslaved Southerners stayed behind on the plantations and often bore the brunt of their owners' new sense of vulnerability and dislocation. While the power of the slave master was waning, the threat of family separation continued during the war, as black men were impressed into the Confederate military or dragged away by owners attempting to stay a few steps ahead of the encroaching Union forces.

Southern white women experienced the dislocation, brutality, and danger of a home front war, which most Northern women were spared. Even in those areas of the South that were not touched by Union troops, the deprivations of war hit the Confederacy harder than the Union. Inflation was higher, food shortages greater, and a larger percentage of men fought on the Confederate than on the Union side. Off to the front, men left their wives, daughters, and sisters behind to tend to the plantations and farms in their stead. Many plantation mistresses found themselves in the uncomfortable position of running large plantations and managing increasingly restless slaves. The planter culture, which required the submissiveness and dependence of its ladies, confronted the needs of wartime, where plantation mistresses were now in positions of great responsibility. Many rose to the challenge, but some gave up in desperation.

Women on both sides immersed themselves in voluntary activities, including raising money for the war effort, rolling bandages, sewing clothing, and nursing wounded soldiers. Such activities were more organized in the Union states, where the federal government established the United States Sanitary Commission. Run by men but dominated by women, the Sanitary Commission bureaucratized volunteer efforts, fund-raising, and professionalized nursing. Many middle-class white Northern women learned important skills in the organization, which they parlayed into careers following the war. Other middle-class Northern women—both black and white—traveled south to work as teachers in Union-occupied territories. They were central to the establishment of freedmen's schools, one of the few and important successes of the federal government in the Reconstruction era.

The Late Nineteenth Century

With the war's end, many women ceded the responsibilities they had taken on during the war to returning soldiers. But many soldiers did not return. The Civil War was the deadliest in American history—more than 600,000 men lost their lives. Thousands of women were left widowed and on the edge of financial ruin, especially in the South, which suffered far greater casualties than the North. For these women, finding and keeping work during and following the war became an absolute necessity. Many middle-class white women found white-collar work as store clerks, office workers, and teachers, as the public education system in the South expanded. Working-class women took jobs in the burgeoning industrial sector, which included textile mills, cigarette factories, and light industry. By 1890, almost half of the workers in the Southern textiles industry were women.

While freedwomen may have seen domesticity as a badge of freedom, in reality many formerly enslaved women had no choice but to work for wages because their husbands and fathers had trouble making adequate wages to support an entire family. African American women's options were doubly limited by race and gender; the vast majority were confined to domestic service, laundry, and agricultural work. Others contributed to their family income by taking in boarders, laundry, or piecework. In the last decades of the nineteenth century, African American women outnumbered men in migrations to Northern cities. But manufacturing jobs remained largely closed to them, and most of these women had few job choices other than domestic service.

The policies of the strengthened federal government, including homestead rights, land grants, and subsidies to railroads and other corporations, encouraged white, western settlement. Thousands of women participated in the geographic mobility of the era, through westward settlement, migration, and immigration. In this process, they continued a long-term development that had begun just after the American Revolution, when land-hungry settlers, no longer limited in their aspirations by British policies like the Proclamation Line of 1763, started to encroach on lands west of the Appalachians. But following the Civil War, with the question of slavery in the territories resolved, the way was cleared for expansion and settlement to the west coast and the exploitation of the land for coveted raw materials that spurred industrial development.

Native American men and women were displaced from their lands on the Plains and in the Far West. Those whose tribes signed treaties with the federal government were forced onto reservations in Oklahoma and other western states. The reservation system was, to say the least, disruptive of every area of Native American life. Among these disruptions were changes to Indian women's roles within the family and community. The Dawes Act of 1887 imposed a bourgeois model of family structure and private property on the reservation. The government divided reservation lands into individual family plots and encouraged a white, bourgeois domestic model with corresponding gender norms. Indian women were encouraged to submit to a role of legal and social dependence on their husbands and to abandon traditional work roles, along with tribal activities and rituals.

The federal government also attempted to foster Native American acculturation through schooling; it established boarding schools like the Indian School of Carlisle, Pennsylvania, to inculcate Native American children with white, bourgeois values and practices. By 1902, there were twenty-five Indian schools in the United States, offering industrial training and English to their reticent students. The course of study also included inculcation in middle-class gender roles and mores; girls were taught domestic skills while boys were trained in industry.

Of course, Native American women responded to the onslaught of acculturation in a variety of ways—some embraced the European model, some rejected it outright and sought to preserve tribal traditions, and some blended old and new traditions in accordance with their needs. One example of this syncretism was the use of western tools to make traditional Indian clothing, beadwork, and pottery. Another was the entry into the market economy through sale of such items to non-Indian consumers. Many Native American women worked off the reservation in menial jobs such as domestic service and agricultural day labor. By and large, Native American women suffered from Western expansion and subjugation. The loss of tribal traditions for many and the restructuring of their economic role meant a loss of autonomy and

influence within the family and tribe. Further, Native American women suffered the general poverty and sense of dislocation that afflicted Native American
communities in general.

While Native American women reacted to white encroachment and subjugation, the European-descended women who moved onto their land experienced a different set of circumstances. Women on the westward trail faced a
particular set of difficulties, including isolation, having to "keep house" in rudimentary circumstances, and having to perform tasks usually relegated to men,
as the men in their group grew tired and sick on the trail. Those who settled in
remote regions of the West had to replicate the household system of production that industrialization had made obsolete in the more established communities of the East. In mining and other boom towns, single women found jobs
as boarding house keepers and in similar jobs to their Eastern counterparts—
domestic service, sewing, and prostitution. As the remote areas of the West
became more integrated into the national market economy, the demands of the
pioneer lifestyle eventually waned, and the lives of women in Western towns
and cities came to look more like those of the East.

The more fluid conditions of the West served in some cases to exagger-
ate women's vulnerability and exploitation and in others to afford them
more autonomy and opportunity than in the more settled societies back
East. Suffrage, for example, came first to women in Western states. In 1869,
the legislature of the Wyoming Territory became the first to extend the franchise to women; Utah, Idaho, and Colorado followed suit by the 1890s.
Entrepreneurship opportunities also accrued to some women in the less
established atmosphere of Western towns. And in some Western territories
like Wyoming and Colorado, women composed a small but significant percentage of homesteaders.

In another major migration stream, women were well represented among
the millions of immigrants entering the United States in the late nineteenth
century. These newcomers came largely from Eastern and Southern Europe
but represented nations and regions around the globe. Their experience upon
arrival and settlement depended, in some cases, upon their country of origin.
Jewish immigrants, for example, settled overwhelmingly in cities, especially
New York, while Scandinavian arrivals gravitated toward the rich farmland of
the Midwest. Italian and Chinese immigrants (who came in large numbers
before the 1882 Chinese Exclusion Act strongly limited further Chinese
immigration until well into the twentieth century) were overwhelmingly
male, whereas Eastern European Jews and Scandinavians tended to come in
family groups or to send for their families after settling themselves in the
United States.

Women continued to make up a large percentage of the industrial work-force. This was particularly true in certain industries, such as the garment industry. After the war, New York City became the center of the garment indus-try—its factories produced the vast majority of the nation's manufactured clothing. As they emerged in the 1870s and 1880s, these "factories" were, in fact, tenement apartments in the immigrant wards of the city. Women per-formed most of this sweatshop labor. The work was backbreaking—women huddled over sewing machines for hours at a time without breaks. The pace was impossible—garment workers worked on quota systems, and their employ-ers demanded a virtually impossible output. Moreover, wages were incredibly low, and the exploitive practices of the labor bosses meant that pay was often withheld or docked for supplies and even for the rental of the sewing machines. Few outlets existed for improvement of these work conditions. The state did not yet regulate factory conditions, and trade unions excluded women from membership throughout the nineteenth century.

Immigrant children also contributed to the family income by working in fields and factories. In some cultures, girls were especially central to the family income. Jewish immigrant families, for example, often sent their daughters out to work in the garment factories of New York City while their brothers con-centrated on their studies. These girls were expected to turn their earnings over to their families, who were dependent upon the additional income.

While their daughters might work for wages to help support the families, married immigrant women by and large tended to the home and worked within it for wages when necessary. Piecework continued to be common recourse for women hoping to supplement the meager incomes earned by their husbands and children. Garment finishing—sewing on buttons and decorations, for example—was a common form of outwork, and the artificial flowers that adorned the hats and clothing of wealthy and middle-class women were pro-duced largely by Italian women in the immigrant tenements of New York City. Clearly then, these tenements served as sites of wage-producing industrial labor, as much as domesticity.

Married working-class women contributed further to the family income by taking in boarders. This practice was particularly important in immigrant neighborhoods, where many young, single men arrived daily and required lodging and food. Boarders added to the already arduous work involved in run-ning a household, including cooking, shopping, cleaning, and laundry. These chores were especially difficult in the tenement districts of the nineteenth-century industrial city, where amenities such as plumbing, elevators, heat, elec-tricity, household appliances, and ventilation were either luxuries of the wealthy or not yet invented. Laundry, for example, involved fetching and hauling buckets of water, a task that often required climbing up and down several flights of rickety tenement stairs. The water then had to be heated, and the clothing beaten and wrung by hand. Finally, women had to hang the heavy laundry to dry on lines above the soot-filled streets, which ensured that it never truly got clean.

In addition to immigrant laborers, native-born women also sought economic opportunity in the nation's burgeoning cities. These "women adrift" lived in boarding houses and apartments; worked in factories, department stores, and offices; and frequented dance halls, amusement parks, and movie theaters, along with the daughters of European immigrants. Such cheap amusements emerged at the turn of the twentieth century, contributing to a heterosocial world of entertainments available to these women of which their mothers could not have dreamed. While amusement parks, dance halls, and nickelodeons provided young working women with a release from the monotony of factory, retail, and clerical work, historians have suggested that consumer culture fostered a lack of labor and gender consciousness for workers who could surround themselves with trappings of a middle-class, "liberated" lifestyle even as their work conditions deteriorated and their vulnerability to sexual exploitation continued.[6]

Many women adrift found work in the growing number of female-dominated occupations of the second half of the 1800s. Corporate capitalism required a huge clerical workforce, and typing and stenography became women's work, providing an entry for women into white-collar labor. Department stores and other retail outlets also developed female-dominated sales staffs and provided some limited professional opportunities for women as buyers and managers. Teaching also continued to be a predominantly female occupation. By and large, jobs in these sectors (clerical work, retail, and teaching) were reserved for native-born, white women, although African American women did find some teaching opportunities in the segregated schools of the South. The white-collar jobs available to women in the retail and sales sectors were cleaner and better paid than those in factories and domestic labor, but the average woman's wage was still half of the average man's, and with few exceptions, women were denied managerial opportunities.

Women did have greater opportunities for higher education in the late nineteenth century. Female academies had formed from the earliest days of the Republic and some American colleges, such as Oberlin, had opened their doors to women as early as the 1830s. But in the second half of the nineteenth century, the percentage of women in the nation's college population rose from 20 to 40 percent. The nation's new land-grant colleges, funded by the Morrill Land Grant Act of 1862, were coed from the beginning. And the late nineteenth century saw the creation of all-women's colleges like Mt. Holyoke, Vassar, Bryn Mawr, Wellesley, and Smith, as well as sister colleges to male universities, including Barnard and Radcliffe.

Distinct from the earlier ladies' academies that prepared young women for roles as wives and hostesses, the women's colleges offered rigorous liberal arts curricula on a par with the nation's elite men's colleges. Although the vast majority of students at these colleges were white, African American women experienced some opportunities in higher education as well. Some of the Northern schools accepted African American women, and some of the nation's all-black colleges such as Tuskegee Institute and Fisk University were coeducational. Thanks to the expansion of women's educational opportunities, women began to make inroads into professions such as law, medicine, and academia during this period. But professional positions for women remained incredibly limited throughout the 1800s.

By the end of the nineteenth century, a fifth of American women worked for wages, in tenement apartments, factories, schools, retail stores, and offices. Many of those who did not earn wages worked for political and social reform. Middle-class women extended and professionalized their reform activities, opening settlement houses, forming national organizations for women's rights and suffrage, and training in the new field of social work. By the late nineteenth century, middle-class women were arguing for an increased role in politics and reform based not on Christian morality but rather on women's "natural" domestic role. If women were to take care of their households properly, the argument for municipal housekeeping went, then they needed to be certain that their families would be safe outside the household as well. This motivation led to middle-class women demanding government reforms such as sanitation reform, antivice crusades, temperance, and agitation for parks and playgrounds. They would lead women into professional reform and eventually the field of social work.

Expanded opportunities for women in education, the professions, and public life were part of a general loosening of gender roles in the late nineteenth century. The abandonment of separate spheres extended from reality to prescription, as middle-class women were encouraged by a host of cultural arbiters to take a greater role in public life through education and reform activities. Middle-class women's role within the family expanded, too, as companionate marriages began to become the ideal and average family size shrank. Moreover, while the vast majority of women married, an increasing number, especially among the college-educated, were choosing not to marry but rather to follow a life of service or employment. Some of these women, such as those who dedicated their lives to higher education or to settlement living, formed their own families, replacing the domestic model with a female world of support and sometimes romantic love.

The settlement house movement drew a number of wealthy and middle-class white women in the 1890s and beyond. The largely female residents of settlement houses like Chicago's Hull House and New York's College Settlement came from families of wealth and privilege. They sought to use their resources and education toward the betterment of social problems and to foster a mutuality of class interests in the Gilded Age city. Settlements offered such services to the poor, immigrant communities they served as day care, industrial education, recreational activities, and advocacy—liaising between their neighbors and the city bureaucracy. These community centers served important roles within their neighborhoods and also for their residents, many of whom went on to illustrious careers as social workers and professional reformers, including Jane Addams, Eleanor Roosevelt, Florence Kelley, and Julia Lathrop.

As they had been in the antebellum period, women were involved in a variety of political movements in the late nineteenth century. Women led the charge for temperance reform. The most powerful and vocal temperance organization in the country, the Women's Christian Temperance Union (WCTU), was entirely organized, run, and peopled by women, including its influential leader, Frances Willard. With more than 160,000 members by 1890, the WCTU sought to prohibit the production and sale of alcohol, of course. But as the largest women's organization in the country, it also sought reform in other areas that affected women, including vice, politics, work, and suffrage. Women were prominent as well in the Farmers' Alliances, the Grange, and the Populist Party that emerged from these movements. They held "parlor meetings," canvassed, lobbied, and joined rallies. Indeed, the movement's rallying cry, "Raise less corn and more hell," was spoken by a woman, Kansan orator Mary Elizabeth Lease.

Women also gained valuable experience and social outlets in the club movement, in which many thousands of middle-class and elite women became involved in the late nineteenth century. By the 1890s, there were hundreds of women's clubs around the country, and in 1892, they formed an umbrella organization, the General Federation of Women's Clubs (GFWC). These clubs were established to provide an intellectual and cultural outlet to their members. They hosted lectures and discussions, sponsored civic improvements and charity endeavors, and pressured legislatures to pass laws concerning women's and children's labor, consumer advocacy laws, and suffrage.

Associational life was not limited to white women. Middle-class African American women also developed a rich group of organizations aimed at reform in general and at improving the position of African Americans in particular. In 1896, the black women's club movement formed its own umbrella organization, the National Association of Colored Women. In part, these clubs were involved in similar activities to white women's clubs, but they followed an additional mission of addressing the particular needs of African Americans. Some of these needs were political: The NAWC investigated lynching and segregation and provided a forum for antilynching crusader Ida B. Wells. Others of their concerns were moral. Like white reformers, the middle-class women of the black club women's movement applied bourgeois standards of morality to the men and women they sought to help. Their message of uplift, encoded in their motto "Lifting as We Climb," was seen by some as condescending and priggish, geared as it was toward chastity, modesty, and sobriety. But in their efforts toward elevating the status of all African Americans, regardless of social class, these women made important contributions to the ongoing struggle for African American equality.

As the nineteenth century ended, American women lived in a nation transformed in less than a century from a rural republic to an imperial, industrial powerhouse. Industrialization and modernization had changed the legal, social, and political position of all American women, regardless of their race, ethnicity, or class. And while gender did not unite American women in sisterhood, it did profoundly shape the way that individual women experienced the shocks, dislocations, promise, and perils of living in an industrial democracy. As they faced a new century, American women could expect even greater changes to their political, social, economic, and cultural lives.

NOTES

1. Influential works on separate spheres include: Barbara Welter, "The Cult of True Womanhood: 1820–1860," *American Quarterly* 18 (Summer 1966), 151–74; Nancy Cott, *The Bonds of Womanhood: "Woman's Sphere" in New England, 1780–1835* (New Haven, CT: Yale University Press, 1977); Carl Degler, *At Odds: Women and the Family in America from the Revolution to the Present* (New York: Oxford University Press, 1980); and Kathryn Kish Sklar, *Catharine Beecher: A Study in American Domesticity* (New Haven, CT: Yale University Press, 1973). For a more positive interpretation of separate spheres in creating supportive networks for women, see Carroll Smith-Rosenberg, "The Female World of Love and Ritual: Relations between Women in Nineteenth-Century America," *Signs* 1 (Autumn 1975), 1–29; and Blanche Wiesen Cook, "Female Support Networks and Political Activism: Lillian Wald, Crystal Eastman, Emma Goldman," *Chrysalis* (1977), 43–61.

2. In a pivotal article published in 1988, Linda Kerber surveyed the paradigms of women's history and complicated the idea of separate spheres. See Kerber, "Separate

Spheres, Female Worlds, Woman's Place: The Rhetoric of Woman's History," *Journal of American History* 75:1 (June 1988), 9–39. For a more recent rejection of separate spheres as an organizing principle, see the 2001 special issue of the *Journal of the Early Republic* 21 (Spring 2001), edited by Mary Kelley, with contributions by Julie Roy Jeffrey, Laura McCall, and Carol Lasser.

3. On working-class women and the uses of the street, see Christine Stansell, *City of Women: Sex and Class in New York, 1789–1860* (Urbana: University of Illinois Press, 1986).

4. On this shift from hired help to domestic service, see Faye Dudden, *Serving Women: Household Service in Nineteenth-Century America* (Middletown, CT: Wesleyan University Press, 1983).

5. On the female-centered world of the slave quarters, see Brenda Stevenson, *Life in Black and White: Family and Community in the Slave South* (New York: Oxford University Press, 1996).

6. Kathy Peiss, *Cheap Amusements: Working Women and Leisure in Turn-of-the-Century New York* (Philadelphia: Temple University Press, 1986). See also Joanne Meyerowitz, *Women Adrift: Independent Wage Earners in Chicago, 1880–1920* (Chicago: University of Chicago Press, 1988); Nan Enstad, *Ladies of Labor, Girls of Adventure: Working Women, Popular Culture, and Labor Politics at the Turn of the Twentieth Century* (New York: Columbia University Press, 1999).

3

Women in Twentieth-Century America

Barbara Winslow

Perhaps one of the most striking features of the twentieth century has been the dramatic transformation of women's status.[1] In 1900, women were excluded from the formal organizations of political and economic life and socially defined primarily by their marital status. With very few exceptions, women could not vote, serve on juries, or hold elective office, and they were legally as well as socially barred from a wide range of professions and occupations. Women had no legal right to contraception or abortion. In some states, only married women could own property. Marriage was deemed to be the only appropriate condition, and divorced women were socially ostracized. Divorced or abandoned mothers had no legal right to custody of their own children. The Fourteenth Amendment, which guarantees equal protection under the law, did not include women as "persons." Yet over the course of a century, women entered all aspects of public life—the workforce, politics, professions, arts, the armed forces, sports, media, and popular culture. Throughout this transformation, several themes have remained constant for women—the protection of mothers and children in the home and workplace and the struggle for equality in the economic and political life of the nation, peace, reproductive rights, and sexual freedom. At the same time, women have been deeply divided by race, class, nationality, ethnicity, and region and have often not acted collectively on these issues. Thus, another important theme of women's history in the twentieth century is the way in which diverse groups of women acted together, while organizing separately.

Women's activism and feminism were driving forces behind the profound transformation of women's status and women's lives in the twentieth century, centering the reform agenda of the pre–World War I Progressive Era. The absence of a *feminist* movement—that is, a conscious movement fighting for women's rights—shaped the great reform period from 1932 to 1940 known as the New Deal and left women and women's rights out of social reform. Women's activism and feminism once again shaped the post–World War II reform period agenda, changing the way in which men and women work, play, think, dress, worship, vote, reproduce, make love, and make war. Women's lives today would be almost unrecognizable to our great-grandmothers.

The transformation of women's lives coincided with the growth of industrialization, which necessitated an inexhaustible supply of waged labor. Women as well as men were needed to fill the demand. At the same time, the expansion of capitalism created new forms of industrial organization, in particular, the corporation, and with it a corporate bureaucracy in need of service, clerical, and domestic workers. Similarly, as federal, state, and local governments expanded, so did their need for service and clerical work. Urbanization necessitated new public and social service industries and jobs—schools, hospitals, communications, retail, and social work. Women entered the expanding areas of service, clerical, and domestic work, which by the end of the twentieth century had all but replaced manufacturing. Women's concentration in these areas maintained the gendered division of labor but moved it from the privacy of the home into the public economic sphere.

The entrance of women into the paid labor force had profound implications for the family structure. Large patriarchal families could not be sustained in the urban metropolis. Mothers, daughters, and sisters left the farms, often by themselves, for the cities and employment. Black women went north, to free themselves from the racial violence and legal segregation of the South. Tens of thousands of immigrant women left the family domicile every day to work in factories, offices, or shops, away from the chaperonage of fathers or husbands. These wives and daughters had the potential to be less dependent on the men of their family since the beginning of the century, when women had won the right to own property and keep their earnings. But while women could free themselves from the authority of their fathers, they still lived under the authority of a patriarchal state.

The first reform period in the twentieth century (1900–1920), called Progressivism, encompassed a wide range of networks, political organizations, and coalitions, some conflicting, some overlapping, but all campaigning to address the wide-ranging cultural, social, political, and economic dislocations and inequities brought about by industrial capitalism. Millions of women entered the social and political arena as reformers and radicals. Some, like Lillian Wald, settlement worker and peace advocate, wanted to reform the economic and political system in order to ameliorate the worst conditions of women's lives; others, like Elizabeth Gurley Flynn, labor radical and feminist, challenged the foundations of capitalism itself, as well as women's sexual oppression. Black women like Mary Church Terrell, founder of the National Association of Colored Women (NACW) and the National Association for the Advancement of Colored People (NAACP), advocated "lifting as we climb," combining the historic experience of African American mutual aid with the promise of upward mobility.

As women's activism and feminism took center stage in every aspect of this reform period, so did the belief that women's historic role as mother, housewife, and nurturer was connected to a wider movement for social change and gave women a unique role as mothers. "Maternalism," as scholar Eileen Boris describes it, is a set of ideas and policies that consider women as primarily responsible for nurturing children.[2] Although feminist maternalism had differing political emphases, depending on class, race, gender, ethnicity and region, it was the dominant discourse of progressive reform.

The political argument for women's suffrage exemplifies the emergence of a form of maternalist feminism. In the nineteenth century, the argument had been based on the assumption that women were entitled to the same legal rights as men. By the early twentieth century, the suffrage movement became a mass movement, and its rhetoric changed. The membership of the National American Women's Suffrage Association (NAWSA), the largest and most influential women's suffrage movement, was made up largely of college-educated, middle-class white women who were already involved in a wide range of women's clubs, temperance societies, and civic and charitable institutions. These women activists presented themselves as the embodiment of civic virtue and based their demand on the essentialist argument of special roles for women. As immigrant, working-class, and African American women increasingly entered industry and joined labor and civic organizations, they, too, became involved in the struggle for women's suffrage. Members of NAWSA advocated a wide range of progressive reforms: protective legislation, equal pay, pure-food regulation, social welfare, higher education, and municipal reforms. In other words, women voters, especially middle-class women voters, would reform political corruption, "Americanize" the immigrant poor, outlaw alcohol and child labor, punish male violence, and end industrial conflict.

Maternalist suffrage rhetoric was often class-based and racist. Southern suffragists promised that (white) women's suffrage would ensure white supremacy in the South. For fear of losing white suffrage supporters, NAWSA meetings were segregated, and despite pleas from black suffragists, the organization never took a stand against lynching.

In response to NAWSA's exclusionary politics, black women formed their own suffrage organizations, marched in suffrage parades, and linked their demands for women's suffrage to the needs of the black community, including antilynching campaigns, and to support of black politicians. Many of the same black suffragists founded the National Council of Negro Women, as well as the NAACP. Working-class, trade union, and immigrant women, excluded from the organized labor movement, formed working-class women's suffrage organizations or worked with NAWSA in the hopes that women's suffrage would result in legislation improving wages and working conditions. Alliances with middle-class reformers were problematic. The Women's Trade Union League (WTUL), a progressive feminist organization founded in 1903 by white middle-class reformers, reflected the tension. The WTUL brought together trade union activists and middle-class reformers for the purpose of educating women about the advantages of trade union membership, supporting women's demands for better working conditions and women's suffrage, and raising awareness about the exploitation of women. Trade union women constantly complained that the dominating presence of middle-class women prevented working-class and immigrant women from full and equal participation.

The campaign for women's suffrage, somewhat stalled by 1914, was reinvigorated after Alice Paul returned to the United States to bring militant, confrontational tactics to the women's suffrage movement. Paul joined with other feminist radicals like Crystal Eastman and Harriot Stanton Blatch in demanding a new definition of womanhood, one based on freedom and equality. For the next five years, and even during World War I, suffrage activists continued their campaigns. During World War I, Paul's militant suffrage organization, the Congressional Union, pursued confrontational tactics, including picketing President Wilson and chaining themselves to the White House gates. In return, the government arrested and then force-fed hunger-striking suffragists. In 1919, the Senate accepted the Nineteenth—women's suffrage–Amendment, which was ratified by the states and became federal law the following year.

Although the struggle for women's suffrage was the most visible, well-organized, and successful political expression of women's activism, progressive maternalism had a wide range of other political emphases. Progressive reformers lobbied municipal officials to improve sanitation in cities and advocated legislation to enforce street cleaning, sewerage, and garbage disposal.

Progressives won the first public welfare program providing state aid to single mothers. Other localized campaigns coalesced into successful reforms. The Pure Food and Drug Act, another example, came about in part because of pressures from the powerful network of women's clubs.

Black women's political activities occasionally intersected with those of white women, especially in areas of health and sanitation. Like their white sisters, they claimed a higher moral authority. Combining religious values with activism, they organized in their communities, campaigned for municipal reform, and supported temperance and suffrage. Unlike white women, however, they had to create and sustain their own institutions, such as playgrounds, community centers, and homes for the aged, services denied to them because of race.

The overriding political belief of maternalist feminism was that governments could produce positive change and that the state could protect women. Nowhere was this better expressed than in the demands for protective legislation for women, for mothers' pensions, and for the creation of women's and children's bureaus at the state and federal levels. Each state had its own set of protective legislation, laws that, for example, guaranteed an eight-hour day for women, prohibited night work for women in certain occupations, mandated weight restrictions, and provided couches or chairs in women's restrooms. Because women could not vote in most states and were not organized in trade unions, these laws were enacted in recognition of women's powerlessness. But the political rationale behind them assumed women's inferiority: that women were inherently weaker and therefore could not do the same tasks as men; that women are essentially mothers, and therefore, workplaces must be conducive for mothers or future mothers; and that certain jobs, for example, jobs requiring night work, were unsafe for women and could call into question their purity.

The world of women's work was a central concern to feminists and progressives. More and more middle-class women were entering the professions. In 1870, professional women represented 6.4 percent of the female labor force; this grew to 10 percent in 1900 and 13.3 percent in 1920, representing almost a million women. At the same time, female education was expanding. From 1890 to 1920, women were 55 percent of all high school students and 60 percent of all high school graduates. By 1890, American women made up a third of all college students.[3] A college education was not solely a mark of class privilege but an indication that middle-class women had aspirations other than marriage and motherhood. New professions, such as sales, clerical, nursing, and social work, attracted middle-class women while others went into teaching or entered male-dominated professions such as journalism, medicine, and law.

The overwhelming majority of women and children who worked did so in a variety of paid, unpaid, illegal, and bartered jobs. In 1900, more than a quarter of a million children under age fifteen were working in mines, mills, factories, and fields. Mexicanas, Chicanas, African American women, and Filipinas worked as hired farm laborers, especially in the South and West.⁴ In towns and cities, women took in boarders, looked after children, and took in washing and other forms of homework. The majority of domestic workers in the South were African American women. As they migrated north, they replaced Irish and German women working as maids in Northern homes. Prostitution expanded with the growth of urban areas. Progressive feminists were moved by the condition of these women, and a key part of their progressive agenda was to ameliorate their poverty and powerlessness.

Changes in industry created the material conditions for working-class and overwhelmingly immigrant women workers to connect progressive feminism to working-class radicalism and to lay their own claim to power. In the textile industry, new machinery, especially sewing and cutting machines, increased productivity and created a new form of industrial organization—the sweatshop. Thousands of women, primarily Italian and Jewish, worked sixteen hours a day in tiny, unventilated, poorly lit shops locked from the outside. It was not uncommon for women to go blind after years of sewing sequins and beads. The pay was so low that most women had to take work home.

In 1908, 15,000 women textile workers, many of whom were members of the Socialist Party, marched through the streets of New York carrying a banner calling for the end to sweatshop labor, the right to vote, child care provisions, and equal pay. These young women proved to the country and to the world that women were a powerful force and that they were determined to have a voice in the struggle for unionization and women's rights.

The next year, the textile industry exploded when even more thousands of women, furious with wage cuts and other grievances, walked out. Clara Lemlich, a young Jewish clothing worker and a veteran of other strikes, made history on November 1909 by passionately calling for a general strike. More than 40,000 workers went out in New York, and the strike soon spread to Rochester, Chicago, Philadelphia, and Cleveland. The Women's Trade Union League supported the strike with money, legal advice, publicity, and womanpower on the picket lines, even risking arrest and jail time. The industry-wide strike brought thousands of women into the International Ladies Garment Workers' Union (ILGWU). While the strikers did not win all their demands, these young women had made themselves a force to be reckoned with. The public consciousness of the plight of working women was accentuated when a year later a fire at the Triangle Shirtwaist Factory, one of the most notorious sweatshops, killed 146 women. The public outrage against the owners of the factory finally brought about factory inspections.

The socialist, anarchist, and radical movements had a different point of view about how best to end women's oppression. Radical labor organizer Mary "Mother" Jones; Elizabeth Gurley Flynn, member of the syndicalist Industrial Workers of the World (IWW); and anarchist Emma Goldman believed that the key to improving women's lot would not come from the vote or from the American Federation of Labor (AFL), but from organizational change at the workplace and sexual liberation through birth control.

Feminists in the first two decades of the twentieth century pursued more than just economic and political reform and often opposed the progressive emphasis on uplift, selfless service, and feminine nurturance. Ida Rauh campaigned for birth control and trade union rights and also acted with the Cape Cod Provincetown players; Crystal Eastman and Harriet Rodman smoked in public and danced at a saloon called the Working Man's Club. Emma Goldman agitated for free love. These New Women, determined to achieve self-determination and personal freedom, connected personal, sexual, and psychological liberation and presaged the radical feminism of the post-1965 period.

During the Progressive period, the campaign for birth control was associated almost exclusively with political and sexual radicalism. Emma Goldman, the anarchist; Dr. Marie Equi and Kate Richards O'Hare, socialists; and Elizabeth Gurley Flynn, member of the IWW, campaigned for birth control information and devices as the key to women's freedom. However, the person most associated with the century-long campaign for birth control is Margaret Sanger, who coined the phrase "birth control" in her newspaper, *The Woman Rebel*. Sanger and her supporters took direct action by opening birth control clinics in Brooklyn, New York, and giving immigrant women information about birth control devices.

When war broke out in Europe in 1914, the maternalist belief in an international sisterhood and motherhood was abandoned. Feminists and reformers supported their own nation-state against "sisters" and "mothers" of other nations. Progressive women reformers like Lillian Wald, while opposing the war and conscription, worked with the government in the administration of wartime activities. Some suffragists promised loyal support for the government in return for the vote. Others, like those in the Congressional Union, continued to engage in suffrage agitation. Some feminists, however, campaigned against the war. Jeannette Rankin, the first woman elected to Congress, cast her first vote in opposition to the U.S. declaration of war. Radical and socialist women worked outside the system in opposing the war, conscription, and the repressive war legislation. For their efforts, Emma Goldman was deported, and others, such as Kate Richards O'Hare and Elizabeth Gurley Flynn, were imprisoned. In 1915, the Women's Peace Party was established. Later that year, American women joined more than a thousand representatives from twelve countries to the International Congress of Women at The Hague. The ICW called for women's suffrage, as well as an end to war. Peace activists, most of whom were already involved in aspects of progressive reform, carried the maternalist arguments about government reform into the arena of war and peace. The formation of the Women's International League for Peace and Freedom (WILPF) stressed the common bond of women as mothers and the importance of motherly values in international relations.

Wars often open up opportunities for women by drawing more women into the paid labor force, loosening the patriarchal bonds of the family, and sometimes forcing the government to intervene and regulate the equality of women's employment, earnings, and working conditions. At the same time, women lose husbands, fathers, sons, and brothers, and they are often left poverty-stricken. Political repression at the end of the war demonized socialist and radical feminism, leaving reform feminists marginalized.

In 1920, women won the right to vote. For feminist activists, women's suffrage was their first great victory. There was some extension of women's rights in the 1920s. White women gained the right to serve on juries in twenty states, and the Sheppard-Towner Maternity and Infancy Protection Act of 1921 was passed, which for the first time provided federal funds for health care.[5] Property, marriage, and divorce laws, however, remained discriminatory.

Women's visibility took new forms. In 1920, American women entered the Olympics for the first time; Glenna Collett was the first woman golfer to break 80 for eighteen holes; Floretta McCutcheon defeated bowling champion Jimmy Smith; Hazel Wightman won U.S. tennis titles. Women's bodies and sexuality became more visible with the rise of movie stars like Mae West, Clara Bow, and Mary Pickford. The Miss America Contest, founded in 1921, made the bathing beauty as American as apple pie. Gladys Bentley, an open lesbian performer, owned her own nightclub in Harlem and married her white girlfriend in a public ceremony. Women drove automobiles, smoked, drank, and danced in public; single women dated without chaperonage.

But in the 1920s, feminism and women's rights were constantly attacked. In 1921, Republican Vice President Calvin Coolidge declared women's colleges to be hotbeds of radicalism; the Daughters of the American Revolution (DAR) accused the Women's Trade Union League and the government Women's Bureau of destroying the family. The conservative political attack was accompanied by a cultural assault. Psychology, an emerging social science, analyzed feminism as neurosis, maladjustment, or immaturity.

The largest women's rights organization, NAWSA, was dismantled and renamed the League of Women Voters. Rather than organizing women voters to pursue specific women's reforms, the League defined itself as training women for the role of citizenship. The National Woman's Party (NWP), founded by Alice Paul, concentrated its efforts on removing laws restricting women's equality. When the NWP introduced the Equal Rights Amendment (ERA) in 1923, it provoked a split with the progressive reformers who had fought for protective legislation, further weakening feminist activities. Temperance, which had united feminists and reformers, divided feminists between those who wished to protect working-class women from the abuses of alcohol and those who defended individual freedom.

The most significant development in the lives of American women was the growing number of married women in the paid labor force. Since 1900, the percentage of married women workers had doubled. Poverty was the main determinant of whether a woman worked; married African American women were five times more likely to be in the paid labor force. Progressive reformers continued to press such issues as equal pay, the eight-hour day, abolition of child labor, services for maternal and infant health, employment boards, a minimum wage, and antilynching legislation. Women entered the paid labor force as new kinds of "white-collar" employment—banking, real estate, retail, and clerical—emerged. But while women continued to enter the workforce, they did so on unequal terms with men. By 1929, a woman earned only 57 cents to a man's dollar. One traditional female profession, midwifery, all but disappeared as states outlawed the practice during the 1920s, and birthing moved from the home to the hospital.

The rise of consumerism, marketed as a way of life that would ultimately free women from domestic drudgery and give them a sense of personal fulfillment, allowed more married women to enter the labor force. Sales of household appliances were booming. Labor-saving devices, however, did not necessarily lead to less work and more fulfillment. Women were expected to do all the shopping, and some services, such as laundry and baking, for example, which had formerly been done outside the home, moved back to the individual woman's kitchen. Middle-class women were told that consumption was a means by which they could exercise both individual freedom and authority in the family as the major purchaser.

Women of color continued to face racial discrimination and segregation. Mexican American women were concentrated in marginally paid work in the fields, textiles, laundries, and bakeries; Japanese women worked mainly in small family businesses or domestic service. All women of color faced racially based employment as well as social segregation.

The lives of African American women changed in the first two decades of the twentieth century as tens of thousands moved from the rural South to the industrial North. Disenfranchisement, segregation, racial violence, poverty, poor educational and employment opportunities, and the day-to-day indignity of living in the Jim Crow South were the impetus for this migration, but racial prejudice followed. Expanding industrial production demanded more unskilled workers, and when the flow of European immigrants declined during World War I, African Americans filled the necessary gaps. The black population of Chicago doubled to more than 100,000, and 150,000 African Americans lived in New York City, making it the largest black center in the world. African American women found jobs in industry and manufacturing, as well as in some professions, nursing, and teaching. The most dramatic change was in the area of domestic labor, as the domestic workforce shifted from Irish or German to African American or Afro Caribbean. In less than thirty years, the gendered occupation of housework had become racialized.

The change from rural to urban life allowed black women to demonstrate differing forms of racial pride and solidarity. Pan-Africanism, an ideology and movement that called for the unification of all Africans into a single African state to which those in the African diaspora could return, was centered in New York City. The largest black organization in modern world history, the United Negro Improvement Association (UNIA), founded by Marcus Garvey, organized black women. There were thousands of women in the general membership; the UNIA had two specific women's sections, the Black Cross Nurses and an all-woman paramilitary, the African Motors Corps, and special organizational positions for women assured their representation at the highest level. Garveyism's promotion of female activism enabled black women to assert racial and gender pride without fear of violent racist backlash. Garveyism collapsed as a result of government persecution. A flowering of black culture known as the Harlem Renaissance paralleled the migration to urban areas and postwar African American activism. Black women singers like Ma Rainey, Ethel Waters, and Bessie Smith and writers like Zora Neale Hurston and Nella Larsen challenged traditional racial, sexual, and gender norms.

Throughout the 1920s, the absence of a feminist movement, the impact of political repression, and the decline of radicalism meant that when the "roaring twenties" crashed on October 24, 1929, women and women's rights had little protection. The economic and social crisis of the Great Depression exacerbated gender, racial, and ethnic discrimination. As women's unemployment rose, so did discrimination against working women, especially married women. In 1936, a Gallup Poll revealed that 82 percent of the population thought wives should not work if their husbands had jobs. In most cities, married women teachers lost their jobs. The New England Telephone and Telegraph and the

Northern Pacific Railroad fired all its married female employees. The AFL agreed that employment preference should be given to men.

Destitution affected a growing number of single women. By 1932, more than 2 million women were unemployed; homeless women roamed the streets and slept in subways. Low-paid women combined several forms of economic activity to support their families by taking in boarders, doing laundry, becoming cleaning women, or setting up bakeries, beauty parlors, or restaurants in their homes. Finally, the Depression cut the upward mobility of working women, forcing them to lower their job expectations and face diminished pay and job satisfaction.

The 1932 election of Franklin Roosevelt gave the unemployed and destitute new hope. His New Deal created social legislation, economic regulations, and governmental apparatus that became the prominent feature of American life during the second half of the twentieth century. First Lady Eleanor Roosevelt was the 1930s model of American womanhood, a devoted wife, mother, and grandmother who was at the same time engaged in civic activism. In the 1920s, she turned her energies to a variety of reformist organizations, including the League of Women Voters and the Women's Trade Union League. She advocated the abolition of child labor, the establishment of a minimum wage, and legislation to protect workers. In the process, she discovered that she had talents—for public speaking, for organizing, and for articulating social problems.

There was, however, no New Deal for women. Women and women's rights were excluded from legislation and policy making. The New Deal administration saw the employment of the male breadwinner as the answer to poverty. The National Recovery Act that set wages and the Social Security Act did not cover the majority of female jobs—domestic, clerical, and agricultural. Unequal pay was mandated from 5 cents to 25 cents in a quarter of its codes. The Social Security Act provided grants for mothers with dependent children, but many of its provisions discriminated against female wage earners, especially married ones. Aid to Dependent Children (ADC), while paying money to widows and a broader group of women living without men, was extremely limited, and in the South, white administrators denied payment to black families. Few women found jobs in the Civil Works Administration or the Public Works Administration. Only 8,000 young women, in contrast to 2.5 million men, gained employment in the Civilian Conservation Corps. Some federal programs provided relief for African American, Chinese, Filipina, Indian, and Latina women, who had been excluded from state and local relief efforts. Overall, women and minority men faced gender and racial discrimination in these programs.

By the 1930s, feminism was identified as a movement for middle-class women that was interested only in narrow individual rights. Most women New Dealers were committed to the older Progressive agenda and campaigned for "special protection" for women rather than equal rights. Very few raised their voices in protest against the gender discrimination of New Deal legislation. Even the radical, trade union, socialist, and communist movements, while supporting women's rights in principle, did not mobilize women around a feminist agenda. There was no protest against the exclusion of married women from the workforce. Women participated in organizing and union activities in spite of strong resistance from men. Stella Nowicki, Chicago Packing House Union activist and Communist Party organizer, complained that her comrades "didn't take up the problems women had nor did they encourage women to come to meetings." The ideology of the Left was that proletarian women were to be supportive of and protected by white male workers.

In spite of such neglect, women gained influential positions in the Roosevelt administration. Frances Perkins became the first woman U.S. cabinet member, secretary of Labor; Nellie Taylor Ross, the first woman director of the Mint; and Florence Allen, the first woman on the U.S. Circuit Court of Appeals. Some New Deal programs, especially the Works Progress Administration, financially supported women artists such as Dorothea Lange, Alice Neel, Margaret Bourke-White, Louise Nevelson, and Hallie Flanagan, which allowed them to paint and write. First Lady Eleanor Roosevelt brought along her own "Negro Cabinet," including Mary McLeod Bethune, who was appointed director of the Division of Negro Affairs. While FDR needed white racist Southerners for his New Deal coalition, his wife was able to bring the support of African Americans into an emerging Democratic Party coalition.

Women were politically active outside the confines of New Deal politics. The antifascist movement revived women's internationalism. Writers and journalists such as Dorothy Parker, Martha Gellhorn, and Lillian Hellman went to Spain in support of the Republican cause. Salaria Kea, an African American nurse, organized against the Italian invasion of Ethiopia as well. Socialist, Communist, and Trotskyist women played leading roles in unemployment councils, food riots, and women's auxiliaries in trade union organizing struggles. As a result of the National Labor Relations Act in 1936, which legalized collective bargaining, more than half a million women workers joined trade unions. Pressure from black women, as well as the Communist Party's activities opposing racial segregation, enabled Jessie Daniel Ames, a former Texas suffragist and feminist, to set up the Association of Southern Women for the Prevention of Lynching. This organization brought women from the National

Council of Jewish Women and the Methodist Women's Missionary Council to investigate accusations of rape, as well as campaign against lynching.

Margaret Sanger's campaign for birth control reflected the decline of radical feminism. By the 1930s, she abandoned her pre–World War I emphasis on women's right to sexual self-determination for the more respectable idea of "planned parenthood," a concept supported by middle-class Republicans. As birth control became associated with the ideas of population control and eugenics as a means for whites to control black and Puerto Rican birthrates, more contraceptive devices and clinics were made available in a number of state public health programs. There was no public opposition to the ideas of eugenics, even from radicals and feminists. In the 1930s, Puerto Rican feminists, public health workers, and *independistas* organized a successful campaign to repeal the anti–sex information Comstock Law. However, they did so because this coalition wanted birth control to deal with the problem of so-called overpopulation.[6]

Even before the formal declaration of U.S. entry into World War II, Franklin Roosevelt shifted priorities from New Deal domestic legislation to preparation for wartime mobilization, which transformed women's roles in the home and workforce. Shortly after the formal declaration of war, the government War Manpower Commission launched a special campaign to recruit women, especially married women, by emphasizing how women war workers supported their husbands on the front lines without losing their femininity or challenging existing gender roles. Norman Rockwell's wartime cover girl, Rosie the Riveter, depicted a confident, muscular woman, wearing denims, eating her lunch with a large riveting tool in her lap and her feet stepping on *Mein Kampf.*

The percentage of women entering the paid labor force with the expansion of wartime industries increased dramatically from 25 percent to 36 percent, the largest increase in forty years. The number of employed women rose from 11 million to nearly 20 million, 5 million of whom had never before worked for wages. Hundreds of thousands of women moved from lower to higher paying jobs. In 1940, one in twenty women worked in the high-wage automobile industry. By 1944, it was one in five. Despite great resistance from employers and white workers, black women, who had been largely confined to domestic and agricultural labor, entered higher paying and unionized factory, clerical, and sales jobs. The proportion of married women and mothers increased; by war's end, married women were the majority of the female labor force. Women's membership in unions doubled from 11 to 23 percent, despite the indifference and hostility of male union members. Unions supported equal pay for women, mainly to protect the higher wages of male unionists, but did not support women's demands for maternity leaves with continuous seniority and improved child care or for ending job segregation and separate seniority lists, which dis-criminated against women. When the war ended and millions of women were fired, the unions raised few objections.

Women also volunteered to serve in the armed forces. After overcoming tremendous hostility from the military, the Women's Army Corps (WAC) was established, attracting thousands of women. However, the army made sure that gender and racial roles were rigidly enforced. The 4,000 African American women who joined the WAC were relegated to kitchen work, lived in segre-gated barracks, and were not sent overseas. Black army nurses were allowed to care for only black soldiers; the WAVES (Women Accepted for Voluntary Emergency Services) remained all white until 1944.

The growth of female employment and the mobilization of women in all areas of patriotic public life did not necessarily translate into a challenge to existing gender roles. The government provided child care for defense workers through the passage of the Lanham Act in 1941, but for the most part, federal day care was inadequate and inaccessible, and most women had to find indi-vidual solutions to child care. There was an acute housing shortage during the war. Rents were high, and wartime inflation ate up the high wages. Landlords discriminated against African American and single women. Women had to make do with rationed food and overcrowded living quarters. The home front was even more inhospitable for Japanese women when 10,000 Japanese were interned in barbed wire camps in the desert. Conditions of camp life led to deterioration of family unity, as harsh barracks life separated mothers from children, men from women.

When the men began marching home in August 1945, thousands of women workers were summarily dismissed. Because there were no working-women's organizations, there was little protest, even though four of five women indicated in a Woman's Bureau survey that they wished to stay in the labor force. Returning soldiers came home to a GI Bill and got their jobs back. Women were fired or demoted in droves, their child care centers were disman-tled, and training programs ended. They found it difficult to enter colleges flooded with ex-GIs matriculating on government money. Yet in spite of all these disappointments, millions of women gained a new sense of self-confi-dence as waged workers. They understood that their horizons had been expanded. In the words of welder Lola Weixel, her experience "was a special thing. At the end of the day I always felt I accomplished something."[7]

Three factors characterized American life after World War II: the postwar baby boom and economic boom and the emergence of the Cold War. From 1946 to 1964, 92 percent of all women of childbearing age had children. On average, a baby was born every eight seconds for eighteen straight years.

Likewise, for almost a quarter century after the war, the United States experienced an unprecedented era of sustained economic growth. Despite a few short recessions, the production of services and goods doubled while unemployment and inflation, for most of the time, stayed below 5 percent. The greatest growth occurred in the public sector. In 1956, for the first time in U.S. history, white- and pink-collar, professional, managerial, clerical, sales, and domestic workers comprised half the labor force. The economic expansion and the accompanying material affluence had a profound effect on women.

While business leaders, politicians, clergy, and other social commentators were insisting that a woman's place was in the home, female employment grew at a rate four times that of men. The postwar shift to clerical and service work would not have been possible without the influx of 20 million women into the labor force. In 1950, women were 31 percent of the total work force; by 1960, they were 42 percent. Forty percent of black mothers with small children worked outside the home; 39 percent of Puerto Rican women who migrated to the mainland after World War II also worked, largely in low-paid, nonunionized employment. Job segregation characterized women's work, keeping women in the lowest paid dead-end jobs. By 1960, 95 percent of the female labor force was confined to five low-paying job categories: light manufacturing (garment work), service, clerical, domestic, and education—categories that, one could argue, represented the extension of women's work in the home into the labor market. Women sought employment because of economic necessity, which was exacerbated by postwar inflation, and a greater emphasis on consumer goods. Even many white middle-class women whose husbands were professionals needed to work in the paid labor force to maintain a middle-class lifestyle.

The gendered division of labor was reinforced by a sexual ideology of the postwar years that celebrated women's domesticity, nurturing, and submissiveness. Women were constantly caught between two contradictory and hostile ideologies: If they worked, they were made to feel guilty for being selfish and neglectful of their husbands and children; yet, as women were encouraged to leave the workplace for full-time devotion to housewifery and motherhood, they were attacked for a "momism" that is overbearing, stultifying, and even emasculating.

The suburban housing tracts of postwar America, a product of the economic boom, sustained the ideology and rigidity of race and gender roles. The suburban lifestyle was designed around the stay-at-home mom who cared for her private home, emphasizing consumption: two cars, so that mom could shop and chauffeur children and dad could drive to work, and modern appliances, washer-dryers, refrigerators, and televisions. Many women loved the

spaciousness and convenience of their new homes, the safety of their neighborhoods, and the access to good schools, even without the urban social services—
laundries, the corner grocery, the bus or subway—that eased the burden of
housework and child rearing.

The material wealth of the postwar economic boom was, however, accompanied by an era of repression and fear. McCarthyism, the name given to the
movement against real and imagined communism at home and abroad, had a
profound impact on women. The overall assault on radicalism in unions weakened labor's ability to fight for its membership. The most vulnerable members,
women and trade unionists of color, suffered the most. McCarthyism stopped
the progress toward a welfare state and prevented public medical insurance,
federally funded birth control, and public housing. The right-wing atmosphere
of the 1950s contributed to the decline of progressive women's organizations.
The Women's Trade Union League disbanded in 1950; the National Consumers
League was barely active; the League of Women Voters and the National
Women's Party lost membership. The Women's Division of the Democratic
Party was disbanded in 1952.

Women's discontent with the prevailing social order bubbled up just under
the surface of 1950s repression, conformity, and complacency. Clara Fraser, a
young Trotskyite electrician on the Boeing Aircraft assembly line, successfully
campaigned for increased involvement of women in the International
Association of Machinists and first-class union membership for blacks. During
the 1948 Boeing strike, she organized a picket line of mothers and babies to
defy an antipicketing injunction. When the strike was broken, Fraser was black-
listed—a condition she endured throughout the McCarthy era. Pauli Murray, a
lawyer active in community and labor politics under the New Deal, worked
with the NAACP in challenging legal segregation. Rosa Parks, a Methodist,
seamstress, and NAACP member, attended the left-wing, integrated Highlander
Folk School in Tennessee, which trained labor and civil rights organizers. Del
Martin and Phyllis Lyon founded the Daughters of Bilitis (DOB) to provide an
alternative culture for lesbians and to "educate the public to accept the Lesbian
homosexual into society."[8] The FBI and CIA infiltrated the organization, terrified that homosexuality threatened the patriarchal social order. The women's
peace movement resurfaced during this period in opposition to the Korean
War and the proliferation of nuclear weapons.

There were other indications that American women were not as happy and
fulfilled as the housewives and mothers in popular television shows such as
Father Knows Best, Ozzie and Harriet, and *Leave It to Beaver.* The media noted
rising divorce rates, increased alcoholism, and women's dependency on tran-
quilizers. At the beginning of the 1950s, Betty Friedan, a leftist working for the

UE (the abbreviation for United Electrical, Radio and Machine Workers of America, a union expelled from the AFL-CIO for its Communist Party leadership), wrote a pamphlet entitled "UE Fights for Women Worker," one of many treatises arguing for greater political and economic rights for women workers. By the end of the decade, she sent out a questionnaire to her well-educated classmates from Smith College asking, "What do you wish you had done different?" Their replies revealed the underlying dissatisfaction of many American women or, as Friedan put it in her path-breaking book, *The Feminine Mystique*, "the problem that has no name."[9]

From 1955 to 1975, contradictory movements of conservatism and political repression, women's activism and feminism, transformed the American landscape. The refusal by Rosa Parks, long-time NAACP activist, on December 1, 1955, to give up her seat to a white man and move to the back of a bus in Montgomery, Alabama, sparked a massive grassroots struggle against the brutality of legal segregation. Reverend Martin Luther King Jr., then a twenty-six-year-old minister in his first pulpit, quickly emerged as the leader and spokesperson for the civil rights movement, but black women, organized in their churches and neighborhoods, were the backbone of the successful thirteen-month bus boycott.

Although the leadership of the civil rights movement was male, African American women were its core. Ruby Doris Smith, Eleanor Holmes Norton, Diane Nash, Gloria Richardson, and Bernice Johnson Reagan organized the student protests. Fannie Lou Hamer led the voter registration campaign in Mississippi. Ella Baker constantly challenged the all-male domination of the movement by the ministers, worked with the Student Non-Violent Coordinating Committee (SNCC), and urged group-centered, as opposed to individual, leadership, a concept that particularly resonated with young people. Throughout the South, black women were recognized as the most dynamic element within the black church and community organizations. Black women may have been militant, outspoken, and courageous, but they were not visible nationally. At the 1963 March on Washington, a huge debate occurred about the presence of women speakers. Josephine Baker, the African American dancer, actress, and supporter of the civil rights movement, was the lone woman's voice. Rather than allowing women activists to speak, the all-male leadership opted for a "Tribute to Women," with Bayard Rustin, a march organizer introducing to the crowd Rosa Parks, Daisy Bates, Diane Nash, Gloria Richardson, Mrs. Herbert Lee, and Myrlie Evers, the latter two being widows of murdered civil rights workers.

For the first time since the New Deal, the massive involvement of young people in politics, beginning with the Civil Rights movement, helped set the stage for the promise of the Kennedy administration. Kennedy's narrow victory was due in part to the votes of women and African Americans. Totally unsympathetic to women in politics and women's issues, he nevertheless knew he had to find some way to repay the Democratic Party's women activists who had worked for his election and who were now demanding that their concerns be addressed.

Throughout the 1960s, these concerns were plentiful and varied. Married women could not borrow money in their own names. Professional and graduate schools imposed quotas on the number of women they would accept; some refused to admit any women. Union contracts continued separate seniority lists. Divorced women could not get credit or even automobile insurance. No women ran large corporations, sat on the Supreme Court, conducted orchestras, worked as firefighters, drove tractor trailors, or repaired telephones. Contraception was illegal in most states; abortion was a crime in all states. Rape was considered a crime that women "asked for." Momism took a particular racial turn in 1965 with the publication of Daniel Patrick Moynihan's report, "The Negro Family: The Case for National Action," which blamed single black mothers for black male unemployment and crime.

In response to women's pressure, Kennedy created the Presidential Commission on the Status of Women (PCSW) in 1961, with Eleanor Roosevelt as its chair. Kennedy hoped that this gesture would keep women quiet. Instead, the PCSW had the opposite effect. When the commission published its results in 1963, the data showed that economic inequality had intensified. In 1960, the full-time year-round wages for women workers averaged only 60.6 percent of those of men, down from 63.6 percent in 1957. Black women fared the worst of all, earning only 42 percent of male wages.[10] Women with college degrees, a growing proportion of women workers, were still earning less than men with only high school educations. Married working women paid an emotional as well as economic price, as popular pundits and scholarly publications claimed that their joining the paid workforce was unnatural and harmful to their families. The report called for equal pay for *comparable* work (it understood that *equal* pay for *equal* work would not be adequate because women so rarely did the same work as men), child care services, paid maternity leave, and many other measures still not achieved.

Equal pay legislation was an urgent concern for Esther Peterson, an early Kennedy supporter, labor organizer, and experienced lobbyist who played an instrumental role in the passage of the Equal Pay Act of 1963. This enabled hundreds of thousands of women to file discrimination charges and marked the first time since 1920 that the federal government passed legislation benefiting women.

Democratic Party women continued pressing for more legislation during the Johnson administration. Title VII of the Civil Rights Act made it unlawful to discriminate against any individual with respect to compensation, terms, conditions, or privileges of employment, because of the individual's race, color, religion, sex, or national origin. Lyndon Johnson signed the bill into law in 1964, with no women present and no mention of equal rights. For almost a decade, the commission charged with handling discrimination, the Equal Employment Opportunities Commission (EEOC), treated sex discrimination with hostility. Its chair, Franklin Roosevelt Jr., assured the public that there would be no massive assault on sex discrimination. It would not be until decades later that Title VII began to play a significant role in challenging discrimination against women, especially in colleges.

Other changes taking place in the 1960s contributed to the explosion of women's activism and feminism. Labor organizing, for example, galvanized thousands of black and Puerto Rican women hospital workers in New York City. Women hospital workers of Local 1199B in Charleston, South Carolina, struck for 113 days, winning collective bargaining. In California, the United Farm Workers' Organizing Committee (UFWOC), led by César Chávez, combined civil rights for Chicanos and union rights for farm workers. Dolores Huerta, then the committee vice president, became a national figure in the women's, civil rights, and union movements. Antipoverty and welfare rights movements challenged prevailing attitudes about race, gender, and sexuality, in particular, the demonization of poor women and the forced sterilization of women on welfare.

Publication of Betty Friedan's best-selling book, *The Feminine Mystique*, coincided with publication of the PCSW's report, *The American Woman*. Both are credited with triggering the formation of the National Organization for Women (NOW), which represented one stream of the post-1945 women's movement. The initial organizers of NOW included leading trade union women and women of color. Pauli Murray, Dorothy Haener of the United Auto Workers (UAW), and Addie Wyatt of the Amalgamated Meat Cutters joined Friedan and other middle-class white women to create this organization. Aileen Hernandez, an African American woman who had worked in the EEOC, was NOW's second president. NOW, made up primarily of adult professional women (and a few male feminists), concentrated mainly on employment issues such as challenging gender discrimination in the workforce, electing women to political office, and lobbying elected officials to support women's rights. In the 1970s, in part because of pressure from the radical women's liberation movement, NOW moved to expand its membership and take on issues such as abortion reform and lesbian and gay rights. In the late 1970s and 1980s, it channeled its energies into an unsuccessful campaign for an Equal Rights Amendment to the U.S. Constitution. For more than forty years, NOW has been the leading organization and voice for liberal feminism; at its peak in the 1970s, it had 250,000 members in 600 chapters in all fifty states and the District of Columbia.

The other stream in the revival of feminism was the radical women's liberation movement. While NOW arose from New Deal Democrats and "old" left (meaning the Communist Party, Trotskyite, socialist, and anarchist left of the 1930s to 1955 generation), the women's liberation movement grew out of the radicalism of the civil rights, antiwar, student, and youth movements called the "new" left. Women organizers of these movements, furious at being marginalized and treated like movement "wives" relegated to coffee making, envelope stuffing, and supporting and sexually servicing male leaders, were the organizers of the first women's liberation groups.

Unlike NOW, which was highly organized, centralized, hierarchical, and reformist, the women's liberation groups developed spontaneously, were nonhierarchical, usually women-only, and comprised of younger, college-educated women. These women brought private, psychological, cultural, and sexual politics into the public sphere. Their political vision was both radical and utopian in that they wanted to overturn and transform every aspect of patriarchal society. The day-to-day issues of women's lives, housework, orgasms, sexual harassment at work, and abortions became public and political. Younger radical feminists used guerrilla theater to challenge entrenched gender notions. In September 1968, the world learned about the movement when radical feminists protested the parade of wholesome sex objects known as the Miss America contest. By the end of the decade, hundreds of thousands, perhaps even millions, of women were organizing at work, in cities, neighborhoods, unions, churches, workplaces, universities, colleges, and schools.

The radicalism of the women's liberation movement became the engine for change in women's organizations and consciousness. NOW became a mass organization openly advocating abortion rights. Shirley Chisholm of Brooklyn, an outspoken feminist, opponent of the war in Vietnam, and champion of civil rights and social justice, became the first African American woman elected to Congress. In June 1969, after the New York City police raided a Greenwich Village gay bar, the Stonewall Inn, lesbians, gay men, and drag queens fought back in the first mass homosexual protest, which gave birth to the lesbian and gay liberation movements. On August 26, 1970, 5,000 women marched down Fifth Avenue demanding Equal Pay for Equal Work, Free Child Care, Free Abortion on Demand, and Freedom of Sexual Expression. "I Am Woman, Hear Me Roar, in numbers too big to ignore," a song written and sung by Helen

Reddy in 1972, was not only a top Grammy-winning hit but also the theme song for the 1975 United Nations Year of the Woman. Women's liberation was having a pervasive effect on every area of American life: music, the arts, media, publishing, politics, sport, medicine, religion, higher education, the economy, work, and family. Women started wearing pants to work. Colleges and universities established women's studies programs. Feminists even changed the language: Firefighters replaced firemen, chairmen became chairpersons, mankind became humanity, and the title "Ms." entered the lexicon, replacing Miss and Mrs. as the preferred appellation for women.

Working-class women and women of color organized, redefined, and expanded ideas of feminist activism. The National Black Feminist Organization (NBFO) formed in 1973. The Boston-based Combahee River Collective, a group of black feminists and lesbians, wrote an influential document arguing that "racial, sexual, heterosexual and class oppression were interlocking."[11] Women involved in the Puerto Rican, Chicano, and Indian rights movements challenged male supremacy and went on to form their own all-women's rights groups.

In the 1970s, federal and state legislation was enacted outlawing gender discrimination. Rape, sexual harassment, and wife beating were criminalized. In 1971, Gloria Steinem, feminist journalist and editor of *Ms* magazine, along with Bella Abzug, Shirley Chisholm, and Betty Freidan, founded the National Women's Political Caucus, an organization promoting the election of more women to political office, including Chisholm, Abzug, Patsy Mink, Patricia Schroeder, and Elizabeth Holtzman, all outspoken feminists. In 1972, Shirley Chisholm ran for president of the United States in the Democratic primary, supported by many groups within the women's movement.

Women entered the professions in large numbers. White women, the major beneficiaries of affirmative action, swelled law and medical schools, as well as academic graduate schools. More women than men of color used the EEOC to challenge unequal pay and other forms of discrimination. Women were organizing everywhere. In 1970, a group of women at the Fiberboard Factory in Antioch, California, organized Women INC, one of the first labor-feminist groups. Union Women's Association for Greater Equality (Union W.A.G.E.) was organized in 1971 to fight for women's rights in the workplace and in the unions. In 1974, more than 3,600 trade union women met in Chicago to form the Coalition of Labor Union Women (CLUW), an organization whose goal was to pressure the male-dominated AFL-CIO leadership to take up women's rights in the workplace and bring more women into labor leadership positions. Women organized caucuses and committees in unions and workplaces. Nonunion white-collar workers organized WOW, or Women

Office Workers, and Nine-to-Five to fight for job dignity. "Raises not Roses" and "More Rank, Less File" were their slogans. For the first time since World War II, women entered the high-paying, highly unionized traditional male industries such as steel, automobile, and truck driving. Even the coal-mining industry, long a male bastion, began to hire women in 1974.

Women changed athletics. The passage of Title IX in 1972, which stated that "no person in the United States shall, on the basis of sex, be excluded from participation in, be denied the benefits of, or be subjected to discrimination under any education program or activity receiving Federal financial assistance," opened high school and college athletics to women and girls. According to the Women's Sport's Foundation, one of twenty-seven girls played sports in the 1980s; by the end of the millennium, one of three girls were involved in sports. When tennis champion and feminist Billie Jean King defeated tennis pro Bobby Riggs at the Houston Astrodome in a so-called Battle of the Sexes in 1973, women's athleticism and feminism took center stage. More women entered colleges and universities on sports scholarships, and by the 1980s and 1990s, women's sports had a mass audience. Today, the U.S. Tennis Center is named after King, outspoken, open lesbian, feminist, and social justice advocate. No other stadium or arena in the world is named after a woman.

Finally, the most personal aspect of women's lives, sexuality and reproduction, became political. Beginning in the 1960s and culminating in 1973, a successful struggle to legalize contraception and abortion was won with the 1973 Supreme Court decision *Roe v. Wade*. Radical feminists worked with black, Puerto Rican, Indian, and welfare activists to oppose coercive sterilization laws and other eugenicist population-control policies. New developments in contraception, combined with the legalization of abortion, gave women more sexual freedom; at the same time, it also absolved men from sexual responsibility. Women demanded sexual self-fulfillment through heterosexual or homosexual relationships, inside and outside marriage.

This sea change in women's lives, families, and sexuality created unease and protest from other sections of society. Conservatives, a quiet but restive minority, began to organize from the grassroots with the goal of reestablishing patriarchal authority, circumscribing women's sexual freedom, outlawing abortion, and restoring "Christian" values to the state and society. Within months of the Supreme Court's decision, conservatives joined with the Catholic Church, Protestant evangelicals, and others to oppose *Roe v. Wade*. Rather than focus on lobbying and statewide action, they built prolife organizations and mobilized their constituents to picket abortion clinics and engage in acts of civil disobedience. Anti–homosexual rights activists began successful campaigns to oppose antidiscrimination laws. The most successful campaign against women's

rights, Stop ERA, was led by Phyllis Schlafly, who argued that feminists deval-
ued mothers and the economic security of older married homemakers.
Schlafly's organization not only defeated NOW's mobilization for the ERA's
ratification but also brought together powerful opposition to every issue of
concern to feminists.

The 1980 election pitting Jimmy Carter, the Democratic incumbent,
against Ronald Reagan, the conservative Republican, marked the beginning of
a critical shift in the political debate over women. For the first time, the
Republican Party reversed its position of support for the Equal Rights
Amendment and embraced an antiabortion political platform. At the same
time, the Democratic Party voted not to support candidates who opposed abortion or the ERA. For the next twenty years, support or opposition to abortion
rights was the "litmus test" for Democratic or Republican political candidates
and federal judges. During his eight years as president, Reagan promised to
defeat more than abortion rights and the ERA. The collapse of the Soviet Union
in 1991 ended the specter of communism as the greatest threat to America.
Women's rights, feminism, and homosexuality filled that void.

The grassroots conservative movement, often referred to as the "New
Right," was overwhelmingly composed of white suburban and exurban evangelical Protestants and working-class Catholics. Talk radio provided the right
wing with a powerful medium for organizing. The New Right appealed to millions of Americans who looked to the "traditional values" of the father-centered
patriarchal family, wanted a "Christian" character to American public life, and
applauded a resurgence of patriotism.

In the 1980s and 1990s, a major focus of the New Right's attack was on
reproductive and homosexual rights. While the courts upheld the essence of
Roe, state and federal legislation limited access and funding. Anti-abortion pro-
testers intimidated and harassed abortion providers and their patients and
invaded, burned down, and blew up abortion clinics. Abortion providers were
murdered. Conservatives opposed young women's right to contraception.
Some anti-abortion pharmacists refused to sell the legal over-the-counter morn-
ing-after pill, on the grounds that it would encourage female promiscuity.
Conservatives held up the Federal Drug Administration's (FDA) approval of
RU 487, an abortifacient, which would eliminate the need for surgical abortions. Republican administrations refused to fund sex education programs,
denied abortions to women in the military, and based international aid on their
anti–birth control and abortion provisions. During the current war in Iraq,
applicants for positions working in the Green Zone in Bagdad were asked
about their position on *Roe v. Wade*. Beginning in the 1970s, social conservatives fought legislation guaranteeing homosexuals equal rights in employment,

benefits, housing, and health care and in the twenty-first century, mounted campaigns against gay marriage.

From the 1980s to the present, women of color and poor women were blamed for poverty, rising crime, drugs, illegitimacy, and single motherhood. Reagan demonized poor black women as "welfare queens." In the 1990s, centrist Democratic President Bill Clinton ended "welfare as we know it" when he signed into law a major revision that ended a sixty-year commitment to poor families with dependent children, the result of which was to move women off welfare and into greater poverty. Patriarchal authority had to be reestablished, according to conservative spokespersons, not only to deny women abortions and contraception but also to deny welfare women or lesbians their right to bear, adopt, or keep their children. Low-income pregnant women who drank or took drugs were prosecuted, fined, jailed, and in some cases, lost custody of babies at birth. Poor women were viewed as uncaring and inadequate mothers if they worked and as lazy welfare cheats if they stayed at home. Single women, whether unmarried or divorced, were looked upon as threats to the social order. Middle-class women were warned of the dangers of postponing marriage; working-class and poor women were considered by conservatives to be sexually suspect and deserving punishment.

Even as feminists found themselves on the defensive, women's roles and activism continued to be front and center in the political arena. Politicians became aware of how women's voting differed from men's. This "gender gap" has been factor in every election since Reagan. "Soccer Moms," or in post 9/11 terminology, "Security Moms," referred primarily to white suburban women, who were courted by both political parties. In a number of elections, women were a decisive voting bloc. The late twentieth century saw a succession of "first women": Geraldine Ferraro, vice presidential candidate; Sandra Day O'Connor, Supreme Court justice; Jeanne Kirkpatrick, ambassador to the United Nations; Carol Moseley Braun, first African American woman elected to the Senate; Madeleine Albright, secretary of State; Condoleezza Rice, first female African American national security advisor and secretary of State; and Nancy Pelosi, speaker of the House. Since 1972, Shirley Chisholm, Patricia Schroeder, Elizabeth Dole, Carol Moseley Braun, and Hillary Clinton have all campaigned for their party's presidential nomination, reflecting the ever-increasing number of women at all levels of government.

Women's working lives have also undergone changes and dislocations. Women conduct symphonies, pilot jet aircraft, play professional basketball, and lead corporations. However, in the ever-changing global economy, the majority of women face new stresses upon themselves and their families. In spite of the conservative rhetoric of a woman's place being in the home, women, especially working mothers, continue to enter and stay in the paid labor force. Two incomes have become necessary for a family's well-being. But the feminization of the workplace has also resulted in lower pay, fewer benefits, and difficult working conditions. The prevalence of shift work in the faster growing occupations present problems for working mothers, as day care is either too expensive or not available. The growth of new high-tech industries has also resulted in lower paying, nonunionized jobs. Working in the home, whether as knitters, telephone solicitors, proofreaders, or consultants, has been one way women have tried to juggle work and home life.

One of the most dramatic examples of the changing visibility of women has been in the military. By the end of the twentieth century, women were 20 percent of the armed forces and 15 percent of all officers. In 1994, the "risk rule," which kept women out of most combat operations, was rescinded, and now 91 percent of all career fields are open to women. While the armed forces promises career advancement and education for women, sexual abuse and violence are also an integral part of the military experience.

Women have also changed the face of higher education. Today's average college student is a thirty-year-old woman, married or divorced with at least one child, who is typically going back to school for career retraining. Women are the majority of students at the elite liberal arts colleges. Half of the populations of law and medical schools are women. There are more women tenured faculty at colleges and universities than at any other point in the history of the academy. Yet at the same time, a study commissioned by the American Association of University Women (AAUW) pointed out that gender discrimination continues to be pervasive in higher education.[12]

At the end of the second millennium, American women are considered full citizens and occupy almost every job category. They have greater personal autonomy than ever before. At the same time, conflict, confusion, and ambivalence persist about gender roles, feminism, and so-called progress for women. Does progress consist of women's replicating men's lives? Or does progress for women entail a fundamental restructuring of social, political, and economic life? Women continue to shy away from the word *feminism*, yet poll after poll shows they want equal pay, equal job opportunities, and more social supports for motherhood and child raising. How these differences and challenges are resolved, if ever, depends in part on how women make history.

NOTES

1. Thanks to Rosalind Baxandall, Carol Berkin, Eileen Boris, and Margaret Crocco for their suggestions, critiques, and encouragement; special thanks to Stephanie Golden, a greater writer and dear friend, for her thoughtful editing. Thanks to the

Professional Staff Congress Women's Studies grant for travel money and reassigned time for this essay.

2. Eileen Boris, "What about the Working of the Working Mother?" *Journal of Women's History* 5: 2, 2004, p. 104.

3. Barbara Woloch, *Women and the American Experience: A Concise History* (New York: McGraw Hill, 1966), p. 214.

4. See, for example, Vicky Ruiz, *Cannery Women, Cannery Lives: Mexican Women's Unionization in the California Food Processing Industry, 1930–1950* (Albuquerque: University of New Mexico Press, 1992).

5. Sheila Rowbotham, *A Century of Women* (New York: Penguin, 1997), pp. 150–151.

6. Iris Lopez, *Sterile Choices: Reproductive Dilemmas of Puerto Rican Women* (New Brunswick, NJ: Rutgers University Press, 2008).

7. Quoted in Rowbotham, p. 268.

8. Lillian Faderman, *Odd Girls and Twilight Lovers: A History of Lesbian Life in Twentieth Century America* (Harmondsworth, England: Penguin, 1992), p. 149.

9. Betty Friedan, *The Feminine Mystique* (New York: Norton, 1963).

10. U.S. Department of Labor, Women's Bureau, "Background Facts on Wome n Workers in the United States." January 1962.

11. "A Black Feminist Statement," quoted in C. Moraga and G. Anzuldua, eds., *This Bridge Called My Back* (New York: Kitchen Table Women of Color Press, 1983), p. 210.

12. "Behind the Pay Gap." Press Release. American Association of University Women, April 23, 2007.

PART II

Conceptualizing Issues in U.S. Women's History

4

Conceptualizing U.S. Women's History through the History of Medicine

Rebecca Tannenbaum

The history of medicine, public health, and reproduction is a rich area for teachers and scholars of women's history. The reverse is also true: Women's history is an excellent topic for investigating and discussing important themes in the history of medicine. Teachers at all levels will find that topics in the history of women and medicine speak to each other in multiple ways, illuminating themes not just concerning women and the body but broader themes in American history as well.

Here I have chosen three broad topics to illustrate these themes: the history of childbirth, nineteenth-century "female complaints and disorders," and the history of abortion and contraception. These topics cover the range of American history from colonial times to the post–World War II era. In women's history, they demonstrate the uneven process of women struggling for authority and autonomy, the body as a site of contested meanings and contested control, the intersecting definitions of race and gender, and women's resistance to male-dominated culture, either through personal expression or through political activism. In the history of medicine, these topics illustrate the gradual professionalization of medicine, the changing dynamic of the doctor-patient relationship, and the ways in which medicine is not just a scientific enterprise but a social construction. Taken together, these themes address broader questions of political, economic, and cultural change.

Probably the first topic that will come into the minds of many students when women and medicine are mentioned together is the history of childbirth. Indeed, this is where individual women confronted ideas about the body, healing, and the medical profession. Childbirth is the biological and social event that has until relatively recently been solely under the jurisdiction of women. As such, it is a perfect topic for teaching the history of medicine as a site of women's autonomy and authority in any time period. When teaching the colonial era in a survey or early America class, the history of childbirth is particularly effective in addressing issues of social control, social hierarchy, and dissent.

In the colonial and early national periods, midwifery was one of the few positions of power available to women. In court proceedings, midwives and other female healers testified as "expert witnesses" in cases ranging from rape and murder to witchcraft. Most commonly, female healers testified to the identity of the fathers of babies born out of wedlock. Such testimony was usually the result of a ritual examination performed "at the height" of a woman's labor. It was a common folk belief that a woman was incapable of lying at that time, and that belief was enshrined in the common law of England and British North America. Once a man was named, he had little defense against being named the legal father of the baby, convicted of fornication, and held liable for the support of the child. This was usually the case even if the woman in question was a poor servant and the father her wealthy master.[1]

Midwives were figures of considerable authority among both men and women outside the courtroom as well. Often, they were called informally by women to adjudicate sexual or reproductive matters—for instance, when a woman claimed to have been sexually harassed or assaulted short of rape. At other times, midwives used their authority to support one side or another in a community quarrel, interpreting evidence in the light most favorable to the side they supported.[2]

Other women looked up to midwives and thought of them as natural leaders of the women's community. A famous example is that of Massachusetts religious dissenter Anne Hutchinson, who acquired the first recruits to her form of Christianity among the women she attended in childbirth and their friends and relatives. Medical practice conferred authority and a certain measure of power.[3]

When teaching this topic, do not romanticize this power. Colonial midwives were not feminist heroines, supporting women in an oppressive patriarchy—they were part of that patriarchy, as were their patients. While midwives (and other healers) could and did act as advocates for their female patients, they also served as social enforcers. The very testimony that enabled midwives to

bring consequences down on male fornicators and rapists entailed the relentless questioning of women at their most pain-filled moments. If a midwife was
not severe enough in her examination, her word would not be accepted. Thus,
the midwife is not just an example of female empowerment but of the fine line
women had to walk when asserting their own authority. A seventeenth- or eighteenth-century midwife could have more power than other women only by participating in the social and political structures that enforced women's secondary
status in the prevailing culture of gender.[4]

Legal and cultural authority was one aspect of the midwife's role; economic
participation was another. Midwifery was one of the few trades open to women
in the seventeenth and eighteenth centuries, and one of the most prestigious.
Although few midwives supported themselves solely through their practices,
they always charged for their skills and services. Their empowerment was
therefore not just cultural but economic as well.

Midwives were often at the center of economic networks that included
men and women alike and served as the link between the (often) invisible bar-
ter economy of women and the cash-based trade of men. The Maine midwife
Martha Ballard was paid in cash, wool, pork, brandy, and spices. A midwife's
records, such as Ballard's, are a crucial resource for describing the ways in
which local, regional, and even international trade shaped lives in rural
America and in documenting women's contributions to and participation in
the economy.[5]

When we shift focus from the role of the midwife to the role of the birthing
woman herself, other themes come into view. The nineteenth century saw
many important changes in medical practice and obstetrics, shifting childbirth
practices above all. Female demand combined with physician salesmanship to
bring about the two most important changes: the routine attendance of male
physicians at childbirth and the use of anesthesia for women in labor. Tracing
these changes illustrates the power of consumers in a developing capitalist culture, as well as the subtle negotiations of power between patients and physicians concerning health care.

Male physicians began conducting routine childbirth in the late eighteenth
century among elite urban women. The key to female acceptance of male practitioners was the perception of safety doctors could offer through their use of
the obstetrical forceps. Forceps enabled some babies to be born alive who previously would have been stillborn or extracted piece by piece as a last resort, and
they no doubt saved the lives of some women who might otherwise have died
of exhaustion and blood loss. Women who could afford to hire physicians over-
came their qualms at having men in the birth chamber in their eagerness to
avail themselves of the new technology. As more men were trained in the

technique, physician-attended birth gradually became the norm for middle-class as well as wealthy women.[6]

It is important to stress in this case that the safety was mostly a matter of perception, not of reality. Although forceps no doubt saved some lives, less skilled physicians inflicted terrible lacerations and infections on women and injured or killed infants. Despite these risks, women soon accepted the presence of a male doctor as a matter of course, whether or not he even used his instruments or did much more than stand and wait for the birth to proceed on its own. Once the physician had been invited into the birthing room, he stayed.[7]

One common misperception is that the replacement of midwives by male physicians was a male conspiracy to disempower women—both the midwives themselves and the women giving birth. Noting that the "obstetrical revolution" was consumer driven is one way of correcting this misperception; discussing the ways in which women remained in control of the process is another. Although the physician was invited in, he was only a guest; the woman and her female relatives and friends retained their roles as directors of the process. Women decided which procedures they deemed acceptable, and which they did not, and followed their own inclinations even when the physician objected. While doctors complained endlessly about "meddlesome" relatives and "ignorant" patients, they were powerless to change procedures until most births moved to the hospital in the mid-twentieth century.[8]

Nothing is more illustrative of the consumer-driven nature of childbirth and women's continuing control over the process than the history of anesthesia in childbirth. Ether was first used in 1847; the first American woman to undergo this process was Fanny Longfellow, wife of the poet Henry Wadsworth Longfellow. Longfellow enthused in a letter that anesthesia was "the greatest blessing of this age."[9] As was the case with forceps, elite urban women were the first to use this new technology. Longfellow's enthusiasm was taken up by thousands of women, yet doctors remained somewhat reluctant to use anesthesia routinely. Some cited medical reasons—the risks of death or disability attendant on the use of any drug. Others cited moral or religious grounds, arguing that pain in childbirth was part of God's plan for human reproduction. Some even went so far as to suggest that women who gave birth painlessly would not love their children. However, all arguments fell before the intensity of women's desire for pain relief. One woman went so far as to buy and administer chloroform herself, despite her physician's objections.[10]

Forceps and anesthesia illustrate the ways in which power was negotiated between physician and patient and between men and women. Male physicians used the power of desirable medical technology to expand their practice into a formerly female-dominated realm. However, women used their power as consumers and as traditional childbirth attendants to set the conditions under which that technology would be used. As such, the history of childbirth offers a vivid case study of both gendered and medicalized power relationships.

The history of childbirth also offers a unique perspective on the intersections of race and gender. As in the history of medical technology for white women and their doctors, childbirth for enslaved women entailed struggles over authority and can highlight the complex power relationships of master-slave relations.

Childbirth under slavery was an event fraught with meanings for women. On the one hand, giving birth was a deeply personal event, both physically and emotionally. The universal ordeal of labor and delivery (usually) produced a deeply beloved child and conferred on the woman the honored status of motherhood. This much she shared with her white mistress. On the other hand, a slave woman's reproductive capacity was not entirely hers to control and define. For slaveholders, slave women were not honored mothers but "breeders" who could produce salable commodities and a future labor force. Such competing definitions of women's bodies created a constant power struggle between enslaved women and slaveholders.[11]

Enslaved mothers created a number of strategies to keep their bodies and their reproductive labor under their own control. Some women went so far as to give birth in secret to avoid the prying eyes of the master and the prying hands of the physician he might hire. Keeping childbirth a private ritual was one way for women to carve out an area of autonomy within a coercive system and to lay claim to their children. In their turn, slaveholders did their best to retain control. Using racial rhetoric and medical practice alike, they asserted authority and control over both the birth process and its product. Claiming that medical intervention was necessary to ensure the safety of mother and child, doctors and slaveholders condemned slave folk practice as ignorance and superstition. Slaveholders were not just protecting women's health but their own economic interest in both mother and child.[12]

The end of slavery did not spell the end of such racialized definitions of women's bodies and the process of childbirth. In the years immediately following World War II, single motherhood became a social problem. However, the nature of that problem varied by race. Ironically, black women's reproductive capacity became a threat and potential economic burden, and black babies were characterized as "valueless" on the adoption market. When a white woman became pregnant out of wedlock, her body in some ways became the property of others. Urged to give birth in secret and to give away or sell their valuable babies, unmarried white women found themselves in a situation not unlike that of enslaved women a hundred years earlier. These two examples in juxta-position provide a vivid example of the ways in which racial and gender defini-tions are historically constructed and change according to circumstance.[13]

Yet childbirth is only one example of the ways that gender and the history of medicine intersect in interesting and teachable ways. Another is the cultural phenomenon of "female complaints and disorders" that generated so much medical writing during the late nineteenth century. Looking at the ways the medical profession defined women—and the ways women responded to that definition—demonstrates in a concrete way that the body itself is a site of con-tested meanings. The women who resisted the influence of mainstream medi-cine resisted not only on a personal level but also through political and social reform movements.

Women had always been defined in part by their bodies, as the history of childbirth demonstrates. However, the thinking of nineteenth-century main-stream physicians represents a particularly extreme example. To cite a much-quoted pronouncement made by a physician in 1870, many doctors felt that "the Almighty, in creating the female sex, had taken the uterus and built up a woman around it."[14] For many nineteenth-century physicians, reproduction was the defining factor not just for women's bodies but for their lives.

This definition had implications that went far beyond the physical. If fol-lowed to its logical conclusion, it means that women were biologically deter-mined to be nurturing mothers and household matrons. To do otherwise would be unnatural and downright unhealthy. Thus, a range of diseases and disorders ranging from infertility to tuberculosis were thought to be caused by women stepping outside of their "natural" role. One prominent physician wrote that education for girls was a major cause of physical and mental illness. A young woman who exercised her brain stinted her reproductive organs of their neces-sary strength, and the result was a young woman who could neither study nor become a mother—a physical and mental wreck with no place in society.[15]

In teaching this material, it is possible to make larger connections to other social issues. On the surface, it appears to be merely an example of egregious nineteenth-century sexism. Yet the biological definition of womanhood—and the condemnation of education for women—coincided with the explosion of women's colleges and women's entrance into the professions, including the medical profession. It is possible to see this kind of thinking not as the heavy hand of social control but a futile protest against changes that had already happened.

It also illustrates a number of other anxieties. Such pronouncements coin-cided with a drop in the birthrate among the middle and upper classes, most of whom were native born and of northern European descent. At the same time, masses of immigrants were arriving from Ireland, and later on Southern and Eastern Europe, who had high birthrates. For mainstream, elite physicians, condemning new social roles for women was a warning aimed solely at native-born women of their own class. Fears of a changing population, a changing class structure, and the loss of their own status fueled these writings as much as the desire to keep women at home. Medical writings about women can give students a unique view of changing ideas about class and ethnicity, as well as gender.

Women doctors accepted the same assumptions about gender as their male counterparts. Discussing these shared assumptions adds nuance to a history of women's entrance into the professions. Pioneering physicians such as Elizabeth Blackwell used the rhetoric of motherhood and women's "natural" nurturing abilities as an argument in favor of women's medical practice. Such assumptions also are manifest in their practices. Women used the rhetoric of feminine gentleness and sympathy to justify their practices, even though women doctors' use of gynecological surgery, forceps in childbirth, and anesthesia was identical with that of their male colleagues.[16] They shared rhetoric with men of their class and educational level, as well as beliefs about the female body. Similarly, some women doctors defended the controversial practice of ovariotomy to cure female ills by saying "the mutilation has been effected [sic] by disease ... before the surgeon intervened....There is not such special sanction about the ovary!" Such arguments demonstrated not just that women doctors shared the values of their male colleagues but that they needed to prove that they shared them to achieve full acceptance into the profession. In a sense, then, women's bodies became a battleground on which some women were able to fight their way into territory previously reserved for men.[17]

In a culture where a woman's role was proclaimed to be a product of her biology, some women used their bodies as a site of resistance. One example that students find riveting is the emergence of anorexia nervosa in its modern form. Anorexia was first given its modern name in 1873 by a British physician. Although instances of deliberate self-starvation have been documented as early as medieval times, it was not until the nineteenth century that the eating disorder took the form that we recognize: young women, often in their teens, refusing to eat to the point where they become emaciated and perhaps even die. Then as now, it was clear that anorexia had cultural as well as psychological roots. The women who became anorexic were using their bodies to comment on their status and on the tenets of conventional femininity—and as such, anorexia was a historically constructed disease.[18]

The manifestations of the disease have changed over time. In the nineteenth century, young women who refused to eat gave different reasons for doing so than similar young women today. Nineteenth-century anorexics defined their behavior as about eating and food and wanted to prove they were beyond physical desires of any kind. Eating too heartily was considered "vulgar" and "masculine," even for women who did not have eating disorders. By overexaggerating this pattern, anorexic women called normal femininity into question and made a subtle, if not entirely conscious, critique of gender norms.[19]

This kind of resistance can be paired with a discussion of the organized ways in which women created and promulgated alternative definitions of women's health and women's bodies. Middle-class women were the driving force behind numerous health reform and alternative medicine movements of the nineteenth century. While many women accepted the mainstream medical assumption that women of their generation and class were sickly, they differed on both the cause and cure of women's illnesses. Rather than defining the female body as pathological and in need of careful medical monitoring, they defined it as naturally healthy. Rather than proclaiming female biology to be the root of women's socially subordinate role, they argued that a healthy woman was a natural equal and partner to men. Finally, they advocated egalitarian marriages, limited childbearing, and meaningful work and education as keys not just to women's happiness but to their health. It should not be surprising, then, that health reform organizations were intimately involved in feminist politics as well as medical issues. Health and politics deeply influenced each other; resistance to medical definitions of women's subordination could not be separated from resistance to women's legal and political subordination. A discussion of women's health can therefore be an engaging gateway to general discussions of nineteenth-century reform, the social vision of reformers, and women's role in reform movements.[20]

The history of abortion and contraception offers insights into the intersections of feminism and medicine. Although women had been using contraceptive and abortive techniques since before Europeans arrived in America, family limitation did not become a public issue until the late nineteenth and early twentieth centuries. The arguments for "voluntary motherhood" promoted by feminists and their allies would remain essentially the same throughout the twentieth century. Different factions of the movement framed their rationales somewhat differently, but the core issue remained the same: Women needed this technology to ensure their autonomy and independence.

In the late nineteenth century, Free Lovers and more mainstream feminists shared ambivalence toward "artificial" birth control. Devices such as condoms and diaphragms were associated in the popular mind with promiscuity and prostitution and were denounced as unnatural and dangerous. Many

public activists, therefore, advocated periodic abstinence or such ancient methods as male withdrawal. Despite their attitude toward contraceptive technology,
the arguments all advocated that women bear only as many children as they
consciously chose, at a time they chose. Women needed to be free from constant childbearing for several reasons: to be better, more attentive mothers; to
preserve their health; and, for a few radicals, to express sexuality freely. Whether
obtained through "natural" or "artificial" means, fertility control was crucial to
women's freedom, autonomy, and well-being.[21]

The history of contraception as a technological product brings together
social and business history. Despite the vocal opposition to technological fixes
and the illegality of birth control and abortion, in the late nineteenth and early
twentieth centuries, the demand was insatiable and created a thriving black
market. The demand for contraceptive devices crossed race and class lines—all
women, it seemed, wanted and needed to control their fertility. This demand
created opportunities for a variety of male and female entrepreneurs, who provided condoms, cervical caps, sponges, a variety of douching solutions, and
when all else failed, abortions. Even while denounced by reformers such as
Anthony Comstock and the mainstream physicians of the American Medical
Association (AMA), these businesses continued to thrive. Some manufacturers, such as Julius Schmidt, a sausage maker turned condom manufacturer,
became quite wealthy.[22]

Big business soon stepped in to tap into the desire for cheap contraception
that could be purchased discreetly. The entrance of big businesses had both
advantages and disadvantages. National brands made contraception more accessible to more women. Once contraception was legal, large drug companies could
put their resources behind development of contraceptive technology, manufacturing more effective products. However, the profit-driven nature of businesses
meant that products were not always adequately tested before they were marketed, resulting in methods that were ineffective and sometimes dangerous.

As early as the 1930s, with the sale of contraceptives still illegal in many
states, companies began marketing "feminine hygiene" products as contraceptives. The most successful of these was Lysol, originally promoted as a surgical
disinfectant. Lysol's manufacturer initiated an advertising campaign in wom-
en's magazines that played on women's fears of unintended pregnancy and the
effect of such pregnancies on marriage. The words *contraception* and *pregnancy*
were never used, but the intent was made clear. Feminine hygiene advertising
headlines read "Calendar Fear," "Can a Married Woman Ever Feel Safe?" and
"Young Wives Are Often Secretly Terrified." The problem was that douching
with Lysol was both dangerous and ineffective. Women often ended up with
severe chemical burns, and douching with any substance is not an effective

form of birth control. However, Lysol continued to be marketed as a "feminine hygiene" product into the 1960s.[23]

Perhaps the most notorious instance of a dangerous and failed contraceptive is the story of the Dalkon Shield intrauterine device. The story of the Dalkon Shield reads almost like a medico-legal thriller, a perfect parable of what happens when business interests overcome ethics. Without revealing his commercial interest in the products, one of the inventors of the device, Hugh Davis, published an "objective" study of his IUD that concluded that the shield was both the safest and most effective of the many IUDs already on the market. A large pharmaceutical company, A. H. Robbins, bought the distribution rights to the device on the basis of that article and ignored mounting evidence that the shield was not as effective as first claimed. The company mounted an aggressive advertising campaign to market the device. More than 2 million women were fitted with the shield. Once the device was sold, it became clear that the shield's design could create serious medical problems for its users, including uterine perforation and pelvic inflammatory disease. Those who became pregnant while using the shield were susceptible to septic miscarriages; those who carried pregnancies to term often gave birth to severely damaged infants. The shield was eventually removed from the market, and the wave of lawsuits that followed bankrupted A. H. Robbins.[24]

The story of the Dalkon Shield might be fruitfully paired with the story of the contraceptive pill. While both the pill and the shield had significant side effects and were the products of big business, the pill is still one of the most effective and popular methods of contraception today. It, too, was aggressively marketed and opposed with equal passion by some feminists, the Catholic clergy, and the Black Power movement. Yet no amount of opposition and no number of warnings about potential side effects have put a dent in the market. Juxtaposing the success (and relative safety) of the pill with the Dalkon Shield disaster and the Lysol campaign could produce a good discussion of the role of big business in medicine, the role of consumers in effecting technological change, and the many reasons women have wanted and needed contraception.[25]

Shifting focus from contraception to abortion brings up some of the same themes: An illegal practice that is in much demand creates a thriving black market. However, abortion has always been the subject of more charged political and social debate than contraception. Abortion was legal in the United States until the middle of the nineteenth century, when a coalition of groups led by the AMA successfully pushed through a series of state laws regulating the practice and making it all but impossible to obtain legally anywhere by 1900. Starting in the 1950s, and gathering steam as second-wave feminism emerged in the 1960s, women and doctors began a movement to repeal these laws. Despite vocal opposition, they succeeded in overturning state laws in sixteen states by 1972, and in 1973 the Supreme Court legalized abortion nationwide in its *Roe v. Wade* decision.[26]

The story of feminist underground abortion networks during the last few years before *Roe v. Wade* provides an important supplement to the familiar political and legal narrative. It is an effective illustration of women reacting against big business and big medicine and asserting their autonomy and right not just to get abortions but to perform them as well. While underground abortion services had existed since legal abortion was abolished, such services became ideologically driven in the late 1960s and early 1970s. For the women of these groups, especially the now-famous "Jane" Collective of Chicago, their services were part of a longer history of groups performing illegal services for a higher moral purpose. Women of the Jane Collective compared themselves with historical figures who liberated an oppressed class from slavery, such as the members of the Underground Railroad.[27]

Abortion was an essential part of women's liberation. It provided autonomy and freedom. True to many of the members' backgrounds in the New Left, the group also saw itself as undermining all forms of authority, including that of physicians and medical personnel. The group began by hiring a doctor to perform the procedures, but they soon learned to do them on their own. This was a crucial part of their group—that any member could perform any job, including the abortions themselves.[28]

The service was also designed to empower their clients and encourage them to "own" their experience. One of the slogans of the group was "We don't do this to you, we do it with you."[29] Similarly, the group decided that they would always charge a fee. Clients had to pay something, even if it was only a dollar or two, as a way of proving that they valued the service and the skill of the practitioner.[30]

While other groups worked on legalizing abortion, underground groups like Jane focused on making it available, much like the underground marketers of contraception. Their story illustrates the politics of the New Left, the many faces of second-wave feminism, and the continuing need for women to control their fertility. It could be placed in the historical narrative of any of these topics as a way of integrating women's history into a broader survey course. Alternatively, it could be taught as part of the history of alternative medicine, self-care, and the mistrust Americans have often felt toward large, elite social institutions such as mainstream medicine.

This essay barely scratches the surface of the history of women, health, and medicine. However, it does give a sense of the multiple ways these topics intersect with each other and with the larger history of the United States. Medicine and health are topics that are part of the lives of all students, and most find the topic both relevant and engaging.

NOTES

1. Rebecca J. Tannenbaum, *The Healer's Calling: Women and Medicine in Early New England* (Ithaca, NY: Cornell University Press, 2002), 103–113.

2. Ibid., 106–113.

3. Mary Beth Norton, *Founding Mothers and Fathers: Gendered Power and the Formation of American Culture* (New York: Knopf, 1996), 203–229.

4. Tannenbaum, *Healer's Calling*, 107–112.

5. Laurel Thatcher Ulrich, *A Midwife's Tale: The Life of Martha Ballard Based on Her Diary, 1785–1812* (New York: Knopf, 1990).

6. Judith Walzer Leavitt, *Brought to Bed: Childbearing in America, 1750–1950* (New York: Oxford University Press, 1986), 36–63.

7. Ibid.

8. Ibid., 87–115.

9. Quoted in ibid., 116.

10. Ibid., 116–141.

11. Marie Jenkins Schwartz, *Birthing a Slave: Motherhood and Medicine in the Antebellum South* (Cambridge: Harvard University Press, 2006).

12. Ibid., 143–186.

13. Rickie Solinger, *Wake Up Little Susie: Single Pregnancy and Race Before* Roe vs. Wade (New York: Routledge, 1992).

14. Quoted in Carroll Smith-Rosenberg and Charles Rosenberg, "The Female Animal: Medical and Biological Views of Woman and Her Role in Nineteenth-Century America," in Judith Walzer Leavitt, ed., *Women and Health in America* (Madison: University of Wisconsin Press, 1984), 13.

15. Ibid.

16. Regina Markell Morantz-Sanchez, *Sympathy and Science: Women Physicians in American Medicine* (New York: Oxford University Press, 1985), 228–230.

17. Ibid., 195.

18. Joan Jacobs Brumberg, *Fasting Girls: The Emergence of Anorexia Nervosa as a Modern Disease* (Cambridge: Harvard University Press, 1988).

19. Ibid.

20. Morantz-Sanchez, *Sympathy and Science*, 28–46.

21. Linda Gordon, "Voluntary Motherhood: The Beginnings of Feminist Birth Control Ideas in the United States," in Leavitt, ed., *Women and Health in America*, 104–116; Andrea Tone, *Devices and Desires: A History of Contraceptives in America* (New York: Hill and Wang, 2001), 1–25.

22. Tone, *Devices and Desires*, 71–92.

23. Ibid., 155–186, quotations p. 162.

24. Ibid., 280–291.

25. Ibid., 209–267.

26. Nancy Woloch, *Women and the American Experience: A Concise History* (New York: McGraw Hill, 1996), 76, 353.

27. Laura Kaplan, *The Story of Jane, the Legendary Underground Feminist Abortion Service* (New York: Pantheon, 1995).

28. Ibid.

29. Ibid., x.

30. Ibid.

5

Conceptualizing U.S. Women's History through the History of Sexuality

Christy Regenhardt

If you say that you teach the history of sexuality, people usually laugh and make a joke. Even among historians, the study of sexuality is generally marginalized. Discussing this topic is not always easy, but the things that make it so difficult are the same things that make it so interesting. Because sexuality is so personal for most people, it helps students understand how much historical context shapes even the most seemingly private experiences. Students can generally learn to put aside questions of whether sexual orientation is natural or learned and instead learn to interrogate those questions in historical context.[1]

The shock value of talking about sex in a college history classroom can be valuable. Many high school teachers will not address the topic at all, fearing trouble with administrators and/or parents. Students think of sexuality as natural and personal, even if they enter the classroom already questioning the meanings of masculinity and femininity. Teaching them to historicize sexuality not only challenges the dichotomy between personal and social but also helps them understand how even those areas of life that have biological causes can still have social meaning and can change over time.

The study of the history of sexuality also helps students break down their desire to see certain historical epochs as "conservative" and others as "liberal" or even "radical." Nothing surprises students more than to learn that the Puritans valued sexual pleasure and then to see a complicated people who were struggling with religion, politics, and personal behavior in ways that do not simply mirror our own. Students are also challenged when they learn about women's rights activists who decried the use of birth control or who stereotyped the sexual behavior of minority groups as they sought to gain power for white women. Certainly, the study of history as a whole seeks to teach the lesson that those struggles don't mirror ours, but because so much of our political culture today focuses on the politics of sexuality, students often enter the classroom with a strong predisposition to view the past in terms of today's debates.

This chapter explores a few examples of how the study of sexuality can enhance our understanding of women's history. For the sake of brevity, I have chosen just three examples, all from the twentieth century: the role played by sexuality in the creation of "modern" America, the key importance of sexuality in social movements that have defined their age, and the history of sexual subcultures as they struggled to create communities and gain civil rights.

Clarifying key terms is important to the study of the history of sexuality. *Sexuality* itself is the first. Sexuality is not limited solely to intercourse. While its role and importance change both historically and between individuals, sexuality can be, and in the twentieth century often was, an important part of people's lives and identities. Entire cultures are built around sexual identities, and describing both these cultures and these identities is part of teaching the history of sexuality. Defining *sex* itself is often difficult, yet these definitions have been historically important. Were women who had sex with other women able to slip past the legal system because most people of their time didn't define what they did as "sex"? Did a taboo around premarital sex in the twentieth century allow young unmarried couples to engage in increasingly sexual behavior, so long as they stopped short of vaginal intercourse?

Terms such as *gay* and *lesbian* also require definition when teaching the history of sexuality. People often ask if some historical figure—Eleanor Roosevelt, Abraham Lincoln, Walt Whitman—was gay. These terms, however, are historically specific. When people before the mid-twentieth century felt affection or desire for members of their own gender, or even physically acted on that desire in some way, they cannot simply be defined as "gay." For example, Walt Whitman lived in a period when men who had sex with men were understood to have engaged in sodomy, not to have adopted a sexual identity. When sexual subcultures began to develop, men could still move in and out of having sex with other men without being defined as part of that culture, so long as they performed the "masculine" role in sex and in society. Even if we had concrete evidence that

Walt Whitman engaged in sex with other men, it would be inaccurate to label him as "gay." Ironically, part of teaching the history of sexuality is getting students to move beyond defining relationships by whether people had sex and to accept that we often do not know what people did behind closed doors.[2]

Finally, studying sexuality also asks students to struggle with concepts of love and friendship and how they relate to sex. Most students initially want to dismiss relationships like the "romantic friendships" of the Victorian era that do not always end with some sort of sexual consummation.[3] However, it is just these relationships that push students to move beyond their personal notions of sexuality and their belief that sex and romance are inherently related. When students begin to recognize the value that nonsexual romantic relationships had for people in the Victorian era, and therefore how different a role sex played in that time, they have truly understood how much of the meaning of sex is historically specific.

Sexuality in "Modern" America

The changes that took place in the late nineteenth and early twentieth centuries had enormous effects on sexuality. The structures of both families and communities changed. Cities exploded, and new forms of communication connected individuals across distant spaces. Industry took work out of the home and helped create a new middle class. The changes in sexuality during this era were not incidental, either; they were central to a new understanding of womanhood itself.[4]

One of the most important shifts in the nineteenth and twentieth centuries was the separation of sex from reproduction. As more people engaged in non-agricultural labor, children's roles in the family changed. On a farm, children provided much-needed labor. For middle-class families in the nineteenth century, however, children increasingly became an economic burden, since they did not generate income and required education as well as basic economic support. Child labor laws in the twentieth century decreased the earning power of working-class children, making them, like middle-class children, drains on the economic resources of their families. All of this led to a drastic decrease in family size over the course of a century. In 1800, married couples on average had more than seven children. By 1900, that number had dropped to 3.54, and within the middle class, the decline was even greater. At the same time, life expectancy increased.[5] This means that women spent more of their adult lives neither pregnant nor raising small children. This also means that couples were either abstaining from sex or finding other ways to prevent conception. Since we have evidence that many people were doing the latter, this shows that heterosexual intercourse must have been taking on roles beyond reproduction.

The importance many Americans placed on pleasure, or sexual satisfaction, increased accordingly. At the turn of the century, a battle raged over the proper role of sex. Birth control advocates, most notably Margaret Sanger, claimed that sexual pleasure was important to marriage and that only birth control could release the family from burdensome births. Others, opposed to birth control, continued to claim that sex was naturally tied to reproduction and that to break this tie through birth control would challenge human nature and result in ill health.[6] The concept of the "companionate marriage," which became popular early in the twentieth century, emphasized sexual satisfaction as an important part of the happy companionship men and women were supposed to achieve within marriage. By the 1960s, the shift in the place of sex in American life had gone so far that birth control became legally available not only to married couples but also to unmarried people. Writers like Hugh Hefner and Helen Gurley Brown argued that premarital sex was both healthy and natural, and they made a fair amount of money promoting this belief. This is not to say that the belief that sex should always be tied to reproduction faded entirely—it remained strongest in the Catholic Church—but that it became somewhat marginal.

Of course, this had enormous effects on women and on women's history. Lower fertility rates translated into time used for wage work, education, reform work, and even leisure activities. The expectation of sexual satisfaction in marriage, as part of general companionship and happiness, led ultimately to liberalized divorce laws and to greater emphasis on heterosocial leisure involving husbands and wives together. That this decline occurred earlier and more dramatically in the middle class, largely native-born white Protestants, also led to fears of "race suicide" by the turn of the century.

Most important, the falling fertility rate also advanced the ideological separation of women from their own bodies. Victorians, and many before them, generally believed that the female body dictated every aspect of a woman's life. Concepts of "neurasthenia" and "hysteria" in the nineteenth century relied on a medical conflation of woman and womb. Under this view of the woman's body, any move beyond the role of wife and mother was illness. In a culture in which these roles were already eroding in importance, this attempt to enforce the link between women and their reproductive function was ultimately unsuccessful, and in the twentieth century this tie eroded.[7] As women's reproductive functions became less central to their lives, they also decreased in their importance to both popular and "expert" conceptions of women.

The 1927 film *It*, best known for tagging its star, Clara Bow, with the title "It Girl," is a wonderful tool for helping students understand the role of sexuality in the early twentieth century. The titular "it" of the film is sex appeal, and the film spends much time judging the sex appeal of its characters. Clara Bow's character, a department store clerk, sets out to win the love of the wealthy store owner. He is already involved with a woman of his own class. In the midst of Bow's seduction attempt, her boss mistakenly assumes that her roommate's child is Bow's and thinks the child is born out of wedlock. When he offers to make her his mistress, she is so insulted she quits both the relationship and her job. After she learns of his error, she sets out again to get him to propose, but when she succeeds, she realizes that she loves him, and the two are reunited. The boss's upper-class girlfriend and the other man who had pursued Bow end the film with the realization that they are "itless its."[8]

The film provides wonderful fodder for discussion and a potent example of how all of the changes taking place in the early twentieth century relate to sexuality. Leisure, consumer culture, and work all revolve around sexuality in this film, and it shows how much the changes of urbanization and industrialization altered the sex lives of Americans. There are two date scenes in the film. The first, at "the Ritz," is a staid dinner, with the date's mother along. The other, at Coney Island, shows the young couple in close physical proximity on amusement park rides, often literally forced together, and without any supervision. Both show the new phenomenon of "dating," and the latter illustrates the growing youth subculture.[9] The film also addresses the social stigma facing an unwed mother and the attempts by social services to take her child away. Students are usually quite interested in the negative portrayal of social workers, who are told in the film that the world would be better off if they stayed home and had children of their own. Finally, the whole concept of sex appeal provides an opening to talk about modern conceptions of marriage and sexual compatibility.

Sexuality in Social Movements

Another place where sexuality is central to women's history is the study of social movements. Such movements have attempted not only to rewrite political policy and laws but also to alter the personal lives of every American. The arguments over sexuality within social movements can help students understand that those movements went beyond broad calls for reform to inspire intensely personal change.

A comparison of Ida B. Wells and Frances Willard near the turn of the century can be very productive in a women's history class. These two women both fought for (among other things) civil rights for women but disagreed vigorously over the causes of lynching and the role of sexuality in Southern social structures. Their fight exposes some of the deep fissures over racial questions within not only women's movements but also among progressives as a whole. Ida B. Wells, a journalist and activist who had to leave her home in Tennessee as her attacks on lynching made her anathema to the white population of the South, argued that the myth of black rapists was used to justify terrorism against the black population of the South and to disguise the real problem of white men raping black women. Frances Willard, the president of the Women's Christian Temperance Union, used the myth of the black rapist to argue that Southern white women needed to be protected from drunken black men by prohibiting the sale of alcoholic beverages. The sparring between the two women over Willard's perpetuation of the myth of the black rapist shook reformers in the United States, as well as in Great Britain, where both women toured to rally support for their causes.[10]

Understanding Wells and the myth of black rapists can help students understand the entire gender system of the South and how the supposed sexual purity of white women and ostensible lasciviousness of all African Americans led not only to sexual abuse of African American women and deadly violence against African American men (and occasionally women) but also to the subordination of white women. Willard, arguably the most politically powerful woman of her day, demonstrates the links between progressive and conservative thinking about the differences between men and women. Willard argued for political rights for women largely by contending that women's difference from men necessitated a separate political voice. Her arguments were premised on an idea of sexual difference between men and women, and often between different racial or ethnic groups. A comparison of these women can help students see how fundamental the differences could be between two reformers who are both remembered as "progressives" and who both argued for women's rights, as well as help students understand how different perceptions of women's (and men's) sexuality underlay many of the ideals to which progressives aspired.

Sexuality likewise played a vital role in the civil rights movement that peaked in the 1950s and 1960s. Within the movement, sexual relationships between men and women, across racial lines or not, created connections as well as tensions within civil rights organizations, especially as activists traveled to Mississippi during Freedom Summer.

Student Nonviolent Coordinating Committee President Stokely Carmichael's famous quip that the position of women in the civil rights movement was "prone" is more telling if students understand how black and white civil rights activists struggled with the place of sexuality within the movement. Of course, since they were challenging a system of racial oppression in which sexuality played a pivotal role, dealing with questions of sexuality was necessary. It was not, however, easy. Historian Mary Rothschild describes the problems surrounding sexuality during the 1964 Freedom Summer in Mississippi. "Whether women volunteers accepted or rejected the advances of black men," she writes, "sex became the metaphor for racial tension, hostility, and aggression. Nearly every project had real problems over interracial sex."[11] White women might be accused of racism for refusing the advances of black men or be seen as harmful to the movement if they slept with multiple men. Sexual relationships between white men and black women might seem reminiscent of the sexual exploitation of the Southern racial system, and some activists treated them with suspicion. All of this took place as civil rights workers lived and worked in a largely hostile environment, which required that any sexual activity within the movement, especially interracial sexuality, remain hidden from the white public.

The backlash against civil rights also took on sexual meaning. Those attacking integration often raised the threat of miscegenation, claiming that desegregation was a scheme concocted by black men to get into the beds of white women. Supposed news articles about miscegenation in magazines like *U.S. News and World Report* reveal the sexual rhetoric of the pro-segregation view for students.[12] Such articles contended that the push for integration was really driven by black male desire for sexual access to white women. They relied, of course, on the same myth of the black rapist that Ida B. Wells had fought so hard to quash, as well as the same belief in the lack of desire on the part of white women.

The study of twentieth-century feminism also benefits from an examination of sexuality that includes and goes beyond birth control. For example, tracing ideas about "vaginal" versus "clitoral" orgasms through the century can help students understand how fundamentally arguments about women's place affected women's personal lives. The idea of the vaginal orgasm, which peaked in influence in the 1940s and 1950s, assumed that women could obtain sexual satisfaction only through the presence of a male phallus and that women were dependent on men for such satisfaction. At a time when psychological theories claimed that sexual satisfaction was central to the mental health of both men and women, scientific proof that women *needed* men bolstered the belief that women who did not desire heterosexual marriage and children above all else were "unnatural." As sexologists in the 1950s and 1960s began arguing for the centrality of the clitoris in female sexual pleasure, beliefs about the healthiest sexual relationships for women changed as well. The most dramatic example combined the focus on clitoral sexual pleasure with the separatism popular in many social movements of the late 1960s and early 1970s in the form of "lesbian feminism." Lesbian feminists generally argued that, to overcome male oppression, women needed to escape heterosexual relationships entirely and embrace the love of women instead. The belief in the importance of the clitoris gave such women fuel to argue that sex between women provided greater sexual satisfaction for women than did sex with men. Questions about sex and sexual preference were heated subjects for debate within the feminist movement of the 1970s and created large rifts between those who argued for lesbian rights and those who, like Betty Friedan, saw lesbianism as "dangerous and diversionary" to feminism.[13]

Looking at sexuality in less radical or cohesive social movements (if they can even be called movements) can also show how widespread social change became. In the 1960s and 1970s, those who might not have self-identified as feminists or imagined themselves as radicals fought to end in loco parentis rules on college campuses and began to accept both premarital sex and cohabitation. In addition, college students pushed their universities for access to birth control, even for unmarried students. Because only a minority of Americans were actively involved in the civil rights movement or the feminist movement, looking at these more widespread calls for change help to contextualize cultural change during these years.

Sexual Subcultures and Women

While it is certainly important to study the history of lesbian communities and movements for their own sake, they are also important in relation to the larger trends in women's history. Through much of the twentieth century, the specter of the "mannish" lesbian threatened the ideal of the feminine heterosexual woman. Within lesbian communities, debates over gender performance, especially over the meaning of butch-femme roles, shed light on social conceptions of femininity at large. In addition, the existence of lesbian communities challenged conservative definitions of womanhood and of female sexuality.

Sexual subcultures became more prominent around the turn of the century. Many of the same changes that led to the decrease in fertility also created space for sexual subcultures. The rise of the city, whose size offered anonymity, and the availability of wage work for women contributed to an environment in which both men and women had greater opportunity to live outside marriage. For college-educated women, this often meant working within progressive organizations or in the few other careers open to women. For working-class women, this meant jobs with abominably low pay in factories or the like, so remaining unmarried often meant consigning themselves to a life of poverty.

Studying the lesbian communities that developed under these circumstances offers a compelling story of adaptation and community creation. The seeming acceptance, or at least tolerance, of lesbians and gay men in early-twentieth-century working-class neighborhoods challenges the traditional narrative in which gay men and lesbians lived fearful, closeted lives before the Stonewall riot in 1969.[14]

Studying the lesbian rights movement of the 1950s helps question students' view of that decade as a conformist era. The Daughters of Bilitis (DOB), the first lesbian rights group in the United States, began their fight in this era. Along with the (predominantly male) Mattachine Society, these activists struggled with gender performance, psychological theories around sexuality, and government crackdowns on gay and lesbian meeting places. These groups picketed, negotiated, and sued for their rights just as the civil rights movement was gaining national prominence and before the boom of social reforms in the 1960s. In addition, many of the same struggles faced by DOB members were commonly experienced by women regardless of sexual preference in the 1950s.[15] For example, most of these women did not rely on a male breadwinner for their income and so inevitably faced gender discrimination in the workplace in an era when even married women were increasingly joining the paid workforce. In addition, the concern about "career woman syndrome" that arose in popular books and magazines in the 1940s often linked career ambition to lesbianism, since they defined both as a failure of femininity.[16] Most women, therefore, had a stake in these issues.

Finally, the challenges that lesbian and gay activists presented to normative sexuality were part of a broader questioning of gender and sexual propriety. "Effeminist" gay men in the late 1960s and early 1970s rejected masculinity, claiming that America's problems and especially the Vietnam War were the result of irrational adherence to violent male culture.[17] Both men and women in the 1970s rejected marriage and heterosexual monogamy as oppressive and tried to imagine new forms of sexual organization—from communal sexuality to serial monogamy, free love to total abstention from sex, hetero and homosexual. Women also fought to gain control of their bodies, not only through birth control but also through laws to protect them from sexual harassment and rape, influence in the medical community, and knowledge. The radical challenges to sexual standards had enormous impact on the lives of women, whose options increased in many areas of their lives in dramatic ways.

Even in the 1980s and 1990s, when parts of the gay and lesbian rights movement espoused more mainstream, even conservative, goals such as marriage, military service, and positive representation in the media, the movement has a lot to teach the student of women's history. The activism that surrounded the AIDS crisis led to an increased focus on economic rights, medical coverage, and legal status for same-sex partners, even among lesbians. The baby boom among lesbians in the 1980s added to this desire for legal, medical, and economic rights. In 1997, when Ellen DeGeneres came out (as did her sitcom character), she did so without ruining her career, and gay and lesbian characters increased their presence in the media as multidimensional characters. Many of these fights paralleled and occasionally joined with feminist fights for better medical care for women, nondiscrimination in military service, and more positive media representation.

Conclusion

Teaching the history of sexuality in the classroom can be complicated, but it greatly enriches students' understanding of women's history. It is important that the environment be one in which students have the opportunity to openly ask questions—even more so than usual. There are so many myths and powerful stereotypes surrounding sexuality that students come to the material with strong predispositions to filter information through their own preexisting beliefs.

This chapter only begins to show the myriad ways in which the study of sexuality can enhance a women's history classroom. The history of sexuality before the twentieth century is equally compelling and just as revealing. Although it is not the easiest of subjects to teach, the rewards far surpass the difficulties. Studying such a personal aspect of the lives of women in the past pushes them to contextualize and demonstrates the interaction between the social and the political and the personal.

NOTES

1. The author wishes to thank Allida Black for her generous help in conceptualizing and editing this piece.

2. George Chauncey, *Gay New York: Gender, Urban Culture, and the Making of a Gay Male World, 1890–1940* (New York: Basic Books, 1995).

3. Carroll Smith-Rosenberg, "The Female World of Love and Ritual: Relations between Women in Nineteenth-Century America," *Journal of Women in Culture and Society* 1, no. 1 (1975), 1–30.

4. Christine Stansell, *American Moderns: Bohemian New York and the Creation of a New Century* (New York: Henry Holt, 2000), 225–308.

5. John D'Emilio and Estelle B. Freedman, *Intimate Matters: A History of Sexuality in America*, 2nd ed. (Chicago: University of Chicago Press, 1997), 58, 174.

6. Ibid., 222–223, 231–233.

7. For more on hysteria and neurasthenia, see Rachel P. Maines, *The Technology of Orgasm: "Hysteria," the Vibrator, and Women's Sexual Satisfaction* (Baltimore: Johns Hopkins University Press, 1999); Allida Black, "Perverting the Diagnosis: The Lesbian and Scientific Basis of Stigma," *Historical Reflections* 20, no. 2 (1994), 201–216; Carroll Smith-Rosenberg, "The Hysterical Woman: Sex Roles and Role Conflict in 19th-Century America," *Social Research* 39, no. 4 (1972), 652–678.

8. Clarence Badger, director, *It* (Paramount Pictures, 1927).

9. Kathy Peiss, *Cheap Amusements: Working Women and Leisure in Turn-of-the-Century New York* (Philadelphia: Temple University Press, 1986).

10. Gail Bederman, *Manliness and Civilization: A Cultural History of Gender and Race in the United States, 1870–1917* (Chicago: University of Chicago Press, 1995), 45–76.

11. Mary Aiken Rothschild, "White Women Volunteers in the Freedom Summers: Their Life and Work in a Movement for Social Change," *Feminist Studies* 5, no. 3 (Autumn 1979), 481; see also Susan Evans, *Personal Politics: The Roots of Women's Liberation in the Civil Rights Movement and the New Left* (New York: Vintage, 1979).

12. See, for example, "Intermarriage and the Race Problem," *U.S. News and World Report* (18 November 1963), 84–93.

13. Friedan, quoted in Daniel Horowitz, *Betty Friedan and the Making of* The Feminine Mystique (Amherst: University of Massachusetts Press, 1998), 232.

14. For histories of gay cultures before Stonewall, see John D'Emilio, *Sexual Politics, Sexual Communities: The Making of a Homosexual Minority in the United States, 1940–1970* (Chicago: University of Chicago Press, 1983); Chauncey, *Gay New York*; Lillian Faderman, *Odd Girls and Twilight Lovers: A History of Lesbian Life in Twentieth-Century America* (New York: Penguin, 1992).

15. D'Emilio, *Sexual Politics*, 101–125.

16. See, for example, Marynia Farnham and Ferdinand Lundberg, *Modern Woman: The Lost Sex* (New York: Harper and Brothers, 1947), 177.

17. Terence Kissack, "Freaking Fag Revolutionaries: New York's Gay Liberation Front, 1969–1971," *Radical History Review* 62 (1995), 120. Some men in the Gay Liberation Front referred to themselves as "effeminists."

6

Conceptualizing Citizenship in U.S. Women's History

Christine L. Compston

Integration of women's experience into U.S. history courses provides opportunities for students to explore how American ideals—equality, justice, and democratic rule—have translated into policies and practices that have shaped the lives of individual women, as well as groups defined by race, ethnicity, and class. Students gain a deeper understanding of the role of the Constitution in American life; they realize that individuals— both those serving in government and those challenging government policies—make a difference; they learn the importance of civil, political, and social rights and the power that comes from asserting those rights. In addition, they discover the importance of perspective in the study of history and how our understanding of the past is influenced by the issues we raise, the sources we use, and the questions we ask.

A central theme in my U.S. history courses is the role of the Constitution in American life. The emphasis is on how the government operates, who makes decisions, what factors influence the decision-making process, and how decisions affect real people. Women's experiences serve as case studies that inform and deepen students' understanding of the Constitution and American government, while acquainting them with the challenges and achievements of women.

Students learn about political status. How has the framework of government shaped the political environment and determined who exercises power? How have the powers been used? How have the decisions taken by policy makers affected the lives of women? To what extent have legislative and judicial decisions affecting women been based on commonly held assumptions or personal values rather than constitutional principles? On what basis have lawmakers justified a double standard for women and men? How have those excluded from political citizenship used their civil rights to challenge injustice and discrimination? What does the gradual expansion of women's rights tell us about the American system? What do the achievements of those denied the full rights and privileges of citizenship tell us about the importance of effective leadership and grassroots movements? What generalizations can we draw about the American system of government and the constitutional guarantees of individual rights, based on the experiences of women?

Woman's status, her access to citizenship, and her ability to exercise the rights associated with citizenship are critical. Civil and political rights determine whether a woman has a voice and the ways in which she can make that voice heard. Is she dependent solely on freedom of expression—speech, press, petition, and assembly—guaranteed in the First Amendment? Or can she exercise political rights, such as jury duty and the right to vote and hold office? To what extent and in what ways has woman's limited political voice determined her access to economic opportunities? How has the expansion of woman's rights affected her role in the marketplace and in the community?

Linking women's history to legal and constitutional issues has served to convince many skeptical students of the legitimacy of examining women's experience. Back in the 1970s, for example, I relied on newspaper clippings to draw the attention of my high school students to the inequalities still imposed on women. I did not seem to be making much headway until I came to an article describing the double standard built into a law dealing with desertion. "That's not fair," blurted out one of the male students. Exactly! The students got the point, and the whole tenor of the class changed at that moment.

Despite decades of scholarly contributions, extensive inclusion of women in the curriculum still requires going beyond the textbook and making frequent use of primary sources—from popular depictions of women in films, advertisements, literature, and news to official records left by political, economic, and social institutions. These materials engage students in ways that secondary texts do not. They also serve as vehicles for teaching students analytical skills that are applicable to resources encountered in daily life as well as academic assignments.

The questions asked and the analysis required to discover the nature of women's experience is often more demanding and radically different from the standard set of tools taught to students. Students must learn to examine assumptions and generalizations based on class, race, and gender and to pay particularly close attention to language. They must also recognize the need to dig deeper. The film *Adam's Rib* provides a classic example. When students discover that the laws at the time made a sharp distinction between how husbands and wives were treated when a spouse decided to take revenge on her or his partner's lover, they become aware of the serious issues underlying what is generally viewed as a comedy.

Themes That Shape the Curriculum

Throughout American history, woman's citizenship has been closely related to her marital status. English common law established the doctrine of *coverture*, which merged the civil existence of a woman with that of her husband. In doing so, the law deprived married women of basic political and economic rights, including the right to vote, make contracts, write wills, sue or be sued in court, and own property. Social and economic conditions, along with legal instruments such as prenuptial contracts, allowed exemptions from the limitations imposed by coverture. Most of the time, however, this doctrine operated to deprive women of rights that were considered "natural" when exercised by men, to excuse women from the duties and obligations generally associated with full citizenship, and to deny both native-born women and immigrants the privileges associated with American citizenship.

Although coverture technically applied only to married women, the assumption that women would marry carried over into laws and policies that affected single women. The assumption that women would be provided for by husbands, despite evidence to the contrary, influenced legislation and judicial decisions, as well as private business practices, well into the twentieth century, thus depriving women of the economic rights of citizenship. A survey of the history of women shows that long after the *law* of coverture had been expunged, the *idea* of coverture persisted.

A second theme builds on the meaning of *citizenship* in a democratic society. Americans adopted the term *citizen* at the time of the Revolution to distinguish themselves from the British, who were *subjects* of the king.[1] Republican ideals embraced principles of self-government and equality. The idea of self-government rests on the political elements of citizenship, including the privileges of voting and holding offices, as well as the duties of serving on juries and defending one's country. Equality under the law has economic and social implications that have, over time, taken on greater importance.

The three aspects of citizenship—civil, political, and social—are worth examining more closely. Civil citizenship consists of "the rights necessary to individual freedom—liberty of the person, freedom of speech, thought, and faith, the right to own property and to conclude valid contracts, and the right to justice." Political citizenship affords the right to exercise political power "as a member of a body invested with political authority, or as an elector of the members of such a body." Social citizenship, a relatively recent phenomenon, is essential to the *exercise* of civil and political rights. It covers "the whole range from the right to a modicum of economic welfare and security to the right to share to the full in the social heritage and to live the life of a civilized being according to the standards prevailing in the society."[2]

A distinct, though related, theme is the contrast between political rhetoric and practical reality. The contrast between political ideals carefully articulated by the Founding Fathers and the experiences of ordinary Americans during and after the war for independence serves to lay the foundation for an ongoing examination of rhetoric versus reality.

Developing the Themes within the Narrative

The egalitarian language used by Revolutionary leaders inspired many colonists to support independence. Only the most radical, James Otis and Benjamin Rush, considered the implications for women. Otis discussed the possibility of women voting in the new republic.[3] Rush, along with feminist Judith Sargent Murray, advocated equal education as a critical step toward economic independence.[4]

The Constitution left states to determine criteria for citizenship and rights granted to citizens. Only New Jersey, which granted suffrage to all residents who met specific property requirements, gave any women the right to political participation. Although a few single women had qualified, the state amended its constitution in 1807 to disenfranchise all women.

British attitudes shaped the thinking of most Americans in the early republic; however, women's role did change. The new model had many traditional elements but new features as well. The republican mother "was dedicated to the service of civic virtue; she educated her sons for it; she condemned and corrected her husband's lapses from it."[5] This role represented an intermediate stage in the process of political socialization, that of the "deferential citizen: the person who expects to influence the political system, but only to a limited extent." It represented "not the negation of citizenship, but an approach to full participation in the civic culture."[6]

Greater participation in public affairs became a hallmark of the Jacksonian Era. Still denied political citizenship, women relied on rights associated with civil citizenship as they engaged in reform movements to improve education, prison conditions, and care for the mentally ill. Referring to the three categories of citizenship can help students recognize the importance of First Amendment rights in achieving the Founders' ideals—equality of opportunity, dignity of the individual, democratic governance—and come to see that civil rights were not enough. Political rights were also needed.

Many of the causes embraced by female reformers had implications for the larger society; others were unique to women. For example, the temperance movement had special significance for women married to alcoholic husbands. Denied control over family property—dowries, personal earnings, and their husbands' assets—women petitioned and testified before state legislatures to pass Married Women's Property Acts. These decidedly political actions demonstrated both the extent of women's civil rights (right to speak and petition) and the limits on those rights (the rights to own property and to sign contracts, as well as dependence on male lawmakers to provide a remedy) resulting from coverture. By 1850, seventeen states had passed laws granting married women rights to own and manage their property and that of their families.

Women also fought for fair treatment in the workplace. The rights of civil citizenship were critical to New England's mill girls, typically young and single, who were drawn into the public forum to protest against long hours and harsh working conditions.[7] During the 1840s, factory women published their own newspapers, petitioned for shorter workdays, and testified before legislative committees. Primary documents capture the energy and determination of the workers and illustrate their political insights and strategies. Lacking the right to vote and the concomitant influence over elected officials, mill girls were ultimately forced to rely on male coworkers to secure needed reforms. They learned that, while civil rights were essential, political citizenship was required. As a result, many female factory workers became suffragists.

Both white and black women became abolitionists, exercising their civil rights to denounce and destroy the institution of slavery. Women circulated petitions, assisted and sheltered fugitive slaves, and wrote political tracts, short stories, and novels attacking the heinous institution. Free African American women sponsored fairs and bazaars to raise money for antislavery societies and the antislavery press.[8] Women attended antislavery conventions and, in a few notable cases, voiced their opposition to slavery in public forums. The hostility they faced when attempting to speak out sparked a realization that their claims to civil citizenship were sharply limited by traditional views of woman's proper role.

Influenced by these experiences, women recognized the need to challenge impositions on women and insist that they be granted rights of political citizenship. Lucretia Mott and Elizabeth Cady Stanton organized the first Women's Rights Convention, held in Seneca Falls, New York, in 1848. Stanton's Declaration of Sentiments, designed to mold public opinion and establish an agenda for subsequent action, listed specific grievances, most of which had their roots in the doctrine of coverture. It concluded by "insist[ing] that [women] have immediate admission to all the rights and privileges which belong to them as citizens of the United States."

What did Stanton mean by this? What did she think others attending the convention would have understood this to mean? What would the general population have thought it meant? The language implied that the "rights and privileges" of citizens were clearly established or, at least, commonly agreed upon. Yet, as late as 1862, the U.S. Attorney General conducted a "fruitless" investigation of rights conveyed by citizenship. He reported, "Eighty years of practical enjoyment of citizenship, under the Constitution, have not sufficed to teach us either the exact meaning of the word, or the constituent elements of the thing we prize so highly."[9]

In one of the few cases involving women's citizenship prior to the Civil War, the Supreme Court in *Shanks v. DuPont* upheld common law doctrine "that no persons can, by any act of their own, without the consent of the government, put off their allegiance and become aliens."[10] Based on this rule, a woman could not lose her native allegiance by marrying a foreigner. However, the influx of immigrants from Ireland and Germany, which began shortly after the Court issued this decision, raised critical questions about married women's citizenship.

In response to growing nativism, Congress passed the Naturalization Act of 1855. The law automatically naturalized immigrant women who married American citizens but excluded women who were Negroes, Indians, and Chinese. Senator Charles Sumner succeeded in amending the law in 1870 to allow women of African descent to become citizens. However, strong resistance from the western states prevented Chinese women from becoming citizens, a policy that was reinforced by the Chinese Exclusion Act of 1882.[11]

The Naturalization Act harked back to the common law doctrine of coverture. According to the bill's sponsor, "By the act of marriage itself the political character of the wife shall at once conform to the political character of the husband."[12] The law naturalized the children of an American father but not of a mother, thus reinforcing its patriarchal underpinnings.

Two years later, the Supreme Court took up the issue of citizenship in *Dred Scott v. Sandford*, denying all African Americans the status of citizen, as well as the resulting rights and privileges.[13] The system of slavery had resulted in denial of virtually all rights to African American women—basic human rights as well as those grounded in the Constitution. The issue of African American citizenship was, in effect, settled by force of arms during the Civil War and formally addressed during Reconstruction by the Fourteenth Amendment. Section 1 declared: "All persons born or naturalized in the United States and subject to the jurisdiction thereof, are citizens of the United States and of the State wherein they reside." Section 2, however, spoke not of persons but of "male inhabitants" and their voting rights, making this the first federal constitutional provision to mention gender.

About the same time, delegates charged with drafting new state constitutions in the South debated whether black women should be given the vote; African Americans were "more apt to support women's suffrage" than their white counterparts. Although these measures were defeated in all of the conventions, black legislators continued to push for woman suffrage in state assemblies, but without success. In contrast to white suffragists, black women saw the vote as a collective privilege, reasoning that husbands, fathers, brothers, and sons would use their vote in the interest of the entire African American community. African American women took part in political campaigns and, on occasion, assumed a "protective role" at political rallies and polling places to discourage violence aimed at black male voters.[14]

They also assumed leading roles in the campaign against lynching, placing their own lives in danger in an effort to attract public attention. A gifted and courageous journalist, Ida B. Wells, relied on First Amendment guarantees of free expression—her civil rights as a citizen—but lacked the political clout needed to secure antilynching legislation.

Freedwomen enjoyed virtually no economic rights. In part, this resulted from the fact that few had either education or skills of any sort. Their status was further undermined by the Freedman's Bureau, which gave former slaves the right to marry legally but imposed the strictures of coverture on black women. Husbands assumed the title of "family head" and acquired rights not only to family property but also to the earnings of their wives.[15]

Black women were relegated to a handful of jobs that no one else would take—domestic servant, laundress, or field hand—where they put in long hours at hard labor for little money. Situated in jobs that offered little opportunity for collective action, they seldom mustered the support necessary to protest successfully against exploitation. Kept "in their place" by de facto as well as de jure segregation, black women remained at the bottom of the economic ladder for generations, ignored by leaders of the women's rights movement.

Stanton viewed the Fourteenth and Fifteenth Amendments as affronts to women, many of whom, she asserted, were better educated and better prepared to assume the responsibilities of citizenship than either newly freed black men or newly naturalized immigrants. Under her leadership, the National Women's Suffrage Association (NWSA) concluded that the Fourteenth Amendment could be used to assert women's right to vote. When Susan B. Anthony cast her ballot in November 1872, she was arrested and tried in federal district court. The judge announced his opinion before directing the jury to bring in a verdict of guilty. Anthony's lawyer protested, at which point the judge discharged the jury and confronted the defendant. Anthony seized the moment. "My natural rights, my civil rights, my political rights, my judicial rights, are all alike ignored. Robbed of the fundamental privilege of citizenship, I am degraded from the status of citizen to that of a subject."[16] The judge imposed a fine of $100 and court costs but refused to imprison Anthony for nonpayment, thus precluding the possibility of appeal.

Less than six months later, the Supreme Court denied Myra Bradwell's petition to practice law. A qualified lawyer, Bradwell based her claim on the fact that she was a citizen of both the United States and the State of Illinois. The Fourteenth Amendment, she pointed out, guaranteed her the "privileges" of citizenship, which, she maintained, included her right to practice her profession. The Illinois Court had rejected her application "by reason of the disability imposed by [her] married condition," in other words, on the basis of coverture.[17]

The Supreme Court, in *Bradwell v. Illinois*, upheld that ruling, explaining that the federal government had no authority to decide who could practice law. Such decisions were left to the states. Justice Bradley's concurring opinion, based on the doctrine of coverture, noted that a married woman was "incapable, without her husband's consent, of making contracts" and therefore could not perform the duties associated with legal practice.[18]

The judicial opinions in this case raise a number of questions: What are the "privileges" of citizenship? What is the difference between state and federal citizenship? What is meant by the "law of nature," "divine ordinance," "civil law," and "constitutional law"? Which of these should be considered by a court of law, and why? To what extent were the justices' assumptions about the relationship between husband and wife valid? To what extent were their assumptions about the role of women in American society valid? To what extent were these assumptions related to a woman's racial and/or economic status? When issued, was the Court's reasoning valid or anachronistic? Was it consistent with democratic values? Was it just and reasonable?

When the U.S. Supreme Court rendered its opinion in the spring of 1873, the Illinois legislature had voted to admit women to the bar. Gradually, other state legislatures followed suit—often in response to state judicial decisions that followed Bradley's line of reasoning.

Despite the fact that state lawmakers were beginning to reconsider woman's status and her rights as a citizen, the Supreme Court remained resolute, as evidenced in their 1875 ruling in *Minor v. Happersett*. Virginia Minor asserted that the First Amendment's guarantee of free speech and the Fourteenth Amendment's protection of a citizen's "privileges" included the right to vote. The Court concluded that this was not an inherent right of all citizens. Rather, as the historical record clearly demonstrated, voting was a right that could be granted or withheld by a state, regardless of whether the individual was a citizen.[19]

Like *Bradwell*, the *Minor* decision calls on students to probe more deeply. Should the "historical record" take precedence over arguments grounded in constitutional language—in this case, the First and Fourteenth Amendments? Should the Equal Protection Clause of the Fourteenth Amendment have trumped the doctrine of coverture?

Angered by the Court's reluctance to adopt an expansive reading of the Fourteenth Amendment, Stanton abandoned universal suffrage and adopted a platform that was xenophobic, racist, and class-based. Francis Willard, whose influence as president of the Women's Christian Temperance Union surpassed that of Stanton by the end of the century, joined the chorus. Ironically, claims that white, educated women were more deserving of the vote than nonwhite, uneducated men "justified" denying suffrage to Mexican Americans—male and female—in the Southwest.[20]

The American Women's Suffrage Association (AWSA) supported state campaigns to give women the vote. Several western states extended the franchise; however, the most successful strategy was the quest for "partial" or "limited" suffrage. Middle- and upper-class women leveraged their civil citizenship to make the case for political citizenship at the municipal level. These women responded to challenges presented by industrialization, urbanization, and a resurgence of immigration by taking on the role of "municipal housekeeper." College-educated women joined settlement houses, campaigned against corrupt political machines, and urged municipal governments to adopt "progressive" reforms. Women's achievements earned them the right to vote in city elections and serve on school boards.[21]

A younger generation of suffragists assumed leadership following the merger of the AWSA and NWSA in 1890. Carrie Chapman Catt, president of the National American Women's Suffrage Association, adopted a "flexible" plan directed at both state and federal governments. While Catt deserves much of the credit for passage and ratification of the Nineteenth Amendment, Alice Paul—founder of the Congressional Union (CU), renamed the Woman's Party—played a significant role in the suffrage movement. So, too, did Harriot Stanton Blatch, who had joined the CU in 1913.

Paul and Blatch, both of whom were influenced by Britain's militant suffragists, maintained that women should be given equal rights—economic as
well as political. This marked a change in how the women's movement defined
the rights of citizens. Paul and Blatch opposed protective labor legislation and
judicial decisions, including *Muller v. Oregon*, which treated women as "depen-
dents."[22] In 1923, they proposed the Equal Rights Amendment and campaigned
for independent citizenship for married women.

The Naturalization Act of 1855 had awarded citizenship to a large number
of married women. At the same time, the law denied a woman the right to
choose whether to retain her native allegiance or become an American.
Citizenship of a married woman became "derivative," inextricably linked to
that of her husband, but automatic naturalization was limited to white and
black women.

Native American women suffered from the "good intentions" of politicians. The Dawes Act (1887) sought to replace the communal Indian culture
with a patriarchal arrangement constructed around the family unit. Women,
who had traditionally farmed the land, lost standing as men became property
owners and farmers. In 1924, the federal government, satisfied with the results
of this "Americanization" process, gave the vote to Native American men and
women.[23]

Asian women faced two major obstacles: traditional attitudes regarding
women's proper role and stereotypes that blended race and gender. From 1882
until 1946, discriminatory laws and enforcement policies restricted immigration and naturalization. Federal law allowed Asian women to immigrate if they
could prove through documentation, supporting testimony, "respectable"
appearance, or convincing responses to probing interrogation that they were
married to men already working in the United States and would be economically dependent on their husbands. A woman who intended to support herself
or was suspected of being a prostitute (loosely defined) had little chance of
admission. An 1875 immigration law that excluded prostitutes was "in many
ways a response to anti-Chinese agitation on the West Coast that had painted
all Chinese women immigrants with the broad brush of moral and physical
contagion."[24] Judicial decisions allowing women to enter the country reflected
a concern for the husbands' rights to their wives' company rather than recognition that the women themselves had rights.[25]

Government policies sharply limiting the number of women who could
enter the United States from Asia created an imbalance among ethnic populations. This fact resulted in Asian women being granted greater—though not
complete—equality within their homes. The gender imbalance among Japanese
was addressed in 1907 by the Gentleman's Agreement, which enabled Japanese

women, usually "picture brides," to immigrate. Responding to negative public opinion, American officials pressured the Japanese government in 1920 to stop issuing passports to women who had married proxy husbands, and Congress acted in 1924 to bar all "aliens ineligible for citizenship" from entering the country.[26]

Because Asian men were exploited in the workplace, women had to contribute to the family economy, further enhancing their status within the home. Outside the home, Japanese and Filipino women were relegated to low-paid field work and domestic service, jobs they managed in addition to household responsibilities. Unable to become citizens, these women, many of whom settled in Hawaii, were highly vulnerable to economic exploitation by the white plantation owners who dominated the local economy.[27]

President Franklin Roosevelt's 1941 Executive Order allowed immigrants from China, India, Korea, and the Philippines—American allies during the war—to become U.S. citizens. The Soldier Brides Act (1947) opened the way for more than 45,000 women to enter the United States as wives of military personnel.[28] In 1952, the McCarran-Walter Act made Japanese immigrants eligible for citizenship.[29]

With passage of the Expatriation Act of 1907, American-born women automatically lost their citizenship if they married foreigners, and they were not able to apply for renaturalization on their own. Since not all nations automatically bestowed citizenship on the wives of their nationals, some women were made stateless by this legislation—unable to exercise rights of citizenship, including entering or leaving the country.

Ethel Mackenzie lived in California, which had granted women suffrage. Having lost the right to vote when she married a noncitizen, she challenged the 1907 law in the Supreme Court.[30] Her lawyers argued that she had been deprived of her citizenship without her express consent, a violation of due process, and challenged Congress's power to denaturalize citizens. Harking back to the doctrine of coverture, the Court, in *Mackenzie v. Hare*, defended derivative citizenship and asserted that the federal government was sovereign over issues of nationality.[31] This defeat was soon to be rectified.

Ratification of the Nineteenth Amendment in 1920 fully granted women the right to vote. In doing so, it dramatically increased the number of women with a "real" political voice and enlarged the number of women who were involuntarily disenfranchised under the 1907 act. In response to lobbying by women's rights groups, Representative John L. Cable proposed legislation repealing most provisions in the earlier bill. The Cable Act (1922) was amended a number of times, eventually providing married women with independent citizenship.[32]

While more conservative groups, including the League of Women Voters, continued to press for protective legislation for working women, radicals pushed for equal rights and opportunities in the workplace. Reasoning from different premises and supporting conflicting agendas, these two factions shared a common commitment to improving the plight of women employed outside the home. Women still received less education, acquired fewer skills, had far fewer employment opportunities, and were paid considerably less than their male counterparts. The notion that women's lives were dominated by domestic responsibilities fled in the face of reality. Even among the middle and upper classes, white women increasingly sought careers outside the home but often ran into roadblocks. Working-class women—native-born and immigrant, white and nonwhite—supplemented family income, but the economic downturn at the end of the 1920s resulted in reactionary policies that denied jobs to women, including those who were sole providers for their families, in an effort to create work for men, who were still perceived as heads of households and primary wage earners.

The Great Depression presented female immigrants with a new set of challenges. Beginning in the 1880s, the government had evaluated immigrants to determine whether they would be able to support themselves and their families. A person who fell short was labeled "LPC"—likely to become a public charge—and denied admission or closely observed after entering the country. Single, divorced, and widowed women typically had few skills and few opportunities in a market that discriminated against female workers. During the Depression, these women had a hard time finding jobs. Demands on public assistance were sufficiently strained to warrant deportation of those who could not support themselves.[33]

The Social Security Act recognized rights associated with social citizenship but awarded more of those rights to men than to women, more to whites than to blacks, more to the economically secure than to the poor. Records reveal a "conscious sense of preserving an appropriate gender balance [that] went into constructing the system" and policies that based the "economic viability" of the system on "the occasional contributions of women and the poor who would never earn enough to collect any benefits." The law discouraged married women from working outside the home and denied domestic servants and farm workers—most black women—opportunity to participate in the program.[34]

Inequities in the Social Security system were finally ruled unconstitutional in 1975 in *Weinberger v. Wiesenfeld*, a case brought by a widower whose wife, the principal wage earner for the family, had died in childbirth. The Court determined that "gender-based generalization[s] cannot suffice to justify the denigration of the efforts of women who do work and whose earnings contribute significantly to their families' support."[35]

In 1961, President John F. Kennedy established the President's Commission on the Status of Women (PCSW). Dominated by Esther Peterson, a supporter of protective labor legislation, the PCSW relied on traditional views of women's role in the workplace. Pauli Murray, a civil rights lawyer and legal scholar, played a critical role through her efforts to equate race-based and gender-based discrimination. Her work served as the basis for the Equal Pay Act of 1963, which required equal pay for identical jobs but rejected equal pay for "comparable" work and, therefore, "protect[ed] men's jobs by ensuring that women would not undermine male wages."[36]

Title VII of the Civil Rights Act of 1964 allowed challenges to social programs and employment practices that denied women the full extent of rights inherent in social citizenship. In *Frontiero v. Richardson* (1973), the Court ruled that laws providing greater benefits to men in the military than to their female counterparts were unconstitutional. It rejected Bradley's reasoning in *Bradwell*; acknowledged discrimination against women in education, employment, and politics; and observed that "statutory distinctions between the sexes often have the effect of invidiously relegating the entire class of females to inferior legal status without regard to the actual capabilities of its individual members."[37]

Although the Court has not been willing to grant equal status to women in other cases involving military service, Congress has amended the law to increase the percentage of women serving in the armed forces, commanding male and female units, and engaging in naval and air combat.[38] These changes have moderated the impact on women of laws giving veterans preference in civil service employment.[39]

As a result of the recent reconfiguration of the Supreme Court, advances in the area of economic equality now appear in jeopardy. The Supreme Court's 2007 decision in *Ledbetter v. Goodyear Tire and Rubber Company*, which relies on a narrow reading of Title VII of the Civil Rights Act of 1964, makes it more difficult—in many cases, impossible—for women to challenge discriminatory pay practices that they were not aware of when the Equal Employment Opportunity Commission clock began to tick. Justice Ruth Bader Ginsburg rejected the majority opinion, charging that it "overlooks common characteristics of pay discrimination" and arguing that women should be able to file claims "based on the cumulative effect of individual acts" that become apparent over time.[40]

Prior to the realignment of the Court, the justices had enlarged political rights and the responsibilities of women. Women had been excluded from jury service, with notable but short-lived exceptions, even after winning the right to vote. Legal challenges had resulted in mixed rulings: Some judges found that the obligation to serve on juries accompanied suffrage; others concluded that the two were discrete and unrelated. Massachusetts, New York, Illinois, and eight other states had granted women the right to sit on juries by 1938, but as late as 1965, only twenty-one states made women eligible on the same terms as men. Others excluded women entirely or granted exemptions to allow women to carry out their domestic duties. Echoes of coverture could still be heard. In *J.E.B. v. Alabama* (1994), the justices recognized the importance of women's participation in the legal process: their own right to equal justice, as well as a shared responsibility to assure that all persons are accorded equal treatment under the law.[41]

Suffrage remains an issue for U.S. citizens—women and men—who live outside the fifty states, including Guam and Puerto Rico. Since the 1970s, Puerto Ricans have sought the right to vote in presidential elections but without success. Federal court rulings based on Article II of the Constitution have consistently held that the right to vote in presidential elections derives from the states, and because Puerto Rico is not a state, this right can be awarded only by means of a constitutional amendment.[42]

In recent years, a new set of questions relating to marriage and citizenship has emerged as lesbians and gays committed to long-term relationships have sought civil rights and the right to marry another person of the same sex. A fundamental yet unresolved legal question is whether a marriage performed in one state must be recognized, under Article IV of the Constitution, by the government of another state. In contrast to past debates, in which a woman's citizenship was dependent on her marital status and derived from her husband's citizenship, the current debate examines the question of whether marriage is itself a right of citizenship.

NOTES

1. Rogers M. Smith, *Civic Ideals: Conflicting Visions of Citizenship in U.S. History* (New Haven, CT: Yale University Press, 1997), p. 14.

2. T. H. Marshall, "Citizenship and Social Class," in *Class, Citizenship and Social Development* (New York: Doubleday, 1964), p. 78, as quoted in Evelyn Nakano Glenn, *Unequal Freedom: How Race and Gender Shaped American Citizenship and Labor* (Cambridge: Harvard University Press, 2002), p. 19.

3. Rosemarie Zagarri, "The Rights of Man and Woman in Post-Revolutionary America," *William and Mary Quarterly*, 3rd ser., 55 (April 1998): 205; and Linda K. Kerber, *Toward an Intellectual History of Women* (Chapel Hill: University of North Carolina Press, 1997), pp. 54–55.

4. Kerber, pp. 24–34.

5. Ibid., p. 58. See also Linda K. Kerber, *Women of the Republic: Intellect and Ideology in Revolutionary America* (Chapel Hill: University of North Carolina Press, 1980).

6. Kerber, *Toward an Intellectual History of Women*, pp. 58–60.

7. Thomas Dublin argues that factory workers claimed both economic and political rights on the basis of their being "daughters of freemen" in *Women at Work* (New York: Columbia University Press, 1979), p. 103.

8. C. Peter Ripley et al., eds., *Witness for Freedom* (Chapel Hill: University of North Carolina Press, 1993), pp. 96–105.

9. Bates as quoted in Patricia Lucie, "On Being a Free Person and a Citizen by Constitutional Amendment," *Journal of American Studies* 12 (1978): 355.

10. *Shanks v. DuPont*, 3 Pet. 242 (1830).

11. Nancy Cott, "Marriage and Women's Citizenship in the United States, 1830–1934," *American Historical Review* 103 (December 1998): 1458–59.

12. *Congressional Globe*, 33d Cong., 1st sess. (January 13, 1854), 169–71, as quoted in Cott, pp. 1456–57.

13. *Dred Scott v. Sandford*, 19 Howard 393 (1857).

14. Evelyn Nakano Glenn, *Unequal Freedom: How Race and Gender Shaped American Citizenship and Labor* (Cambridge: Harvard University Press, 2002), pp. 96–97.

15. Nancy F. Cott, *Public Vows: A History of Marriage and the Nation* (Cambridge: Harvard University Press, 2000), p. 93.

16. Kathleen Barry, *Susan B. Anthony: A Biography of a Singular Feminist* (New York: Ballantine, 1988), p. 255.

17. Virginia G. Drachman, *Sisters in Law: Women Lawyers in Modern American History* (Cambridge: Harvard University Press, 1998), pp. 16–25.

18. *Bradwell v. Illinois*, 83 U.S. 130, 141 (1873).

19. *Minor v. Happersett*, 88 U.S. 162 (1875). See also Alexander Keyssar, *The Right to Vote* (New York: Basic Books, 2000), pp. 172–83. Men who had declared their intent to become citizens were often given the vote.

20. Glenn, p. 162.

21. Keyssar, p. 186.

22. *Muller v. Oregon*, 208 U.S. 412 (1908). See also Nancy Wolloch, ed., *Muller v. Oregon: A Brief History with Documents* (Boston: Bedford, 1996).

23. Cott, *Public Vows*, pp. 122–23.

24. Martha Gardner, *The Qualities of a Citizen: Women, Immigration, and Citizenship, 1870–1965* (Princeton, NJ: Princeton University Press, 2005), p. 51.

25. Ibid., p. 18.

26. Ibid., p. 44. See also Yen Le Espiritu, *Asian American Women and Men: Labor, Laws, and Love* (Thousand Oaks, CA: Sage, 1997), p. 18.

27. Espiritu, p. 9. See also Glenn, p. 212.

28. Cott, *Public Vows*, p. 184.

29. Gardner, p. 212.

30. Candice Lewis Bredbenner, *A Nationality of Her Own: Women, Marriage, and the Law of Citizenship* (Berkeley: University of California Press, 1998), pp. 63–64.

31. Ibid., pp. 65–66; *Mackenzie v. Hare*, 239 U.S. 299, at 300 (1915).

32. Bredbenner, pp. 80–122.

33. Gardner., pp. 89, 176–83.

34. Alice Kessler-Harris, "Designing Women and Old Fools: The Construction of the Social Security Amendments of 1939," in Linda K. Kerber et al., eds., *U.S. History as Women's History: New Feminist Essays* (Chapel Hill: University of North Carolina Press, 1995), pp. 101–3.

35. *Weinberger v. Wiesenfeld*, 420 U.S. 636, at 645 (1975).

36. Alice Kessler-Harris, *In Pursuit of Equality: Women, Men, and the Quest for Economic Citizenship in 20th-Century America* (New York: Oxford University Press, 2001), pp. 215–35.

37. *Frontiero v. Richardson*, 411 U.S. 677, at 685, 686–687 (1973).

38. Clare Cushman, ed., *Supreme Court Decisions and Women's Rights* (Washington, DC: CQ Press, 2001), pp. 98–108.

39. *Personnel Administrator of Massachusetts v. Feeney*, 442 U.S. 256 (1979). See also Linda K. Kerber, *No Constitutional Right to Be Ladies: Women and the Obligations of Citizenship* (New York: Hill and Wang, 1998), pp. 221ff.

40. Justice Ruth Bader Ginsburg, *Ledbetter v. Goodyear Tire and Rubber Company*, No. 05-1074 (29 May 2007).

41. *J.E.B. v. Alabama ex rel. T.B.*, 511 U.S. 127 (1994). See also Kerber, *No Constitutional Right*, pp. 124ff.

42. José D. Román, "Trying to Fit an Oval Shaped Island into a Square Constitution: Arguments for Puerto Rican Statehood," 29 *Fordham Urban Law Journal* 1681–1713 (April 2002), excerpted on http://academic.udayton.edu/race/02rights/citizen01.htm.

7

Conceptualizing U.S. Women's History through Consumerism

Jennifer Scanlon

Early studies of consumer culture in the United States viewed women as dupes of advertising and other media entities: Women received the message that they were "born to shop," and they followed that dictate without considering its gendered economic or political consequences—or its suitability for their lives. In the history of consumer culture, such marginalization of women as historical actors has operated on two planes, depicting women as the passive recipients of men's dictates about money and power, and marking the work women do, purchasing products for themselves and their families, as an activity to be mocked ("Women's place is at the mall") and as a meager social undertaking rather than an essential economic contribution. Such understandings leave us with a woefully inadequate picture of Americans' historical relationships to the getting and spending of money. This chapter explores how teaching about consumerism from a gendered historical perspective can provide students with a richer and more complex engagement not only with the history of women but also with the history of the development of consumerism and consumer capitalism in the United States.

It is difficult for students to imagine a life outside almost relentless invitations to participate in consumer culture. They encounter myriad advertisements each day as they walk through school buildings or down the street, read newspapers or magazines, log on to their computers, or even open their closets. When I initially engage students with questions of consumerism, and ask how much an individual student was paid to wear those Air Jordan sneakers, that New England Patriots cap, or those Juicy Couture jeans, they look at me with incredulity—until something clicks. Contemporary consumer culture is sufficiently ubiquitous to seem unremarkable (we are all walking advertisements), but like other quintessential elements of American life, it has a fascinating and important history, one that can be made visible. Students who recognize the importance consumerism holds in their own lives engage readily with this history and learn a great deal about gendered relationships and about the relationship between "conspicuous" and "consumption" in American history and life.

One of the first questions students bring to this subject deals with chronology: When did the acquisition of goods assume prominence in the American imagination and in daily life? When did our nation's citizens come to identify as Americans, in part at least, through the things we own? It is no easy task to identify a date, a decade, or even a century in which consumerism became part and parcel of life in the United States. Historians argue that consumerism took on its basic shape in the Western world in the seventeenth and eighteenth centuries, and modern consumerism resulted from the development of industrialization and then corporate capitalism in the late nineteenth and early twentieth centuries. The industrial revolution transformed the production of everyday goods, and the combination of cheap labor, cheap energy, an abundance of natural resources, advances in technology, rapidly expanding transportation networks, and more modern forms of capital investment ensured the advancement of not only the production but then also the consumption of these goods. In the years between the Civil War and the turn of the century, the nation's productive capacities increased tremendously. Manufacturers sought, at home and abroad, new markets for their products. Purchasing increasingly came to be equated not only with social mobility and middle-class status but also with the very notion of citizenship: To be American was to be a consumer. "By the end of the century," writes historian Kathleen Donohue, "the nation's phenomenal productive capacities had convinced all but the most recalcitrant that the real threat to a capitalist economy was not too much consumption but too little."[1]

The process expanded further in the early decades of the twentieth century, with a culmination in the 1920s not only of postwar prosperity but also of new forms of consumer participation, from the installment plan to the mass purchasing of automobiles, from the advent of national advertising to the consumer invitations and implications of Hollywood films. Each of these elements of consumer culture has a rich history of its own and provides an opportunity for lectures and for student research and individual and group presentations. Each of these topics illustrates, too, that consumer participation is a cultural, economic, social, and gendered practice. During the decade of the 1920s, energy use tripled, electricity reached 60 percent of American homes, and the institutionalization of the assembly line made not just everyday goods but even automobiles affordable for tremendous numbers of working people. Car sales tripled between 1916 and 1929, and federal support ensured that roads and highways were built to accommodate the growing presence of automobiles. During this time period, large numbers of consumers could for the first time make purchasing decisions based on considerations other than price.[2] In addition, with the implementation of a shorter working week, more and more citizens had increased time to spend both thinking about consumer goods and actively acquiring them. New products became available, and they were promoted in ways both direct and subtle. During the Golden Age of Hollywood, for example, from the late 1920s through the 1940s, moviegoing became a regular form of entertainment, as well as a showcase for fashion and consumer goods for American women. In 1933, *Esquire* magazine was founded with the goal of spreading what were considered female practices of acquisition to women's brothers, husbands, and sons.

When students' understanding of the chronology of consumerism becomes more complicated, they will be ready to be challenged as well in their definition of the fabled consumer, the "average American" they might envision making these purchases and assuming this consumer identity. Not all groups of people have benefited equally from the processes of consumerism, so this topic provides an important means of exploring differences among Americans at the same time that we explore a surface uniformity. In the early twentieth century, for example, certain sectors of women's employment, including domestic work, agricultural work, and textiles, remained low paying, and these women workers as a group fell outside the national consumer frenzy of the day. Class differences among Americans dictated that while many people began to define themselves and their neighbors by the brand names they purchased, others continued to struggle to acquire basic necessities. Manufacturers and advertisers made assumptions about the consumer abilities of African Americans that prevented this group of Americans from receiving consumer invitations even when their pocketbooks supported that participation. The development of national advertising in women's magazines, which tended to reach more urban and Northern than rural and Southern readers, ensured that consumer identity developed inconsistently across lines of region, as well as lines of race, class, and gender. Even during the supposedly wealthy postwar period of the 1950s, consumer participation proved uneven, with certain Americans receiving governmental support for consumer participation while others met only obstacles to increasingly important markers of identity, such as higher education and home ownership.

The increasing significance of goods as markers of American identity has led to the "ugly American" phenomenon, in which U.S. citizens appear more interested in shopping than in politics or issues of local or global citizenship. Nonetheless, although consumerism has led to acquiescence to certain identities or cultural aspirations, it has also led to some forms of political activism. As Americans increasingly felt they deserved not only survival but also the pleasure that goods provide, they came to equate consumerism with economic justice rather than juxtapose the two. In short, participation in consumer culture came to be viewed as a right of citizenship rather than a privilege of wealth. The equation of social justice, economic justice, and the acquisition of goods might seem strange at first to students, but discussions of historical as well as contemporary examples make the connections apparent. After all, many shoppers today deliberately purchase fair trade coffee or sweatshop-free clothing. Students will be interested to know that such consumer practices have a long history. Before the Civil War, a group of abolitionists opened "free produce" stores to market goods produced outside the slave economy. Women textile workers went on strike in Lawrence, Massachusetts, in 1912 with the slogan "Give us bread but give us roses, too," which indicated their dual desires for food on the table and beauty in their homes and lives. African Americans at various moments in the twentieth century supported black-owned businesses as one response to the racially based lending practices of banks that kept communities of African Americans from full participation in American economic life. Importantly, in most consumer movements in the United States, women have played active if not leading roles in defining and communicating expectations and demands.

Students can also profitably explore their own family histories of consumerism, investigating through oral history their families' processes of Americanization or social mobility through consumption. What changes occurred in the family's relationships to consumerism from generation to generation? What political as well as economic roles did female family members play as holders of the family purse? If a student's family owned a home, how and when did they become home owners? Who was the first family member to purchase a car? Might some of their gendered expectations about who earned money and who spent it, and the relative importance of those activities, be challenged by their own family histories of getting and spending?

One of the key issues related to consumer culture in U.S. history has to do with values. Many people worry today that consumerism makes us all hedonists, takes away our social consciousness, and controls our decision-making processes, both personal and economic. Such worries are long-standing. Consumer participation seemed from early on to transform not only the practices of daily life but also the values that governed them. To many late-nineteenth- and early-twentieth-century observers, "Victorian" values of thrift and industriousness appeared to give way rapidly to more selfish values associated with the pursuit of pleasure. In 1928, Frenchman Andre Siegfried wrote that for Americans, the standard of living was "a somewhat sacred acquisition" and that Americans were all too ready to "make many an intellectual or even moral concession in order to maintain that standard."[3] In 1930, American philosopher John Dewey concurred, arguing that thrift, that "old-fashioned ideal," had been rendered obsolete by people's increased purchasing, which had become the nation's economic "duty."[4] The process he noted, however, both began decades earlier and remained incomplete at the time of his observation. At the core of the nation's Protestant, capitalist culture lie the competing interests and values of frugality and excess, saving and spending. Interestingly and importantly, the history of consumer culture suggests that leisure time and discretionary income were often deemed natural elements of upper- and even middle-class life but viewed as threatening to the social order in the hands of the less privileged classes or in the hands of women generally.

Women as Consumers

Unlike many other arenas of tremendous national development and import, such as democracy or capitalism, women rather than men have formed the nucleus of consumer culture. Women shopped for their families; women spent the consumer dollars. Contemporary unease about women's political, economic, and familial agency in the late nineteenth and early twentieth centuries, however, ensured that women would be portrayed in the popular press and envisioned in the popular mind more as vulnerable to the invitations of consumer capitalism and less as economic actors in their own right. By 1910, women were called the nation's "chief purchasing agents," but this definition of agency was tempered by the degree to which they were considered impulsive, easily influenced, and naive—responsible for the nation's values but also prone to abandon appropriate, thrifty, family-based values when seduced by the latest fashions, the newest colors, or the keenest sales promotions. Women of all classes and races took their own spending seriously and engaged in consumer advocacy, promoting consumer education, engaging in product or company boycotts, and pushing for federal legislation to protect consumers from useless or dangerous products. Nevertheless, women's actions have been seen

FIGURE 7.1. Participation in consumer culture continues to be an area in which, under the direction of others, women's desires seemingly outweigh reason, even in matters of national importance. (*The Born Loser*, © Newspaper Enterprise Association, Inc. Used by permission.)

as adjunct to rather than an essential element of the economy within which they operate. Such ideas about women have proved lasting, as a *Born Loser* comic strip, published nationally on Election Day in 2000, makes clear (figure 7.1).

In virtually all explorations of the development of industrial capitalism, men have been deemed traditional political and economic subjects and women the objects of other people's directives. Women were thought to exercise 85 percent of the consumer dollars in the early twentieth century, and their spending today suggests that they influence the American economy in enormously significant ways, but most often they appear vulnerable rather than powerful in their deliberations and actions. Women's active participation in consumer culture is made problematic, too, by the degree to which they themselves, as much as any merchandise they purchase, become commodified. The earliest department stores, for example, founded in the 1860s and 1870s, relied on women of sufficient means to purchase the goods they offered. They also relied on a certain commodification of those female shoppers, whose bodies, dress, and even their presence in downtown shopping areas suggested not so much their own power as the significance of the stores, the value of the men who provided the spending money, and the increasing centrality of consumer spending and consumer goods to American life.[5] Today, of course, women's bodies continue to be used to sell products to women and men alike, although with different messages: Women are invited to imagine they assume the identity of the women they see in ads; men are invited to imagine that the purchase of the product also conveys possession of the commodified female image.

When teaching this material, it is important to move beyond the dichotomy of women as historical actors, engaged in consumer culture's activities, and women as passive recipients of the messages of manufacturers, advertisers, and the men in their individual lives. To complicate the relationship between women and consumerism, to make women actual subjects of study rather than objects of circumstance and gender relations, teachers can make use of the work of recent historians. In my own classes, I rely on two particularly effective approaches: engaging in resistant readings of sources commonly consulted and looking for new sources of information about women and their lives as consumers. The remainder of this chapter focuses on these approaches, first reading traditional sources in new ways, and second, looking for new sources to provide information about people seemingly missing from the existing historical narrative.

Resistant Readings: Women and Consumerism's Dictates

Women's magazines and advertising continue to serve as two of the most widely consulted sources for the history of women and consumer culture, and with good reason. The founding of the "big six" magazines in the late nineteenth century (*Ladies' Home Journal, Woman's Home Companion, Good Housekeeping, Delineator, Pictorial Review,* and *McCall's*) provided women, at least the white, middle-class women who could afford them, a means of establishing a national identity as American women. These magazines, importantly, created an "average American woman," an iconic consumer who came to stand in for the many women in the United States whose differences became subsumed in her seeming ubiquity. Magazines and the advertisements they hosted offered aesthetically pleasing, direct, and profitable ways both to reach female consumers and to suggest that American female identity and consumer identity were one and the same. According to these magazines, men earned the money, women spent it, and women gained pleasure from this arrangement and its consumer possibilities. These entities, magazines and advertising, proved so successful in equating women with spending that this history seems too simple and too accurate even to note. Yet like so many others, this history can be deconstructed in the classroom and in outside readings.

Because these materials are so accessible online, in print form, and on microfilm, magazines and advertisements provide an excellent way for students to engage with primary historical materials. They also provide an important training ground for teaching students to read critically. Students can examine a piece of text for the overt message and read with the grain, but they can also explore the inconsistencies in a text and explore what remains unstated. Close readings of these artifacts of consumer culture, including magazine articles, advertisements, and editorials, reveal more tension and less agreement about the seemingly easy, seemingly "natural" formula of male breadwinner and female consumer than appear at first glance. The editor of the *Ladies' Home Journal*'s Girls' Club, for example, encouraged women in the 1910s to work as subscription agents for the magazine to make some money. Although her suggestions for employment led to little in the way of earnings, and she did not wish women to see themselves primarily as breadwinners, her acknowledgment in the magazine that she had received 144,000 inquiries suggests that women's desires to earn money may well have eclipsed their desires to abide by the rules of gendered consumerism. Similarly, the magazine revealed that a 1916 discussion of married women's employment generated 4,000 letters of inquiry within a week, 10,000 within thirty days.[6] The sheer number of times the magazine's editor, Edward Bok, admonished women for seeking employment in his editorials also suggests that the issue was by no means a settled one for the readers of this leading women's magazine. The editor's recognition, even when he gave his readers a talking to, that they had sincere complaints about the gendered dynamics of money earning and money spending reveals that women resisted at least some of the dictates of the day. Examinations of women's lives benefit by looking at what remains unstated, or merely suggested, as well as what comes across clearly, in sources about women's lives.[7]

Historians and students of consumer culture also do well to employ resistant readings of the advertising present in women's magazines. Images of the good life for women came across through advertising in increasingly technically sophisticated, visually appealing, textually seductive packages. And the ads as a whole seem to have done the job they set out to do, as women responded to the invitations of consumer culture in increasing numbers and with increasing diligence. The following automobile ad from 1920 serves as a case in point (figure 7.2). On the one hand, women who believed that the Liberty Six would deliver what it promised, namely, independence, wealth, and sophistication, certainly played into the hands of advertisers. But what might a resistant reading of an advertisement like this one reveal, and how might such revelations attribute other levels of agency to female consumers?

Read against the grain, this particular advertisement appealed to what certain groups of women had at the time, increasing purchasing power, but even more to what they lacked, namely, a fulfillment of their desires. American society in May 1920, when the ad was launched, was on the verge of granting women the vote but still limited on so many levels women's liberty or autonomy. Advertisers of the time, like the J. Walter Thompson agency that produced this ad, researched what made women happy but also, more important, they investigated what made them unhappy, and then designed ads to address what I call elsewhere women's "inarticulate longings," their often unspoken, socially unrecognized desires for personal autonomy, intimacy, sensuality,

Women who enjoy the use of a car, prefer the Liberty—and almost always drive it themselves.

They have found that there *is* a difference in the way the Liberty rides and drives—a difference as pronounced and distinctive as Liberty beauty and inner quality are pronounced and distinctive.

To them, of course, this difference expresses itself in the utter *ease* of everything a driver is called upon to do.

Liberty Motor Car Company, Detroit

LIBERTY SIX

FIGURE 7.2. Automobile and other advertising lured women with promises that consumer goods, if not the culture at large, provided them with a "distinctive" identity. (*Ladies' Home Journal*, May 1920, p. 55).

economic independence, and social recognition. When we examine ads such as this one against the grain, we discern not only what was promised, or perhaps what was delivered, but also what remained unfulfilled in women's lives generally and in their engagements with consumer culture specifically. In this case, the intended audience may well have dreamed about owning a classy car and using the identity it provided to escape more mundane responsibilities. Neither the ad nor the automobile could deliver the life the ad suggested, but they both reveal that women desired more than the simple domesticity the magazine championed.

One of the surprising lessons in reading print and visual sources against the grain is that many of the themes in women's lives that we think of as modern appear in these sources of a century ago. One particularly effective exercise is to give students magazine ads, editorials, or advice columns with the dates removed and ask them to attribute dates to the sources. Most often, when they encounter women's desires for professional lives, sexual autonomy, or shared domestic responsibility, even when couched in consumer-related promises, students believe the sources are far more recent than they really are. Students can be asked to consider whether this enormously successful culture, consumer culture, displaced women's concerns for a time, as it effectively encouraged women to attempt to meet their larger social needs through consumer goods and practices. Reading well-worn sources with new lenses provides important insights into the gendered lives of women and the complicated history of Americans' acceptance of consumer culture as American culture. These sources have the potential to unlock stories, to complicate simple understandings, to acknowledge women's agency in the arena of consumer culture, however incomplete or contested it might prove to be.

Locating Absent Women, Telling Their Stories

Women's magazines and advertising reveal interesting and complicated histories of the women we most commonly associate with consumer culture, namely, the "average American woman" that consumer culture helped to create. This woman, sometimes real and often imagined or envisioned, is white, middleclass, fairly happily married, and not employed outside the home. We can read her story with the grain, and we can read her story, more problematically, against the grain. But what of the individuals who seem entirely absent from the history of consumer culture—the woman who pursued higher education and professional life, or the woman deemed undeserving of consumer culture's invitations because she was too poor, or African American, or part of another marginalized group? The discovery that the most well-used sources tell only part of the story about that "average" woman may encourage students to look more deeply in those sources, as well as in new ones, to discover more about the women who do not fit established patterns. If women at home expressed desires to be out in the work world, might some of them have ended up there? If African American women saw only white women in advertising images, to which invitations did they respond as consumers? The remainder of this chapter explores how teachers can, by bringing more Americans' histories to the classroom, further enhance the telling of our collective and contested past.

The retelling of the "average American woman" story, which depicts the early-twentieth-century woman as married and working only in the home, obscures the lives of whole groups of women who worked, ironically enough, in the same consumer culture industries that made them invisible. The women who wrote articles for women's magazines provide one example of this phenomenon; the women who wrote the ads provide another. The advent of national women's magazines provided a host of employment opportunities for women who wrote personal advice columns, recipe columns, housekeeping hints, and short magazine fiction. Other women found employment within the advertising agencies that grew in tandem with the magazines. Our culture's gendered description of the advertising professional as an "ad man" may have been historically accurate to a degree, but women did work in the field, promoting consumer participation among other women and earning a living doing so. Men certainly were the majority of people working in positions of power in both women's magazines and advertising in the late nineteenth and early to middle twentieth centuries. Nevertheless, women, too, found employment, particularly in writing advertising copy. What do their lives teach us? Reading company records and taking female employees' stories seriously, no matter how small their numbers, provides one way of complicating gender and history alike.

The J. Walter Thompson Company was the most successful advertising agency of the early twentieth century. It stood out not only because of its enormous business success but also because it led the field in employing women. In a 1924 publication, the company claimed as one of its thirteen most important attributes, "The J. Walter Thompson Company employs more women in creative, responsible positions than does any other agency."[8] Although the numbers remained small, women in the agency certainly proved influential; organized into a separate women's department and concentrating on products aimed primarily at women, they generated, in the late 1910s, more than half of the revenue of the entire agency. An examination of their stories, which include work lives, family lives, and relationship to the consuming women they advertised to and often resisted becoming themselves, provides compelling new ways of seeing women, consumerism, and the trajectories of history.

Company records reveal that the women employed in advertising at J. Walter Thompson seemed to have little in common with the magazine readers who responded to their invitations to purchase goods. These women pursued higher education, sought the financial autonomy that careers rather than jobs provided, often identified as feminists, and shopped as infrequently as did their male counterparts. They viewed advertising as a social force and entered the profession with the intention of using it to further women's place in society. They hoped to pose challenges, through the ads they created, to the "stand pat" woman featured so often in the *Ladies' Home Journal*.[9] They hoped even more directly to recognize women's longings and bring those into public discourse through advertising. A group of women at J. Walter Thompson celebrated, for example, when they contracted suffrage leader Alva Belmont to provide an endorsement for Pond's Cold Cream. They praised the "woman at home," but their meeting notes and personnel files reveal that they believed in creating more options for women, women like and women unlike themselves. Students, who already have read these ads against the grain and see in them the complaints as well as the aspirations of women's magazine readers, may through this exercise become even more inclined to give the complaints of those readers greater credence. The desire for "more out of life" seems problematically linked to consumer goods as these various groups of women enter the historical framework. Whether middle or upper-middle class, lesbian or heterosexual, single or divorced, these female advertising agents lived lives distinctly different from the "average American woman" their ad copy addressed and arguably helped to create. Their inclusion in the discussion of women and consumer culture complicates the ways in which we define women's work, the degree to which we see women as victims of male decision making, and the degree to which we believe the woman pictured in advertising represents more than a cultural construction.[10]

Another absence in traditional historical scholarship is the legions of women whom advertisers failed to court in mainstream magazines. African American women in the early twentieth century, for example, found themselves in the pages of the *Ladies' Home Journal* only on the jokes page as examples of deficient housekeepers, or in the ads as women who seem to live primarily to make the lives of white women easier. Students of consumer culture might be prompted to attribute these women's absence, or extremely limited presence, as a simple feature of their economic status: Once they reached sufficient levels of economic power, surely they, too, would find themselves in the pages of women's magazines. Unfortunately, cultural understandings about race prevented such a progression; advertisers avoided targeting African American women even when their own research indicated the group's enormous purchasing power. Black women in the *Journal* and other women's magazines of the day provided an important juxtaposition: White women purchased products not only to appear worldly but also to appear far from black, or immigrant, or poor.

More recently, however, scholars have unearthed additional sources that shed light on black women's consumer participation. Historian Noliwe Rooks discovered that between 1891 and 1950 there were at least eight African American women's magazines in circulation.[11] One of these, *Half-Century*, was named to mark the fifty-year anniversary of the enactment of the Emancipation Proclamation. These publications provided political content as well as advice about cooking, fashion, and other consumer-related pursuits. Ads in the "big six" magazines that feature African American women as servants can be juxtaposed with evidence Rooks and others provide about African American women's decision making around consumer choices and practices. Learning about such figures as Madame C. J. Walker, widely considered the nation's first self-made black female millionaire, also complicates the idea that black women largely imitated white women's consumer practices as their financial situations improved.[12]

Like their white counterparts, black women in American history most often held the family purse strings. They mobilized as consumers during the 1930s, demanding not only affordable consumer goods but also racial justice. In Chicago, for example, women used their purchasing power, however ignored it may have been by national advertisers, to threaten boycotts and demand that African American salesclerks be hired and that their skin be dark enough for their racial identity to be unmistakable.[13] In a variety of cities, black women established Housewives' Leagues, with members pledging to support black businesses and professionals, buy black-produced products, and help train young people for careers in business.[14] Like their white counterparts, black women have always exercised agency when it comes to consumerism; they used their dollars to participate in a central component of American life, but they also used those dollars to claim identities, state preferences, and protest injustices. The same is true, of course, of women from other ethnic and racial groups. In different but complementary ways, for example, Jewish women in New York City and Mexican American women in southern California in the early twentieth century developed their skills as consumers both to maintain cultural traditions and to assist or resist elements of their families' processes of Americanization.[15] Today, teachers who live in regions where ethnic newspapers or magazines are available can use those historical sources, in hard copy or perhaps online, to explore the ways in which women were solicited as purchasers, were used as commodities in the effort to sell products, and claimed consumer participation on their own terms.

Conclusion

Women continue to serve as the nation's chief purchasing agents, but their agency in the process is, in popular discourse, given little more respect now than it was a hundred years ago. Attempts to recognize or make political these activities on the part of women are often refused, and women's economic activity, rather than gain significance from its association with money, continually falls into a category of "natural" behavior, so insignificant as to warrant only jokes. Advertisers seem increasingly adept at encouraging us to "fix our desires out there, beyond where we are," and to spend, spend, spend.[16] But women have always actively participated in the work of consuming. As they purchase things for themselves and for others, they engage with identity formation, dreaming, and economic decision making. Historians, by reading traditional sources in new ways, refusing to allow silences to dictate, and looking for new sources to fill gaps, can help complicate women's agency as citizens and as consumers. Students who are encouraged to explore these issues and these contested histories in a classroom setting most often prove adept at such engagements. They also, most often, become enriched intellectually in the process.

NOTES

1. Kathleen G. Donohue, *Freedom from Want: American Liberalism and the Idea of the Consumer* (Baltimore: Johns Hopkins University Press, 2003), 81.

2. Susan Strasser, *Satisfaction Guaranteed: The Making of the American Mass Market* (New York: Pantheon, 1989), 28.

3. Andre Siegfried, "The Gulf Between," *Atlantic Monthly* (March 1928): 289–96, quoted in Leach, *Land of Desire: Merchants, Power, and the Rise of a New American Culture* (New York: Pantheon, 1993), 266.

4. John Dewey, *Individualism Old and New* (New York: Minton, Balch, 1930), 43–44.

5. Sociologist and economist Thorstein Veblen argued that the woman shopper was one of the greatest commodities of the Gilded Age; see Thorstein Veblen (1899), *The Theory of the Leisure Class* (Boston: Houghton Mifflin, 1973).

6. "What 35,000 Girls Have Told Me," *Ladies' Home Journal* (March 1914), 54.

7. For more on Edward Bok's admonitions to his readers, and ways of reading their concerns and his responses, see Scanlon, *Inarticulate Longings: The Ladies' Home Journal, Gender, and the Promises of Consumer Culture* (New York: Routledge, 1995).

8. "The J. Walter Thompson Company Portfolio Comprising of Facts and Figures," 1924, J. Walter Thompson Company Archives, Duke University Library, Durham, North Carolina.

9. *News Bulletin*, July 11, 1916, 2. J. Walter Thompson Company Archives, Duke University Library, Durham, North Carolina.

10. To learn more about these women and their work, see Scanlon, *Inarticulate Longings.*

11. Noliwe Rooks, *Ladies' Pages: African American Women's Magazines and the Culture That Made Them* (New Brunswick, NJ: Rutgers University Press, 2004).

12. See Beverly Lowry, *Her Dream of Dreams: The Rise and Triumph of Madam C. J. Walker* (New York: Knopf, 2003).

13. Cohen, *A Consumer's Republic: The Politics of Mass Consumption in Postwar America* (New York: Knopf, 2003), 46.

14. Ibid., 51. On black-owned businesses and economic nationalism, see also Robert E. Weems, "Consumerism and the Construction of Black Female Identity," in *The Gender and Consumer Culture Reader*, ed. Jennifer Scanlon (New York: New York University Press, 2000), 166–178.

15. See, for example, Andrew Heinze, "Jewish Women and the Making of an American Home," in *The Gender and Consumer Culture Reader*, ed. Jennifer Scanlon, 19–29; and Vicki Ruiz, "'Star Struck': Acculturation, Adolescence, and Mexican American Women, 1920–1950," in *Unequal Sisters: A Multicultural Reader in U.S. Women's History*, ed. Vicki Ruiz and Ellen Carol Dubois, 3rd ed. (New York: Routledge, 2000), 346–361.

16. Vincent Miller, *Consuming Religion: Christian Faith and Practice in a Consumer Culture* (New York: Continuum, 2004), 124.

8

Conceptualizing U.S. Women's History in Medicine, Law, and Business: The Challenge of Success

Virginia G. Drachman

The history of nineteenth-century women and their entrance into medicine, law, and business is an intriguing story of discrimination, strategies for success, and the quest for equality and autonomy in American society. At the heart of this narrative is an enduring challenge: how to reconcile gender difference with women's desire for equality with men. Nineteenth-century women were believed to be naturally pious, pure, emotional, and domestic; their place was at home, the caretakers of husbands and children. In contrast, men were understood to be naturally strong, rational, and aggressive; they belonged beyond the boundaries of the home, in the competitive world of work. Although reality often deviated markedly from cultural ideals for immigrant women, African American women, and even middle-class women, the ideology of gender created significant hurdles for women seeking to enter male domains.

On the one hand, the belief in gender difference excluded women from entry into medicine, law, and business. Paradoxically, this same belief in gender difference paved the way for women's entry into these male-dominated arenas, providing women with a way to claim their place and superiority. The most obvious challenge faced by women of the nineteenth century was institutional and cultural discrimination. The prominent nineteenth-century physician Charles Meigs summed it up in 1847: Women were totally unsuited to be doctors, lawyers, entrepreneurs, in fact, practically anything other than wives and mothers. Lecturing to the all-male class of medical students at Jefferson Medical College, he explained that one need only look at a woman's head to see that it was "almost too small for intellect but just big enough for love."[1] A quarter century later, in 1873, Justice Joseph Bradley of the U.S. Supreme Court echoed Meigs's view, arguing that women were "unfit...for many of the occupations of civil life." Insisting that women's "destiny and mission" was "to fulfill the noble and benign offices of wife and mother," he ruled that a woman did not have a right to carry on a profession in any state.[2]

Meigs and Bradley expressed the prominent views of the day that women and men were inherently different and that women did not belong outside the boundaries of the home. Moreover, these attitudes reflected and reinforced the rigid institutional barriers that impeded nineteenth-century women's entrance into medicine, law, and business. Women could not vote, own property, or gain admission to college. Women who wanted to be doctors were excluded from medical schools and hospital training programs; aspiring women lawyers were excluded from law schools and state bars; and would-be women entrepreneurs, though not seeking professional training, were excluded from most industries and denied capital crucial to launching their own businesses.

Beyond discrimination, the history of women in medicine, law, and business is also a story of the struggle to balance gender and professional identity. This was no simple task in the nineteenth century, when views about women's place, as expressed by men like Meigs and Bradley, were so deeply rooted in society. As women strove to forge careers in traditionally male professions and business, they encountered a perplexing dilemma: how to be at once a woman— the caretaker of home and family—and a doctor, lawyer, or entrepreneur in the world of men. Paradoxically, despite the prevailing ideology about women's proper place, women's domestic duties—that is, childrearing, nursing the sick, balancing the family budget, and negotiating family conflict—provided them with excellent training for the practice of medicine, law, or business. Ultimately, women found ways to forward their careers by embracing, rather than rejecting, their traditional gender roles.

The history of women in medicine, law, and business is also a story of family ties, marriage, and motherhood. For women doctors, lawyers, and entrepreneurs, public and private life have always been inextricably linked. Their careers evolved in relationship to, not independent of, their roles as wives and mothers, or single women. For women in the nineteenth century, marriage was a major turning point. Under the common law doctrine of *feme covert*, when a woman married, she lost the legal right to own property, make a contract, or buy and sell property in her own name. Throughout the nineteenth century, states gradually passed legislation that dismantled women's legal disabilities. As a result, legal rights for married women were uneven across the country.

Marriage changed women's lives in other profound ways. In an age before the availability of reliable methods of birth control, marriage and motherhood were inextricably linked. And motherhood forced all married career women to juggle the constant demands of their personal lives with the responsibilities of their work. Ultimately, how a married woman fared typically depended on whom she married. Some husbands were supportive of their wives' career aspirations; others were not. As a result, marriage could either terminate a promising career or propel a woman to success. Meanwhile, for those who remained single, a career was often far more than a route to fulfillment; it was a necessity of survival.

The challenges of overcoming discrimination, balancing gender and professional identity, and juggling career with private life are integral to the history of women in male-dominated professions and business. Yet, while women doctors, lawyers, and entrepreneurs shared these challenges, they often confronted them differently, depending on their particular area of work. Women doctors responded to the gender discrimination in the medical profession that excluded them from medical schools and hospitals in a unique way; they created their own separate all-women's medical institutions.[3] In doing so, they accepted, rather than rejected, the prevailing belief in gender differences and argued that they belonged in medicine, not because they were the same as men, but precisely because they were different. Medical practice, they insisted, was a natural extension of women's caring responsibilities. They, not male doctors, were the natural caretakers of children and of women because they would protect a sick woman's modesty and virtue in a way that a male physician simply could not do.

In creating all-women's medical schools and hospitals, women had the support of influential male doctors and leading male reformers such as abolitionist William Lloyd Garrison in Boston and journalist Horace Greeley in New York. So, from the start, the gender discrimination that barred women from men's institutions provided the cornerstone for the founding of a range of all-women's medical institutions, including women's medical colleges in Philadelphia, Baltimore, and Chicago and all-women's hospitals in New York and Boston.[4] These institutions enabled women to bypass the closed doors of the male-run medical institutions and offered women hard-to-find education and clinical training. By 1880, there were already more than 2,400 women doctors, and their numbers increased to more than 4,000 in 1890. By 1910, there were more than 9,000 women doctors, representing 6 percent of all physicians in the country.[5]

Gradually, the separate all-women's medical institutions encountered a new challenge as male-run medical schools and hospitals began to admit women in the late nineteenth century. By the 1890s, the doors were open to women at Johns Hopkins, Cornell, and Tufts, as well as at male-run medical schools throughout the country, from Buffalo and Syracuse to Denver and Los Angeles. At the same time, women began to gain internships at major urban hospitals, including Bellevue in New York, Cook County in Chicago, and Blockley in Philadelphia. This integration of women into the male-run medical schools and hospitals provoked a new challenge for women doctors: Should they close their separate medical institutions now that women had gained a foothold in the medical mainstream, or should they keep them open?

There was no simple answer. Many believed that with the opening of the male-run institutions, the all-women's medical institutions had outlived their usefulness. This was often the view of a generation of younger women who, at the end of the century, enjoyed options for medical school and hospital internships that were unavailable to the pioneer women doctors. While fourteen all-women's medical schools closed before 1910, some women fought to maintain separate all-women's institutions. The Woman's Medical College of Pennsylvania in Philadelphia and the New England Hospital in Boston continued to offer twentieth-century women the option of learning and practicing medicine apart from men.

Despite a strong but minority belief in the continued value of the all-women's medical institutions, the trend in the early twentieth century appeared to be toward professional integration into the medical mainstream. Among women who studied medicine in the 1910s, 80 percent attended coeducational medical schools. This shift toward professional integration extended beyond medical school, as women increasingly took internships at male-run hospitals and began to enter traditionally male laboratory specialties, including otolaryngology, ophthalmology, and even surgery. A survey of women doctors in 1927 optimistically proclaimed that there was "unlimited opportunity for success."[6]

But on closer examination, this optimism was misplaced. The integration of women into the mainstream of medicine was far more tenuous than it appeared. The most obvious sign was the decline in the numbers of women doctors. To be sure, women could apply to many of the mainstream medical schools by the end of the nineteenth century, but they were rarely admitted. Indeed, the enrollment of women in eighteen male-run medical schools, including Tufts, Johns Hopkins, University of Michigan, and University of Buffalo, dropped between the 1890s and early years of the twentieth century.[7] Meanwhile, the optimistic closing of the all-women's medical schools left women with no alternative but male medical institutions. The result was a precipitous decline in the number of women doctors from a peak in 1910 of 9,015 (representing 6 percent of all doctors) to 7,219 (5 percent) in 1920 to 6,825 (4.4 percent) in 1930.[8]

By the 1910s, the percentage of women doctors in typically male laboratory specialties had already begun to decline. By 1912, the percentage of women in otolaryngology, ophthalmology, and surgery had reached 8 percent, 13 percent, and 3 percent, respectively. But by 1921, women were only 6 percent of otolaryngologists and 4 percent of ophthalmologists. The percentage of women in surgery had dropped to zero. Instead, the trend was for women doctors to congregate in typically female specialties such as internal medicine, pediatrics, and gynecology and in the service areas of medicine, including infant and children's health, tuberculosis, and venereal diseases.[9] As one women doctor explained, women's greatest opportunities in medicine were "in connection with promotion of the health of children, of girls and women in industry, of the community, and of the home."[10]

Ultimately, the integration of women into mainstream medicine was more illusory than it appeared. The all-women's medical schools and hospitals, once the only gateway into the profession, were abandoned by a generation who had the option of professional integration. But a new version of gender discrimination, inequality, and separatism accompanied the integration of women doctors into the mainstream, as women congregated in the low-status areas of practice. As one woman doctor astutely observed, "A generation earlier, women doctors were on the outside standing together. Now they were on the inside sitting alone."[11] Despite the opportunity for integration, most women doctors worked within the mainstream of American medicine—but remained isolated from men.

While the history of women doctors reveals how women used separatism to overcome gender discrimination, the history of women lawyers brings into clear relief the struggle to balance gender and professional identity.[12] Nineteenth-century law was even more impenetrable to women than medicine: By 1920, when women represented 5 percent of all doctors, they were only 1.4 percent of all lawyers.[13] There were two important reasons for this discrepancy. First, while nineteenth-century women founded their own all-women's institutions, no comparable institutions existed to ease their entry into the legal profession. Instead, each woman had to enter the profession through often-hostile male-controlled institutions—law schools, courts, bar associations, and law firms—on her own.

Second, women lawyers faced a unique obstacle: Their profession made and interpreted the laws that denied women access to the rights of equal citizenship, including the practice of law. The very act of gaining admission to practice law demanded that women change the law of the land. Women had to persuade male judges and legislatures to reinterpret the male-constructed jurisprudence that made their entry into the legal profession not only unthinkable, but illegal. In 1873, the U.S. Supreme Court ruled against Myra Bradwell's attempt to practice law. Two years later, Justice Edward G. Ryan of the Wisconsin Supreme Court echoed Bradley. Blocking Lavinia Goodell's efforts to gain admission to practice law in Wisconsin, Ryan proclaimed "the common law wise in excluding women from the profession of the law."[14] The pervasiveness of gender discrimination in the legal profession and the absence of separate institutions to shield women lawyers posed a particular challenge. As women faced the daunting task of entering the legal profession with, rather than apart from, men, they confronted a deep and persistent challenge: to resolve the tension between their gender and professional identity.

While women doctors could claim a special role in medicine because compassion and caretaking were part of medical care, law was different. Not only did it demand cold objectivity and mastery of facts, it also required cunning, toughness, and the ability to deal with a sordid world. Moreover, medical practice occurred in a hospital, which resembled a home where the sick sought rest, quiet, and care. In contrast, law practice occurred in a boisterous courtroom, much like a saloon with spittoons, noise, and raucous behavior. Here, criminals and individuals of illrepute were brought to justice for their deception, greed, and crimes. Before a male judge and an all-male jury, male lawyers squared off against each other in merciless legal combat, flaunting their most manly qualities—assertiveness, combativeness, competitiveness, and hard-hearted objectivity. The prevailing view held that the courtroom was no place for a woman.

Many nineteenth-century women lawyers agreed. Just as women doctors identified women's and children's health as their special province, women lawyers embraced the ideal of gender difference, avoided the courtroom, and claimed the office as their ideal workplace. Office work mirrored the work of the home: It demanded the same focus on organization and efficiency that was expected of the nineteenth-century housewife; it relied on negotiation rather than conflict; and it was private, taking place behind closed doors rather than in the public arena of the courtroom. While many male lawyers argued publicly in court, women lawyers in an office devoted their time to drafting legal documents such as wills, deeds for real estate conveyances, and contracts.

But some women lawyers preferred the courtroom, with its activity, publicity, and potential for lucrative financial success. For these women lawyers, the challenge of balancing their professional and gender identities was especially acute. This was highlighted by a unique problem that every woman lawyer encountered once she crossed the threshold to the courtroom—that is, what she should wear in court. While fashion may have been a frivolous pastime for the leisured woman with money to spend, for the nineteenth-century woman lawyer, it was a serious matter that embodied the debate over woman's place in the legal profession and in society at large. Before a woman lawyer left her home each day, she had to carefully select an outfit that would convey at once seriousness and softness, professionalism and femininity. With this in mind, women lawyers who went to court typically chose a simple black suit or dress, usually accented with jewelry or lace. Its simplicity and color mirrored the suits of men and revealed women's professional identification with their male colleagues. The extra adornments conveyed the message that these women, while lawyers, were still ladies.

Women lawyers faced a more perplexing fashion dilemma when it came to their hats. A hat was part of the proper attire for any nineteenth-century lady who ventured forth in public. But male lawyers removed their hats whenever they entered a courtroom. Here was the dilemma for the woman lawyer of the day: Social etiquette required that she wear a hat in public; professional etiquette demanded that she remove her hat when she entered the courtroom. There was no consensus on the matter. Some women emphasized their femininity and wore hats in the courtroom; others accentuated their professional equality and removed theirs. This confounded women throughout the nineteenth century and into the early decades of the twentieth, revealing just how deeply the challenge of balancing gender and professional identity permeated even the minutest details of women lawyers' daily lives.

The challenge of balancing professional and gender identity permeated the inner sanctum of women's lawyers' personal lives, shaping intimate decisions about marriage. Women lawyers were well aware that marriage could radically alter the course of their professional lives. With this in mind, some chose not to marry, preferring to remain single and independent. Some married and willingly gave up their careers. But others married, hoping to be both wife and lawyer. Most women agreed that marriage to another lawyer was the easiest route to follow. Together, husband and wife could successfully transplant the traditional gender division of labor from home to office; the wife would work in the office, modestly and unobtrusively behind the scenes, while her husband went to court and worked aggressively in the public eye.

But it took more than marrying another lawyer for a woman to successfully balance marriage and career. How a woman fared depended for the most part on the character of the man she chose. Sometimes a woman learned this the hard way. Mary McHenry, the first woman to graduate from Hastings College of Law in San Francisco in 1882, had a successful law practice before she married and moved with her husband to Berkeley. Though she told her husband she wanted to resume her practice, he "laughingly" responded, "Not much you will," and not surprisingly, she never did.[15] Sometimes women lawyers flourished when they married. Catharine Waugh McCulloch deliberately looked for a husband who would be "proud that his wife was a lawyer."[16] Her efforts paid off. Frank McCulloch brought his wife into his law practice; encouraged her career, even as she raised four children; and supported her road trips on behalf of women's suffrage, happily washing dishes and preparing dinners while she was away. His message to Catharine was a supportive "Don't worry about anything."[17] While marriage often hindered or destroyed a woman's career, for some women, marriage actually supported and sustained their professional lives.

The history of women business owners of the nineteenth century provides an intriguing comparison with women doctors and lawyers.[18] These women embraced the American dream of success and founded and ran businesses throughout the nineteenth century, proof that the ideal of the self-made man included women. In some ways, women entrepreneurs may have had it easier than their counterparts in medicine and law, because they needed neither special education nor professional training to launch a business. Instead, what they needed to achieve success was a good idea, the capital to finance it, and the willingness to work hard and take risks. Still, women entrepreneurs encountered discrimination, struggled to juggle gender and work identity, and faced the burden of reconciling public and private life.

Even the most successful women business owners encountered institutional and legal obstacles that impeded their success. Throughout much of the century, many could not own property, a serious hindrance for an entrepreneur. In addition, they were excluded from the largest and most powerful industries, including oil, steel, railroads, and automobiles; they had trouble getting capital to finance their businesses; and they were denied access to the men's clubs and organizations where businessmen socialized, networked, and made the big deals. One social critic in 1935 summed up the second-class status of women entrepreneurs in *Fortune* magazine: "There is no American woman whose business achievement would properly rank with the first, or the second, or even the third line of male successes."[19]

Like women doctors and lawyers, a woman business owner confronted traditional ideas about gender and woman's proper place that forced her to straddle two worlds. As a woman, she belonged at home, the caretaker of the family; as an entrepreneur, she belonged outside, the builder of a business. As a woman, she was dependent on her husband for financial security; as an entrepreneur, she stood on her own. As a woman, she had to protect the family's emotional needs; as an entrepreneur, she had to be rational and ready to take risks. As a woman, she had to be nurturing and self-sacrificing, placing the needs of others before her own; as an entrepreneur, she had to be independent and acquisitive, seeking profit for herself.

It was a tall, but not insurmountable, order. Nineteenth-century women understood all too well that the very gender roles that supposedly made women unfit for a life of competition and finance actually prepared them for business. They claimed that their ability to keep detailed account books, manage myriad household tasks, and keep everyone happy was excellent training for business. This was particularly the case when women created businesses geared specifically to other women.

Women entrepreneurs capitalized on the widespread belief in gender differences. Marketing their unique understanding of women's needs and desires, they carved out a separate female niche, products for women, children, and the home. Lydia Pinkham made a fortune in the nineteenth century by selling herbal medicines that promised women painless, noninvasive relief from their "female ailments" in an era when doctors, male or female, were unable to relieve many of women's gynecological problems. Meanwhile, Ellen Demorest built a fashion empire, selling expensive fashions to the wealthy elite in her New York City emporium and paper dress patterns to women in towns and villages across the country.[20] By the early twentieth century, this separate, female niche exploded into a thriving arena of business run by women for women, as fashion and beauty became important consumer industries. Beauty entrepreneur Helena Rubinstein extolled the advantages of the cosmetics industry for women. "Here [women] have found a field that is their own province—working for women with women, and giving that which only women can give—an intimate understanding of feminine needs and feminine desires."[21] By the early twentieth century, Rubinstein and other beauty entrepreneurs, including Elizabeth Arden and Martha Matilda Harper, had made fortunes as they turned the cosmetic industry into a cornerstone of the American economy.

While most women entrepreneurs created enterprises geared specifically to women, some owned traditionally male businesses. For the most part, these women inherited, rather than initiated, their businesses, revealing once again the powerful connection between work and family ties for women. Widowhood could unexpectedly transform a conventional wife into an unlikely entrepreneur and thrust her into a traditionally male arena of business. Rebecca Lukens and Martha Coston planned traditional domestic lives as wives and mothers but became business owners when their respective husbands suddenly died. Lukens inherited her husband's iron mill and manufactured iron plate for ships and locomotives in the early nineteenth century. Coston manufactured her husband's pyrotechnic flares and sold them to the U.S. Navy, which used them to great advantage during the Civil War.[22]

Marriage could help or deter women entrepreneurs. Myra Bradwell, who had been unsuccessful in her case before the Supreme Court to practice law, founded the *Chicago Legal News* with her husband and built a legal publishing enterprise with a national reputation. In the early twentieth century, Ida Rosenthal established an unconventional division of labor with her husband; he was the creative one, she took care of financial matters. It was an ideal partnership, and together they built a thriving lingerie business, the Maiden Form Brassiere Company. But marriage hindered others, including beauty entrepreneurs Elizabeth Arden and Madam C. J. Walker, who divorced their husbands and then went on to expand their beauty businesses.[23]

Madam C. J. Walker's story reminds us that not all successful women business owners were white. Rather, race is an integral part of the history of women business owners. Seizing upon the ideal of the American dream, African American women identified the particular needs of their race and built businesses to address them. In doing so, they also redefined the path to success, elevating the collective power of the black community to moderate the virtues of individualism and independence.

Following the model of women entrepreneurs who founded businesses for women, Madame C. J. Walker carved out a special market within the separate arena of women's business, the beauty needs of black women. The founder of a hair care venture with products designed specifically for the women of her race, Walker made a personal fortune, while simultaneously providing work and the possibility of financial independence to thousands of black women who sold her products. Maggie Lena Walker (no relation) moved beyond the separate arena of women's business and left her mark on the world of finance. The leader of a black insurance company, the founder of a black department store, and the first woman bank president in the country, Maggie Lena Walker encouraged African Americans, especially the women in her native city of Richmond, Virginia, to invest and spend inside the black community. Indeed, she had a goal for the women of her race: They would "put their mites together, put their hands and their brains together and make work and business for themselves."[24]

Ethnic diversity is also central to the history of women entrepreneurs. In the late nineteenth and early twentieth centuries, thousands of Jews, including Hattie Carnegie and Jennie Grossinger, emigrated from Eastern Europe in search of opportunity. They brought with them the values of their Jewish culture, which encouraged women to work and earn money to help support the family. Henrietta Koningeiser founded a fashion company that defined sophistication and style for the American woman of means. Along the way she shed her ethnic identity, reinvented herself as Hattie Carnegie, and built an empire as the arbiter of fashion and taste.[25] Jennie Grossinger turned a modest boardinghouse in the Catskill Mountains of New York into the family-run resort Grossinger's. Unlike Carnegie, who deliberately masked her Jewish identity, Grossinger embraced it. In an era of anti-Semitism, when resorts were closed to Jews, her hotel welcomed Jews, inviting them to celebrate their religious and cultural identity. It was good business. Grossinger's became the major resort in the Catskills and one of the largest resort complexes in the country.[26]

Race and ethnicity continue to shape the history of women entrepreneurs. Mexican-born Maria de Lourdes Sobrino is the founder of Lulu's Desserts, the first company in the United States to sell prepared gelatin products. Linda Alvarado, a Hispanic woman, has succeeded at the highest levels of commercial construction and professional sports. Founder of Alvarado Construction, she built the Colorado Convention Center and Mile High Stadium, home of the Denver Broncos, and she is part-owner of the Colorado Rockies baseball team. And Oprah Winfrey has left an indelible mark on the entertainment and communications industries. She defines the pinnacle of success for African American women, indeed, for all women entrepreneurs in America.

This history of women doctors, lawyers, and entrepreneurs focuses on the pioneer generation, the women who broke barriers and forged the first paths into the male-dominated arenas of medicine, law, and business. While their story began more than a century and a half ago, they leave a legacy with continuing relevance today. The debate over separate or integrated institutions continues. Just as most, though not all, women doctors in the late nineteenth century rejected the all-women's medical schools and hospitals in preference for the newly opened male-run medical institutions, most young women today prefer coeducation, but single-sex colleges like Wellesley and Smith continue to thrive. Women lawyers continue to seek to balance their gender and professional identity when they go to court. While they have given up the hat of their predecessors, they still search for the ideal courtroom attire, weighing the merits of a dress, suit, or pants. Aspiring women entrepreneurs continue to use female culture, whether it is cooking, child care, or beauty and fashion, as a springboard to establish new business ventures.

And there are new challenges. In an era of gender discrimination and closed doors, nineteenth-century women defined entry into medicine, law, and business as their primary goal. By the early twentieth century, they sought integration alongside men. By the end of the twentieth century, women finally achieved their long-time goal of access to professional schools in equal numbers with men. They entered hospitals, law firms, and corporations in larger numbers than ever before and with new expectations of success. But they discovered a new obstacle, a "glass ceiling" that impeded their climb to the top. So, in the early twenty-first century, women face new goals, namely, crashing the glass ceiling, achieving positions of power and leadership, and dealing with the enduring challenge of work and family life.

But even with all the progress over the last 150 years, the old challenges remain, though in different forms: Women still encounter discrimination and obstacles to equality with their male peers; they continue to face the tensions between femininity and work identity; they still debate the merits of gender difference and equality in their careers; and the enduring challenge of balancing work and family remains unresolved. Make no mistake, the history of women in medicine, law, and business is not just a story about the past. It is a powerful and poignant story that brings into better focus the challenges that confront women in the professions and business today.

NOTES

1. Charles Meigs, *Lecture on Some of the Distinctive Characteristics of the Female, Delivered before the Class of Jefferson Medical College,* January 1847 (Philadelphia: Blanchard and Lea, 1847), 67.

2. See Virginia G. Drachman, *Sisters in Law: Women Lawyers in Modern American History* (Cambridge: Harvard University Press, 1998), 19.

3. On the history of women doctors, see, for example, Mary Roth Walsh, *"Doctors Wanted: No Women Need Apply": Sexual Barriers in the Medical Profession, 1835–1975* (New Haven, CT: Yale University Press, 1977); Virginia G. Drachman, *Hospital with a Heart: Women Doctors and the Paradox of Separatism at the New England Hospital, 1862–1962* (Ithaca, NY: Cornell University Press, 1984); Regina Markell Morantz-Sanchez, *Sympathy and Science: Women Physicians in American Medicine* (New York: Oxford University Press, 1985); Virginia G. Drachman, "The Limits of Progress: The Professional Lives of Women Doctors, 1881–1926," *Bulletin of the History of Medicine* 60 (1986): 58–72; Gloria Moldow, *Women Doctors in Gilded-Age Washington: Race, Gender, and Professionalization* (Chicago: University of Illinois Press, 1987); and Ellen S. More, *Restoring the Balance: Women Physicians and the Profession of Medicine, 1850–1995* (Cambridge: Harvard University Press, 1999).

4. For an analysis of the history of one all-women's medical institution, see Drachman, *Hospital with a Heart.*

5. See Walsh, *"Doctors Wanted,"* 186 and chap. 3; and Drachman, "Limits of Progress," 60.

6. Drachman, "Limits of Progress," 70.

7. Walsh, *"Doctors Wanted,"* 193.

8. Ibid., 186.

9. Drachman, "Limits of Progress," 70.

10. Elizabeth Kemper Adams, *Women Professional Workers* (Chautauqua, NY: Chautauqua Press, 1921), 65.

11. Drachman, "Limits of Progress," 71.

12. On the history of women lawyers, see Drachman, *Sisters in Law*; and Virginia G. Drachman, *Women Lawyers and the Origins of Professional Identity in America: The Letters of the Equity Club, 1887–1890* (Ann Arbor: University of Michigan Press, 1993). See also Ronald Chester, *Unequal Access: Women Lawyers in a Changing America* (South Hadley, MA: Bergin and Garvey, 1985); and Douglas Lamar Jones, "Lelia J. Robinson's Case and the Entry of Women into the Legal Profession in Massachusetts," in Russell K. Osgood, ed., *The History of Law in Massachusetts: The Supreme Judicial Court, 1692–1992* (Charlottesville: University of Virginia Press, 1992), 241–74. For an interpretive biography of a woman lawyer, see Dorothy M. Brown, *Mabel Walker Willebrandt: A Study of Power, Loyalty, and Law* (Knoxville: University of Tennessee Press, 1984). Jane M. Friedman, *America's First Woman Lawyer: The Biography of Myra Bradwell* (Buffalo: Prometheus, 1993), and Karen Berger Morello, *The Invisible Bar: The Woman Lawyer in America, 1638 to the Present* (Boston: Beacon, 1986) provide useful information but lack a sophisticated historical analysis.

13. Drachman, *Sisters in Law*, table 3, 254.

14. Ibid., 9.

15. Ibid., 107.

16. Ibid., 105, 106.

17. Ibid., 109.

18. On the history of women business owners, see Virginia G. Drachman, *Enterprising Women: 250 Years of American Business* (Chapel Hill: University of North Carolina Press, 2002).

19. Drachman, *Enterprising Women*, 107. See also Kathy Peiss, "'Vital Industry' and Women's Ventures: Conceptualizing Gender in Twentieth-Century Business History," *Business History Review* 72 (1998): 219–41.

20. On Lydia Pinkham and Ellen Demorest, see Drachman, *Enterprising Women*, chap. 2.

21. Helena Rubinstein, "Manufacturing-Cosmetics," in Doris E. Fleischman, ed., *An Outline of Careers for Women: A Practical Guide to Achievement* (New York: Doubleday, Doran, 1934), 327–31, quotation at 331.

22. On Rebecca Lukens and Martha Coston, see Drachman, *Enterprising Women*, chap. 2.

23. On Myra Bradwell, see *Enterprising Women*, chap. 2. On Ida Rosenthal, Elizabeth Arden, and Madam C. J. Walker, see *Enterprising Women*, chap. 3.

24. Drachman, *Enterprising Women*, 131. See also Elsa Barkley Brown, "Womanist Consciousness: Maggie Lena Walker and the Independent Order of Saint Luke," *Signs: Journal of Women in Culture and Society* 14 (1989): 610–32, quotation at 618.

25. On Hattie Carnegie, see Drachman, *Enterprising Women*, chap. 3.

26. On Jennie Grossinger, see Drachman, *Enterprising Women*, chap. 4.

9

Conceptualizing the Intersectionality of Race, Class, and Gender in U.S. Women's History

Erica L. Ball

In 1982, Gloria T. Hull, Patricia Bell Scott, and Barbara Smith edited a collection of essays titled *All the Women Are White, All the Blacks Are Men, but Some of Us Are Brave: Black Women's Studies.*[1] The book included discussions of black feminist theory, analyses of African American women writers, essays on teaching black women's history, and concluded with a series of syllabi and annotated bibliographies for instructors. At the time it appeared, the number of publications in women's studies and African American studies was growing rapidly, and the fields were gaining legitimacy in the academy. But as the editors of *But Some of Us Are Brave* saw it, the two areas of study were hampered by a "women-and-minorities" paradigm that relied on a racially exclusive definition of *women* and masculine interpretations of race. Consequently, neither the race-based nor the gender-based scholarship of the day fully addressed the specific experiences and concerns of women of African descent.

The editors of *But Some of Us Are Brave* hoped to make an important scholarly intervention, one that would disrupt this women-and-minorities paradigm.[2] And since that time, scholars have done much to incorporate the perspectives of working-class women and women of color into the larger women's history narrative. This process of making the stories of "invisible" women "visible" has not simply been a project of reclamation and recovery. It has required scholars to become more attentive to the ways that the dynamics of race, class, and gender work together—a process that theorists have called "intersectionality."[3] By utilizing this theoretical concept, historians have been able to explore the myriad ways that race and class have shaped women's lives. Moreover, by focusing on the ways that intersectionality has functioned on a structural level, they have been able to highlight the ways that competing notions of masculinity, femininity, and constructions of race have informed some of the most well-known political, social, and economic developments in U.S. history. In the process, scholars have demonstrated that gender and women's history belongs not at the margins, but at the center of historical analysis.

Using African American women's history as a case study, this chapter explores ways that instructors can incorporate intersectionality into the classroom. It begins by discussing ways to conceptualize the political consequences of "invisibility"—the central dilemma that immediately concerned those theorists who first coined the term intersectionality. It continues by examining how intersections of race and class have defined African American women's lives, shaping their familial relationships, their labor, and their community service and activism. Throughout, the chapter highlights key moments where a focus on intersectionality can challenge long-standing assumptions about U.S. history and culture and enable students to better grapple with the complexities of the past.

Conceptualizing Intersectionality in the Classroom

Throughout the 1980s, feminists of color interrogated the complex ways that race, gender, and class intersected in women's lives, defining their identities, drawing the boundaries that limited them, coloring the nature of their oppression, and shaping the societal roles they were expected to fulfill.[4] Although they took very different approaches to the subject matter, their work had one major commonality: the premise that categories of identification like race, class, and gender were neither competing nor additive but, instead, thoroughly integrated into an individual's overall sense of self. As Beverly Smith put it in an interview in *This Bridge Called My Back*, "Women don't live their lives like, 'Well this part is race, and this is class, and this part has to do with women's identities.'"[5]

Most students will intuitively agree with Smith's statement. Given their tendency to claim multiple interests and identities for themselves (whether it be through their extracurricular activities and musical preferences or their increasingly mixed racial and ethnic backgrounds), students often personally identify with the notion that multiple social constructs help define one's sense of self and affect the ways that one is perceived by others. Therefore, before they can begin to discuss how race, class, and gender have shaped important historical moments, they must be reminded that sustained attention to intersectionality is a relatively new phenomenon in the United States.

Discussing the invisibility of African American women is a useful way to begin this process. Asking students to discuss recent and contemporary examples of moments when the term *women* has really meant "white women" and the phrase *African American* has really meant "African American men" can often yield fruitful discussions about the ways we continue to render women of color invisible in everyday life.[6] One example is the media coverage of the 2008 Democratic presidential primary race, when pundits repeatedly insisted that "African Americans" invariably supported candidate Barack Obama while "women" preferred candidate Hillary Clinton. Students will be quick to critique the ease with which political analysts ignored the role of African American women and obscured the diversity of the larger female population. When pressed, they are likely to find other examples of this tendency in contemporary American culture. These initial conversations can serve as a starting point for an examination of the ways that the women-and-minorities paradigm can conceal the multiple intersecting identities of all women and obscure the experiences of women of color.

A well-chosen example can also help students appreciate the practical impact and historical importance of this trend. Take, for example, the experiences of middle-class African American women in the years immediately following Reconstruction. In an effort to keep black male passengers from coming into contact with white female passengers, railway companies began barring African Americans from riding in first-class compartments (often called the "Ladies Car") in the 1870s and 1880s. Because African American women were not specifically addressed by these rules, it was up to the conductor to decide whether individual African American women would be defined as middle-class ladies who purchased first-class tickets and deserved access to the Ladies Car, or excluded from these gender and class privileges because of their race. Not surprisingly, conductors often defined these women in racial terms alone, and ordered them to leave the Ladies Car.[7] Incidents such as these serve as stark reminders of the ways that U.S. law and custom can render women of color all but invisible.

Challenging Assumptions

Critical attention to key moments when race, gender, and class work together can challenge students' assumptions about the past in profound and important ways. And nowhere is the relationship between race, class, and gender more apparent than in the context of North American slavery. For decades, scholars discussed antebellum slavery in masculine terms, relegating women to the periphery of the story or even excluding women from analysis altogether. Like these early scholars, students may initially think of the "typical" slave in masculine terms. So a discussion of the importance of enslaved women's labor will challenge many of their preconceived notions about the institution.

The vast majority of enslaved African American women spent their days as agricultural laborers engaged in the tilling, planting, and harvesting integral to the economy of the Old South. Moreover, as a system of production, slavery was predicated on the reproductive labor of women, for it was women's role as child bearers that provided one of the fundamental characteristics of American racial slavery—its perpetuity.[8] A discussion of enslaved women's reproductive labor, in turn, opens the door to analysis of the culture of the slave community. For it was reproductive labor that transformed "women" into "mothers" who established, nurtured, and preserved family connections and traditions to the best of their abilities. By exploring both the forced labor enslaved women performed for their owners and the "labors of love" they performed for their family members, students can place women at the center of the slave community. Once there, enslaved African American women emerge not just as laborers but as mothers, sisters, and daughters, keepers of cultural traditions, and fictive kin who resisted the institution of slavery to the best of their abilities. By doing this, students can see the ways that women were not simply "additional" members of the slave community, but individuals whose labor was critical for both the economic viability of the institution *and* the resilience of its people.[9]

If we return to the example raised earlier—the ad hoc segregation of trains in the 1870s and 1880s—the utility of this analytical approach becomes even more apparent. In the years after Reconstruction, middle-class African American women refused to take the abuse they received at the hands of conductors without complaint. Some middle-class African American women asserted their right to be considered "ladies," only to be dragged from the compartment by conductors and passengers. On several occasions, African American women sued the railway companies that excluded them from the rights of their sex and their class, and won. These lawsuits caused a considerable amount of confusion in the southern courts. Since middle-class black women could sue and win on the grounds that they were indeed ladies, southern state legislatures felt compelled to close these legal loopholes. Ultimately, they did so by imposing "absolute racial separation" on African Americans through an elaborate web of Jim Crow legislation. Awareness of these women's stories challenges students' assumptions about the nature of African American resistance to racism in the post-Reconstruction era and recasts the long-standing interpretation of the legal and cultural phenomena at play on the road to *Plessy v. Ferguson* (1896) and the subsequent rise of Jim Crow.[10]

Students can also profit by exploring the ways that race, class, and gender informed collective protest and activism at the turn of the last century. For too long, scholarship on the Progressive Era focused on the white men who controlled the ballot. In the last several decades, white middle-class women were incorporated into the narrative as reformers and woman suffrage advocates. But despite these historiographical developments, the narrative continued to cast white Americans as the agents of change, with black and immigrant women and men as victims, wards, and obstacles for the nation to overcome. An examination of late-nineteenth- and early-twentieth-century African American women's activism can challenge students' understanding of the roots, goals, and results of a traditional political movement like Progressivism.[11]

Female African American activists like Mary Church Terrell (the first president of the National Association of Colored Women), Ida B. Wells (the intrepid newspaper reporter, suffragist, and antilynching activist), and Mary McLeod Bethune (head of the National Council of Negro Women and member of President Roosevelt's "Black Cabinet") left a significant body of primary source material, including the constitutions and bylaws of their organizations and newsletters and minutes from their meetings.[12] Women such as these also published speeches, newspaper columns, essays, and autobiographies that provide great insight into their personal lives and public activities. These serve as useful primary sources for reading and class discussion.[13]

Examining the words and activities of these women allows students to analyze the ways that race, class, and gender dynamics work together to inform the culture of women's activism. In this case, students can see that African American women activists typically worked for the welfare of both their race *and* their sex. For example, middle-class African American clubwomen saw their community work, their own personal advancement, expanded opportunity for their sex, and the political aspirations of the entire race as inextricably intertwined.[14] As Paula Giddings argued in *When and Where I Enter*, one of the founding texts on the history of African American women's activism, African American women "could understand the relationship between racism and sexism because they had to strive against both."[15] Their interest in improving the condition of their race and their sex led these women to establish relationships with progressive white female reformers; organize on behalf of temperance, woman suffrage, and federal antilynching legislation; and adopt an extraordinarily broad and wide-ranging political agenda that simultaneously embraced campaigns for women's rights and civil rights. Rather than distancing themselves from their poorer sisters, members of the National Association of Colored Women embraced the motto "Lifting as We Climb." They pooled their resources and raised funds to provide ample support for their churches and establish newspapers, libraries, schools, and homes for the aged in their communities. They were also particularly intent on countering the prevailing racist ideologies that characterized African American women as sexually promiscuous and unwomanly, in marked contrast with white women who were idealized as virtuous and pure. Consequently, throughout the late nineteenth and early twentieth centuries, female activists from the black middle class designed their activism around their own intersectionality, positioning themselves as the "best women" of the race, serving as "ambassadors" of a sort to the white community, building institutions in their own communities, and striving to live impeccably virtuous lives that challenged racist stereotypes.[16]

Stories such as these can have a dramatic impact on the way instructors diversify their courses. African American voices often disappear from U.S. history surveys immediately after Reconstruction and emerge again only when it's time to discuss the developments of the 1960s. But those African American women whose intersectionality defied prevailing assumptions about race and class reveal the vibrant history of African American women's organizations and the activism and community-building efforts that predated and, in fact, laid the groundwork for the emergence of the Civil Rights movement after World War II.

Dealing with Difference and Disrupting the Narrative

Analyzing the ways that race and class intersect in African American women's lives allows instructors and students to complicate the women-and-minorities paradigm in a fundamental way. But attention to African American women's history is only one way to investigate the experiences of "other" American women. Since the 1990s, the stories of Native American women in the colonial era, Latinas living in the borderlands between the United States and Mexico, and Chinese and Japanese women in California have all been researched under the rubric of women's history. These historiographical developments have shed much needed light on the many ways that the experiences of women vary according to class and race and across region and time.[17]

While this diversification of women's history is extraordinarily exciting, it also poses a number of potential challenges for instructors, particularly for those who are concerned about the issue of coverage. Faced with a growing number of women to discuss, instructors struggle to give equal time to an array of women whose historical experiences have varied so greatly. As Christine DiStefano puts it:

> In the United States today, we have five major racial groups: Native American, African American, Asian American, Hispanic or Latino, and White. Each of these categories contains extremely diversified cohorts; the cultural and political diversity drowned within each boggles the mind. When does the specification stop?...At what point do we all become endlessly particular individuals, each with a particular story to tell?[18]

The issue of "difference" itself can also be problematic. Some have argued that focusing on the differences among women can obscure the underlying similarities that women shared across class and racial lines, destabilize gender as a category of analysis, and rend the fabric of the women's history narrative into unrecognizable shreds.[19] Others find that perfunctory acknowledgment of the diversity of women's experience simply "renormalizes" the experiences of white middle-class heterosexual women, reinforcing the idea that middle-class white women's experiences were the norm and that other women's experiences were either "exotic" or "deviant."[20]

But even these difficulties provide opportunities for transforming our understanding of the conventional U.S. history narrative. If there is one thing scholarship of the 1980s and 1990s has demonstrated, it is that race, class, and gender are not stable, biological, or transhistorical entities.[21] Rather, they are complex processes and social constructs subject to historical change. Moreover, as the concept of intersectionality insists, these categories are interrelated and mutually defining. With these developments in mind, analyzing difference itself can reveal much about the "interconnectedness" of women, while simultaneously shedding light on the creation and maintenance of caste and class lines in the United States.[22] As Elsa Barkley Brown puts it, "Middle-class white women's lives are not just different from working-class white, Black, and Latin women's lives." Rather, white and middle-class women's privileges are directly connected to the social and economic status of working-class women and women of color.[23] In other words, group identities are formed in relation to each other, and the differences between women can serve to establish and reinforce boundaries and hierarchies of race and class.

By examining the life cycles, family relationships and responsibilities, labor, and community networks of women in a comparative way, students can gain greater understanding about the race and class hierarchies that separate groups of women. They can also learn more about the ways that women have helped to define the rituals, practices, ideals, and politics of their own particular class and race. If we apply this type of comparative analysis of intersectionality to our discussions of women and slavery, for example, students can debate the possibilities and limitations of the shared dependence experienced by free and enslaved women in the antebellum South. Both free white and enslaved black women occupied positions below the master in the patriarchal, hierarchical household system of the antebellum South. And because of their shared dependency, individual black and white women could, at times, forge bonds across racial lines. But enslaved women's status as chattel—that is, personal property to be bought, sold, and used according to their owners' will—placed them in a fundamentally different category than white women. On a material level, it was family ownership of enslaved African Americans that undergirded the economic and social status of white plantation mistresses. Additionally, it was the characterization of enslaved women as sexually promiscuous jezebels and beasts of burden that helped to shape and shore up the mythology of the plantation mistress ideal.[24]

Careful attention to the differences among groups of women can also give explanatory power to large-scale social and economic developments. This is most apparent in early American history. English settlers in the seventeenth-century Chesapeake worked out the difference between indentured servitude and slavery by imposing one set of legal and cultural gender conventions on African women and another on European women. While white female indentured servants might be put into the field to cultivate tobacco during their term of service, the prevailing cultural assumption was that such work was unsuitable for respectable women. African women, however, were routinely depicted in a manner emphasizing their physical "distinctiveness" and expected to engage in agricultural labor. Moreover, those few African women who were able to secure their freedom, marry, and set up housekeeping remained tithable in colonial Virginia, a tax reflecting the prevailing assumption that they—unlike their English counterparts—would remain field laborers throughout their lives. Eventually, English notions that only "nasty wenches" engaged in field labor merged with the practice of putting enslaved African women to work outdoors. Thus, by first characterizing and codifying African women as different from and less civilized than European women, English colonists began the process of articulating the racial ideology that would ultimately underpin North American chattel slavery.[25]

As these examples demonstrate, comparative analysis has allowed scholars to give critical attention to the ways that intersectionality functions on a structural level. In the process, they have recast major social and economic developments like the transition from indentured servitude to slavery and the cultural framework of the antebellum South. These methodological strategies have important pedagogical implications for those teaching U.S. history. They reveal what women's historians have long argued: that women's history is at the heart of the U.S. history narrative.

Finally, growing interest in the study of race, class, and gender has also led to more robust understandings of the identities, activities, and prerogatives of American men. Like ideals of femininity, ideals of masculinity have been fluid rather than fixed, and they have been formed and redefined in relation to women and children.[26] Constructions of manhood also intersect with constructs of race and class. As historian Gail Bederman demonstrates, turn-of-the-century constructions of middle-class white masculinity were created in relation to men of African, Asian, and Native American descent, men that white Americans characterized as primitive "others."[27] Moreover, major revisions in male gender ideals have tended to occur at the same time as major economic and demographic developments and changes in family roles and practices. By taking a comparative approach to the study of male intersectionality at critical points in U.S. history, historians have further revised the interpretation of several major historical events, from English encroachment on Native American territory in the colonial era, to African American participation in the Civil War, to the rise of modern American ideals of masculinity.[28] As scholars work through these comparative, racialized notions of gender and masculinity, it seems likely that our approaches to classroom instruction will continue to be refined.

Attention to race, class, and gender has made it clear that there is no universal narrative for women in the United States. Women's experiences as paid and unpaid laborers, as activists, and as daughters, wives, and mothers have been defined by their class and their race as much as by their gender. Attention to the ways these categories have intersected in individual women's lives has created a much more detailed and complex picture of women's history. This new scholarship has helped to reveal the multicultural history of the United States, given us greater insight into the ways that women's experiences have differed, and provided a more vibrant palette for U.S. history instructors.

Ultimately, however, theories of intersectionality have done even more than incorporate the experiences of women of color into the U.S. history narrative. They have made it possible to disrupt and revise some long-standing interpretations of critical moments in American history. Topics such as colonial settlement, the growth and perpetuation of slavery, the transition to Jim Crow, and the politics of the Progressive Era can be fully understood only by analyzing the dynamics of race, gender, and class. Indeed, many of the endeavors traditionally defined in male terms—such as wars, battles, or early-twentieth-century electoral politics—have been framed around these mutually reinforcing constructs.[29] And when we utilize these approaches in the classroom, we can move multicultural interpretations of gender and women's history from the margins to the center of the U.S. history curriculum, underscoring the dynamism and complexity of our shared past.

NOTES

1. Gloria T. Hull, Patricia Bell Scott, and Barbara Smith, eds., *All the Women Are White, All the Blacks Are Men, but Some of Us Are Brave: Black Women's Studies* (New York: Feminist Press, 1982).

2. Other pioneering collections and anthologies on African American women's history include Gerda Lerner, ed., *Black Women in White America* (1972; reprint, New York: Vintage Books, 1992); Bert James Lowenberg and Ruth Bogin, eds., *Black Women in Nineteenth-Century American Life: Their Words, Their Thoughts, Their Feelings* (University Park: Pennsylvania State University Press, 1976); Sharon Harley and Rosalyn Terborg-Penn, *The Afro-American Woman: Struggles and Images* (1978; reprint, Baltimore: Black Classic Press, 1997); Dorothy Sterling, ed., *We Are Your Sisters: Black Women in the Nineteenth Century* (New York: W. W. Norton, 1984).

3. See Kimberle Crenshaw, *Demarginalizing the Intersection of Race and Sex* (Chicago: University of Chicago Press, 1989). As Crenshaw put it in respect to African American women, "the intersection of racism and sexism factors into Black women's lives in ways that cannot be captured wholly by looking at the race or gender dimensions of those experiences separately." Kimberle Crenshaw, "Mapping the Margins: Intersectionality, Identity Politics, and Violence against Women of Color," *Stanford Law Review* 43 (July 1991), 1244.

4. Key texts include Cherríe Moraga and Gloria Anzaldúa, eds., *This Bridge Called My Back: Writings by Radical Women of Color* (New York: Kitchen Table and Women of Color Press, 1981); Angela Y. Davis, *Women, Race, and Class* (New York: Vintage, 1981); bell hooks, *Feminist Theory: From Margin to Center* (Boston: South End Press, 1984); Filomina Steady, ed., *The Black Woman Cross-Culturally* (Cambridge, MA: Schenkman, 1981); Patricia Hill Collins, *Black Feminist Thought: Knowledge, Consciousness, and the Politics of Empowerment* (New York: Routledge, 1990).

5. Moraga and Anzaldúa, eds., *This Bridge Called My Back*, 116.

6. Evelyn Brooks Higginbotham, "African-American Women's History and the Meta-language of Race," *Signs* 17 (Winter 1992), 251–74.

7. Barbara Y. Welke, "When All the Women Were White, and All the Blacks Were Men: Gender, Class, Race, and the Road to *Plessy*, 1855–1914," *Law and History Review* 13 (Fall 1995), 261–315.

8. Jennifer L. Morgan, *Laboring Women: Reproduction and Gender in New World Slavery* (Philadelphia: University of Pennsylvania Press, 2004).

9. Works that discuss black women during antebellum slavery include Angela Y. Davis, "Reflections on the Black Woman's Role in the Community of Slaves," *Black Scholar* 3 (December 1971), 2–15; Herbert G. Gutman, *The Black Family in Slavery and*

Freedom, 1750–1925 (New York: Pantheon, 1976); David Barry Gaspar and Darlene Clark Hine, eds., *More Than Chattel: Black Women and Slavery in the Americas* (Bloomington: Indiana University Press, 1998); Leslie A. Schwalm. *A Hard Fight for We: Women's Transition from Slavery to Freedom in South Carolina* (Urbana: University of Illinois Press, 1997); Deborah Gray White, *Ar'n't I a Woman? Female Slaves in the Plantation South* (New York: W. W. Norton, 1985); Elizabeth Fox-Genovese, *Within the Plantation Household: Black and White Women of the Old South* (Chapel Hill: University of North Carolina Press, 1988); Stephanie Camp, *Closer to Freedom: Enslaved Women and Everyday Resistance in the Plantation South* (Chapel Hill: University of North Carolina Press, 2004); Sharla M. Fett, *Working Cures: Healing, Health and Power on Southern Slave Plantations* (Chapel Hill: University of North Carolina Press, 2002); and Jennifer Morgan, *Laboring Women.*

10. Welke, "When All the Women Were White," 267.

11. Glenda Gilmore, *Gender and Jim Crow: Women and the Politics of White Supremacy in North Carolina, 1896–1920* (Chapel Hill: University of North Carolina Press, 1996), 150.

12. Work on black women's activism at the turn of the century is vast and growing. Key publications include Evelyn Brooks Higginbotham, *Righteous Discontent: The Women's Movement in the Black Baptist Church, 1880–1920* (Cambridge: Harvard University Press, 1993); chapter 5 of Linda Gordon, *Pitied but Not Entitled: Single Mothers and the History of Welfare, 1890–1935* (New York: Free Press, 1994); Rosalyn Terborg-Penn, *African American Women in the Struggle for the Vote, 1850–1920* (Bloomington: Indiana University Press, 1998); Stephanie Shaw, *What a Woman Ought to Be and to Do: Black Professional Women during the Jim Crow Era* (Chicago: University of Chicago Press, 1996); Cynthia Neverdon-Morton, *Afro-American Women of the South and the Advancement of the Race, 1895–1925* (Knoxville: University of Tennessee Press, 1989); Deborah Gray White, *Too Heavy a Load: Black Women in Defense of Themselves, 1894–1994* (New York: W. W. Norton, 1999); Victoria W. Wolcott, *Remaking Respectability: African American Women in Interwar Detroit* (Chapel Hill: University of North Carolina Press, 2001); and Michele Mitchell, *Righteous Propagation: African Americans and the Politics of Racial Destiny after Reconstruction* (Chapel Hill: University of North Carolina Press, 2004).

13. Key documents from the period include the *Woman's Era*, the ladies' columns in the African American press, the *National Notes*, the official organ of the National Association of Colored Women, Mary Church Terrell, *A Colored Woman in a White World* (Washington, DC: Ransdell, 1940); and Alfreda M. Duster, ed., *Crusade for Justice: The Autobiography of Ida B. Wells* (Chicago: University of Chicago Press, 1970).

14. For an example of the distance between white female reformers and their charges, see Christine Stansell, *City of Women: Sex and Class in New York, 1789–1860* (New York: Knopf, 1986).

15. Paula Giddings, *"When and Where I Enter": The Impact of Black Women on Race and Sex in America* (New York: William Morrow, 1984), 6–7.

16. See Hazel Carby, *Reconstructing Womanhood: The Emergence of the Afro-American Woman Novelist* (New York: Oxford University Press, 1987); Higginbotham,

Righteous Discontent; Glenda Gilmore, *Gender and Jim Crow*, and Paula Giddings, *"When and Where I Enter"* for a discussion of these tactics.

17. Examples include Ramon Gutierrez, *When Jesus Came, the Corn Mothers Went Away: Power and Sexuality in New Mexico, 1500–1846* (Stanford, CA: Stanford University Press, 1990); Judy Yung, *Unbound Feet: A Social History of Chinese Women in San Francisco* (Berkeley: University of California Press, 1995); George Anthony Peffer, *If They Don't Bring Their Women Here: Chinese Female Immigration before Exclusion* (Urbana: University of Illinois Press, 1999); Valerie Matsumoto, *Farming the Home Place: A Japanese American Community in California, 1919–1982* (Ithaca, NY: Cornell University Press, 1993); Vicki Ruiz, *From Out of the Shadows* (New York: Oxford University Press, 1987); Theda Perdue, *Cherokee Women: Gender and Culture, 1700–1835* (Lincoln: University of Nebraska Press, 1998); Helen C. Roundtree, "Powhatan Indian Women: The People Captain John Smith Barely Saw," *Ethnohistory* 45 (1998), 1–29; Linda Gordon, *The Great Arizona Orphan Abduction* (Cambridge: Harvard University Press, 2000); and Vicki L. Ruiz and Ellen Carol DuBois, eds., *Unequal Sisters: A Multicultural Reader in U.S. Women's History*, 3rd ed. (New York: Routledge, 2000).

18. Christine DiStefano, "Who the Heck Are We? Theoretical Turns against Gender," *Frontiers: A Journal of Women Studies* 12 (1991), 92.

19. Bonnie Thornton Dill, "Race, Class, and Gender: Prospects for an All-Inclusive Sisterhood," *Feminist Studies* 9 (Spring 1983), 131–150, 138.

20. Elsa Barkley Brown, "'What Has Happened Here': The Politics of Difference in Women's History and Feminist Politics," *Feminist Studies* 18 (Spring 1992). Reprinted in Darlene Clark Hine, Wilma King and Linda Reed, eds., *"We Specialize in the Wholly Impossible": A Reader in Black Women's History* (Brooklyn, NY: Carlson Publishing, 1995), 43.

21. Joan Wallach Scott, *Gender and the Politics of History* (New York: Columbia University Press, 1988); Barbara Jeanne Fields, "Slavery, Race and Ideology in the United States of America," *New Left Review* 181 (May–June 1990); Carol Lasser, "Gender, Ideology and Class in the Early Republic," *Journal of the Early Republic* 10 (Autumn 1990); David R. Roediger, *The Wages of Whiteness: Race and the Making of the American Working Class* (New York: Verso, 1991); Noel Ignatiev, *How the Irish Became White* (New York: Routledge, 1995); and Gail Bederman, *Manliness and Civilization: A Cultural History of Gender and Race in the United States, 1880–1917* (Chicago: University of Chicago Press, 1995).

22. Evelyn Nakano Glenn, "From Servitude to Service Work: Historical Continuities in the Racial Division of Paid Reproductive Labor," *Signs* 18 (1992), reprinted in Ruiz and DuBois, *Unequal Sisters*, 459. Emphasis mine.

23. Brown, "What Has Happened Here," 42.

24. For comparative discussions of black and white women in antebellum slavery, see Elizabeth Fox-Genovese, *Within the Plantation Household: Black and White Women of the Old South* (Chapel Hill: University of North Carolina Press, 1988); Patricia Morton, ed., *Discovering the Women in Slavery: Emancipating Perspectives on the American Past* (Athens: University of Georgia Press, 1996); and Brenda Stevenson, *Life*

in Black and White: Family and Community in the Slave South (New York: Oxford University Press, 1996).

25. For discussions of African American women in southern colonies, see Joan Gunderson, "The Double Bonds of Race and Sex: Black and White Women in a Colonial Virginia Parish," *Journal of Southern History* 52 (August 1986); chapter 2 of Carol Berkin, *First Generations: Women in Colonial America* (New York: Hill and Wang, 1996); Kathleen M. Brown, *Good Wives, Nasty Wenches, and Anxious Patriarchs: Gender, Race, and Power in Colonial Virginia* (Chapel Hill: University of North Carolina Press, 1996); and Jennifer Morgan, *Laboring Women.*

26. E. Anthony Rotundo, *American Manhood: Transformations in Masculinity from the Revolution to the Modern Era* (New York: Basic Books, 1993).

27. See Bederman, *Manliness and Civilization.*

28. Brown, *Good Wives, Natsy Wenches, and Anxious Patriarchs;* James Cullen, "'I's a Man Now': Gender and African American Men," in Catherine Clinton and Nina Silber, eds., *Divided Houses: Gender and the Civil War* (New York: Oxford University Press, 1992), 76–91; Bederman, *Manliness and Civilization;* and Kristin Hoganson, *Fighting for American Manhood: How Gender Politics Provoked the Spanish-American and Philippine-American Wars* (New Haven, CT: Yale University Press, 1998).

29. See Kathleen M. Brown, "Brave New Worlds: Women's and Gender History," *William and Mary Quarterly*, 3rd ser., 50: 2 (April 1993), 311–28.

10

Conceptualizing the Female World of Religion in U.S. Women's History

Barbara Welter

I teach the history of religion in the United States and the history of women in the United States as part of the same continuum of change, continuity, individuals, and ideas. I find that the questions posed in both subjects are similar, but even more interesting is the fact that the questions are never really answered—the next generation poses them again, in a slightly different context, from slightly different perspectives, but impelled by similar needs. Like Gertrude Stein's last words: It is not the answer we seek in the study but the questions themselves. The students I teach are either completely without religious knowledge, have some cultural but little historical knowledge of their own religion, or, in rare cases, are better trained in biblical exegesis than I am and far more willing to debate its merits.

"Woman's History *Is* American Religious History," historian Ann Braude asserts in an essay examining the decline, secularization, and feminization of American religion.[1] Women were perceived to be more naturally good than men, and this piety was a critical component of the True Woman. However, as the theology and social rituals of religion itself became domesticated, kinder, gentler, and, in a word, more feminine, its prestige and importance declined. The rhetoric of religion remained, but it was left to the women of early

America, who did not produce wealth and did not pursue happiness through politics, to maintain religion in an increasingly materialistic and secular society.[2] As women predominated in the American institution of religion, it became less valuable in terms of power, status, and money.[3]

The intersection of women's history and the history of American religion is most obvious in the major figures, ideas, and events of both fields. Anne Hutchinson, Sojourner Truth, Frances Willard, Mary Baker Eddy, and Aimee Semple MacPherson can be found in most textbooks. There is a large literature of their spiritual autobiographies, as well as an increasing number of scholarly biographies.[4] In the nineteenth century, Transcendentalism, the Second Awakening, Seneca Falls and other reforms, the religions of positive thought, the missionary movement, evangelism, and the "Americanization" of old-world religions are markers for the history of religion and women. But religion and women were also engaged in such traditional themes of American history as western expansion, imperialism, immigration, and urbanization. The women who contributed to these ideas and these events were dissenters as well as conformers. While women were and, to some degree, still are regarded as the conservators of tradition and traditional values, their active role in change and reform can be traced from colonial times to the present. I always start my course with a discussion of the witches of Salem, partly because there are few historical subjects more appealing to students, but also because the ways in which religion is invoked to explain, defend, or rationalize the situation in Salem are echoed throughout the course. In fact, this repetition and lack of resolution in both fields is for me one of the most valuable lessons of the course. Students inevitably say "but that's still the way things are," with a kind of wonder at the intransigence of the problem.

Deference, agency, and the search for personal identity in a new nation involved not only those American men that French observer Hector Crèvecoeur called the "new man" but also new women. Although these women were expected to obey St. Paul's injunction, "Wives be subject to your husbands," the actual experience of American life made submission a nuanced virtue. Teachers of history have restored active roles to previously marginalized groups; the enslaved person, not just the abolitionist, is given credit for winning freedom. The submissive and passive woman is seen as empowered to effect change, while at the same time preserving family order. Religion was her balance wheel between the need for courage and activity in a harsh land and her apparent biblical humility before God and man. One of the enduring questions posed by this tension is: Was religion "good" for women, or did it add to their oppression?[5]

One of the changes in Protestant theology, and a response to this question, was the doctrine of individual reception of grace and the ability of the prepared soul to hear God's voice. God did not discriminate against gender and perhaps not against race when he spoke, and his "transcendence" of these differences suggested that mere mortals should be equally unbiased. Those sects that accepted this doctrine and relied on the individual's call or vocation rather than on the curriculum of the seminary, from which women were excluded, could accept women as ministers. An equal opportunity Divine Being became a significant argument for racial, ethnic, and gender tolerance. The Society of Friends (Quakers) epitomized, at least in theory, this dual right of women to speak in public when they had the divine mandate of a "concern" and, if given a similar mandate, to preach. Many of the first generation of female activists were raised as Quakers or converted to that sect, and it was no accident that the meetings preceding the 1848 meeting at Seneca Falls, the first public call for the vote for women, coincided in time, place, and membership with a group of reform-minded Progressive Quakers.[6]

Women's religious organizations, in mainstream Protestant churches, were sanctioned by nineteenth-century society and allowed women to gain the experience and skills necessary for involvement in the plethora of antebellum reform movements. These reforms themselves owed much to the religious imagination in rhetoric and motive.[7] It is easy to get lost in the thicket of these overlapping organizations hoping to change everything from diet to divorce.[8] All of them become part of the "ferment" of the new nation's growth in the nineteenth century, and all of them involved women, working (and praying) for both change and continuity. I discuss abolition, women's rights, and temperance, with a few words on diet and dress reform, to illustrate the overlapping of individuals and families, as well as the particular female spin that characterized their participation.[9] The use of religion on both sides of an issue, and the differing approaches of women to still unresolved problems, is seen in The Woman's Bible, published in two volumes in 1896 and 1898, with Elizabeth Cady Stanton as its primary author. Stanton believed that the Bible, correctly explicated (by women), would validate God's gender equity, although some passages remained irretrievably offensive and atavistic. Prominent religious women begged to differ.[10]

Frances Willard, president of the Woman's Christian Temperance Union (W.C.T.U.), was a leader of the loyal opposition and, since her organization's endorsement of the ballot for women "as a weapon for the protection of the home" in 1880 was perhaps the single most important step in middle-class acceptance of the drive for the franchise, she had good reform credentials even when she rejected Stanton's biblical criticism.[11] Some of these multiple reforms were successful at least in terms of legislation, but real change often eluded even the passage of constitutional amendments and emerged generations later as variations of the same unhappy themes.

No teacher of American history can ignore its less than admirable aspects and its unresolved recurring problems. Deciding how to present them in context with as little judgmental comment and as many primary sources as possible is an admirable, even necessary, goal. That both religion and women were often involved in the country's less than salubrious moments needs to be acknowledged. At the same time, demonizing one side or another ignores the historical reality that both groups saw themselves as reformers. Nineteenth-century Protestants could denounce Catholics because they had slavish devotion to papal authority, did not accept voluntarism in biblical interpretation, and "incarcerated" women in convents. Mormons were a threat because polygamy was a sin against women and the family. The missionary movement, with its pious women who saw themselves as divinely called to help their "heathen" sisters, was at the very least co-opted into tools of American imperialism.

And yet Catholics could show how their devotion to God's mother gave dignity and value to women, and Catholic sisters performed many good works; Mormons believed that they were participating in a gospel of perfection for family life and eradicating the loneliness and dependency of single women; missionary women risked their lives to bring education and medicine as well as the promise of salvation to a waiting world.[12]

Other themes in the nation's history present similar negative, as well as positive, connections to religion and to women. Women and men braved the Overland Trail in search of land and prosperity but proclaimed their primary desire to Christianize the West, even if the Native Americans were subjugated to federal and religious control.[13] Immigration was not only the refuge of the tired and the poor, but an opportunity to denounce these wretched refugees, whose religions and customs were strange and whose men, feminists felt, were entirely too fond of alcohol and opposed to suffrage. The immigrant woman's life was bounded by her ethnicity and the religion. How would these new enclaves affect urban politics? Would feminism put women "at odds," as historian Carl Degler put it, with their own culture?[14] Benevolent organizations, usually religious in origin, proliferated to mitigate the dangers of the city. But they might also bring about a loss of cultural and religious identity, if not in the immigrants themselves, then in the next generation.[15] In teaching these paradoxical positions, I find many of my students unresponsive. In their minds, nothing trumps indigenous culture. Immolation of widows? Genital mutilation? Perhaps not, they may concede, but in the words of Edna St. Vincent Millay, "they know but they do not approve," and I am not sure I have ever really convinced them. At least we always have a lively discussion.

The new realities of the latter part of the nineteenth century required changes in established religion and new religions. Christian Science, founded by Mary Baker Eddy in 1879, gave a religious dimension to the realistic need in a competitive, fast-changing nation for long working hours and to a reliance on will rather than on the dubious medical advice available. Hard work promised economic mobility. In its early years it gave equal authority to women and men. The Science of Health praised each individual, without concern for gender, as "God's Perfect Child." The idea of the Father-Mother God, which existed in pre-Christian times and was periodically resurrected, was a constant in its theology.[16] Spiritualism allowed women, whether through individual mediums, Universalism, or Theosophy, to speak with the authority of the entity they channeled, frequently a male. Catholicism and Judaism, the religions of many of the new immigrants, were Americanized in their crossing of the Atlantic.[17] These new and changed religions helped maintain religious traditions while adjusting to a new country and a new century.

African Americans also used religion during their enslavement and after emancipation. Margaret Walker's poem, "We Have Been Believers," published in 1938, is the epigraph for a book of readings in African American women's spiritual biography.[18] The contributions of these women, and the complex ways in which they achieved agency in their churches, illustrate women's access to power through individual and communal religious experiences. They speak also to the importance of religion to their sense of identity.[19] And yet presenting this religious tradition to students brings back the old question of whether religion is "good" for women. Did religion, with its emphasis on a better life hereafter, encourage passivity and resignation? The importance of religion to the twentieth-century Civil Rights movement would suggest a more proactive role, but some students are not easily convinced of this. They believe in the Marxian "opiate of the people" definition of religion, whether they have ever heard the words, just as some of them believe that missionaries acted only to destroy indigenous culture and promote imperialism.

A more agreeable and accessible analysis of religion is the role of ritual. Religious rituals are still a part of many people's lives, at least at birth, marriage, and death, and their value as a conferrer of respectability, as well as a marker for class, ethnic, and gender identity, is both a historical and contemporary phenomenon. Looking at religion gives it a new dimension, and it means looking at its women: at the sober colors of Quaker dress, the habits of Catholic sisters, the impressive hats in African American congregations, and the veiled heads of Muslim women as outward signs of inward grace and status. It means going to the churches, synagogues, and mosques and observing the iconography, the ritual, and the roles of the congregation.[20] The popular culture of religion, ritual, and women is evident in many pieces of literature, from Harriet Beecher Stowe to Judy Blume. Hymns are examples of how religion was internalized and domesticated in music. The development of a religious press both informed and entertained congregations, and religious objects decorated their homes as a proud statement of the family's identity.[21]

All religions increasingly sought to do good as well as to be good. The nineteenth century's Social Gospel was a response to urbanization and diversity. Its proponents argued that justice in this life was a necessary precursor to justice in the next, a tenet that literally stood predestination on its head.

Religion, like many American institutions, was valuable when it was pragmatically viable, when it worked, and when it was useful. Urban reforms required women to carry them out because families, the primary recipients of these reforms, were more accessible to women than to men. Although Saint Paul warned against women preaching, usurping authority over men, or adorning themselves with jewelry and braided hair, he lavished praise on the "useful woman," adorned only with her good works.[22]

Religious rhetoric continued to dominate even secular reforms such as Hull House. Ellen Gates Starr, cofounder with Jane Addams, spent her last days as an oblate of the Third Order of Saint Benedict. Josephine Shaw Lowell, whose crusades included the House of Refuge for Women and the women's auxiliary of the Civil Service Reform Association of New York State, insisted that reform work "should only be entered into with a feeling of consecration." The urban reforms of the Salvation Army combined religious rhetoric with military organization and allowed women full participation in both. Frances Willard, speaking of her own and other women's organizations, understood that Christian activism, however valuable for those it served, was most useful for the women reformers themselves, giving them "knowledge of their own power," making them "eager to clasp hands for a more aggressive work than such women had ever before dreamed of undertaking."[23]

Fundamentalism and evangelicalism increased in the first decades of the twentieth century. Both groups emphasized the importance of women, but evangelicals generally took a more liberal view of their role in the church. Fundamentalists were as fervent in their praise of women as any Victorian eulogizing the "Angel in the Home," returning to woman's traditional role as wife, mother, and guardian of virtue.[24] This return to earlier standards of women's behavior was a backlash against the "new woman" and the fear that moral standards were being lowered as hemlines were raised.[25] More instances of the woman problem redux occurred in this transitional period: Should all Protestant denominations ordain women? Should women control the boards and the finances of their own missionary and reform organizations? What role should religion play in the proposed amendments for woman suffrage and prohibition? Here again, trying to present both sides of these arguments is not easy. Students have real difficulty believing that any decent human being, particularly a woman, could oppose the vote or, for that matter, the right to drink alcohol. It is always necessary to differentiate individual or particular women from the generic woman, and in presenting these arguments, it is necessary (although not usually successful) to present the differences among classes, ethnic and racial groups, and even regions.[26]

Were wars, as well as religion, good for women? This question has been asked by historians about the American Revolution to the present conflicts. The wars of the twentieth century, and the role that women and religions played in them, are becoming increasingly contentious. In the aftermath of World War I, President Warren G. Harding called for a return to "normalcy"; for many listeners, that infelicitous word implied a return to the traditional role of women. Subsequent decades saw the fundamentalist reinvention of the ante-bellum True Woman. Indeed, the growth of the Religious Right in the period following World War II saw a similar attempt to remove Rosie the Riveter from her factory and put her into a nice suburban house complete with a newly coined "family room." One advocate of this position called it a "Focus on the Family," with all that phrase implies.[27]

The latter part of the twentieth century saw a new wave of feminism and a new set of religious options so that women with raised consciousness could maintain some religious or at least spiritual connection. Many women wanted a religion less patriarchal, less judgmental, but capable of providing solace and sustenance, and one in which their individual identities, as well as their ethnic and racial heritage, would be respected. Traditional religions, both in new and sometimes in their most conservative form, were reexamined; these religions are still evolving. Religions newer to the North American context, such as Islam, Buddhism, and Hinduism, grew, as large numbers of migrants from Africa, Asia, and the Middle East entered the United States as a result of changes in the immigration law in 1965.

The emergence of Wicca brings full circle a course that begins with a discussion of witchcraft.[28] The old questions are still being asked, and the new answers still do not satisfy everyone. Perhaps the best parting advice to give to a generation of students who wish to understand the history of American religion and the role women have played in it, and their own relationship to religious and gender identity, would be the words, probably apocryphal, of the suffragist leader to a new recruit: "Trust in God, my dear, and SHE will protect you."

NOTES

1. Ann Braude, "Women's History *Is* American Religious History," in Thomas A. Tweed, ed., *Retelling U.S. Religious History* (Berkeley: University of California Press, 1997), 87–109, is the best succinct summary.

2. David S. Reynolds, "The Feminization Controversy: Sexual Stereotypes and the Paradoxes of Piety in Nineteenth-Century America," *New England Quarterly*, 53, no. 1

(March 1980), 96–106; David G. Hackett, "Gender and Religion in American Culture, 1970–1950," *Religion in American Culture* 5, no. 2 (Summer 1995), 127–157.

3. Ann Douglas, *The Feminization of American Culture* (New York: Knopf, 1977; Richard D. Shiels, "The Feminization of American Congregationalism, 1730–1835," *American Quarterly* 39 (1981), 45–62; Nancy F. Cott, "Young Women in the Second Great Awakening," *Feminist Studies* 3 (Fall 1975), 15–29.

4. Roger Lundin and Mary A. Noll, eds., *Voices from the Heart: Four Centuries of American Piety* (Grand Rapids, MI: William B. Eerdmans, 1987); Daniel B. Shea, *Spiritual Autobiography in Early America* (Princeton, NJ: Princeton University Press, 1968); Estelle C. Jelinek, *Women's Autobiography: Essays in Criticism* (Bloomington: University of Indiana Press, 1980).

5. Much of this argument is based on Carol Gilligan's differentiation between the voice of relationship and the voice of individuation. Gilligan argues that because of woman's traditional role as self-sacrificing caregiver, she sees morality in terms of relationships and community, whereas men are socialized to evaluate themselves through intellect and power. Carol Gilligan, *In a Different Voice* (Cambridge: Harvard University Press, 1982). Concerning the debate whether religion is "good" for women, see Elizabeth Weiss Ozorak, "The Power but Not the Glory: How Women Empower Themselves through Religion," *Journal for the Scientific Study of Religion* 35, no. 1 (March 1996), 17–29. Susan Starr Sered addresses the same question in "Ideology, Autonomy and Sisterhood: An Analysis of the Secular Consequences of Women's Religion," *Gender and Society* 4 (December 1994), 486–506. Her conclusion in this study of worldwide religions is that while most religions provide "transient help" for a few women, only a small number "affect or at least work toward permanent and structural advantages," 486.

6. James E. Block, *A Nation of Agents: The American Path to a Modern Self and Society* (Cambridge: Belknap Press of Harvard University Press, 1992). Women are rather conspicuously absent from this 658-page volume.

7. Mary P. Ryan, *Cradle of the Middle Class: The Family in Oneida County, New York, 1790–1865* (Cambridge: Cambridge University Press, 1981); Lori D. Ginzberg, *Women and the Work of Benevolence: Morality, Politics and Class in the Nineteenth Century United States* (New Haven, CT: Yale University Press, 1990); Anne M. Boylan, "Women in Groups: An Analysis of Women's Benevolent Organizations in New York and Boston, 1797–1840," *Journal of American History* 71 (December 1984), 497–523; Barbara Leslie Epstein, *The Politics of Domesticity: Women, Evangelism, and Temperance in Nineteenth-Century America* (Middletown, CT: Wesleyan University Press, 1981).

8. Robert H. Abzug, *Cosmos Crumbling: American Reform and the Religious Imagination* (New York: Oxford University Press, 1984), chap. 8, "The Woman Question," and chap. 9, "Woman's Rights and Schism," 183–229.

9. The five volumes of *The Dictionary of Notable American Women*, published from 1971 to 2004, are rich sources for women's religious lives.

10. Elizabeth Cady Stanton published the two volumes of *The Woman's Bible* in 1895 and 1898. The leadership of the National American Woman Suffrage Association (NAWSA) voted to disassociate the organization from it, largely because Stanton posed

the question: Have the teachings of the Bible advanced or retarded the emancipation of women? While the text of the work is interesting, the letters in support and opposition published in the appendix provide an excellent cross-section of American women's ambivalence to questioning both the truth and the authority of the Bible.

11. Janet Zollinger Giele, *Two Paths to Women's Equality* (New York: Twayne, 1995); Jack S. Blocker Jr., *"Give to the Winds Thy Fears": The Women's Temperance Crusade, 1873–1974* (Westport, CT: Greenwood, 1985); Ruth Bordin, *Woman and Temperance: The Quest for Power and Liberty* (Philadelphia: Temple University Press, 1981); Frances Grace Carver, "With Bible in One Hand and Battle-Axe in the Other: Carry A. Nation as Religious Reformer and Self-Promoter," *Religion and American Culture* 9 (Winter 1999), 31–65; Ruth Bordin, *Frances Willard: A Biography* (Chapel Hill: University of North Carolina Press, 1986).

12. This argument was first made by David Brion Davis, "Some Themes of Countersubversion: An Analysis of Anti-Masonic, Anti-Catholic, and Anti-Mormon Literature, *Mississippi Valley Historical Review* 47 (September 1960): 205–224.

13. Peggy Pascoe, *Relations of Rescue: The Search for Female Moral Authority in the American West, 1874–1939* (New York: Oxford University Press, 1990); Cynthia Grant Tucker, *Prophetic Sisterhood: Liberal Women Ministers on the Western Frontier 1880–1930* (Boston: Beacon, 1990).

14. Carl Degler, *At Odds: Women and Family in America from the Revolution to the Present* (New York: Oxford University Press, 1980).

15. Sydney Ahlstrom, "Mary Baker Eddy," *The Dictionary of Notable American Women*, vol. 1, Edward T. James, ed. (Cambridge: Belknap Press of Harvard University Press, 1971), 551–561. Robert David Thomas, *"With Bleeding Footsteps": Mary Baker Eddy's Path to Religious Leadership* (New York: Knopf, 1994); Caroline Fraser, *God's Perfect Child: Living and Dying in the Christian Science Church* (New York: Henry Holt, 1999); Susan Hill Lindley, "The Ambiguous Feminism of Mary Baker Eddy," *Journal of Religion* 64, no. 4 (October 1984), 318–381.

16. Ann Braude, *Radical Spirits: Spiritualism and Women's Rights in Nineteenth-Century America* (Boston: Beacon, 1989).

17. Judith Weisenfeld and Richard Newman, eds., *This Far by Faith: Readings in African-American Women's Biography* (New York: Routledge, 1996), 1.

18. Delores C. Carpenter, "Black Women in Religious Institutions: A Historical Summary from Slavery to the 1960s," *Journal of Religious Thought* 46 (Winter–Spring 1989–1990), 7–27; Evelyn Brooks Higginbotham, *Righteous Discontent: The Women's Movement in the Black Baptist Church 1880–1920* (Cambridge: Harvard University Press, 1993); Hans A. Baer, "The Limited Empowerment of Women in Black Spiritual Churches: An Alternative Vehicle to Religious Leadership," *Sociology of Religion* 54 (Spring 1993).

19. Robert S. Orsi, *Thank You, St. Jude: Women's Devotion to the Patron Saint of Hopeless Causes* (New Haven: Yale University Press, 1996), xi; James K. Kenneally, *The History of American Catholic Women* (New York: Crossroad, 1990); Carol K. Coburn and Martha Smith, *Spirited Lives: How Nuns Shaped Catholic Culture and American Life, 1836–1920* (Chapel Hill: University of North Carolina Press, 1999). For women in Judaism, see Ellen M. Umansky, "Spiritual Expressions: Jewish Women's Religious

Lives in the Twentieth-Century," in Judith R. Baskin, ed., *Jewish Women in Historical Perspective* (Detroit: Wayne State University Press, 1991), 265–288; Ann Braude, "The Jewish Woman's Encounter with American Culture," in Rosemary Radford Ruether and Rosemary Skinner Keller, eds., *Women and Religion in America, I* (San Francisco: Harper and Row, 1981); and Charlotte Baum, Paula Hyman, and Sonya Michel, *The Jewish Woman in America* (New York: New American Library, 1977).

20. Nina Baym, "Reinventing Lydia Sigourney," *American Literature* 62, no. 3 (September 1990), 385–404; Charles H. Foster, *The Rungless Ladder: Harriet Beecher Stowe and Puritanism* (Durham, NC: Duke University Press, 1954) emphasizes religion in Stowe's novels. For hymns, see June Hadden Hobbs, *"I Sing for I Cannot Be Silent": The Feminization of American Hymnody, 1870–1920* (Pittsburgh: University of Pittsburgh Press, 1997); Sandra S. Sizer, *Gospel Hymns and Social Religion: The Rhetoric of Nineteenth-Century Revivalism* (Philadelphia: Temple University Press, 1978).

21. Washington Gladden, *Applied Christianity* (Boston: Houghton Mifflin, 1886); Angelina E. Grimké, *Letters to Catherine E. Beecher, in Reply to an Essay on Slavery and Abolition, Addressed to A. E. Grimke* (Boston: Isaac Knapp, 1838), 30; Janet Forsythe Fishburn, *The Fatherhood of God and the Victorian Family: The Social Gospel in America* (Philadelphia: Fortress, 1981); Susan Curtis, *Consuming Faith: The Social Gospel and Modern American Culture* (Baltimore: Johns Hopkins University Press, 1991); Ida M. Tarbell, *The Business of Being a Woman* (New York: Macmillan, 1921); and Charlotte Perkins Gilman, *His Religion and Hers* (New York: Century, 1923). Josephine Shaw Lowell is quoted in Carolyn De Swarte Gifford, "Women in Social Reform Movements," *Women and Religion in America* I (San Francisco: Harper & Row, 1981), 297. For women in the Salvation Army, see Diane Winston, *Red-Hot and Righteous: The Urban Religion of the Salvation Army* (Cambridge: Harvard University Press, 1999).

22. Frances E. Willard, *Glimpses of Fifty Years: The Autobiography of an American Woman* (Chicago: Woman's Temperance Publishing Association, 1892), 470–471.

23. Dana L. Robert, "The Influence of American Missionary Women on the World Back Home," *Religion and American Culture* 12, no. 1 (Winter 2002), 59–89; and Robert, *American Women in Mission: A Social History of Their Thought and Practice* (Macon, GA: Mercer University Press, 1996); R. Pierce Beaver, *All Loves Excelling: American Protestant Women in World Mission* (Grand Rapids, MI: William B. Eerdmans, 1968).

24. Margaret Lamberts Bendroth, *Fundamentalism and Gender, 1875 to the Present* (New Haven, CT: Yale University Press, 1993); Betty A. DeBerg, *Ungodly Women: Gender and the First Wave of American Fundamentalism* (Minneapolis: Fortress, 1990); Brenda Brasher, *Godly Women: Fundamentalism and Female Power* (New Brunswick, NJ: Rutgers University Press, 1998).

25. Jerome L. Himmelstein, "The Social Basis of Antifeminism: Religious Networks and Culture," *Journal for the Scientific Study of Religion* 25, no. 1 (March 1986), 1–15; Christel Manning, *God Gave Us the Right: Conservative Catholic, Evangelical Protestant and Orthodox Jewish Women Grapple with Feminism* (New Brunswick, NJ: Rutgers University Press, 1999). It is interesting to note that Christian fundamentalists

and feminists have become allies in opposing trafficking in women, prostitution, and sex work.

26. For female clergy, see Patricia M. Y. Chang, "Introduction to Symposium: Female Clergy in the Contemporary Protestant Church: A Current Assessment," *Journal for the Scientific Study of Religion* 36 no. 4 (December 1997), 565–573; Elizabeth Cazden, *Antoinette Brown Blackwell: A Biography* (Old Westport, NY: Feminist Press, 1983); Mary S. Donovan, *Women Priests in the Episcopal Church: The Experience of the First Decade* (Cincinnati: Forward Movement, 1988); Blu Greenberg, "Is Now the Time for Orthodox Women Rabbis?" *Moment: The Magazine of Jewish Culture and Opinion* 18 (December 1993), 50–53, 74.

27. R. Laurence Moore, "Reinventing American Religion: Yet Again," *American Literary History* 12 (Spring–Summer 2000), 318–326; Cynthia Eller, *Living in the Lap of the Goddess: The Feminist Spirituality Movement in America* (New York: Crossroad, 1993); Ruth A. Wallace, "The Mosaic of Research on Religion: Where Are the Women? 1995 Presidential Address," *Journal for the Scientific Study of Religion* 36, no. 1 (March 1997), 1–12.

11

Conceptualizing Radicalism in U.S. Women's History

Ronald G. Walters

"Why bother studying radicals?" a recalcitrant student once asked, adding, "They always lose, anyway." One answer comes from a frequently seen bumper sticker: "Well-Behaved Women Seldom Make History." Nineteenth-century American radical women refused to be well-behaved, made history, and did not always lose. They are also among the most fascinating people of the period. For example, just juxtapose President Chester A. Arthur (1829–1886), a machine politician, and his contemporary, Victoria Woodhull (1838–1927), whose views on sexuality were so extreme that a critic dubbed her "Mrs. Satan."

This chapter is less about colorful individuals like Woodhull than it is an attempt to answer the student's question by suggesting various ways in which teaching nineteenth-century radical women's lives reveals things about American history, society, and culture that students might otherwise see less clearly, or not at all.[1]

Before going further, however, let's examine three pairs of crucial terms: *radical* and *reformer*, *presentism* and *perspective*, and *social class* and *social control*. Whether or not these words are explicitly discussed in the classroom, they embody concepts and assumptions that shape any consideration of nineteenth-century radical women.

The most crucial term, naturally, is *radical*. The word sometimes stands in distinction to *reactionary*, on the assumption that radicals are extremists on the left and reactionaries are extremists on the right. I don't find that distinction especially accurate, in part because notions of left and right are both historically specific and slippery. More fruitful—although still problematic—is the commonly made distinction between radicals and reformers. One of my courses begins by asking the class to define each term. What usually emerges is a distinction based on the degree of change a person seeks. Radicals want the world to be different in almost every respect—politically, economically, socially, and culturally. They want the old order swept away. In contrast, reformers seek less drastic change, perhaps only in one aspect of society and perhaps achieved incrementally, with much of the old order remaining intact. By this logic, someone who believes that banning alcohol is the key to a purer America is a reformer, and someone who advocates overthrowing the government and modeling the United States after a utopian community is a radical. According to this commonsense definition, many of the people called radicals in this essay might more properly be considered reformers. In practice, however, the distinction often breaks down, especially regarding race and gender, central issues for many nineteenth-century women radicals. If, for example, inequality between men and women, and whites and blacks, is a fundamental part of a society, are people who oppose it radicals or reformers? Moreover, simply for women to speak authoritatively on public issues was itself a radical act in the minds of many nineteenth-century Americans. Finally, ideas that seem radical in one era—like Victoria Woodhull's about sex and marriage—become widely accepted in a later one. From a twenty-first-century perspective, many of the radicals in this chapter look like reformers, except for a few like the anarchist Emma Goldman, who did indeed want to overthrow the political and economic system and pretty much everything else. In their own day, however, they seemed much more dangerous to the status quo and therefore appear here as radicals.

Rather than despair at arriving at a precise, fixed definition of *radical*, I see the problem of doing so as an opportunity to discuss two other significant concepts: presentism and perspective. By presentism, I mean reading the past strictly in terms of the present, without respecting differences between the two. There is always a risk of doing this, but the danger is especially strong when dealing with people, like radicals, who arouse strong positive or negative feelings. It is tempting, for example, to read nineteenth-century women's rights activists as the grandmothers of modern feminists, a reading that obscures vast differences in attitudes toward such crucial things as sexuality, family, and religion. In the classroom, however, I try to move beyond warnings about presentism to a far more useful topic for discussion, that of perspective—of the need to understand historical figures like the women in this chapter on their own terms while simultaneously measuring them from the vantage point of our moment in time. My goal here is not specific to radical women; it is rather to encourage students to think of history as an ongoing dialogue between past and present, one that respects differences across time and cultures, as well as continuities and commonalities.

Many things shape a person's perspective, including social class, an unavoidable issue when teaching the history of radical women. By the end of the nineteenth century, for many of them social change was *about* class (as well as gender), in particular about economic, social, and political inequalities between rich and poor, the working class and capitalists. But class figured into nineteenth-century reform and radicalism in subtler ways as well. Any kind of social movement requires free time, money, and inexpensive means of communication. By the 1830s, these were increasingly available to what historians commonly, and loosely, characterize as an emerging middle class, located primarily in small towns and in major urban areas.[2] Its numbers included many men and women prominent in the antislavery, temperance, women's rights, and other major reform movements of the day. From that observation, it is tempting to suggest two somewhat misleading conclusions. The first is that all the more moderate women in this chapter were middle class and that the extreme radicals were from the working class and perhaps were immigrants like Emma Goldman (1869–1940). As is usual with history, reality was far messier, with only a rough correlation between class and ethnicity and the degree of radicalism of nineteenth-century women. The second misleading conclusion is that the great movements of the period were about "social control," meaning that they were attempts by middle-class Americans to discipline and to impose their values on immigrants and the working class.[3] To a large degree that point is not so much wrong as obvious and not very helpful. It would be very hard to have any kind of movement for change that did not seek to make some group behave differently or eliminate it altogether. To focus exclusively on social control, moreover, obscures many important things about a radical commitment, including its social and political consequences, as well as the way it becomes a transformative part of a radical woman's life and identity.

Sometimes to make my point about social control, along with a few others, I ask my students to design their own radical movement—to figure out what they would have needed in the nineteenth century to create one. At an early stage in the process, some form of social control necessarily becomes a part of the agenda, but as a given rather than as something central to it. Perhaps only for a brief moment in the 1960s, and then only in some places, would it have been possible to organize a movement on the principle of "whatever." The exercise of designing a radical movement also gives life and substance to the other key concepts, which are crucial to have in mind but often boring if discussed only in the abstract.

But the student's question still stands—what can we gain by studying radicals, in this case radical women? There are at least three questions implied in his deceptively simple one: *why* study them? And then two further questions that all of us who teach have to face: *how* to bring them into the classroom? And *what* will they add to the curriculum? The pages that follow give a personal set of answers to those questions, based on three decades of experience pondering them.

Five Reasons *Why*

Embedded in my own courses are at least five answers to the why question, although the first is pedagogical and more for teachers than for students. It is that their lives are valuable teaching devices because they embody, often flamboyantly, important but otherwise abstract points about American history.

The second of the five answers is that some radical women are inspiring, often heroic figures. Take, for example, Isabella Van Wagenen (1797–1883), born a slave in New York state. After becoming a free woman, she joined a religious community in New York City in the 1830s. When it dissolved in a lurid scandal, she embarked on a long life as an abolitionist and militant advocate for the rights of all women, living out the new name she chose for herself, Sojourner Truth.

Beyond sometimes serving as role models, radicals reveal the friction points in American society—the places where the system was not working and the issues not being addressed satisfactorily. They sometimes did that in more complicated ways than appear at first glance. A case in point is the so-called temperance movement, a diverse campaign against alcohol that began in the early nineteenth century and culminated with Prohibition in the 1920s. While abuse of alcohol was a serious problem in the nineteenth century, women like the bar-smashing Carry Nation (1846–1911) and Frances Willard (1839–1898), the great leader of the Women's Temperance Union, also used temperance as a reproach to men, who were the great majority of drunkards. In their hands, temperance was both against a real problem and, more subtly, a challenge to masculine authority.

Radicals also tell us about the boundaries of a culture—the extreme edges of what is imaginable within it. A good example is the woman's suffrage movement of the second half of the nineteenth century, easy to fault from a present-day perspective for focusing primarily—although not exclusively—on voting rights, rather than on the much broader agenda of political, economic, and personal issues that emerged in twentieth-century feminism. But the fact that such issues were *not* as vigorously articulated earlier says much about what was conceivable within nineteenth-century American society, just as the fact that they became central later says much about our recent history.

My fifth and final reason for studying the lives of radicals has to do with a fundamental fact about American politics: our division of powers, both among the executive, legislative, and judicial branches of government and among federal, state, and local authorities. One result is a large amount of inertia; it is a system designed not to change course quickly. Because of that, it is important to have people who challenge the status quo, who force the public to face things it would have otherwise ignored, to take action when it might have preferred inaction, and to see new alternatives it would not otherwise have considered. When the first meeting of the nineteenth-century woman's rights movement gathered in Seneca Falls, New York, in 1848, the suggestion that women ought to have voting rights equal to men's was a radical one. Less than a century later, it was the law of the land and a basic reality of political life.

Teaching Strategies

If the *why* question has five parts, the answer to the *how* question is somewhat simpler but no less crucial because it speaks to how we organize our courses. I'll give the two approaches I use: the *light* and the *heavy* strategies.

I'll start with the light strategy, which is little more than inserting radical women as occasional figures in courses on other subjects. My inspiration for doing this comes from historian Leon Litwack, whose advice to fledgling teachers was "always tell stories." But these are not pointless stories but ones that reveal something significant about historical events. Radical women appear in my courses not because they are interesting or heroic but because they provide alternative viewpoints or function as a kind of Greek chorus, commenting on events and foretelling a better future. One example comes when teaching about America's extraordinary economic growth in the late nineteenth century. I find it effective to use the voices of women radicals to balance that success story with an assessment of its costs in human terms and to show that there were alternative American visions of how the world should be. Anarchist Emma Goldman always serves that purpose, but sometimes it is better to put students on the trail of less well-known critics of industrial capitalism. Instead of Red Emma, why not focus on her more obscure, but equally intriguing, colleague and rival, Voltarine de Cleyre (1866–1912), whom Goldman herself once called "the most gifted and brilliant anarchist woman America ever produced"? Some of de Cleyre's writings are available on line, including her attempt to reconcile

Anarchism and American Traditions. Or if not Goldman or de Cleyre, why not Lucy Parsons (1853–1942), wife of one of the anarchists hung in 1887 in the aftermath of the Haymarket Square riot in Chicago a year earlier? While few of Parsons's writings exist, the ones that do are especially intriguing because she was an African American woman married to a white man. For her, the realities of racism, as well as economic inequality, were not mere abstractions.[4]

The heavy strategy may be less available for teachers in institutions with rigid curricula, but perhaps not impossible. In my case, it involved creating a course titled "Race, Radicalism, and Reform in America: 1789–1919." Radical women are crucial characters in it, although they mix with male counterparts and some antiradicals and reactionaries. A basic premise of the course is that it is important for Americans to try to step outside their own culture and see it though the eyes of its critics. One way of doing that is to use the accounts of foreign observers, but focusing instead on radicals and reformers, and especially women, also lets me bring in fresh and outside perspectives on the past.

However odd it might seem to begin a nineteenth-century course in 1789 and to end with 1919, that period gives it a clear chronology. The course begins with changes unleashed by the American Revolution and ends with an ironic moment. In 1919, some of the agenda of nineteenth-century radicals was ful-filled: Slavery was gone (although not racism), soon alcohol would be banned, and women would have the vote (although not equality). Yet rapid urban growth and industrialization created massive new social problems and set new agen-das for radicals. By 1919, moreover, a combination of events narrowed the spectrum of American political debate by cutting off its most leftward edge. The question of whether the United States should enter World War I divided and weakened radicals. At the same time, the successful communist revolution in Russia emboldened conservatives to mount a counteroffensive against radi-cals, especially those opposed to the war. The legal campaign against them cul-minated in 1919–1920 in a "Red Scare" that gutted radical organizations and led to the prosecution and deportation of "alien" radicals, reinforcing, in the process, the notion that to be radical is to be "un-American."

Stopping at 1920 does not necessarily make for a happy ending, but it gives a narrative structure to the course while allowing the class to discuss major themes in nineteenth-century American history by examining proponents and opponents of change. Although that chronology works well for my purposes, other ways of framing a course dealing with radical women might be equally fruitful under other circumstances. For example, treating the period from Reconstruction through the 1960s allows an especially productive discussion of the tangled relationship between gender and race over a century in which both African Americans and women challenged political, social, and cultural inequality.

The first part of my heavy strategy, then, is to pick a reasonably coherent time period that encompasses significant historical events and then to figure out a practical, day-to-day pedagogy. I almost exclusively use primary source materials and rely on a few general works and on minilectures to provide students with the contexts they need to interpret the documents critically. At this point, it is hard not to sing hymns of praise for the Internet. It makes resources available that I could not, in 1980, have imagined ever being able to use in the classroom, such as the online American Periodical Series (APS), which reproduces in computer-searchable form an enormous number of nineteenth- and early-twentieth-century magazines and newspapers. Some of these databases, including the APS, are accessible only through libraries that have subscriptions to them, but publicly available sources such as those of the Library of Congress and the Gilder Lehrman Institute are so abundant that I could shift entirely to primary materials even without access to a research library. To return to an earlier example, when the course began, I could not have assigned Voltairine de Cleyre's *Anarchism and American Traditions*. Now it is available on the Internet, as are every extant ex-slave narrative and sources one might not immediately think of as useful for teaching about radical women. Among the latter is music, sometimes used to debate controversial issues in the nineteenth century. Several excellent online collections have sheet music covers, and often lyrics and music as well, weighing in on controversial issues such as women's rights, temperance, and slavery, often mocking radicals.[5] Even the act of looking for materials on radical women is a learning experience, especially if students learn to use Web sites judiciously. For example, an Internet search on "mrs. satan" and "woodhull" yields a strange variety of references, including to an opera about Victoria Woodhull (an honor accorded few women radicals).

My overall answer to the *how* question, therefore, comes down to pursuing alternative strategies, ranging from occasional insertions of radical women into conventional courses to creating a more general course in which they are major figures. It also embraces a positive aspect of the Internet—its wealth of source material on nineteenth-century American women radicals, including less known ones.

What's Gained?

What might teaching about women radicals add to the curriculum? In addition to helping students see American history from unfamiliar angles, I hope to encourage them to think more deeply about social change in the United States—about how, why, and when it occurs. There are at least two different ways I go about doing that. The first is more particular, focused, and adaptable for a unit within a general course. The second is essentially the technique used in my "Race, Radicalism, and Reform" course, although its components could be dismantled and appropriated piecemeal for courses on other subjects.

The first approach I will only outline because it is more intuitively obvious. It is to focus on one or all three of the great nineteenth-century social movements in which women had an exceptionally strong influence and to ask why and how gender mattered in them and how radical they were by the standards of the day. The three are antislavery, the women's rights movement after its founding convention at Seneca Falls in 1848, and the temperance movement, especially in its later stages, when women predominated and its focus widened to encompass other issues like voting rights for women. Each opens the way for treating significant questions about how women made their influence felt, what arguments they used, and what connected the cause to their individual lives. In sometimes surprising ways, students may be able to link these causes—especially temperance—to their own communities or families. (How did Chico, California, come to have a Frances Willard Avenue?) Moreover, because all three movements had male as well as female participants and each located men as being at the root of the problem, they provide excellent venues for talking about nineteenth-century gender roles and relations. I do not want to belabor this approach but simply suggest that it is possible to look at particular nineteenth-century social movements, and twentieth-century ones as well (the Civil Rights movement, for example), and ask how different history looks from a woman's perspective, especially a radical woman's one.

My second answer to the *why* question is more abstract and less connected to particular reform and radical movements. It rests on a desire to help students acquire tools to analyze past and present movements for social change. To do that, at the outset of my "Race, Radicalism, and Reform" course, I pose a question that I want them to ask about everyone they study: "Where did this person believe change begins?"

The answers are varied for the nineteenth century, and exploring them helps students understand significant continuities and changes between past and present social movements. Although the answers overlap to a degree and many nineteenth-century radical women would have given more than one, they would have been "with religion," "with the individual," "within the political system," "with a utopian community," "with violence and revolution," and "with expertise"—responses that might be given today, but minus a twenty-first-century one: "with the Internet" (or alternatively, "with a celebrity's endorsement"). I will discuss each briefly to give a clearer sense of how they represent different ways Americans have thought about changing their own society and history.

Religion and Social Change

Although nineteenth-century women were barred from becoming ministers, religion was an obvious starting point for women radicals and reformers. Women were a majority in most nineteenth-century Protestant congregations and deeply involved in religiously inspired organizations, such as missionary groups to convert the heathen in America and abroad. But by the 1830s, a major shift within many Protestant churches, usually called the Second Great Awakening, encouraged men and women to apply their religious principles to social issues such as drunkenness, prostitution, and slavery. Religion—especially the kind of evangelical Protestantism unleashed in the Second Great Awakening—provided radicals and reformers with three things: The first was a burning conviction that men and women could strive to bring Christ's kingdom to earth. The second was an organizational structure that could be adapted to secular causes. And the third was the old religious notion of a conversion experience—a sudden, dramatic transformation of an individual's consciousness. That model, sometimes expressed in secular language, lay behind a second nineteenth-century answer to the question of where social change begins.

One Person at a Time

Although the term *moral suasion* sounds odd in contemporary America, the concept is still with us and was powerful in nineteenth-century radical movements. Much like the notion of religious conversion, it was a belief that radical change proceeded one person at a time, beginning with an individual's immediate commitment to follow the path of righteousness. Thus the task of abolitionists who believed in moral suasion was to persuade Americans to renounce slavery immediately, not to compel them to do so. While men as well as women advocated moral suasion, it was an especially suitable tactic for the latter for two reasons: The first was practical. Disfranchisement meant that women had little leverage in using the political system to bring about reform, so focusing on changing the hearts and minds of individuals was a reasonable alternative. The second appeal of moral suasion was cultural. It was a commonplace in nineteenth-century America that men excelled in the realm of rational thought but that women were superior in moral judgment. It was possible for women, therefore, to make authoritative claims to speak on moral matters even while denied the vote.

Moral suasion required being able to get the message out to as many people as possible. In doing so, nineteenth-century radical women took advantage of every opportunity the period offered to move the public, including cheap print technologies, public meetings, protests, and occasional acts of civil disobedience. They also made use of popular culture in the form of songs, poetry, short stories, plays, and novels (the nineteenth-century's best-seller was Harriet Beecher Stowe's [1811–1896] antislavery novel *Uncle Tom's Cabin*). One particular instrument of change, however, deserves special mention and even attracted attention from European observers such as Alexis de Tocqueville (1805–1859), who noted an American penchant for joining together to create small private organizations called "voluntary associations." These were locally based but sometimes affiliated with national, even international, organizations, dedicated to a variety of purposes, ranging from purely social clubs to grassroots activist groups promoting causes like antislavery, temperance, and women's rights. Although men as well as women made use of them (usually in separate organizations), they were particularly significant for the latter because—lacking the vote, unable to become ministers, and facing strictures against speaking in public—they had little access to crucial political, economic, and social institutions controlled by men. Through voluntary associations, as in no other venue, women could try to change the minds of their fellow Americans.

Moral Politics

Moral suasion by itself often proved inadequate and frustrating. It was not, however, inconsistent with another approach, that of prodding the political system to take action. There was a small distance from voluntary associations persuading sinners to stop sinning to lobbying state legislatures to pass laws against slavery and drunkenness. One result was a turn in American reform and radical circles, visible by the 1840s, to use the government to enforce change rather than rely on moral suasion to convert individuals. While then, as now, some radicals viewed the state as the enemy, others began to see it as an effective means to their ends.

The turn toward coercion rather than conversion produced a number of political successes, notably in the 1840s and 1850s a spate of "Maine Laws," curbing the sale of alcoholic beverages. It was similarly embodied in campaigns, also underway by the 1840s, to build new kinds of institutions to house criminals, the insane, wayward children, and poor people. From a contemporary perspective, these sound custodial and punitive, not like instruments of reform. The women and men who pressed for them, however, argued that such institutions, if properly constructed and managed, could cure damaged human beings and thereby make America a more perfect nation.

When it came to envisioning the political system as an engine of change, Victoria Woodhull was at the extreme. She was born Victoria Claflin in Homer, Ohio, in 1838, the seventh child in a large and disorderly family. At age fifteen, she entered the first of two unstable marriages (a third turned out better) and embarked on a colorful series of careers as an actress, spiritualist, and in partnership with her younger sister, Tennessee (or Tennie C.), as the first women members of the New York Stock Exchange.

With that unlikely background, and a host of friends in radical and reform circles, Woodhull became the first woman candidate for president in 1872, running as the choice of a newly formed Equal Rights Party, with the vice presidential nomination offered to the great African American radical, Frederick Douglass (1818–1895), who appears not to have accepted it. The party was an eclectic mix of radicals, reformers, and general do-gooders, with a platform that encompassed multiple causes, such as racial justice, women's suffrage, temperance, world peace, and economic justice for workingmen and women. The campaign was a fiasco, and the press vilified Woodhull in every possible way, including her private life and her support for "free love"—the position that relations between men and women should be governed by attraction and mutual consent, not by marriage and legislation.

The futility of Woodhull's candidacy obscures two important points about it: The first is that both the party and her own speeches and writings proposed sweeping changes in the structure and role of the U.S. government, with equal rights for all as the starting point. The second is that it exemplifies the degree to which some nineteenth-century women were determined to turn a political system that excluded them to their own ends.

Heaven on Earth

There was another, vastly different approach to social change open to radical women: ignoring politics altogether and creating small-scale utopian communities, inspiring change by setting an example for the rest of the world to emulate. Even though religiously inspired communities began to appear in North America by the early eighteenth century, utopia-building flourished in the first half of the nineteenth century, with well over a hundred of them (some quite ephemeral) founded.

Part of the problem in assessing the vogue of creating utopian societies is that they had diverse origins—some religious and some secular—and could play contradictory roles. Some sought a complete withdrawal from the world in the name of personal salvation. In that sense, they offered a retreat from radicalism. Others, however, proclaimed that the right way to change the world was to present an alternative—to create a perfect human society in miniature, a model for the rest of humankind to imitate. If the measure of radicals is the degree of change they seek, those communitarians rank among the most radical Americans before the Civil War.

The range and occasional weirdness of antebellum utopian societies also masks the degree to which they reflected extreme responses to common discontents. The most obvious one was with gender inequality. Several of the most famous utopian communities radically reordered marital and sexual practices, the Shakers, for instance, by practicing celibacy and having male and female leaders, and the scandalous Oneida community through its notions of plural marriage and planned reproduction. Another similarly radical discontent was with economic inequality. Many expressed this by eliminating private property, either on the model of a Christian community of equals or in an early version of secular socialism articulated by European radicals like Robert Owen and Charles Fourier.

It was, however, rare that a utopian community addressed the most glaring inequality in nineteenth-century America—racial. The great exception was a venture called Nashoba, located on land in western Tennessee purchased in 1825 by a remarkable young Scotswoman, Frances Wright (1795–1852). She eventually became so infamous for her outspoken opposition to the oppression of women, to the economic exploitation of working people, and to established religions that "Fanny Wrightism" passed into the language as a pejorative term for radicalism, especially among women. Fanny Wright's notoriety, nonetheless, was only beginning to build when she planned Nashoba in 1825. She, in fact, conceived of it as a gift to her beloved adopted country. The one great stain on America's republican honor, she argued, was slavery. Nashoba would demonstrate a practical way to end it without violence. The project's rapid failure underscores the fragility of that dream. Nashoba itself, however, was a sign of how thoroughly persuaded some nineteenth-century radical women were that a tiny model of a perfect society could change the world.

Revolutionary Violence

As Fanny Wright demonstrated, the Atlantic was never a barrier blocking the migration of radicals or radical ideas. After the Civil War, this transoceanic exchange intensified. Among the newcomers to the United States were European versions of socialism, communism, and anarchism. They came in many varieties, some quite mild and respectable. From the 1890s through World War I, the Socialist Party, for example, was a legitimate political force in

America, electing local and state officials and gathering more than 900,000 votes for its presidential candidate, Eugene V. Debs, in 1912. Other ideologies were far more extreme and uncompromising in their assaults on private property, the state, religion, and marriage. Among these was European anarchism, which answered the question of where change begins in a way that most Americans did not want to hear—with revolutionary violence. By far the most famous anarchist of her day was a Lithuanian-born Jewish immigrant, Emma Goldman. When she and a sister left for America in 1885, she was sixteen years old and already a rebel in spirit, soon to be a vigorous participant in radical debates.

Among the many beliefs that made Goldman anathema to most Americans was her belief in violence as a tool for social change, but to focus on that aspect of revolutionary anarchist ideology is to miss important things about nineteenth-century radicalism and about her. The first is that anarchist advocacy of violence was part of a broad critique of oppression, one conclusion of which was diametrically opposed to the messages of Fanny Wright or the women's suffrage movement. For Goldman and her allies, America was not evolving toward republican perfection and was not a model for the rest of the world, as Wright had believed. It was just another oppressive capitalist state. Anarchists maintained, moreover, that contrary to what most Americans, including members of the Socialist Party, assumed, the present political system would not and could not end injustice. Violence, therefore, was the only weapon of the oppressed, an opinion shared by others in later generations.

To leave it at that, however, does nothing to counter a common early-twentieth-century caricature of anarchists that does Goldman a major injustice. The image was fanatical, joyless, hate-filled bomb throwers. In contrast, the real Goldman was a lively, charismatic free spirit who shocked and fascinated mainstream Americans with her corrosive attacks on marriage and her advocacy of birth control and sexual freedom. She also loved parties (showing up at one dressed as a nun), a side of her embodied in a quotation often attributed to her to the effect that "if I can't dance, I don't want to be in your revolution." The spirit is Goldman's, even though the exact words are not.

There is a paradox here: Someone who loved life and lived it passionately helped add violence to the American radical list of starting points for change.

Leaving It to Experts

In the last decades of the nineteenth century, a new answer to the "where does change begin?" question emerged. It was "with expertise and the application of specialized knowledge to social problems"—a central assumption in

Progressivism, the major political movement of the early twentieth century. This answer drew on the rising prestige of older professions such as law and medicine and newer ones like engineering and social work. For women, this had mixed implications. While they were excluded from many of these professions, notably law, medicine, and engineering, they were centrally involved in others. For instance, two exemplars of this new approach, Jane Addams (1860–1935), the first American woman to win a Nobel Peace Prize, and her colleague, Florence Kelley (1859–1932), are imposing figures in the history of American social work. Women could, moreover, claim their own kind of expertise as women and mothers, thus empowering them to speak authoritatively on a number of "women's issues."

To place faith for social change in the hands of experts marked major changes in the history of nineteenth-century American reform and radicalism. It represented a shift from more religious to more secular language, and away from the millennialistic and utopian optimism of the antebellum period toward a belief that problems could be managed, rather than cured, and treated piecemeal rather than as part of bringing God's kingdom to earth. Antebellum radicals also mistrusted professionals, whereas their late-nineteenth-century counterparts often saw them, and their methods of gathering and analyzing data, as crucial to promoting social change. In that respect, the new turn toward expertise seems moderate, even potentially conservative, when compared with the strands of utopianism in pre–Civil War movements. Although that is correct in some respects, two other things are also true: One is that expertise and special knowledge could be used by radicals as well as reformers or reactionaries. Indeed, Karl Marx (1818–1883) and Friedrich Engels (1820–1895) themselves advocated a "scientific socialism." The other thing is that some women who endorsed the new approach were genuine radicals. Florence Kelley—who acquired a great deal of political influence in Illinois and nationally—was a socialist. As a young woman, she translated Marxist tracts into English and corresponded with Engels.

By the eve of World War I, however, the map of American radicalism was far different from what it had been in the early nineteenth century, and the options for women radicals and reformers were more extensive, with older modes of changing the world still around, and newer ones—whether on the socialist left or in the form of social engineering—emerging.

Conclusion

There is a useful artificiality in asking students to pose the question "where does change begin?" In practice, radical women often would have given multiple answers over the course of their careers. Victoria Woodhull is a prime example. She practiced moral suasion through her speeches and in the newspaper she and her sister edited, *Woodhull & Claflin's Journal.* She was willing to work with voluntary associations to support women's suffrage and her presidential campaign. The latter, moreover, exemplified a faith that women would eventually be able to work directly through the political system. Even Emma Goldman, perhaps the most radical woman discussed here, saw no incompatibility in using moral suasion to promote violence and revolution. For most nineteenth-century women radicals, the paths to perfection were multiple, if sometimes conflicted.

Yet asking the question of where change begins helps take us into the minds of radical women and into the larger society of which they were a part. It also helps students see—from different perspectives—how profoundly the United States itself changed over the course of the nineteenth century, as did the causes and tactics of radical women. By 1900, the problems of an urban, industrial society dominated in ways that could not have been foreseen in 1800. While old instruments of reform persisted, new technologies were present or on the horizon by 1900, and even more by 1919, when my long nineteenth century ended. Cinema was in its infancy, and radio was waiting in the wings, with equally revolutionary means of communication appearing throughout the twentieth century. Whether these new technologies could be turned to radical ends was—and remains—an open question.

Looking beyond 1919, some of the great achievements of women radicals look like hollow victories: Banning alcohol proved to be a fiasco, voting rights for women did not immediately translate into political power, and ending slavery was only a step toward racial justice yet to be achieved. In their struggle to make the world a better place, nineteenth-century radical women obviously did not always succeed, at least not in their lifetimes. They nonetheless brought to light some of America's darkest problems and proposed compelling alternatives. In so doing, they help us and our students to understand our common past more deeply, to think more clearly about how social change occurs, and to imagine alternative Americas. Even if they did not always win, radical women made a difference.

NOTES

1. No single book treats the history of nineteenth-century radical women, but the following general works provide background material for parts of the century: Paul Buhle, *Marxism in the USA: From 1870 to the Present Day* (London: Verso, 1987); Lori D. Ginzberg, *Women in Antebellum Reform* (Wheeling, IL: Harlan Davidson, 2000); Steven Mintz, *Moralists and Modernizers: America's Pre–Civil War Reformers* (Baltimore:

Johns Hopkins University Press, 1995); Timothy Messar-Kruse, *The Yankee International: Marxism and the American Reform Tradition* (Chapel Hill: University of North Carolina Press, 1998); Nell Irvin Painter, *Standing at Armageddon: The United States, 1877–1919* (New York: W. W. Norton, 1987); and Ronald Walters, *American Reformers: 1815–1860*, rev. ed. (New York: Hill and Wang, 1997 [1978]). The bibliographies of these books serve as guides to the many biographies of women mentioned in this article. In addition, most of them are the subjects of various Web sites that give both primary sources and (mostly accurate) biographical information.

2. A concise commentary on the rise of a new middle class in nineteenth-century America is Stuart M. Blumin, "The Hypothesis of Middle-Class Formation: A Critique and Some Proposals," *American Historical Review* 90, no. 2 (April 1985): 299–338.

3. A sophisticated defense of the "social control" view, as well as a major work on nineteenth-century reformers, is Paul S. Boyer, *The Urban Masses and Moral Order* (Cambridge: Harvard University Press, 1978).

4. Works by de Cleyre and Parsons, as well as other primary source material, are available at the Anarchy Archives, http://dwardmac.pitzer.edu/Anarchist_archives/index.html.

5. The Sheet Music Consortium posted an extremely helpful set of links to online collections at http://digital.library.ucla.edu/sheetmusic/.

12

Thinking Globally about U.S. Women's History

Mary E. Frederickson

Thinking globally about women's history in the United States expands our understanding of the social, political, and economic changes that have taken place throughout the world and provides new perspectives on major topics in American history. A global focus, in contrast to traditional national or continent-centered history, contextualizes the experiences of American women across time and place and uncovers the shared histories of women around the world. Contemporary globalization has increased the interconnectedness of capital and labor and transformed the lives of women on every continent in terms of family, work, and culture. Witnessing these changes today alerts us to the importance and potential of examining patterns and lessons of global exchange in the past.

Over her long career, Eleanor Roosevelt recognized the interdependence of women around the globe and saw women in the "vanguard of change," as leaders in seeking social and economic justice as a foundation for world peace. In 1919, she attended the International Congress of Working Women in Washington, D.C., with representatives from nineteen nations. In 1933, she addressed a group of several thousand women from across the world, called for the creation of "a new social order," and argued that "we must either cooperate as a whole and rise...or go down [together]." In 1960, two years before her death, Roosevelt reflected that while "differences exist among people...in families...within nations and...in the world," she believed strongly that "the dignity of women's equality...is important the world over."[1]

The global perspective endorsed by Eleanor Roosevelt provides a powerful model for a new way of teaching women's history in the United States. When the focus in women's history widens to incorporate a global approach, our understanding of American history broadens as well. Students see the United States as one nation among many, with a history shaped by the movement of people, ideas, capital, and culture back and forth across national boundaries and far-flung regions of the globe. Twenty-first-century contemporary politics demand that we teach the history of the United States in the context of economic, political, and social changes that have taken place around the world.

What do historians mean when they talk about global approaches to the study of the past? Global history, also called world or transnational history, is a relatively new field developed in the 1980s that opens, as one scholar put it, "a world of comparative possibility," by claiming that historical processes evolve in different locations and are constructed in the "spaces between," as people and ideas move from one place or region to another.[2] Global history has become increasingly important as globalization—the increased interconnectedness and mobility of capital, technology, labor, and goods and services throughout the world—has accelerated dramatically in the twenty-first century.

A global approach to women's history is well illustrated in three major movements: antislavery activism and women's rights, the international peace movement, and women's labor history. The global history of these movements demonstrates how American women have been influenced by cultures and societies outside the United States and how American women have shaped social and political changes abroad. Women activists in the United States have never operated in a vacuum. On issues from theology to slavery, from suffrage to free speech, from international peace to economic justice, American women have drawn on their own unique and diverse cultural experiences and simultaneously learned from women of other nations.[3]

Antislavery Activism and Women's Rights

Many students of the American past encounter women's history for the first time when they learn that the movement for women's rights in the United States emerged out of antislavery and abolitionist organizations in the early nineteenth century. As students engage this material, they become familiar with a range of historical figures, such as Elizabeth Cady Stanton, Lucretia Mott, Maria Stewart, Sojourner Truth, and Frederick Douglass, who all feature prominently in American reform movements both before and after the Civil War.[4] Often the actions and experiences of these women and men are studied within the confines of American history, but what happens when students are encouraged to look across the Atlantic and analyze antislavery and women's movements in comparative perspective? How did the larger Atlantic world affect American activists? Did reformers from the United States influence political change in Great Britain and Europe, and vice versa? What benefits derive from a comparative approach to American women's political activism?

The antislavery and women's rights movements clearly illustrate the process of transnational exchange. The Enlightenment tradition argued that because of their moral and rational natures, all individuals were entitled to the same rights of freedom and equality. Opponents of slavery in the eighteenth and nineteenth centuries, including significant numbers of black and white women, collectively developed a sophisticated antislavery ideology, which eventually resulted in widespread organization to dismantle the system of enslavement that had shaped economic, social, and political structures throughout the Atlantic world.

At the same time, ideas of women's equality emerged in continental Europe, Great Britain, and the United States that promoted powerful new ideas about the advancement of women's rights. Early American women such as Judith Sargent Murray and Mercy Otis Warren read Mary Wollstonecraft's *Vindication of the Rights of Woman*, published in Great Britain in 1792. Women activists and writers in the burgeoning new republic became supportive allies of British and European proponents of women's rights, including Frances Wright, whose book *Views of Society and Manners in America* (1821) painted a positive view of American women and their access to higher education; Charles Fourier, who criticized limitations on women's talent; George Sand, who penned radical critiques of traditional marriage; Harriet Martineau, who underscored the leadership and courage that American women brought to the antislavery movement; and Harriet Taylor Mill, who reported for the British press on American suffrage conventions in the mid-nineteenth century, and her husband, John Stuart Mill, who promoted women's suffrage in his book *The Subjection of Women* (1869).[5]

British and European women traversed the Atlantic and toured the United States, where they found receptive audiences among Americans eager for new ideas about women's rights, antislavery, and suffrage. American women, in turn, crossed the Atlantic in the opposite direction, where they absorbed new ideas about social and economic reform, antislavery, and women's rights from their counterparts in Britain, France, and Germany.

One international incident with tangible consequences for the U.S. women's rights movement occurred when Lucretia Mott and Elizabeth Cady Stanton led a delegation of American women to the World's Anti-Slavery Convention in London, in June 1840. The American women, along with their British counterparts, were forced to sit behind a "bar and curtain" in the balcony, where they could be neither seen nor heard.[6] Lucretia Mott viewed such treatment from the conservative British antislavery activists with outrage. She scoffed at this so-called World's Convention, the name of which was, in Mott's words, "merely a 'poetical license'—(alias—a rhetorical flourish)," because only men were allowed to participate.[7] Called the "lioness of the meeting," Mott's experience in London was transformative. She wrote Maria Weston Chapman from Dublin in late July 1840, "I have sometimes shrunk from a defense of our rights, when others have gone forward."[8] After the humiliation she experienced at the Anti-Slavery Convention, Mott hardened her resolve to work for universal rights by abolishing slavery and simultaneously advancing the cause of woman's rights. Her experiences in Britain opened Mott's eyes to new forms of activism and a broader constituency of women. Reticent no longer, Mott returned to the United States ready to do battle as an advocate for all those Americans denied access to basic human political and economic rights.

Comparisons of the American and British antislavery and women's rights movements reveal striking similarities and differences that remain invisible if we do not look at U.S. women's history in a context that transcends national boundaries. The Atlantic world of the eighteenth and nineteenth centuries shaped an American ideology grounded in Enlightenment ideas of equality and freedom. Those beliefs provided the impetus for emancipating enslaved Americans and extending the rights of citizenship to all men and women.

Ideas and people flowed back and forth across "the wide water," as Lucretia Mott put it, and antislavery activists and early feminists in the United States, Britain, and Europe expanded their worlds as they read each other's writings, welcomed visiting speakers, and witnessed differences in gendered public practice.[9] As Mott and Stanton discovered at the World's Anti-Slavery Convention, the exclusion of women delegates galvanized their determination to return home and transform the American political system. This international incident set the stage for the first U.S. woman's rights convention that Stanton, Mott, and others organized at Seneca Falls, New York, in 1848. Women's rights conventions held in Worcester, Massachusetts, in 1850 and 1851 followed shortly, and then a series of women's rights meetings in Ohio, New York, and Massachusetts.[10]

Antislavery activists in the United States did not speak in one voice. Out of a broad range of views on slavery, emancipation, racism, and prescriptions for gendered behavior, women as different as African American journalist Maria Stewart of Boston and New York; the Grimke sisters, white women from an aristocratic South Carolina slave-owning family; and Sojourner Truth, a former slave who became a preacher, abolitionist, and women's rights activist, all assumed crucial leadership positions within the movement.

Exposing themselves to frequent ridicule and tarnished reputations, a few vocal American women and their British counterparts openly addressed the sexual violation of female slaves known to be widespread, particularly in the southern United States. On both sides of the Atlantic, the story of Margaret Garner, a young Kentucky slave woman who in 1856 escaped across the Ohio River with her husband and children, revealed the horror of slavery and the consequences of sexual violence through the act of seeking freedom through infanticide. When Margaret Garner slit her two-year-old daughter's throat to prevent her from being returned to slavery, she was put on trial in Cincinnati, in one of the lengthiest, costliest, and most dramatic cases of the 1850s fugitive slave era. White abolitionist Lucy Stone visited Margaret Garner in prison and testified on her behalf, defending the "deep maternal love" that saved her child from the "degradation" to which "female slaves must submit."[11] As they worked tirelessly for more than three decades, antislavery feminists, and even those nonfeminists within the movement, shaped a new political culture that revolutionized the way American and British women, slave and free, saw themselves and were seen by others.

The International Women's Peace Movement

American women first became engaged in international work through their involvement in antislavery and women's rights movements. As we have seen, their interaction with similar movements across the Atlantic broadened their perspectives, sharpened their arguments, and honed their resolve for social change and political transformation at home. No movement illustrates the transformative power of international participation better than U.S. feminists' dedication to international peace during the late nineteenth and early twentieth centuries.

As imperialism and war increasingly dominated Europe, Africa, and Asia in the late nineteenth century, U.S. women from a broad range of backgrounds worked with women from around the world to build cross-cultural alliances and foster internationalism. Turning their attention and organizing skills to reshaping an international culture in which wars were seen as acceptable ways to resolve disputes, U.S. women played crucial roles in founding the International Council of Women in 1888 and the feminist International Alliance of Women in 1904. Delegations of American women regularly traveled to The Hague for peace conferences from 1899 until the beginning of World War I.[12]

American, British, and Western European women forged the first of these international alliances and were soon joined by women from Eastern Europe, Asia, Indochina, the Middle East, Africa, Australia, and New Zealand. Documents collected in the International Archives of the Women's Movement in Amsterdam and later in the U.S. World Center for Women's Archives recount a history of peace activism in which American women from social activist and reformer Jane Addams, to African American educator Mary Church Terrell, to suffragist Carrie Chapman Catt, to socialist Kate Richards O'Hare played prominent roles. Membership lists reveal local grassroots chapters of peace organizations across the United States, which promoted a counterdiscourse of viable alternatives to arms races, standing armies, and military responses marked by conflict and death.[13]

When World War I broke out in Europe in August 1914, women pacifists collaborated out of "a burning desire to do something." Women from the Netherlands, Belgium, Britain, Germany, and Hungary met in Amsterdam in February 1915 and issued the "Call to the Women of all Nations" to participate in an International Congress of Women to be held at The Hague in April 1915. American Jane Addams presided over the Hague Congress, which drew 1,300 women from over a dozen nations, those already at war, as well as those, like the United States, that still remained neutral.[14] The women attending passed a series of bold resolutions that called for continuous mediation, the expansion of women's suffrage, an international society of nations, a congress of women, and a controversial plan to send envoys to specific nations in an attempt to end the war.

In sharp contrast to the widespread belief that war was inevitable, women peace activists argued that "a permanent peace" could be realized. They wanted nothing less than total and universal disarmament. To this end, they established an International Committee of Women for Permanent Peace, which at war's end took the name Women's International League for Peace and Freedom (WILPF). The league moved its headquarters to Geneva (home to the League of Nations) and pledged to work for the goals of both world peace and women's equality.[15]

As women from the United States became engaged in international work for peace, their sense of American exceptionalism diminished. On a trip around the world in 1911–1912, Carrie Chapman Catt, for example, at first reported on "women's awakening in the East," but then tempered her remarks, noting that she was finding "millions [of women in the Orient] who have always enjoyed more personal freedom than was accorded to most European women a century ago, and more than is now permitted to thousands of women under our boasted Western civilization."[16]

Despite WILPF's creed condemning discrimination on the basis of race and color, in the first decades of the twentieth century, the women's international peace movement was dominated by white Western European and American women who often unconsciously established and reinforced ethnic, class, and language barriers that made it difficult for women from Eastern Europe, Asia, Latin America, and Africa to participate. Women from around the world who spoke multiple languages often noted the "linguistic disabilities of their English-speaking colleagues," referring to the "poor monolingual Americans."[17]

Racism in the United States hindered the participation of women of color, and few African American women participated in the international meetings organized by peace activists. Mary Church Terrell, for example, described herself as the only delegate to the 1919 WILPF congress "who had a drop of African blood in her veins." She complained of having to carry the burden of "representing the women of all the non-white countries in the world."[18]

While often hampered by these internal conflicts and contradictions, women's transnational alliances and policy initiatives were instrumental in the creation of internationalism in the twentieth century. Jane Addams and Emily Greene Balch, awarded Nobel Prizes in 1931 and 1946, respectively, for their work as international activists, sustained the concept of the League of Nations in the interwar years and developed innovative new forms of world cooperation, including international waterways and air routes and designated protected regions throughout the world. During World War II, women activists worked to help the victims of Nazi persecution and later supported Eleanor Roosevelt in her work to draft the Universal Declaration of Human Rights and her insistence that women's equal rights be included in the United Nations Charter adopted in 1948.[19]

For those teaching and writing about U.S. women's history, studying the international collective identity created by women in the first half of the twentieth century opens new possibilities for evaluating the long-term impact of transnational connections among women. The first international women's movement flourished between 1830 and 1860; the second in the period from 1885 to 1920. Women around the world began to organize again in response to the spread of nuclear weapons in the 1950s and 1960s, and a third global women's movement developed in the 1970s, defining itself through four world conferences: Mexico City in 1975, Copenhagen in 1980, Nairobi in 1985, and Beijing in 1995.[20]

These world conferences, which have drawn as many as 5,000 official delegates from 189 countries around the world, paralleled those meetings organized by women activists in the late nineteenth and early twentieth centuries. To break new ground in terms of women's struggle for advancement, the agenda of the contemporary global women's movement initially focused on women's specific concerns about economic security, employment, violence, and access to health care and education. Since 1995, the more comprehensive global agenda for change that has evolved focused on the impact of trade networks on gender and social development. In collaboration with women around the world, U.S. women have called for more corporate accountability, a reexamination of U.S. trade policy, and an analysis of the gendered dynamics of agriculture and the global food supply.[21]

A Global Perspective on Women's Labor History

Women's labor history provides an excellent example of a field in which our understanding of gender and work has been enhanced by transnational and global approaches. Patterns of work, labor migration, worker organization, ethnic and racial identities, and cultural production become clearer from a global perspective that takes into consideration economic, political, and cultural forces that operate across national boundaries.

During the nineteenth and twentieth centuries, the American economy thrived because of the large number of immigrant workers who entered the country to work in both agriculture and industry. Gendered work patterns varied across the United States, and industrialization transformed the lives of men and women alike. A majority of American trade union leaders came out of immigrant communities, and the ideology of the late-nineteenth- and early-twentieth-century American labor movement incorporated many ideas from abroad, ranging from the British concept of guilds in the building trades, to Eastern European critiques of capital and labor, socialist principles of cooperative economics and collective action, and strategies such as strikes and walkouts.[22]

Immigrant union activists included women like Rose Pesotta, born Rakhel Peisoty in Ukraine, who became vice president of the International Ladies Garment Workers Union, and Swedish-born Mary Anderson, who directed the Women's Bureau of the Department of Labor for more than a quarter of a century. Rose Schneiderman immigrated from Russian Poland at age five, organized Local 23 of the United Cloth Hat and Cap Makers' Union in 1903, and helped found the International Ladies Garment Workers Union in 1914, three years after the Triangle Shirtwaist fire in 1911.[23] Schneiderman also served for many years as president of the National Women's Trade Union League and in that capacity developed a close relationship with Eleanor Roosevelt, who credited Schneiderman with teaching her "all she knew about trade unionism."[24] The impact of women labor activists on the Roosevelt administration was clearly evident when the National Industrial Recovery Act granted American workers the right to bargain collectively with their employers in 1933.

American women workers, from the nineteenth century on, have played active roles in transnational labor organizations that called for "common standards of hours and payment." The International Federation of Working Women drew delegates from nations in North and South America, Europe, and Asia. In 1923, these meetings included textile workers, garment workers, and agricultural workers from more than a dozen nations who discussed the eight-hour day, child labor, maternity insurance, night work, unemployment, hazardous occupations, and immigration. Labor activist Alice Henry wrote later that the discussions were "trying and testing," but all in attendance "sincerely intended to think and to speak and to vote as world citizens."[25]

The reform agenda established by these early international organizations set a course for women activists, labor reformers, and trade unionists during the first half of the twentieth century. As the number of women entering the paid workforce increased, trade unions found it increasingly difficult to ignore both the needs of women workers and the activism of women union members. Across the decades, gendered resistance by women labor activists has had a powerful ripple effect in workplaces and communities where women transformed their autonomy as workers into acts of confrontation. Women workers in the United States have a long history of gradually changing the terms of their employment by speaking their minds, whether quietly to each other, openly to their employers, or more forcefully, by staging walkouts and strikes.

As global interdependence increases, transnational feminist organizations are working more actively than ever before to address systematic changes in the world economy. Activists in the United States participate in a broad range of organizations, including established groups like the YWCA and League of Women Voters, both of which have new global initiatives that target women and build leadership skills through education and exchange programs, and the Coalition of Labor Union Women (CLUW), which has endorsed a "Women in the Global Economy" campaign that fights sweatshops and supports trade that improves wages, living standards, and working conditions.[26]

New labor alliances have formed as well, particularly as U.S. industries have moved their factories into Mexico and Central and South America: The Coalition for Justice in the Maquiladoras, Women on the Border, the Colectiva Feminista Binacional and La Mujer Obrera, the Association for Women's Rights in Development (AWID), and the Comité Fronterizo de Obreros (CFO)– Committee of Women Workers all sponsor cooperative programs that foster the transnational organization of women workers. Women Organizing for Social Justice in Central America—STITCH—and other female-sponsored social justice organizations affirm the experiences of individual women workers and the power of the collective; they run leadership training, research, and education programs with a transnational focus in communities affected by global industrial development.[27]

Twenty-first-century globalization promises higher standards of living and education for women around the world, but it also has the power to transform traditional cultures, draw women into low-wage jobs, and increase unemployment, prostitution, sexual slavery, and trafficking in women and children. The legal ownership of humans ended in the United States in 1865, but in 2008 more than 50,000 enslaved people lived in the United States, and more are brought into the country each year. Worldwide, the number of slaves has increased dramatically since the end of World War II, and the price of slaves has plummeted to a fraction of what it was in 1850. The number of enslaved people alive today surpasses the total population stolen from Africa during the transatlantic slave trade. A new generation of antislavery activists is currently fighting a global system that enslaves 27 million people.[28]

As in the nineteenth century, the largest percentage of enslaved people today works in agriculture. But a significant number of women and children are sold each year into the global sex trade or for work in households not only in India, Pakistan, and Cambodia but also in London, New York, Paris, Los Angeles, and Tokyo. The trade in women and children for sexual slavery has drawn the attention of international activists for many decades, but these efforts intensified in 2003, when the United Nations "Protocol to Prevent, Suppress and Punish Trafficking in Persons, Especially Women and Children" went into effect. Twenty-first-century antislavery activists, many of them women, are working to end global slavery by legally prohibiting the profits and products linked to the slave trade.[29]

As this effort continues, these contemporary activists follow in the footsteps of a long line of women reformers, from Lucretia Mott, Sojourner Truth, and Elizabeth Cady Stanton, who allied themselves with British antislavery activists in the 1840s, to Eleanor Roosevelt, whose work a century later resulted in the Universal Declaration of Human Rights statement that "No one shall be held in slavery or servitude; slavery and the slave trade shall be prohibited in all their forms," to women delegates at the Fourth World Conference on Women in Beijing in 1995, who called again for the "enforcement of international conventions on trafficking in persons and on slavery."[30]

Twenty-first-century U.S. women activists are attempting to raise awareness about the importance of "fair globalization," which will increase the accountability of multinational corporations, regulate international trade and migration, and increase opportunities for decent jobs and social equality. This effort mirrors that of American women like Rose Schneiderman and Rose Pesotta, who spoke out forcefully about the human costs of industrialization in previous generations. The significance of U.S. women's labor activism has not changed across time. Globalization requires new forms of organization, but as United Electrical, Radio and Machine Workers of America (UE) member Lynda Leech wrote recently about her union's "Hands across the Border" initiative to organize women workers in the new global economy: "Let history repeat itself," she wrote, "as oppression is overcome."[31]

A New Global Paradigm for U.S. Women's History

What happens when we examine the narrative arc of women's experience in the United States from a global perspective? First, this work provides a healthy antidote to viewing the American experience as exceptional or unique. Second, we find that U.S. history is more similar to other national histories than different from them. At times, U.S. women have broken new ground and set new patterns; at other historical moments, they have followed the lead of activists in other parts of the world. Third, a global paradigm invigorates the teaching of women's history by opening new research areas and showing us different ways of understanding the history of a particular region or nation.

Teachers can better prepare students for the twenty-first century by giving them access to a history that is as complex and interconnected as the society in which they live and work. Women in the United States have never lived in isolation from the rest of the world, although their history has often been taught as if that were the case. When U.S. women performed on a world stage at the London antislavery meeting in 1840, the International Congress at The Hague in 1915, and at the Beijing Conference in 1995, they brought home initiatives that altered the domestic debate. For example, the delegation of U.S. women to the United Nations Conference on Women in Beijing in 1995, led by Hillary Rodham Clinton, returned home determined to advance the goals of "equality, development and peace for all women everywhere in the interest of all humanity."[32] Clinton's statement at the Beijing conference that "human rights are women's rights and women's rights are human rights, once and for all" echoed back to the 1948 United Nation's Universal Declaration of Human Rights and forward to her own campaign for president in 2008.[33]

A global view of U.S. women's history changes the overall narrative, as well as the specific details of what we see as U.S. history. The story is recast from one that moves sequentially from one presidential administration to the next, and from one war to another, to a more complicated analysis of diverse political and economic struggles to extend American citizenship across the boundaries of gender, race, and national origin. New historical players emerge, many of them women and not all of them American. International organizations, a number of which have been operating since the nineteenth century, take center stage. When we study U.S. women's history from a global perspective, we begin to see how transnational ideas about politics and reform have affected the United States and how worldwide labor systems have transformed American society and culture.

This brings us back to Eleanor Roosevelt's belief that women in the United States must join forces with women around the globe to work for a lasting peace realized through economic justice and collective political responsibility. These words present even more of a challenge in post-9/11 America than they did in the twentieth century. The United States faces daunting complexities that transcend national boundaries: an ongoing "war on terror," an unyieldingly competitive transnational economy, extraordinary global health crises, and relentless poverty throughout the world. In this context, thinking globally about U.S. women's history expands our understanding of the American past and provides new perspectives on major topics: antislavery reform, women's rights, citizenship, war, the labor movement, and work. A global approach to U.S. women's history reveals long-standing patterns of transnational intellectual, political, and cultural exchange that demonstrate what can happen when American women see themselves as citizens of the world.

NOTES

I thank the editors and Brigid O'Farrell, Eleanor Roosevelt Papers, George Washington University, for insightful readings of this chapter.

1. Blanche Wiesen Cook, *Eleanor Roosevelt*, volume 2, 1933–1938 (New York: Viking), 119. Eleanor Roosevelt Speech, May 8, 1960 at Brandeis University, Waltham, Massachusetts, cited by Lys Anzia, "Endless Work for a Peaceful World." Women News Network, August 26, 2006 at http://womennewsnetwork.net/2006/08/26/endless-work-for-a-peaceful-world/ (accessed August 25, 2008). Eleanor Roosevelt, "My Day Column," April 30, 1962, available in the "The Eleanor Roosevelt Papers

Project" at http://www.gwu.edu/~erpapers/myday/displaydoc.cfm?_y=
1962&_f=md005101 (accessed February 29, 2008).

2. See C. A. Bayly, Sven Beckert, Matthew Connelly, Isabel Hofmeyr, Wendy
Kozol, and Patricia Seed, "AHR Conversation: On Transnational History." *American
Historical Review*, 3, no. 5 (December 2006), 1440–1464. Patricia Seed referred to
transnational history as a new field that offers a "world of comparative possibility." For
a comprehensive overview of recent work in global women's history, see Bonnie G.
Smith, ed., *Women's History in Global Perspective*, volumes 1–3 (Urbana: University of
Illinois Press, 2004, 2005); and Bonnie G. Smith, ed., *Global Feminisms since 1945*
(London: Routledge, 2000).

3. Bonnie S. Anderson, *Joyous Greetings: The First International Women's
Movement* (New York: Oxford University Press, 2000), p. 3.

4. See Jean Fagan Yellin and John C. Van Horne, eds., *The Abolitionist Sisterhood:
Women's Political Culture in Antebellum America* (Ithaca, NY: Cornell University Press,
1994), especially Kathryn Kish Sklar's "Coda: Toward 1848" on antislavery women in the
international sphere and " 'Women Who Speak for an Entire Nation': American and
British Women at the World Anti-Slavery Convention, London, 1840," 301–333.

5. Eileen Hunt Botting, "Wollstonecraft's Philosophical Impact on Nineteenth-
Century American Women's Rights Advocates." *American Journal of Political Science*,
48, no. 4 (October 2004), 707–722; Elizabeth Ann Bartlett, *Liberty, Equality, Sorority:
The Origins and Interpretation of American Feminist Thought: Frances Wright, Sarah
Grimke, and Margaret Fuller* (Brooklyn, NY: Carlson, 1994); John Stuart Mill and
Harriet Taylor Mill, *Essays on Sex Equality*, Alice S. Rossi, ed. (Chicago: University of
Chicago Press, 1970).

6. See Sklar, " 'Women Who Speak for an Entire Nation,' " 301–306.

7. *Slavery and "The Woman Question"* [Lucretia Mott's Diary], Frederick B.
Tolles, ed. (Haverford, PA: Friends' Historical Association, 1952), 29.

8. Lucretia Mott to Maria Weston Chapman, July 29, 1840, Boston Public Library.

9. Ibid.

10. Ellen C. DuBois, *Feminism and Suffrage: The Emergence of an Independent Women's
Movement in America* (Ithaca, NY: Cornell University Press, 1999); for an international
analysis of suffrage, see Caroline Daley and Melanie Nolan, eds., *Suffrage and Beyond:
International Feminist Perspectives* (New York: New York University Press, 1994).

11. Levi Coffin, *Reminiscences of Levi Coffin* (Cincinnati: Western Tract Society,
1876), 565. For more information about Margaret Garner, see Steven Weisenberger,
Modern Medea: A Family Story of Slavery and Child—Murder in the Old South (New
York: Farrar, Straus and Giroux, 1999).

12. Margaret H. McFadden, *Golden Cables of Sympathy: The Transatlantic Sources of
Nineteenth-Century Feminism* (Lexington: University of Kentucky Press, 1999), 172–176.

13. Leila Rupp, *Worlds of Women: The Making of an International Women's
Movement* (Princeton, NJ: Princeton University Press, 1997), 52–81.

14. Ibid., p. 27.

15. Linda K. Schott, *Reconstructing Women's Thoughts: The Women's International
League for Peace and Freedom before World War II* (Stanford, CA: Stanford University

Press, 1997). Information on current WILPF work at http://www.wilpf.org/ (accessed July 5, 2007).

16. Rupp, *Worlds of Women*, 73.

17. Ibid.

18. Ibid.

19. See "The United Nations Commission on the Status of Women: 60 Years of Work for Equality, Development and Peace" at http://www.un.org/womenwatch/daw/CSW60YRS/index.htm (accessed July 5, 2007); and Mary Ann Glendon, *World Made New: Eleanor Roosevelt and the Universal Declaration of Human Rights* (New York: Random House, 2002).

20. J. Friedman, "Gendering the Agenda: The Impact of the Transnational Women's Rights Movement at the UN Conferences of the 1990's." *Women's Studies International Forum*, 26, no. 4 (July 2004), 313–331. Information on the UN Conferences on women is available at: http://www.un.org/womenwatch/ (accessed July 5, 2007).

21. The Global Women's Project History; see http://www.coc.org/system/files/gwp_project_history.pdf (accessed August 24, 2008).

22. Alice Kessler-Harris, *Gendering Labor History* (Urbana: University of Illinois Press, 2007).

23. See Rose Pesotta, *Bread upon the Waters* (Ithaca, NY: Cornell University Press, 1984); Rose Schneiderman and Lucy Goldthwaite, *All for One* (New York: P. S. Eriksson, 1967).

24. See Rose Schneiderman, Eleanor Roosevelt National Historic Site, at http://www.nps.gov/archive/elro/glossary/schneiderman-rose.htm (accessed February 29, 2008).

25. Alice Henry, *Women and the Labor Movement* (New York: G. H. Doran, 1923), 217–223.

26. Mary E. Frederickson, "A Place to Speak Our Minds: Locating Women's Activism Where North Meets South." *Journal of Developing Societies*, 23, no. 1–2 (2007), 59–70.

27. For programs sponsored by the Coalition of Labor Union Women (CLUW), see http://www.cluw.org/. Information about the Coalition for Justice in the Maquiladoras is available at http://www.coalitionforjustice.net (accessed March 27, 2006); regarding Women on the Border, see http://www.womenontheborder.org (accessed March 27, 2006); for the Association for Women's Rights in Development, see: http://www.awid.org (accessed March 27, 2006); and for material on the work done by the Comite Fronterizo de Obreros (CFO)–Committee of Women Workers, see http://www.cfomaquiladoras.org/english%20site/index_en.html (accessed August 24, 2008). For information about STITCH: Organizers for Labor Justice, see http://www.stitchonline.org (accessed March 26, 2006).

28. Kevin Bales, *Disposable People: New Slavery in the Global Economy* (Berkeley: University of California Press, 1999), 3–4; and *Ending Slavery: How We Free Today's Slaves* (Berkeley: University of California Press, 2007), 10–13. The articles in Barbara Ehrenreich and Arlie Russell Hochschild, eds., *Global Woman: Nannies, Maids, and*

Sex Workers in the New Economy (New York: Henry Holt, 2002), provide extensive discussions of the globalization of child care and housework and the transnational market for domestic workers, child care providers, and sex workers who increasingly migrate or are trafficked to developed nations to fulfill women's traditional roles as caregivers.

29. Emma Christopher, Cassandra Pybus, and Marcus Rediker, eds., *Many Middle Passages: Forced Migration and the Making of the Modern World* (Berkeley: University of California Press, 2007), 216–218.

30. Fourth World Conference on Women, Beijing, 1995, "Platform for Action," at http://www.un.org/womenwatch/daw/beijing/platform/declar.htm (accessed February 29, 2008).

31. The UE's strategic organizing alliance with the Mexican Frente Autentico del Trabajo (FAT) (http://www.fatmexico.org/ (accessed August 24, 2008) is a relationship based on organizing, but it is also one that celebrates art and literature rooted in working-class traditions that transcend national borders and cultural boundaries. The union sponsors the work of mural artists, including Juana Alicia, and writers such as Lynda Leech, whose poem spoke to Alicia's *Hands across the Border* mural.

32. Quotation from the Fourth World Conference on Women Beijing Declaration at http://www.un.org/womenwatch/daw/beijing/platform/declar.htm (accessed February 29, 2008).

33. Patrick E. Tyler, "Hillary Clinton, in China, Details Abuse of Women," *New York Times*, September 6, 1995, A1.

PART III

Teaching and Learning Women's History

Strategies and Resources

13

Redesigning the U.S. Women's History Survey Course Using Feminist Pedagogy, Educational Research, and New Technologies

Michael Lewis Goldberg

In the last fifteen years, advances in educational technology and research on learning have provided historians with new approaches and methods for deepening students' historical understanding. With an ever-expanding choice of digital communication tools, we have a variety of new ways to engage students and assess their work. This potent combination enables instructors to enhance key feminist pedagogical goals. Recent scholarship has begun to explore the challenges of combining traditional feminist pedagogical objectives with scholarly rigor and promoting student agency.[1] The advances in educational technology and learning offer instructors interested in introducing feminist pedagogical goals into their course the means for producing more complex understandings of women's multicultural history.

This chapter describes how I redesigned my U.S. women's history college survey course by using educational technology and research on student learning to improve student achievement within a feminist framework. This feminist framework calls for empowering students, decentering authority in the classroom, creating cohesive learning communities, and honoring students' diverse experiences. I provide a discussion of the entire process so that interested instructors can benefit from the lessons learned. The course described here went through three iterations before it arrived at its present version. Course assessment and redesign requires patience and planning; however, the process can also provide instructors with an opportunity to make a significant impact on their students' lives while reaffirming and strengthening the pedagogical principles that inspire their teaching.

An understanding of the students' backgrounds is an important part of course redesign. Not surprisingly, most of my students are women, although the percentage of men has varied from 8 percent to 20 percent. Because the average age of students on my campus is twenty-seven (and because non-traditional-age women seem especially interested in the course), the ages of those in the course vary from late teens to mid-sixties. Many students have little knowledge or understanding of history in general or U.S. history in particular, and almost none have any prior exposure to women's history. Because between a third and half of the students take the course to fulfill the U.S. history requirement for their K-12 teaching certification, U.S. women's history may well be their only basis for historical thinking when they become teachers themselves. Perhaps a third more come from the business program to fulfill their elective requirement. Although white suburban lower-middle-class and middle-class students predominate, students also vary by geography, ethnicity and race (mostly Asian, with a few Hispanic, Native American, and African American students), immigrant status (mostly Asian and East European), religion, politics, profession, and life experience.

My Multicultural Women's History Course, Phase One

I used feminist principles and new technology to guide the original course design. Feminist teachers strive to create communal, supportive, peer-centered learning environments. My course met twice a week for two hours a day. I controlled the first hour, providing what I assumed to be the requisite coverage in the form of a lecture. In the second hour, two or three students read short "thought pieces" intended to launch discussion from the assigned readings. The students presenting their papers were expected to guide discussion, with my role limited to being an occasional provider of information and synthesizer. Students extended the in-class discussion through an online "newsgroup," where they were encouraged to link their historical insights to their personal experiences. Because of my perceived need to cover the full range of multicultural women's history, I crammed as many readings and topics into the course as I felt my students could handle without open rebellion (although grumblings were common). Besides the short papers, students were assessed by analytical essays written for midterm and final exams.

Although the course was moderately successful in terms of student evaluations and grades, I was dissatisfied in number of ways. One area of concern was the limited success of the feminist-oriented learning goals. Student-led discussions were inconsistent. Despite my reminders that students should contextualize their subjective insights, many comments made vague references to historical phenomena as an excuse to discuss personal concerns in a fairly superficial manner. The rhetorical gestures added little to the discussion and tended to annoy students eager to engage the course material.[2] Clearly, students needed to become more "critically self-reflective."[3]

I was also concerned with students' understanding of the underlying concepts and content related to multicultural women's history. Many students skimmed the material, which led to weak command of details and superficial discussions. When I reviewed the final exams, I found students making certain mistakes consistently. Many students had difficulty understanding that cultural groups could be both similar and different. Another common problem was mixing up analysis, evaluation, and moral judgment, especially when writing about women's political or social groups that did not achieve their stated goals (a fairly common situation for oppressed groups). Another concern was the unevenness of students' reading comprehension, argumentation, and writing skills, which undercut their ability to lead discussions. All these problems frustrated my feminist pedagogical goals for the course that focused on empowerment of my students.

Redesigning the Course

I came to understand that the feminist and women's history learning outcomes I sought were intertwined. The previous version of the course had asked students to step in as instructors from the beginning. To empower students, I needed to provide them with the intellectual and emotional capacities necessary to take on an effective teaching role. In the new course, I drew on learning scholarship that suggested ways for moving students from novices toward experts, enabling more of them to be more "teacherly" and allowing me to gradually shift responsibility and authority to them.

This shift requires careful planning, an understanding of proven learning practices, and where applicable, appropriate technology. Providing students with "critical thinking skills" is not enough. Instructors are experts who need to unpack and make visible the underlying practices and concepts of a discipline.[4] As educational psychologist Samuel Wineburg has argued, "historical thinking" is an "unnatural act" that must be articulated and taught.[5] Based on my analysis of student work, I identified the skills necessary for success in this course, which included historical thinking concepts, interpretation of scholarly sources, use of logic and evidence, and writing skills. In focusing on these skills, I sought to foster effective collaborative learning; create coherent, supportive learning communities; and integrate students' comments into the discussion to enable a more nuanced appreciation of multicultural women's history.

This set of requirements mandated significant changes to my previous course structure. First, I moved to a problem-based learning model. Each week the class explored a historical problem requiring command of both content and historical concepts.[6] Second, I adopted a blended learning environment, swapping one of the in-class meetings for online interaction spread out over a number of days. The in-class meeting was used for activities best suited for face-to-face dynamics, including a problem-posing lecture, a critical review of the readings, and a meeting of permanent collaborative learning groups to initiate the upcoming online discussion.

The online portion made use of an asynchronous Web discussion board, which is not dependent on users communicating at the same time. This approach allowed me to stretch time and provide more space for student reflection, instructor feedback, and group interaction.[7] I also developed a multipart posting process that balanced analysis with subjective self-reflection. The use of collaborative learning methods supported by accountability assignments, the third redesign element, was prompted by my desire to create more coherent, stable communities based on mutuality, trust, and respect that would enable a deeper engagement with the material than a larger class group alone. The final redesign element, an iterative writing process stressing formative assessment within the online environment, was the glue that bound the different learning goals together: It enhanced feminist pedagogical goals by fostering student empowerment, enabling the eventual decentering of authority in the classroom, providing an academically beneficial place for students' subjective experiences, and improving their communal learning experience.[8]

The redesign of the course also required that I move away from the usual coverage model for a survey course. The course essentially lost one class per week of assigned reading, which meant a number of topic areas would not be covered. For multicultural women's history, this is a serious dilemma. Adopting such practices made representing the full range of American women's experiences even more difficult. However, coverage does not equal long-term understanding or even basic retention.[9] By stressing a deeper conceptual understanding of multicultural women's history, students are more likely to be able to retain their knowledge and transfer it to other situations.

Concepts, Content, and Historical Thinking Skills:
A New Approach

Integrating historical thinking skills with content is central to providing students with the necessary intellectual tools to take productive leadership roles in the classroom, thus decentering authority without sacrificing learning. Scholars have identified many historical thinking concepts—the National Center for History in the Schools' *U.S. History Standards* lists more than forty, and the list is not exhaustive.[10] Some of the concepts chosen for my course—such as *cause and effect, chronology,* and *continuity and change*—are crucial for basic historical understanding. Others, such as *cultural diversity and similarity, historical empathy,* and *evaluation,* map particularly well onto the concerns of a multicultural women's history course. Concepts are introduced in the order that best allows students to use their command of a previous concept as a foundation for better understanding a new one; this strategy is known as "scaffolding."[11] In this section, I offer several examples to demonstrate how this works in practice.

The first week's problem explores how the Anglo-American domestic ideal affected the relationship between Native American women's control of economic resources and their political and social power during the eighteenth and nineteenth century, focusing on the Cherokee and Seneca tribes.[12] To be successful, students must be precise about the many *cause-and-effect* elements in their *chronological* order. They then must consider the *cultural differences and similarities* in both cases and the *motivations* of the historical individuals and groups. For example, with the Cherokee, the actions of European American missionaries, settlers, and governmental entities initiated changes that certain Cherokee men took advantage of to leverage their power within the tribe. Without this precision, students often asserted simple (and ahistorical) sexism as the *motivation* for all Cherokee men without considering the complex series of *causal* interactions that took place.[13] *Causal* and *chronological* precision is also important when considering cultural diversity and similarity in the cases of the Seneca and Cherokee women, with students tending to overemphasize the similarities between the Cherokee and Seneca women, as well as among all whites (for example, the missionaries and the settlers).

During the second week, the more challenging concept of *historical agency* is introduced in exploring the problem of slavery and power within the family and community. Because students have already encountered and begun to develop foundational historical concepts, they are better able to tackle this complex problem. The readings for the week offer seemingly opposing views on the question of slave women's historical agency, which also provides the opportunity for introducing the concept of *historiography*.[14] Students in the preredesign course tended to overemphasize the reading that viewed slaves largely as victims. By focusing on the specific instances where slaves caused certain changes to occur and those instances where change was not possible, students developed a more complex comprehension of the contextual and contingent nature of agency.[15]

By themselves, mastering historical concepts are not enough to provide most students with the requisite level of expertise to enable the instructor to cede some control to the students. Most need to improve their reading comprehension and learn critical source assessment and constructive problem posing. Many need to improve their ability to apply evidence and logic, to write with clarity and precision, and to generate original analysis.

This process involves four key parts: preclass preparation, in-class instruction, in-class group work, and online group discussion. In the first stage, students complete a participation preparation form asking them to identify the main argument, subarguments, and conclusions; to evaluate the supporting logic and evidence; and to characterize the author's ideological perspective.[16] Most students achieve the first objective by the fourth week, the second objective by the sixth week, and the third objective by the eighth week. Although this exercise does not take the place of critical note taking, which is also encouraged (but not assessed), it does provide students with the opportunity to improve comprehension skills while moving beyond simply acquiring knowledge. It also means that most students come to the classroom, and the initial group discussion, with a baseline level of preparation.[17]

The second part of the process places the instructor at the center of the learning experience. First, students receive a framing lecture that presents the larger problem to be addressed that week, reviews the historical context, and introduces (or reinforces) the appropriate historical concepts. After responding to requests for clarification, the instructor works with students to review the preparation form and address other issues of basic comprehension and assessment. By assuming strong control during these instructional phases, the instructor is better able to assure that more students can take control more quickly during the discussion phase.

The remaining class time shifts to cooperative learning groups. Now that students have a stronger basic understanding of the material, the historical concepts to apply, and the larger framing problem, the groups can begin to take a more active role in their education. They do this by developing a specific problem that they address during their online discussion. They then create supporting questions and share their first takes on the material. In the first few weeks, the instructor provides the specific problem and questions. Students subsequently generate their own problems and questions, shape them in conversation with the instructor in class, and then finalize them online. Most students find it more difficult to compose problems and questions that support a thoughtful, critical response than to answer them.

In their first attempts, students often provide a very general problem with questions that are most likely to be answered by repeating the content in the scholarly sources. For example, in the week that addressed the early woman suffrage movement, the framing problem was "Historical Agency, Historical Context, and the Question of Power: Winners and Losers in the Early Suffrage Movement." One group suggested the specific problem "How would you assess the ramifications of the activists' decisions when faced with new obstacles?" Because the problem lacked specificity, students were encouraged to provide more focus and depth, drawing on the framing problem. After some negotiation, the group's problem was changed to "Determine the degree of Stanton and Anthony's *historical agency* given the external *causal* factors that impacted the suffrage movement, and then assess (*evaluate* and *judge*) Stanton and Anthony's strategic decisions after considering the role of external forces versus their degree of historical agency." This problem led students to supporting questions that required critical thinking rather than simple repetition of the source material.

The online discussion board allows students to gain the necessary competence and confidence to move from novice learners to newly empowered coteachers. For this transformation to take place, students are asked to follow a protocol that is fairly restrictive in its first stages but then gradually allows for greater creativity and agency. Students may either initiate a discussion thread (Step One) by presenting a well-reasoned argument from their own perspective, using historical evidence, or by responding to Step One posting by extending and/or challenging a response (Step Two). All students must then post at least one additional piece that can be more informal and open-ended and can include personal experiences or insights and information from other courses or from sources outside the course (Step Three). However, the postings must remain engaged with the original postings and maintain scholarly rigor. Step Three enables students to listen to each other in ways that promote complexity. At a certain point in the conversation (usually the fifth day), one student per group is assigned the responsibility of providing concluding comments for the week's discussion (Step Four). This step closes the circle on the process: Now that students have shared perspectives, the concluding statements provide closure to the exploration of the original problem.[18]

Creating coteachers requires that most students get practice writing well-organized and clearly written arguments supported by logic and evidence. Through practice and a de-emphasis on grading, students get feedback and rewards for their improvement. After each posting, students receive an e-mailed assessment using three broad categories (strong, competent, and poor), along with succinct, specific suggestions for improvement. They also receive a mid-term assessment (with a transitional grade to let them know where they stand), as well as a final summative assessment and grade. Students who move up a level or who make significant progress within a level receive a supportive notice. Students seem less competitive over grades, focusing on improvement through regular, written feedback.[19]

The online asynchronous environment makes it possible to disseminate feedback more systematically to more than one student at a time. When a student makes an error that generates feedback that would be beneficial to many students, the instructor posts it to the group's general discussion. This type of social learning helps to avoid repeated and common errors. However, because students typically experience feedback individually and privately, instructors must be careful to explain the rationale for this approach in the beginning. Peer feedback can also serve as important formative assessment and enhance students' appreciation of their learning community.

Providing clear learning outcomes and criteria for assessing them is essential to this process. Students receive the criteria for historical thinking concepts during the in-class lectures, where the concepts are introduced. Criteria for the online postings are listed in the assignment. The course Web site also contains models of each level of assessment for Step One and Step Two postings, along with the reasons for the assessments. Students are encouraged to check their postings against the models.[20]

The effectiveness of this approach can be easily measured. By the third week of postings, few students remain at the lowest level on a consistent basis. Students who do occasionally submit poor postings (or no posting at all) after the third week usually do so because of time pressures. Students generally move much more slowly to the strong level, which requires them to generate original analysis rather than repetition of content, a new experience for some of them. By the last class, more than 70 percent are able to provide strong postings for the discussion.[21] This approach enables more students to lead the discussion effectively.

Having more voices closer to the expert level allows the discussion to become complex quickly. In the seventh week, the course turns to issues of domesticity, work, and power, this time within the matrix of race, ethnicity, class, gender, and region and during overlapping but differing time periods.

The readings address urban housewives during the Depression, interned Japanese women during World War II, and African American, Latina, Asian American, and Native American women in the South, Southwest, and Far West involved in paid reproductive labor during the twentieth century.[22] In the redesigned course, students grasped the connections among these concepts more readily than in the earlier version of the course.

One group provided the problem "Examine the relationship between socially constructed gender norms relating to domesticity and systems of paid and unpaid productive and reproductive labor, and consider how they affected the historical agency of individuals and cultural groups." Two of their supporting questions were "Compare and contrast the intersection of changing social conditions and the dominant ideas about gender norms on Japanese and white working class families/women during the Depression, assessing both the short-term and long-term gains and losses for individual women and the communities they were a part of" and "How does [the argument] that the racialization of paid reproductive work has disempowered women of color challenge or deepen [the argument] that links Black women's paid reproductive work from after slavery to the present to communal empowerment, and visa versa?"

The quality of students' thinking had deepened markedly. In one group's discussion, students used the concept of cultural diversity and similarity to challenge what they saw as overgeneralizations in the source material regarding minority women's reproductive labor. Although the source material argued that the racialization of paid reproductive labor had disempowered women of color, some students argued that black women had historically used paid reproductive labor as the basis for their social empowerment within the black community relative to men, and therefore increased their historical agency. While not diminishing the effect of racism on black women within society, they argued that this distinction, especially when compared with the more patriarchal cultures of Mexican Americans and especially Japanese Americans, enabled black women to play important roles within various community-based movements, including the Civil Rights movement. Others countered that the Civil Rights movement was made necessary because of the job discrimination and occupational segmentation experienced by African American women. Students led and participated impressively in the discussion in ways that had not occurred in the earlier version of the course. Their newly developed skills had enabled them to assume a greater control of their classroom, thus enhancing the learning experience of the entire class.

Experts on cooperative and collaborative learning have demonstrated that instructors must establish student accountability, provide groups with ground rules, and allow sufficient time for the discussion of group process.[23] A key part of this process is the construction of the groups. This course creates groups of eight to ten members to achieve a wide variety of perspectives and enrich the overall discussion. The asynchronous nature of the online environment, which expands time to allow more voices to be considered and responded to, can support the large group size effectively. To create groups with a relatively balanced level of writing and thinking skills, students are asked to submit a writing sample before the groups are formed. Students also complete a group member information form, which enables the creation of heterogeneous groups based on their self-assessment of participation level, background in history and gender issues, ideological perspective, and other factors.[24] Although groups have almost always worked through their ideological or other differences, some groups have experienced difficulties because of too many weak writers or undercommitted students.[25]

Group members also evaluate each other and themselves at the midterm and the conclusion of the course based on criteria discussed during the second week of class. Although the forms are not shared with other students, after the midterm evaluation each group discusses its shared perceptions of the group's process and considers ways to improve it. The evaluations and subsequent discussions generally improve group coherence while providing individual students with important skills in cooperative learning.[26]

The value of heterogeneous voices becomes especially apparent when students move to Step Three in the posting process. By moving from narrowly focused analytical argumentation to a more expressive, complex conversation, students were able to anchor their subjective experience within the community's ongoing scholarly discussion. Rather than smother creativity and expression, this step allows students to become more self-reflective. In the redesigned course's student evaluations, none raised subjective students' comments as a problem, and more than two-thirds of the evaluations praised their peers for their contributions to their learning experience.

Although the evidence from course evaluations and grades strongly suggests that students benefited from the redesigned course in a number of ways, I do not mean to suggest that it is somehow perfect or necessarily even superior to other approaches. Every pedagogical choice about course design, process, or student-teacher interactions comes with costs and benefits. As noted, this course sacrifices coverage for depth. By focusing solely on scholarly sources rather than including primary sources, the direct voices of the historical actors are excluded.[27] Further, while the online writing-and-discussion format offers many benefits, it lacks the spontaneity, risk taking, emotionalism, and humor that extended in-class discussions can deliver. Rather than attempting to re-create the entire format, interested instructors might consider adopting parts of the approach described here in light of their own teaching contexts.

The course redesign enabled me to fulfill my feminist objectives of empowering students, decentering authority in the classroom, building supportive learning communities, and effectively integrating students' subjective experiences. As important, the newly enhanced feminist-oriented methods deepened students' knowledge of and appreciation for multicultural women's history. My experiences should benefit instructors desiring to combine new pedagogical approaches and technologies with feminist objectives to teach this subject.

NOTES

1. This chapter positions itself within the feminist discussions concerning instructor responsibility and authority and its relation to student empowerment. See, for example, Jacqueline Foertsch, "The Circle of Learners in a Vicious Circle: Derrida, Foucault, and Feminist Pedagogic Practice," *College Literature* 27, no. 3 (2000). See also Jodi Wetzel, "Assessment and Feminist Pedagogy," in *Meeting the Challenge: Innovative Feminist Pedagogies in Action*, ed. Maralee Mayberry and Ellen Cronan Rose (New York: Routledge, 1999).

2. In one version of the course, "other students" were noted as an aspect of the course limiting their learning more than the instructor's actions, which is unusual.

3. For a discussion on this phenomenon and the general challenge of integrating subjective experience productively, see Amie A. Macdonald, "Feminist Pedagogy and the Appeal to Epistemic Privilege," in *Twenty-First-Century Feminist Classrooms : Pedagogies of Identity and Difference*, ed. Amie A. Macdonald and Susan Sâanchez-Casal (New York: Palgrave Macmillan, 2002).

4. On expert versus novice, see John D. Bransford, Ann L. Brown, and Rodney R. Cocking, *How People Learn: Brain, Mind, Experience, and School*, expanded ed. (Washington, D.C.: National Academies Press, 2000). "Metacognitive" learning encourages students to "think critically about thinking." Samuel S. Wineburg, *Historical Thinking and Other Unnatural Acts: Charting the Future of Teaching the Past* (Philadelphia: Temple University Press, 2001).

5. Wineburg, *Historical Thinking and Other Unnatural Acts.*

6. See, for example, Barbara J. Duch, Susan E. Groh, and Deborah E. Allen, eds., *The Power of Problem-Based Learning* (Sterling, VA: Stylus, 2001).

7. Asynchronous online communication does not require immediate responses, as opposed to synchronous online communication, like chat and MOO (Multiuser domain Object Oriented) formats.

8. The latest version of the course may be found at http://faculty.washington. edu/mlg/courses/463W07/index.html, which also includes all of the forms, criteria, and other support material discussed in this chapter.

9. Bransford, Brown, and Cocking, *How People Learn.*

10. National Center for History in the Schools, *National History Standards* (1996); available from http://nchs.ucla.edu/standards.html. See also Peter N.

Stearns, "Getting Specific about Training in Historical Analysis: A Case Study in World History," in *Knowing, Teaching, and Learning History: National and International Perspectives,* ed. Peter N. Stearns, Peter C. Seixas, and Samuel S. Wineburg (New York: New York University Press, 2000); Mario Carretero and James F. Voss, *Cognitive and Instructional Processes in History and the Social Sciences* (Hillsdale, NJ: Erlbaum, 1994).

11. Stearns, "Getting Specific about Training in Historical Analysis."

12. Joan Jensen, "Native American Women and Agriculture: A Seneca Case Study," in *Unequal Sisters,* ed. Vicki L. Ruiz and Ellen Carol DuBois (London: Routledge, 1990); Theda Perdue, "Cherokee Women and the Trail of Tears," in *Unequal Sisters: A Multicultural Reader in U.S. Women's History,* 2nd ed., ed. Vicki L. Ruiz and Ellen Carol DuBois (London: Routledge, 1994). Note: I use essays from all three editions of *Unequal Sisters* because they offer useful contrasts.

13. In the preredesign course, more than a third of the students made this error in their postings (12 of 35, or 34.2 percent). In the latest version of the redesign course, only 4 of 34 (11.8 percent) made this error.

14. Brenda Stevenson, "Distress and Discord in Virginia Slave Families, 1830–1860," in *Unequal Sisters: A Multicultural Reader in U.S. Women's History,* 3rd ed., ed. Vicki L Ruiz and Ellen Carol DuBois (London: Routledge, 2000); Deborah White, "Female Slaves: Sex Roles and Status in the Ante-Bellum Plantation South," in *Unequal Sisters: A Multicultural Reader in U.S. Women's History,* 2nd ed., ed. Vicki Ruiz and Ellen Carol DuBois (London: Routledge, 1994).

15. In the preredesign course, 23 of 35 students (65.7 percent) discussed only Stevenson's article, which presents a strong view of slave disempowerment; 7 students (20 percent) referenced only White's more positive article; and 5 students combined the two. Only the students who used White (three students) or combined the sources (four students) presented a view of slave women's historical agency that was not characterized as either complete disempowerment or complete empowerment. In the redesigned course, five and four students (14.7 percent and 11.8 percent) referenced Stevenson and White exclusively, and only six students (17.6 percent) held a simplistic view of historical agency. Note: This project has been accepted as exempt from human subjects review by the University of Washington Human Subjects Division.

16. Because the course is based entirely on scholarly sources, the source comprehension and assessment exercise does not include skills needed for primary sources. An excellent primer on assessing primary sources may be found at the "Making Sense of Evidence" page on the *History Matters* Web site: http://historymatters.gmu.edu/browse/makesense/.

17. This process is greatly expedited by using a course-management system or other online tool to collect the assignments. Students are responsible for uploading each form, which can then be tracked easily. I provide brief feedback (strong, acceptable, and not acceptable) after the first week (to create a benchmark) and then a midterm and final grade based on spot-checking. I can quickly identify students who

are not completing the forms and communicate with them by using the tools of the CMS.

18. The full assignment, with assessment criteria, can be found at http://faculty. washington.edu/mlg/courses/463W07/463W07posting.doc, which includes the rubric for the online postings as a downloadable Word document. This approach brought together several different methods. Readings that served as the basis for my approach included C. McLoughlin and M. Panko, "Multiple Perspectives on the Evaluation of Online Discussion," in *Proceedings of World Conference on Educational Multimedia, Hypermedia and Telecommunications 2002*, P. Barker and S. Rebelsky, eds. (Chesapeake, VA: AACE, 2002) (2002); M. Moallem, "An Interactive Online Course: A Collaborative Design Model," *Educational Technology Research & Development* 51, no. 4 (2003); M. Roblyer, "A Rubric to Encourage and Assess Student Engagement in Online Course Conferences," in *Proceedings of Society for Information Technology and Teacher Education International Conference 2002*, ed. C. Crawford et al. (Chesapeake, VA: AACE, 2002) ; L. Sherry, S. H. Billig, and F. Tavalin, "Good Online Conversation: Building on Research to Inform Practice," *Journal of Interactive Learning Research* 11, no. 1 (2000). I created this approach as part of an online faculty colloquium on new approaches to online group learning. I am indebted to the organizers of the colloquium, Andreas Brockhaus, Carol Leppa, and Julie Planchon-Wolff, as well as my colleagues who participated in the colloquium, Andrea Kovelesky and Walt Freytag.

19. Because Blackboard provides an e-mail link to the author of each post, it is easy to e-mail these assessments and keep track of them by using folders in an e-mail management system such as Microsoft Outlook. I can then quickly find past assessments of students and compare them to their current level of achievement.

20. These are posted on the course Web site.

21. In the first week of postings, 13 of 34 (38.2 percent) postings were rated poor, and only 3 postings (8.8 percent) were rated strong. After the third week of postings, only 3 postings (8.8 percent) were assessed as poor. In the last week of postings, no postings were rated poor, and 25 (73.5 percent) were rated strong.

22. Evelyn Nakano Glenn, "From Servitude to Service Work: Historical Continuities in the Racial Division of Paid Reproductive Labor"; Valerie Matsumoto, "Japanese Women during World War II"; and Annelise Orleck, "'We Are That Mythical Thing Called the Public': Militant Housewives during the Great Depression," all in *Unequal Sisters: A Multicultural Reader in U.S. Women's History*, ed. Vicki Ruiz and Ellen Carol DuBois (London: Routledge, 2000).

23. Elizabeth F. Barkley, K. Patricia Cross, and Claire Howell Major, *Collaborative Learning Techniques: A Handbook for College Faculty*, 1st ed. (San Francisco: Jossey-Bass, 2005). There is a fairly vast literature on collaborative/cooperative learning, but this volume provides sufficient information for instituting a range of collaborative learning activities.

24. Students are strongly encouraged to not include any information that they are not comfortable with sharing.

25. On group formation, size, and similar issues, see Barkley, Cross, and Major, *Collaborative Learning Techniques.*

26. In their course evaluations, only 3 of 27 students (11.1 percent) complained about the group process, and 18 of 27 praised it (66.7 percent). The remainder did not mention it.

27. The format of the course could easily be adapted to include some combination of primary and secondary sources.

14

Teaching Women's History with Visual Images

Tracey Weis

I subscribe to the adage "Never walk into a classroom without a picture."[1] Bringing pictures into the classroom allows me to address several significant and pressing problems that my students and I face when we study women's history. First, using visual evidence offers a window into student thinking. Using images to identify and discuss the knowledge, beliefs, and emotions that students bring into the classroom is particularly useful when women, gender, and power are concerned. Second, looking at drawings, prints, portraits, paintings, and cartoons enables students to "see" complicated historical processes and developments in ways that reading other texts might not. Third, today's students have grown up with visual images and may be more comfortable with them than with printed texts. Fourth, the increasing abundance and availability of visual images in digital archives make this approach particularly attractive but "do not guarantee historical understanding."[2] I see my job as teaching students how to analyze and deconstruct these images so that they are not passive consumers of this fare. Like many other thinking skills, however, visual literacy—and, in particular, the specific skill of reading images—needs to be taught across different disciplines and throughout a student's academic career.[3]

Pioneer women's historian Gerda Lerner's persistent query—if women were at the center of our analysis regarding any event or period, how would our account and our analysis be changed?—can be reframed: If visual evidence were at the center of our analysis of gender and historical agency, how would our account and our analysis be different? To accomplish this shift, students and instructors must work together to devise new ways of reading images that are as rigorous and rewarding as the strategies used with written texts.[4]

In what follows, I present a detailed description of my efforts to integrate visual evidence and modes of presentation in "Women in U.S. History," a sophomore-level survey course that I teach each fall at Millersville University, a mid-size public comprehensive university in south-central Pennsylvania. Many students in history courses at Millersville are preparing to be teachers. Although I am discussing a specific course, my broader understanding of "the problem of the visual in women's history" is grounded in teaching women's history in summer workshops for K-12 instructors, undergraduate electives, and graduate seminars. I hope that the questions I raise, the problems I confront, and the strategies I present will be useful to instructors and students at various levels in different kinds of institutions.[5]

How to Use Images in the Classroom: Notes from the Field

I have been carrying pictures into the classroom ever since I first started teaching as a graduate student in the women's history program at Rutgers University in the late 1980s. My use of images in those early days, however, was variable, occasional, and idiosyncratic. Only much later in my teaching career, as a participant in Learning to Look, a faculty development program sponsored by the American Social History Project at the City University of New York, did I become aware that my haphazard approach to including pictures in my lessons was inadequate. Sharing my efforts to "make images central" in a sophomore-level survey course in African American history with secondary and postsecondary instructors in summer workshops and institutes, I realized that I needed a protocol for analyzing images that my students and I could apply in a methodical manner. Chronicling my students' responses to my experiments with using visual evidence in the classroom helped me to understand what worked that went beyond the anecdotal.[6] I shared stories about what my students were learning about using images to understand slavery with other instructors. We compared notes and tried to assess the messy complexity of what happened when our students encountered images in the history classroom.[7] Challenged by colleagues to rethink how I read images, I had to grapple with larger questions about what constituted historical understanding and how to present history in the classroom.

The most important consequence of that collaborative gaze at students' visual thinking, detailed in "Ways of Seeing: Evidence and Learning in the History

Classroom, an Introduction," has been the generation of new questions.[8] A recursive look at our own teaching practice moved us beyond our initial pedagogical question: *Why* do we use visual approaches in the classroom? Our new questions concerned the value of visual evidence and modes of presentation that extended beyond the conventional historical essay: How can visual evidence inform, or provide alternative perspectives to, our traditional teaching practices? What kinds of historical narratives can our students visualize, construct, and present that demonstrate that "images *reveal* as well as *define* events"?[9] Beyond these framing questions, however, was another important insight that reoriented my teaching and that continues to shape my practice today: Image use and analysis in the classroom needs to be sustained, systematic, and collaborative.

I applied the lessons I learned about how my students made sense of visual evidence and how they used visual modes of presentation to the design of my women's history course. My revised protocol relies extensively on an approach used by art historians: the juxtaposition of images. Juxtaposition is a pedagogical strategy that *models* a type of disciplinary analysis and *invites* the demonstration of student understanding. First, I selected a text that combined narrative interpretation, a healthy dose of documents, and substantive documentary and visual essays. The sixteen visual essays in *Through Women's Eyes*, studded with a wide variety of visual resources, pose provocative questions and encourage students to "see" history as a dynamic process of interpretation rather than a static set of facts.[10] By integrating images as evidence that informs the narrative rather than including images simply as illustrations, this text models the rigorous protocol of sourcing practiced by historians and encourages the sustained investigation of visual evidence.[11] Second, I reorganized the sequence of course content and process so that we could "begin with the end in mind." I start the semester with the last chapter of the textbook; this foreshadowing of the present heightens student apprehension of historical change and continuity. Also, although the essays on visual sources appear at the close of each chapter, I begin the deliberation of each topic with the visual essays and present the visual sources as evidence to be interrogated; this initial inspection sharpens the subsequent reading and discussion of the narrative portions of the text. Third, I devised a set of sequenced exercises to address the difficulties my students experienced when they set out to analyze images: (1) understanding the relationship between the image and the historical context; (2) examining the role of prior knowledge, belief, and emotion in historical interpretation; and (3) incorporating visual evidence in historical analysis. Working through these supplemental exercises in pairs, in small groups, and in class forums allows me to uncover two vital features of historical practice that are often hidden from students: revision and collaboration.

We began the semester with the visual essay in chapter 10, "Modern Feminism in American Society." Half the students were assigned the essay "Lesbians in Postwar America," and the other half read the essay "American Women in the World" in preparation for discussion.[12] Juxtaposition was built into the text. For example, students exploring the impact of World War II on the creation of urban lesbian communities were asked to compare and contrast a photograph of the 1965 Mattachine Society picket line in front of the White House with a 1970 Gay Liberation Front poster and to think about the changing nature of gay protest. The questions at the end of the first essay called students to engage in another level of comparison and contrast. Instructed to examine the newspaper photographs of the 1909 New York City shirtwaist strike, the 1913 Lawrence textile workers' strike, and the 1913 suffrage parades in New York City and Washington, D.C., they pondered the continuities and changes in women's use of public space for protest. Similarly, those who delved into the consequences of economic globalization for women workers across the world were invited to compare and contrast a contemporary photograph taken by a border patrol officer of a Mexican woman captured while crossing the California border with the photographs taken by Jacob Riis of immigrant women and children in New York in the 1880s and 1890s and to contemplate the connections between patterns of immigration, production, and consumption in two different eras. The questions at the end of the second essay urged students to consider how increasing global integration might bring some women in the United States closer to some women in other parts of the world, even as it increased the distance and inequality between others.

Next, I asked students to design a lesson plan for ninth graders on the topic of the visual essay they had read. Which images would they choose to open up discussion of the diversity among American lesbians? Would they select the antisweatshop campaign poster designed to promote solidarity with Guatemalan seamstresses or the photograph of the 1977 National Women's Conference in Houston to probe the impact of globalization on relationships among women around the world? Students had to read an image and understand it in its historical context to defend its use in the proposed lesson plan.

I wanted to make students' prior knowledge, beliefs, and emotions about gender more explicit so that we could all see how these shaped our analytic efforts to "compare and contrast differing sets of ideas, values, personalities, behaviors, and institutions" in the past.[13] The next "check for understanding" required students to select song lyrics that expressed how young women and men defined contemporary women's issues and concerns, as a way of annotating the documents by Third Wave activists on the feminist revival of the 1990s provided in the textbook.[14] In addition, I asked them to write a paragraph explaining how a contemporary film or television show "gets modern feminism right" and whether the film or TV show omits any significant issue. Connecting contemporary culture to liberal feminism and women's liberation movements of the 1960s and 1970s and to the feminist revival of the 1990s was relatively straightforward. Many young women and men are eager to explore how cultural forces such as punk or hip-hop represent female sexuality. Having students select and reflect on visual representations of women in music videos and television programs encourages them to go beyond the textbook to test their understandings of the documentary evidence. Constructing brief commentaries that connect the visual and textual sources allows them to practice the skills of historical analysis.

Maneuvering from the present (the lyrics and graphics of contemporary musicians such as Ani DiFranco, Christina Aguilera, and Pink) to the past (the archaeological record of artifacts created by indigenous groups prior to the collision of cultures in the 1500s), however, required tremendous intellectual agility. Comparing and contrasting the effigy pipes and bottles from Spiro (Oklahoma) and Cahokia (Illinois) Mounds with drawings of John White and Theodor de Bry—our next juxtaposition—was even more demanding because few students were experienced in analyzing material artifacts from the colonial era.[15] Attributing authorial intent to the anonymous producers of domestic objects proved particularly daunting and difficult. Nonetheless, placing the effigy pipes and the engravings side by side yielded both insights and questions about the economic contribution of Native American women to their communities and the impact of European colonization on the sexual division of labor in native societies, even as it problematized Disney's presentation of Pocahontas.

I then asked students to select two images from the visual essay "Images of Native American Women" for an exhibition on that topic to be mounted in the university's student center. Directed to designate two images that would instruct their peers, students had to think about the intent or motivation of the authors or producers. Whose intent would they privilege and why? They had to contemplate the connections among genre, authority, and status as they compared and contrasted the artifacts created by indigenous artisans and the drawings by European illustrators. Learning to identify the conventions of the different types of visual evidence and to recognize the limitations and biases of various sources was another essential step.

Similarly, the next assignment, based on the visual essays "Portraits of Revolutionary Women" and "Gendering Images of the Revolution," called students to create their own juxtapositions by choosing images for an article for the student newspaper that addressed the question "What do Millersville students need to know and understand about women, gender, and the American Revolution?" Yet again, the students had to attend to authorial intent and audience as they deliberated whether to pick portraits of well-known elite white women such as Mercy Otis Warren and Abigail Adams or lesser known African American women such as Phillis Wheatley and Elizabeth Freeman. What point could they make if they selected the 1774 cartoon "A Society of Patriotic Ladies" or one of the various depictions of women as icons of Liberty? How might the portraits of Wheatley and Freeman launch an exploration of the impact of race on the revolutionary process? What could portraits contribute to an analysis that caricatures could not?

In my end-of-unit review, I pose yet another set of juxtapositions. When I place John Singleton Copley's portrait of Mercy Otis Warren, for instance, alongside John Trumbull's painting of General Warren, I encourage students to rethink the gendered meanings of patriotism and virtue.[16] Similarly, when I set Susan Anne Livingston Ridley Sedgwick's watercolor portrait of Elizabeth Freeman, an enslaved woman who achieved her freedom by petitioning the State of Massachusetts in 1781, against Jean-Baptiste Le Paon's portrait of General Marquis de Lafayette accompanied by his orderly, James Armistead, I urge students to ask questions about how images "molded expectations and shaped experiences" as well as "shed light on assumptions of the day."[17] By comparing and contrasting representations of women and men, residents of New England and the Chesapeake, free and enslaved persons, students can start to formulate queries about the significance of gender, region, race, and status on participation in revolutionary processes. By looking at Revolutionary-era portraits produced by both women and men, they can begin to ask critical questions about who portrayed whom and why, questions that lead to further investigation.

At this point, some readers may be thinking, "This sounds wonderful, but I don't have a textbook that puts images at the center, and I don't have time to devise detailed lesson plans that include images. How can I get started?" Web-mounted lesson plans can be used to either extend or supplement classroom investigations; some of these digital lessons may even feature images included in textbooks. Identifying relevant visual evidence to revise a single lesson might be a modest and manageable way to deepen learning. For example, "George Washington: Images of History," a Web-based lesson that invites students to contemplate how artists' depictions of George Washington have shaped perceptions of "the father of our country" in different eras, can be usefully paired with an online lesson based on the 1774 cartoon "A Society of Patriotic Ladies" to deepen student understanding of the nuances of how women and men were portrayed and how women and men participated in revolutionary activity.[18]

These online lessons and activities can, in turn, entice students and instructors alike to explore the extensive digital archives that contain the primary sources featured in the lessons.[19]

To interject another layer of comparative analysis into our study of women in the American Revolution, I would ask students to "read" *Imaging the French Revolution: Depictions of the Revolutionary Crowd*, an experiment in visual scholarship that includes forty-two images of crowds and crowd violence in the French Revolution.[20] This visual archive serves multiple uses. First, it enables scholars and students to determine the nature and extent of women's revolutionary activity. Second, the varied visual evidence (i.e., caricatures, documentary prints, and allegories) works to supplement, reinforce, or even contradict the documentary evidence of contemporary responses to women's expanded public role in revolutionary settings. Third, as sources that shed light on assumptions, images of revolution help scholars and students alike to investigate the link, in the minds of eighteenth-century publics, between female enthusiasm and violence.[21] Comparing and contrasting the representation of Anglo-American and French women in revolutionary settings enables students and scholars to probe the differences and similarities between artistic representations and historical interpretations of revolutionary women.

Moving from the portraits and propagandistic images of the revolutionary era to the prescriptive literature of the antebellum decades, we probed the ideology of true womanhood, the industrialization of textile production, and the expansion of slavery by singling out illustrations from contemporary women's magazines that amplify images in the visual essays on *"Godey's Lady's Book"* and "Early Photographs of Factory Operatives and Slave Women." Students embarked on two comparative excursions. First, they read across *place* as they compared and contrasted "true" women, factory workers, and enslaved laborers. The contrast between the images of true [white] women preserved in the illustrations and paintings and the representations of factory operatives and enslaved women presented in the photographs propelled students to return to earlier conversations about the limits of concepts such as the sexual division of labor and separate spheres. Placing various images of diverse groups of women side by side complicates and collapses rigid categories of "women" for novice historians. Second, they read across *time* as they compared and contrasted the visual representations of women in nineteenth century with those produced in the modern era. Students shared images from magazines such as *Elle, Cosmopolitan, Essence, O the Oprah Magazine, Self, Shape*, and *Vibe Vixen* that commented on or corresponded to advertisements and illustrations in *"Godey's Lady's Book"* and the photographs of Lowell operatives and enslaved domestics. They observed, often with disappointment and displeasure, some changes but mostly continuities in prescriptions for women's health, beauty, fashion, work, and family responsibilities, even as they noted differences in how native-born, immigrant, and enslaved women were portrayed in earlier eras. The juxtaposition of visual evidence prompted students to see both similarities and differences among women that textual sources may merely hint at. Directed to find relevant contemporary images, students worked to refine essential skills of information literacy and historical practice: the ability to locate, evaluate, and effectively use needed information.[22]

To conclude our consideration of the pedestal (domesticity), the loom (industrialization), and the auction block (slavery), I asked students to write several sentences that explained the complex and multiple relationships among the variables pictured in figure 14.1.

Presenting historical questions in a graphical form such as the triangle in figure 14.1 makes it easier for students to see the problem. Extending this assignment to have students locate additional nineteenth-century images that illuminate those proposed relationships would enable students to test hypotheses derived from visual evidence against the documentary record. An elaboration of the in-class activity positions students to assemble visual evidence to investigate the disputed relationships among marriage, prostitution, pornography, and coerced labor that prevail in the twentieth and twenty-first centuries.

Students in my women's history class, however, seemed unable to bring their multiple competencies together when the time came to synthesize what they had learned in their end-of-unit projects: a collaborative visual research report of fifteen to twenty PowerPoint slides accompanied by a narrative—a script—for class presentation. I told the students to think of the slides as "visual paragraphs" that were meant to portray the relationships between the

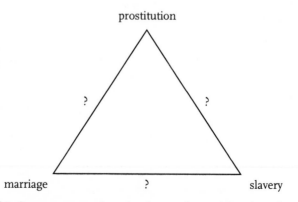

FIGURE 14.1. This diagram was used to stimulate student writing about the relationships among these concepts.

documentary and visual evidence that students selected from digital archives, the scholarship they encountered in the course textbook and other readings, and the arguments they developed as they maneuvered back and forth among the sources. As I watched students construct single slides for earlier assignments, I saw that they grasped, in a theoretical sense, the tension between showing (demonstrating) and telling (narrating). Usually inexperienced in working with primary sources of any kind, however, students frequently employed a cut-and-paste approach to images.[23] They either extracted an image as a freestanding item devoid of context or pulled an image and its accompanying scholarly commentary as a unified and coherent item into their own analyses. Accustomed to report-like explanations that emphasize description rather than analysis, these novice historians seemed stymied and unsettled by the messiness and multiplicity of meanings that the visual summaries involved.

Although many of them had started the semester with the conviction that "pictures speak for themselves," by mid-semester most of them began to admit, "It's more complicated than I thought," as they sought to incorporate, rather than merely include, images in their presentations.[24] Even with this more sophisticated understanding, students still struggled to present nuanced and open-ended analyses of the texts and images they had selected. Although I had sought to provide even more scaffolding for students in my women's history class, I still needed to do more to prepare them to take the next step in narrative construction in order to create coherent and comprehensive explanations of causation and consequence.

Enhancing Effectiveness and Engagement: Three Tactics for Using Images

I employed three tactics to help students maneuver between evidence and argument in a more comfortable and competent fashion. First, I drew on principles of backward design to incorporate *essential questions* in my lessons.[25] Each day in class we worked—as individuals, in pairs, and in small and large groups—to formulate essential questions that addressed the deepest issues that humans confront, to devise and revise queries that precluded simple answers, and to move beyond questions that began with *who, what, when,* and *where* to questions that started with *how, why,* and *which.* In short, we intensively practiced recasting knowledge-based questions into understanding-based questions. For example, we might start with a rather conventional query—*What* were the impacts of the American Revolution on different groups of women?—and reframe that question in a way that put visual evidence at the center: *How* can the portraits of women of this era or the 1774 cartoon "A Society of Patriotic Ladies" and depictions of women representing Liberty enhance our understanding of how gender, race, region, and class shaped the experiences of women at this time?

Second, I developed a template for a *complex slide* to assist their analysis of visual evidence. Complex slides require the juxtaposition of two pieces of evidence: two images, an image and an excerpt from a textual source, or two excerpts from textual sources. I had previously drawn on the National History Standards and the Pennsylvania Academic Standards for History to propose a set of terms that students employed to elaborate the relationships between historical agents, events, and processes: (1) cause versus consequence, (2) change versus continuity, (3) comparison versus contrast, and (4) cooperation versus conflict.[26] Students used PowerPoint slides to portray their observations and questions about the relationships between the various pieces of textual or visual evidence.[27]

Fortified with a focus question and a format for a complex slide that encouraged (even if it did not guarantee) the juxtaposition of evidence, students, I imagined, would be more likely to go beyond description to analysis in the production of their visual essays. Accustomed to the ubiquity of the visual, however, most students still treated images as ahistorical illustrations that were simple "there" rather than as evidence that had been created by historical agents in particular times and places. Clearly, despite their exposure to visual images, students were ready to read visual sources in the same way they read textbooks: for information or content knowledge rather than for understanding or for contextual clues. How, then, do we get students to read images for understanding rather than for information?

My third tactical ploy to get students to rethink the relationships between visual evidence and argument, developed in direct response to this problem, was to expand the *peer review* of assignments, even at the risk of compromising coverage. I often include a peer review component in class presentations. Watching my students include rich visual evidence as mere illustrations in PowerPoint presentations made me realize that they needed frequent practice in reading—and interpreting—images to deepen their analysis of this type of historical evidence. They also needed to rehearse, again and again, using images to build arguments about the past.

Thus, I injected several more layers of scrutiny into the peer review process. Most critical was the individual slide review. First, student reviewers had to determine whether the slide in question was, in fact, complex. At this stage, students debated, in a rather heated fashion, whether a particular image or textual excerpt was a primary source. The sourcing protocols, introduced earlier in the semester, suddenly assumed new significance and value. Students prompted each other to justify their selections of images and texts: Why did you select this image? What point were you trying to make? How does that image relate to this excerpt from a primary document? Challenged to defend the choice of a specific image or quotation, students had to return to the original print or electronic location to verify details—a practical and powerful object lesson in the importance of accurate citations.

The second level of scrutiny involved reviewing the analysis of the primary source. Instructors can easily download worksheets from institutions such as the National Archives and Records Administration for help with analysis of photographs, cartoons, and maps; they and their students can also consult more detailed guides for the interrogation of political cartoons, advertisements, and documentary photographs.[28] Moreover, many Web-mounted lesson plans invite students to formulate research queries based on the images (What questions does this photograph raise in your mind? Where could you find answers to them?) rather than merely answering questions about the images. Directed to think about the motivation of the author or producer or ponder the reaction of various audiences, students were drawn deeper into an examination of the assumptions of the past, even as they noted the beliefs and emotions that the images elicit in them. Introducing students to the systematic interrogation of images as evidence helps them go beyond the illustrative to the interpretive.[29]

The third level of scrutiny—citation check—compelled students to confront the issue of context as they retrace the steps they'd taken to locate an image or quotation on the Web. Although I always provide students with a list of reputable digital archives for each unit of study, some students invariably insist on going directly to the World Wide Web to find images and quotations. One student's project on communism and civil rights in the Cold War era included the well-known photograph of Rosa Parks being fingerprinted by a deputy sheriff in Montgomery, Alabama. When we checked the citation for the photograph in class, we discovered that it had been used to illustrate "Red Rosa: Background on Rosa Parks and the Montgomery Bus Boycott," an online article hosted on a Web site maintained by National Vanguard, a white separatist group. Comparing the narrative on the National Vanguard site with the analysis presented on "'With an Even Hand': *Brown v. Board* at Fifty," a Library of Congress online exhibition that also featured the photograph, led to a productive exchange about how the same image could be used to promote very different interpretations of Rosa Parks's actions and subsequent arrest.[30] The wealth of primary documents on the World Wide Web has made it easier for instructors to supplement the documentary collections, anthologies of classic and cutting-edge scholarly essays, and narrative analyses that serve as the mainstay of women's history courses.[31]

Implications of Using Visual Evidence to See Women as a
Force in History

To move ahead in making women and power visible within the national narrative, we must ask ourselves a series of questions:

- How can we use visual evidence to gain access to students' prior knowledge, beliefs, and emotions about gender and power?
- Which images can help our students probe the particularities and comprehend the complexities of women's historical experiences?
- How can visual evidence inform our analyses of women's agency and the gendered workings of power?
- How can we use visual evidence to illuminate complex historical processes such as the cultural construction of sexuality or the role of women's agency in transnational encounters and empire?

Talking with other history instructors in more sustained and systematic ways about what happens when we bring pictures into our classrooms is crucial. Juxtaposing historical and contemporary visual sources that provide images of women from different times and places allows us to do more deliberate comparative work. Finally, bringing pictures into our classrooms permits us to meet the most pressing demand of feminism: that we develop "an increasingly complex understanding of the ways by which differences among people have been constructed in such a way as to give some people power and privilege over others."[32]

NOTES

1. James H. Madison, "Teaching with Images," *OAH Magazine of History* 18 (January 2004), 65; Louis Masur, " 'Pictures Have Now Become a Necessity': The Use of Images in American History Textbooks," *Journal of American History* 84 (March 1998), 1410.

2. Michael Coventry, Peter Felten, David Jaffee, Cecilia O'Leary, and Tracey Weis, with Susannah McGowan, "Ways of Seeing: Evidence and Learning in the History Classroom, an Introduction," *Journal of American History* 92 (March 2006), 1375.

3. Visual literacy is one component of a broader new media literacy that is premised on recent scholarship in cognitive science, semiotics, linguistics, media literacy, and literacy in general. See Larry Johnson, "The Sea Change before Us," *EDUCAUSE Review* 41 (March–April 2006): 72–73.

4. Recent work by historians has focused on women photographers and photography. See, for example, Linda Gordon, "Dorothea Lange: The Photographer as Agricultural Sociologist," *Journal of American History* 93 (December 2006): 698–727;

Laura Wexler, *Tender Violence: Domestic Visions in an Age of U.S. Imperialism* (Chapel Hill: University of North Carolina Press, 2000).

5. Feminist critics, artists, and activists have contributed critical analyses of visual culture over the past thirty years. For recent feminist scholarship in visual studies, see "Introduction," in "New Feminist Theories of Visual Culture," eds. Jennifer Doyle and Amelia Jones, special issue, *Signs: Journal of Women in Society and Culture* 31, no.3 (Spring 2006): 607–615. Useful overviews of major feminist theories of the visual include Amelia Jones, *The Feminism and Visual Culture Reader* (New York: Routledge, 2002); Lisa Gail Collins, *The Art of History: African American Women Artists Engage the Past* (New Brunswick, NJ: Rutgers University Press, 2002); and Lisa Bloom, *With Other Eyes: Looking at Race and Gender in Visual Culture* (Minneapolis: University of Minnesota Press, 1999).

6. Mariolina Rizzi Salvatori, "The Scholarship of Teaching: Beyond the Anecdotal," *Pedagogy* 2 (Fall 2002), 298.

7. For guidance in using images in a historical interpretation, see Katherine Martinez, "Imaging the Past: Historians, Visual Images, and the Contested Definition of History," *Visual Resources* 11, no. 1 (1995): 21–45.

8. Coventry et al., "Ways of Seeing," 1402.

9. Masur, " 'Pictures Have Now Become a Necessity,' " 1410.

10. Ellen C. DuBois and Lynn Dumenil, *Through Women's Eyes: An American History with Documents* (New York: Bedford/St. Martin's, 2005); Ellen DuBois, "*Through Women's Eyes*: The Challenges of Integrating Women's History and U.S. History in the Writing of a College Textbook," *OAH Magazine of History* 19 (March 2005): 7–9.

11. Sam Wineburg, *Historical Thinking and Other Unnatural Acts: Charting the Future of Teaching the Past* (Philadelphia: Temple University Press, 2001), 232–255. Additionally, as the National Standards for History urge, students must develop competencies to interrogate "a variety of visual sources such as historical photographs, political cartoons, paintings, and architecture in order to clarify, illustrate, or elaborate upon the information presented" in written narratives. National Center for History in the Schools, *National Standards for History*, 1996; see http://nchs.ucla.edu/standards/ (October 7, 2006).

12. DuBois and Dumenil, *Through Women's Eyes*, 677–692.

13. Standard 3B Historical Analysis and Interpretation, *National Standards for History*; see http://nchs.ucla.edu/standards/thinking5-12_toc.html (October 7, 2006).

14. Jennifer Baumgardner, Amy Richards, Kathleen Hanna, Rebecca Walker, and Catherine Orenstein, "Feminist Revival in the 1990s," documentary essay in DuBois and Dumenil, *Through Women's Eyes*, 665–676.

15. For an excellent guide to analyzing material objects, see Daniel Waugh, "Material Culture/Objects," *World History Matters*, Center for History and New Media, at http://chnm.gmu.edu/worldhistorysources/unpacking/objectsmain.html (October 21, 2006).

16. John Singleton Copley's portrait of his own family can be examined for social ideas about family and gender roles. See "Copley Family Portrait," an online module

designed by Paula Petrik for George Mason University's *Exploring U.S. History*, at http://chnm.gmu.edu/exploring/18thcentury/copleyfamily/index.php (March 30, 2007).

17. Masur, "'Pictures Have Now Become a Necessity,'" 1410; the original portrait of Elizabeth Freeman, completed by Susan Anne Livingston Ridley Sedgwick in 1811, is held by the Massachusetts Historical Society and is featured in their online collections: http://www.masshist.org/database/onview_full.cfm?queryID=25 (March 30, 2007); a reproduction of the watercolor of Elizabeth "Mumbet" Freeman is on display in the main rotunda of the National Archives: http://www.archives.gov/exhibits/charters/charters_of_freedom_5.html# (July 23, 2008).

18. See "George Washington: Images of History," a Web-based lesson developed by Sue Luftschein and David Jaffee as part of the Learning to Look Faculty Development program at the Graduate Center, City University of New York, at http://historymatters.gmu.edu/d/6876 (March 30, 2007); and "Society of Patriotic Women at Edenton, North Carolina [1774]," an online module designed by Paula Petrik for George Mason University's *Exploring U.S. History*, at http://chnm.gmu.edu/exploring/18thcentury/patrioticwomen/index.php (March 30, 2007).

19. Many cultural institutions and historical repositories now provide Web-mounted resources for students and instructors. The most notable include the National Archives and Records Administration "Digital Classroom," at http://www.archives.gov/education/ (April 2, 2007); the Library of Congress's "Learning Page," at http://memory.loc.gov/learn/ (April 2, 2007); and "EdSITEment," the National Endowment for the Humanities, at http://edsitement.neh.gov/ (April 2, 2007).

20. *Imaging the French Revolution: Depictions of the Revolutionary Crowd*, a project of the Center for History & New Media, George Mason University, and the Department of History, University of California, Los Angeles, for the *American Historical Review*, offers an archive of forty-two images of crowds and crowd violence in the French Revolution, essays by seven scholars, and excerpts from an online discussion by the scholars on issues of interpretation, methodology, and the impact of digital media on scholarship. "Imaging the French Revolution," *American Historical Review* 110 (February 2005); see http://chnm.gmu.edu/revolution/imaging/home.html (October 7, 2006).

21. Joan B. Landes, "Representing Women in the Revolutionary Crowd," in "Imaging the French Revolution," 1.

22. "Information Literacy in the Disciplines: History," Association of College and Research Libraries, American Library Association, at http://www.ala.org/ala/acrlbucket/is/projectsacrl/infolitdisciplines/history.htm (April 15, 2007).

23. David Jaffee, "Thinking Visually as Historians: Incorporating Visual Methods," *Journal of American History* 92 (March 2006), 1378.

24. Peter Felten, "Confronting Prior Visual Knowledge, Beliefs, and Habits: 'Seeing' beyond the Surface," *Journal of American History* 92 (March 2006), 1384.

25. Essential questions uncover a subject's controversies, they address philosophical foundations of a discipline, and they raise questions across subject-area

boundaries. Framed to provoke and sustain student interest, these questions are at the center of a three-stage curriculum development process of backward design that aligns learning goals, assessments of student understanding, and learning activities. See Grant Wiggins and Jay McTighe, *Understanding by Design* (Alexandria, VA: Association for Supervision and Curriculum Development, 1998).

26. *National Standards for History,* http://nchs.ucla.edu/standards/thinking5–12.html (April 4, 2007); *Pennsylvania Academic Standards for History,* http://www.pde.state.pa.us/stateboard_ed/cwp/view.asp?Q=76716 (April 4, 2007).

27. The notion of a complex slide was inspired by Thomas Thurston, "Hearsay of the Sun: Photography, Identity, and the Law of Evidence in Nineteenth-Century American Courts," in special issue "Hypertext Scholarship in American Studies," ed. Roy Rosenzweig, *American Quarterly* 51 (June 1999), at http://chnm.gmu.edu/aq/ (September 20, 2006). Thurston's system of using HTML "anchor" tag and "frame" to keep all of the pieces (argument, footnotes, sources, illustrations) of an essay on a single screen has been superseded by more recent XML technology; see William G. Thomas III and Edward Ayers, "The Difference That Slavery Made: A Close Analysis of Two Communities," *American Historical Review* 108 (December 2003): 1299–1307. Available online from the Virginia Center for Digital History at http://www.vcdh.virginia.edu/AHR/ (April 15, 2007).

28. For document analysis worksheets, see "The Digital Classroom," U.S. National Archives and Records Administration, http://www.archives.gov/education/ (October 14, 2006). For examples of guidelines for analyzing primary documents, see Center for History and New Media, *Making Sense of Evidence,* http://historymatters.gmu.edu/browse/makesense/ (October 14, 2006). For a useful set of questions to ask about the production and use of images, see Irene Bierman, "Material Culture/Images," *World History Matters,* Center for History and New Media, http://chnm.gmu.edu/worldhistorysources/unpacking/imagesmain.html (April 20, 2007).

29. Martinez, "Imagining the Past," 35.

30. Jeff Hook, "Red Rosa: Background on Rosa Parks and the Montgomery Bus Boycott," *National Vanguard,* November 7, 2005; "Woman fingerprinted. Mrs. Rosa Parks, Negro seamstress, whose refusal to move to the back of a bus touched off the bus boycott in Montgomery, Ala." (1956), *New York World-Telegram & Sun Collection.* Online Catalogue of the Prints and Photographs Division of the Library of Congress, at http://hdl.loc.gov/loc.pnp/cph.3c09643 (April 20, 2007). "The Aftermath," "'With an Even Hand': *Brown v. Board* at Fifty" (August 10, 2004), Library of Congress, at http://www.loc.gov/exhibits/brown/ (April 20, 2007).

31. "A Selection of Web Resources for Gender History," *OAH Magazine of History* 19 (2005), at http://www.oah.org/pubs/magazine/gender/webresources.html (April 22, 2007); Susan K. Freeman, Donna J. Guy, Nancy Hewitt, and Martha S. Jones, "Perspectives on Teaching Women's History: Views from the Classroom, the Library, and the Internet," *Journal of Women's History* 16 (2004): 143–176; Renee M. Sentilles, "Catching It All on the Web: Crafting Cohesive American Women's History in the Age of the Internet," *Journal of Women's History* 15 (2003): 175–177; Kriste Lindenmeyer, "Using Online Resources to Re-Center the U.S. History Survey: Women's History as a

Case Study," *Journal of American History* 89 (2003): 1483–1488; Heather Lee Miller, "Getting to the Source: The World Wide Web of Resources for Women's History," *Journal of Women's History* 11 (1999): 176–187.

32. Gerda Lerner, "U.S. Women's History: Past, Present, and Future," *Journal of Women's History* 16 (2004), 24; Lerner, "A Reply to Responses," *Journal of Women's History* 16 (2004), 63.

15

History You Can Touch: Teaching Women's History through Three-Dimensional Objects

Anne M. Derousie and Vivien E. Rose

Where visual or other documentary evidence is scant, the power of objects to reveal the unknown and unnoticed is of particular use. Like nutritious and healing weeds in a suburban lawn, three-dimensional objects offer previously unnoticed benefits to instructors inviting students to consider an inclusive perspective as they reframe and remember U.S. history. The variety and multiplicity of women's experiences can be touched through three-dimensional primary sources, engaging students with different learning styles; cementing skills of observation, analysis, and construction of narrative; and fostering awareness of what the objects around them can say about race, class, and gender.

Susan Glaspell's 1917 short story, "A Jury of Her Peers," illustrates a farmwoman's actions through the objects of her daily life.[1] In these objects, the wives of officials searching her home and barn for clues about her husband's death find powerful motivation for murder and credible evidence of temporary insanity as they wait while their husbands gather evidence against her. Without a word to their husbands, they find her "not guilty." Glaspell's story is a powerful resource for teachers wanting to understand women's experiences through three-dimensional evidence. Glaspell provides one of the best and most immediate descriptions of the skills of observation and inference needed to decode objects' meanings, while introducing three different types of three-dimensional evidence: artifacts, structures, and landscapes. Readers are shown the female characters' physical interactions with the accused's tools, furniture, home, and surroundings. They hear as the female characters struggle to put words to what they see. They witness the construction of two very different narratives as the women carefully examine the accused's belongings, which the men ignore and criticize in their search for a clue to the motive for murder. In short, the story leads students to an awareness of objects as evidence as few other written pieces can. We strongly recommend reading the piece before continuing with this chapter, as it is a powerful translation device between our experiences and the experiences of instructors unfamiliar with objects as evidence.

Educators and psychologists posit that engagement with objects offers resolution, density of information, scale, authenticity, and value; that is, objects are real, retain a human scale, and truly were created and handled by historical people. Their value as evidence lies in the combination of these characteristics, which leads to a different kind of analysis as well. Optimal tools to provide entry into the underdocumented lives of American women of all races and classes, to teach use of primary sources, and to invite students to write historical narratives of the past, objects engage kinesthetic senses little used in the analysis of visual or auditory evidence. Even the language of this body-based skill is different, for grasping the meaning of an object with the mind implies a familiarity with texture, shape, and heft, all difficult to acquire by viewing an artifact. The mental muscle developed in the act of apprehension seems to us to be complementary to and different from that developed by analysis of the kinds of visual materials that make up the bulk of primary sources.[2]

A wealth of such primary source material is available at local historical societies and museums, in buildings, and in streetscapes and landscapes. Our experience as classroom teachers and staff at historic sites related to the 1848 First Women's Rights Convention suggests that such work cements learning and invites new areas of question. We know curators and education staffers to be quite happy to work with students and schools. In places without historical sites associated with women, the local museum or historical society may be able to lend or bring to the classroom historical objects owned by local women.

In our experience, three-dimensional objects unmediated by a photographer, artist, or inventory maker offer students an opportunity to develop new skills of observation, analysis, hypothesis making, and conclusion drawing. They connect students with women's lived experience and expand students' literacy of different types of primary sources while engaging multiple learning styles. Another benefit is that they immediately involve students in hypothesizing about a historical subject. In a national telephone survey, respondents reported that participation in the creation of historical narratives created an attachment to the past. Survey participants found history classes with recitation of facts boring and preferred activities requiring discovery and integration of information. Wanting "direct engagement with the 'real' stuff of the past and its self-evident relationship to the present," respondents wanted to create meaning out of the evidence around them. Three-dimensional objects offer students the opportunity to interact with "real stuff," acting as historians with instructors as guides and expert witnesses.[3]

Using objects or requiring analysis of buildings or landscapes once may have been extraneous in a U.S. history survey course or even in a higher level topics course, but not any more. When including the history of women in a survey class for the first time, objects, structures, and landscapes can make women's experiences visible to students in ways that documentary sources may not. We observed that students who visited historic buildings related to the antebellum women's rights movement demonstrated a better grasp of that movement on a final examination than those who did not, and high school students who viewed artifacts from Progressive Era woman suffrage campaigns came to different understandings of the meanings of citizenship than had previous classes.[4]

Three-dimensional primary sources can be classified broadly into three types: material culture (objects or artifacts), historic architecture (buildings), and cultural landscapes (buildings and surroundings). Although technical specialties exist within each of these fields, use of three-dimensional objects in classroom exercises is easiest to introduce through a human scale. Material culture is things made by humans; historic architecture is buildings built by and lived in or worked in by humans; cultural landscapes are the built or natural environment through which humans move. All share with written documents and visual images the quality of being made by or used by humans.

Introducing Objects as Evidence of Women's Lives: Glaspell's "A Jury of Her Peers"

Susan Glaspell's 1917 short story offers students an entering wedge into the world of objects as primary sources for understanding women's pasts. As the sheriff, the county attorney, and the neighbor first on the scene of the crime search a house and barns for the motive that will convict a farm wife of her husband's murder, the wives of the sheriff and neighbor examine the sugar bucket, kitchen table, clothes, cookstove, cupboard, birdcage, quilt blocks, and sewing basket of the accused. These objects testify to the accused's living and working conditions and to the effect of her husband's actions on her, vividly portraying an event so disturbing to the accused that she strangled her husband in their bed. The cold house, dark landscape, broken stove, dirty dishes and towels, half-cleaned table, damaged birdcage hinge, and erratically sewn quilt block spell out deprivation and mental cruelty to the waiting women. In a little painted box in the sewing basket, the women find a canary whose neck has been broken. This final piece of evidence convinces them of the husband's guilt for these conditions and of the accused's responsibility for his death.

As the men return to the kitchen where women are waiting, the county attorney says that juries will not convict without strong evidence. His casual interest in the quilt blocks and his repeated questions about how the quilt is to be finished indicate that he may understand the meaning of the canary in the box. The women conspire to remove this piece of evidence when left alone again. Apprehending the rest of the evidence, which the county attorney has not, they find the accused not guilty by virtue of temporary insanity.

Classroom discussion of this story and of the actions of the two women accompanying their husbands can be heated, with students arguing over whether the main characters owed their husbands or the law more allegiance than the accused. Instructors may lead discussion about whether the actions of the sheriff's wife and neighbor's wife indicate trust that the accused will receive a fair trial. Here the story's title provides additional context, pointing in the direction of the history of women's jury service in the United States. In 1917, most states excluded women from jury service. Written three years before suffrage was won on the national level, Glaspell's short story is as much a claim for equality of citizenship rights and responsibilities as a description of an event or scene.[5]

As the men's reaction demonstrates, merely seeing objects does not reveal the information they hold. To derive full benefit from this story as an entry into the use of three-dimensional objects as historical evidence, instructors must engage students in a consideration of how the main characters find evidence and analyze it to reach the conclusions that lead to their actions. The process by which the waiting women use the three-dimensional evidence before them to create a historical narrative starts with what objects say about themselves, their wear patterns, their materials, their edges.[6]

The core processes of historical inquiry, observation, and analysis are applied to three-dimensional resources to derive historical information from them. Leading students through a discussion about the bare facts of each object is the first step in separating observation from analysis and apprehension. What is known about the material, size, shape, color, construction, and markings or condition of the kitchen the women describe? Of the rocking chair? Stove? Table? Cupboard? Birdcage? Quilt blocks? Sewing basket? Can they bring these objects firmly to their mind's eye? Can they draw or otherwise represent these objects? Can they demonstrate that they understand the heft, weight, height, or shape of an object they have read about? Noting the bare facts of the objects on a table gives students an opportunity to compare and contrast the kind of information derived from the descriptions given.[7]

When the objects have been described fully, it is time to move on to an analysis of their meaning, or of what they can tell us about women's experiences. By themselves, do the objects in Glaspell's piece shed light on the life of an isolated farm wife? Or is it their condition of use that provides additional information? Do the main characters bring knowledge to bear on their analysis of the objects left behind? How do the main characters infer the meaning they ascribe to each object? The instructor will want to carefully guide conversation at this point, illustrating the difference between the evidence the object presents in and of itself, the evidence derived from its condition of use, and any additional information that leads the main characters to their conclusions.

Glaspell's short story provides another opportunity for instructors to discuss the construction of historical narrative. Cultural norms literally blind her male characters to historic fact. As the men in this story perceive them, the objects of the accused's life are stereotypical representations of assumed experiences. They do not see evidence in them of tasks interrupted or poorly executed, or question the effect of substandard and broken tools on the farm wife.

If approached as stereotypical, representative brooms, spinning wheels, aprons, and other kitchen tools can become signifiers of student assumptions about gender rather than evidence of the past. Instructors and students will want to consider together whether comprehension of primary sources is required to construct a historical narrative and whether awareness of one's own possible limits of perception are important as one goes about making sense of the past.[8]

The Material Reality of U.S. Women's History

Just as some instructors keep copies of primary sources for classroom use, others maintain a teaching collection of objects. Handkerchiefs and aprons provide entrée to discussions of social customs, hygiene, and women's handwork; clothing to fashion history, as well as to issues of attire by race, class, and gender; and kitchen implements to the creation of family through rituals of feeding. A curator can assist with demonstrating the skills of "apprehending" the objects, but if necessary, instructors can present items to students one by one.

Without touching the objects, students are asked to reach out with their minds to hold and handle the objects and to describe the physical characteristics of each object. The bare facts of material, size, shape, color, construction, and markings are noted until all objects are considered. Then, students can be invited to directly examine objects. Here a curator will be helpful in providing gloves and tips for careful handling of possibly fragile artifacts and in guiding students in apprehending wear patterns and other physical attributes that visual examination may not reveal.

Where additional documentary evidence is available about the object or its owner, guiding students through the process of adding information to the bare facts of an object allows them to learn or infer more meaning to it. Often students are more aware of the importance of visual or written sources for historical analysis and more experienced with using them as sources than they are with three-dimensional sources. Student familiarity with document-based exercises and standard examinations will provide a foundation for using documents to provide context and fuller meaning to three-dimensional sources. Written material is generally assumed to express the conscious intention of the producer, with objects as mere tools to be used in that expression. As Glaspell's story illustrates, however, objects can say as much about embodied experience and actions as written documents can about intent. Understanding that visual sources are different from three-dimensional sources opens dialogue with students about ways of knowing, as well as the similarities and differences between the sense of sight, the sense of touch, and embodied knowledge. Students can also be asked to consider what it would be like for them to use the objects they are viewing and touching. It is worth asking students to consider how it might affect a wife, like the one in Glaspell's story, to have only worn and shabby clothing. How might the owner of the objects being viewed have felt about them? Finally, how does the practice of standing in someone else's shoes affect students' understanding of the past?

Historic Architecture and Cultural Landscapes

Glaspell's short story can be used to introduce two categories of larger three-dimensional objects: buildings (or historical architecture) and grounds (cultural landscapes). Repeating the observation and analysis exercises with a focus on the house and then on the cultural landscape of Glaspell's farm wife illustrates similarities in observation and analysis skills needed to draw information from these sources of evidence. Structures contain added layers of spatial complexity, with relationships between various aspects of the structure becoming sources for investigation. Cultural landscapes have yet another layer of complexity—relationships between built elements within the landscape and between those elements and the landscape itself.

Historic Architecture

Buildings offer students an opportunity to observe women's experiences within space, illuminating assumptions about appropriate gender roles through room size, arrangement of internal space, placement of stairways and hallways, and locations of entries and exits. Examination of these spatial arrangements via visits to historic structures or review of floor plans can reveal segregation of some building users from others or separation of functions by gender. The farm wife in Glaspell's novel appears to have had very limited control over or access to resources within the house and farm buildings. Through comparison of physical evidence, students can literally "inhabit" a different period in time.[9]

Structures associated with women's history have often been significantly altered and may not be recognizable as the building in which a significant event happened or person lived. Subsequent generations may make changes to suit different purposes, leaving multiple layers of evidence of women's roles. Through these alterations, historic structures with much to tell about women's experiences may be hidden in plain sight and in close proximity to high school or college classrooms.[10]

Instructors can approach the use of structures as primary evidence in several ways. Students can be encouraged to use documentary evidence like city directories and census records to investigate the creation and use of a nearby building over time. Students may also be asked to create floor maps of the areas of the building in which class is held and to consider the unmapped areas for functional divisions of appropriate activity by gender or race operating in their own lives and thus sensitize them to historic experiences. By far the best exercise for students, however, is to walk through a historic building to experience the spatial relationships of the people who lived and worked there, attending to evidence of gender roles and class differences. As an example, historic houses often include back stairs, entrances, work spaces, and quarters for women engaged as household help, while the front of the house was reserved for the owner, family, and visitors. Instructors may wish to compare a historic house visit with examination of tenement floor plans showing common bathrooms off hallways and shared sleeping and working space within apartments. The spatial relations between elements in each of these building types reveal assumptions about appropriate roles for women of various classes and races.[11]

Historic house tours are often limited to the "public" side of the house, but instructors can ask for a tour of the "production" side of the house—the kitchens, cellars, and attic rooms where the work of the household was performed. These hidden corners typically reveal much plainer architectural elements, well-trodden wooden stairs from kitchen to cellar, and simpler furnishings. In some museums, instructors and students will find that the "servants' quarters" are now work spaces for staff and researchers, leading to questions about what is preserved and why.

Structures where women lived, taught, worked, worshipped, and banded together to create social change and a nurturing environment for their professional ambitions are still being discovered. Every community has architectural evidence of women's lives and work, including homes, schools, hotels, religious institutions, and women's club and service buildings. Through federal designation of historic buildings as regionally or nationally significant, the National Register of Historic Places and National Historic Landmark Survey list structures by county and state. Instructors may also locate nearby historic sites related to women in *Susan B. Anthony Slept Here*, offering 2,000 sites important to women's history in every state.[12]

Building elements and types can also change with changing gender roles. In the late 1890s, settlement houses, or group homes built for and run by women, proliferated. The most well known of these may be the Young Women's Christian Association or YWCA buildings found nationwide. At least ninety homes for working women were in operation in forty-five cities by 1898, and many still fulfill the function of temporary housing for women workers. Places of work, like factories and stores; headquarters of social, political, and labor reform movements; and homes of their leaders and membership are sites rich in women's history as well.[13]

Libraries, schools, and college campuses also contain evidence of women's lives. As women entered the library profession in the late 1890s, library interiors changed to allow supervision of front desk staff, as well as public access to open stacks. The shape, size, and placement of buildings on women's college campuses followed changes in educational philosophy and accepted roles for women. Likewise, commemoration of women's leadership in memorial buildings dedicated to them may not be evident to today's viewer, especially in formerly female colleges that are now coeducational.[14]

Women's history trails in Denver, Boston, and Portland, Maine, demonstrate one method of using buildings to teach about women in the local community. Created as student projects, the trails required students to investigate areas near their schools to learn about the women who lived and worked there. In Boston, students presented their buildings to an assembly of schools and voted for the most important sites to be places on the trail. Online resources are available to assist in student projects to research nearby buildings and create walking tours.[15]

Cultural Landscapes

Cultural landscapes include both buildings and environment. Where a person or group of people worked, a cultural landscape resulted. In Glaspell's work, the cultural landscape is the road, the fields, the relationship between the barn and house and road, and the natural elements that shaded the area. Cultural landscapes can also be gardens, college campuses, neighborhoods, rivers and settlements, shoreline and condos. Although girls and women may occupy the same space as boys and men, much can be learned about gender roles by differential use and experience of space. Analysis of urban landscapes demonstrates that they can be hostile environments, exposing people using them to the race, class, and gender biases of advertisers, business owners, and others using the same space.[16] These considerations allow students to consider the different experiences of women in the cultural landscape and their effect on the cultural landscape.

Women's labor shaped small farms in all regions of the United States. Women were the primary gatherers of natural resources in many indigenous nations. The Grand Portage historic gardens, planted by Ojibwe women and French voyageur men in the late 1700s, demonstrate two cultures and approaches to nature. Women played a strong role in the preservation of natural spaces in the American West by advocating and supporting the creation of national parks, including Joshua Tree National Park, Organ Pipe National Park, and Indiana Dunes National Park. The General Federation of Women's Clubs spent nearly a decade focused on lobbying for national parks under the leadership of Mary Belle King Sherman.[17]

Studying the cultural landscape can help students understand the complex interaction of women's experiences and place. In two coal-mining towns straddling the Virginia–West Virginia border, a historian found that women of one community ironed, cooked, and provided meals for miners and management. Socially and economically segregated by class, women in the town reserved for upper management rarely came to the other town, while women in the town built for low-level supervisors and miners had regular access to both towns as servants and cooks.[18]

Students comprehend the differential use of space by class, race, and gender most directly through mapping their own cultural landscapes and inquiring into how and by whom the same landscape is inhabited by other humans.

Where is it safe or appropriate for certain classes of people to be? Where are the restrooms? Where are the dining facilities? Where are community resources like libraries and stores? What open space exists and who benefits from it? Who has access to the use of the natural resources in the area? Students might also be asked to map the cultural landscape of Glaspell's farm wife. Where did she go? What were the limits of her experience? Finally, instructors can use historic maps and photographs to invite students to examine women's cultural landscapes across race and class in their own local area. Where were the women? What building resources and access to open land did they have? What did they use them for? Questions like these help students locate themselves in a landscape and to see landscapes as evidence of women's lives.[19]

Class, Race, and Gender

A few examples of things and places attached to particular women demonstrate that objects, buildings, and landscapes reflect class, gender, and racial norms, as well as determined efforts by women to change those norms. As an African American businesswoman and millionaire, Madam C. J. Walker affected the cultural landscape of Indianapolis, Indiana, when she constructed a building that served as factory, school for her sales agents, and theater and community center for Indianapolis's black community. She also built Villa Lewaro, a New York mansion, for herself and her family. A biography might tell her story, but her hair care products say a great deal about her desire for economic success for black women, and her buildings speak to her understanding of community and responsibility to family. Although direct experience of three-dimensional evidence generally offers better opportunities for students to understand women's experience, students can view images of her buildings and product line packaging online.[20]

Ida B. Wells, born in Holly Springs, Missouri, in 1862, fled her Memphis newspaper office and home after she challenged lynching in a fiery 1892 editorial. Her press and office destroyed, she campaigned to end lynching in the United States. Her long life was devoted to equal rights as a founding member of the NAACP, of the African American women's club movement, and of woman suffrage movements. She founded Chicago's first African American women's club and, in 1913, founded the Alpha Suffrage club for African American woman suffrage. Ida B. Wells's press is marked with a historical marker; historic maps of Memphis could be used in exercises to understand the neighborhood she inhabited, as Jim Crow laws and violence enforced segregation in the South. Her home in Chicago is marked as well, a fortress-like structure that speaks to her national stature as a defender of African American rights.[21]

Susan Gaskin and James Robinson had six children, all born into slavery. During the Battle of Manassas in 1862, Robinson's house served as a Union Army hospital. A porch opened on the back of the house to work areas for food production. The house was remodeled several times since the 1860s before being destroyed by arson in 1993. Structural and archaeological investigations conducted after the fire provided evidence of Robinson's purchase of three of his sons, of home production of food for family use, and of common consumer goods and porcelains. The Web site dedicated to this family illustrates the use of cultural landscapes, historic structures, objects, and archaeological sites to understand this family's past.[22]

Nearly every topic covered in the U.S. history survey course can be approached through consideration of objects, buildings, and cultural landscapes that provide evidence of women's lives. Using these sources offers instructors new avenues for teaching the observation and analysis skills essential to framing a historical narrative. They offer students an opportunity to use different sets of visual skills to master new material that relates to lived, everyday experiences of people in the past. Finally, they provide evidence of women's activities in shaping and forming the communities, customs, and achievements that mark the history of the United States.

NOTES

1. Susan Glaspell, "A Jury of Her Peers," was originally published in *The Best Short Stories of 1917*, Edward J. O'Brien, ed. (Boston: Small, Maynard & Company, 1918),256–282. It is now available online at http://www.learner.org/interactives/literature/story/fulltext.html.

2. Gaea Leinhardt and Kevin Crowley, "Objects of Learning, Objects of Talk: Changing Minds in Museums," in Scott G. Paris, ed., *Perspectives in Object-Centered Learning in Museums* (Mahwah, NJ: Erlbaum, 2002), 304–305. Some useful Web sites are from the Washington State Historical Society (http://www.historylab.org/curriculum/artifacts_toc.htm) and Middle Tennessee State University (http://www.mtsu.edu/~then/Objects/).

3. Roy Rosenzweig and David Thelen, *The Presence of the Past* (New York: Columbia University Press, 1998). For the quotation, see the afterword at http://chnm.gmu.edu/survey/afterroy.html.

4. Upper-level high school and university students visiting the Women's Rights National Historical Park generally study the late-nineteenth-century suffrage campaign or antebellum abolitionist and women's rights activities. College students were better able to place the activities of antebellum women's rights reformers in social and political context than were their fellow students, and high school students confronted

with the objects of the New York suffrage campaign in the 1910s debated natural rights with an understanding that political rights developed only slowly for many citizens.

5. Women were excluded from jury service in most states until as late as the 1980s. For a review of the meaning and extent of women's jury service in the United States, see Gretchen Ritter, "Jury Service and Women's Citizenship before and after the Nineteenth Amendment," *Law and History Review*, Fall 2002; http://www .historycooperative.org/journals/lhr/20.3/ritter.html (22 May 2007).

6. Steven Lubar and Kathleen Kendrick, "Artifacts Tell Their Own Stories," reveal the process of using artifacts as evidence at http://smithsonianeducation.org/ idealabs/ap/essays/looking2.htm.

7. Instructors may prefer to use a worksheet provided by the National Archives. See http://www.archives.gov/education/lessons/worksheets/artifact_analysis_ worksheet.pdf.

8. Historians who use material culture as primary sources in their written scholarship on women include Joan Jensen, Claudia Kidwell and Valerie Steele, Laurel Thatcher Ulrich, and Edith P. Mayo. Through artifacts and inventories, Joan Jensen discovered that women's butter production was important to the Brandywine River Valley economy between 1750 and 1850. Claudia Kidwell and Valerie Steele demonstrated changing gender roles through examinations of clothing. Laurel Thatcher Ulrich considered looms, cupboards, quilts, and coverlets to determine that a family farm–based "age of homespun" in the Early National period was a uniquely American myth. First Ladies' gowns, political campaign ephemera, and White House china revealed manipulation of this honorary role to serve political ends in many administrations. See Joan M. Jensen, *Loosening the Bonds: Mid-Atlantic Farm Women, 1750–1850* (New Haven: Yale University Press, 1986); Claudia Kidwell and Valerie Steele, *Men and Women: Dressing the Part* (Washington, DC: Smithsonian Institution Press, 1989); Laurel Thatcher Ulrich, *The Age of Homespun: Objects and Stories in the Creation of an American Myth* (New York: Knopf, 2001); Edith P. Mayo, *The Smithsonian Institution Book of the First Ladies: Their Lives, Times and Issues* (New York: Henry Holt, 1996).

9. For an online lesson plan and resources related to one house, see the Smithsonian Institution's "Within These Walls" site at http://americanhistory.si.edu/ house/home.asp. Online lesson plans from the National Park Service's Teaching with Historic Places program are available at http://www.cr.nps.gov/nr/twhp/.

10. For an overview of sites associated with women, see Heather Huyck, "Beyond John Wayne: Using Historic Sites to Interpret Women's History," in Lillian Schlissel, Vicki L. Ruiz, and Janice Monk, eds., *Western Women: Their Land, Their Lives* (Albuquerque: University of New Mexico Press, 1988).

For essays on how historic sites discuss the experiences of the women associated with them, see Polly Welts Kaufman and Katherine T. Corbett, eds., *Her Past around Us: Interpreting Sites for Women's History* (Malabar, FL: Krieger, 2003).

11. A general overview of building styles can provide basic vocabulary for students' descriptions of their observations. Middle Tennessee State University Center for Historic Preservation's The Heritage Education Network (T.H.E.N.) at http:// histpres.mtsu.edu/then/Architecture/ includes a pictorial glossary of architectural

terms for use in the classroom. The Lower East Side Tenement Museum provides tours of apartments of immigrants at 97 Orchard St., New York City. See http://www .tenement.org/index.htm for information about the museum and its programs.

12. Although the database cannot be sorted for whether women's experiences are the basis for a listing on the National Register of Historic Places, information about National Register buildings by state and county can be found at http://www.cr.nps. gov/nr/research/index.htm. Lynn Sherr and Jurate Kazickas, *Susan B. Anthony Slept Here: A Guide to American Women's Landmarks,* 2nd ed. (New York: Times Books, Random House, 1994).

13. Ibid., 97–98.

14. Helen Lefkowitz Horowitz, "Women and Education," in Miller, ed., *Reclaiming the Past: Landmarks of Women's History* (Bloomington: Indiana University Press,1992), 129–30; Abigail A. Van Slyck, "On the Inside: Preserving Women's History in American Libraries," in Gail Lee Dubrow and Jennifer B. Goodman, eds., *Restoring Women's History through Historic Preservation* (Baltimore: Johns Hopkins University Press, 2003).

15. See http://www.bwht.org/ for the Boston Women's Heritage Trail and instructor resources; http://www.state.nj.us/dep/hpo/1identify/whttrail2.htm for the New Jersey Women's Heritage Trail; http://www.cr.nps.gov/nr/travel/pwwmh/ womlist.htm for women's history sites in New York and Massachusetts; http://www .heritageny.gov/women/index.cfm for the New York Women's Heritage Trail; http:// www.cwhf.org/programs_ctwh.php for the Connecticut Women's Heritage Trail; and http://dll.umaine.edu/historytrail/ for the Augusta, Maine, women's history trail. Arizona and Indiana are presently researching women's heritage trails for their states. Katherine T. Corbett provides a series of articles on the structures associated with African American, religious, and other women in *In Her Place: A Guide to St. Louis Women's History* (St. Louis: Missouri Historical Society Press, 1999).

16. Dolores Hayden, *Redesigning the American Dream: The Future of Housing, Work and Family* (New York: W. W. Norton, 1984). From landscape architecture and historical geographers come two relevant works: Paul Groth and Todd Bressi, eds., *Understanding Ordinary Landscapes* (New Haven: Yale University Press, 1997); John R. Stilgoe, *Outside Lies Magic: Regaining History and Awareness in Everyday Places* (New York: Walker, 1998).

17. For information about the Grand Portage gardens, see http://www.nps.gov/ grpo/historyculture/the-historic-gardens.htm. Polly Welts Kaufman, *National Parks and the Woman's Voice: A History* (Albuquerque: University of New Mexico Press, 1996), 32–43.

18. Susan M. Pierce, "Women in the Southern West Virginia Coalfields," in Dubrow and Goodman, eds., *Restoring Women's History,* 161.

19. The Cultural Landscape Foundation Web site at http://www.tclf.org/whatis. htm provides definitions of cultural landscapes, information about types of landscapes, and student exercises.

20. See http://images.indianahistory.org/cdm4/browse.php?CISOROOT=/ m0399 for online resources related to the Walker business; http://www.cr.nps.gov/nr/ travel/pwwmh/ny22.htm for information about Villa Lewaro; and http://tps.cr.nps.

gov/nhl/detail.cfm?ResourceId=1817&ResourceType=Building for National Historic Landmark Survey information about the Walker Manufacturing Center in Indianapolis.

21. See http://www.ci.chi.il.us/Landmarks/I/IdaBWells.html for the Chicago residence; for a guide to collected papers, see http://ead.lib.uchicago.edu/view. xqy?id=ICU.SPCL.IBWELLS&c=w; for a historical marker in Memphis, see http://www.hmdb.org/marker.asp?marker=140; for information related to women's clubs, see http://www.lib.niu.edu/ipo/2003/iht1020311.html.

22. The Web site http://www.cr.nps.gov/archeology/robinson/index.htm gives an overview of the history of the house and the Robinson family and includes cultural landscape maps as drawn by Robinson descendants; http://www.nps.gov/rap/exhibit/mana/text/rhouse08.htm provides information about the archaeological evidence found on the site. Archaeological sites throughout the United States related to the experience of African-Americans are partially cataloged at http://www.cr.nps.gov/archeology/visit/AfricanAmerarch.htm. These sites find African American women active in plantations, business districts, schools, and other locations. Porcelain and other household items of Harriet Williams, an Alexandria, Virginia, bondswoman (found in her privy in a 1978 excavation) reveal access to better goods than those of free black families a few blocks away. The Williams site is at http://oha.alexandriava.gov/archaeology/ar-exhibits-witness-1.html.

16

Teaching Women's History through Oral History

Margaret S. Crocco

One of the best ways to generate excitement about history among high school and college students is to get them involved in doing oral histories. Students experience the challenges confronting historians in piecing together an understanding of the past—the incomplete and often contradictory nature of evidence, the role of perspective, and the challenge of writing coherent narratives. Some scholars have argued that oral history served as the engine that launched women's history in the 1970s.[1] Over the years, oral history collections focused on women from diverse backgrounds have grown considerably. Engaging students in doing oral history will add to the complex picture we are developing of past women's lives.

The Power of Oral History in Teaching Women's History

Ronald J. Grele has defined oral history as the "interviewing of eyewitness participants in the events of the past for the purposes of historical reconstruction."[2] Oral history began in the United States after World War II as an elite enterprise. Nevertheless, scholars increasingly saw oral history as a vehicle for writing history "from the bottom up." In particular, women's historians saw the possibilities for using oral history to capture the voices of a group that they believed had been marginalized in American history. During the 1970s and 1980s, many feminist scholars employed the metaphor of voice to express women's emergence onto the public stage as actors, authors, and agents of significance to the historical record. As women's voices began to be heard more clearly throughout public as well as private spaces, oral history was there to record them. Today, oral history is used as a method of research in a variety of disciplines, with large-scale projects implemented by interdisciplinary groups of scholars, as in the case of the Telling Lives project at Columbia University. This collaborative effort investigated the trauma inflicted on students, teachers, and other adults—both men and women—in Chinatown as a result of the tragedy of September 11, 2001, in New York City.[3]

Using oral history to teach women's history can take at least two paths—either through interpreting the oral histories available online and in archival collections or by requiring students to conduct their own oral histories. Both types of encounters with oral history may stimulate conversations about the ways in which history gets constructed, whose voices are heard in historical narratives, and how notions of historical significance shape what gets recorded for posterity. Doing oral history can be powerful in promoting excitement about the past and developing deeper understanding of the challenges of reconstructing it, especially when considering nonelite people who left few, if any, records. In doing oral history, even young students may find it possible to make original contributions to knowledge—about local, state, and sometimes national history, and especially their often-forgotten women's history.

Oral history serves as a corrective to the lopsided gendered accounts found in most history textbooks, especially those destined for the secondary school market, which contain about ten references to men for every one to a woman.[4] In this sense, oral histories can round out our understanding of the past by avoiding the part-whole fallacy that men's lives can stand in for women's lives in historical representations.

Oral history can also provide a welcome antidote to a narrative flattened by preoccupation with chronicling the history of groups. When women enter the historical narrative, they often do so as part of social history. The emphasis in social history is typically on groups and movements rather than individuals. This orientation may have the ironic effect of reducing the texture, variation, and personality of women's history. Oral history can provide a welcome antidote to a narrative flattened by preoccupation with groups and bring the actors back on stage, whether they are working in social movements, tending the home fires in time of war, or participating in altered patterns of consumption and commerce.[5]

History is inevitably focused on power and conflict, but a central tenet of women's history is that historical forces affect differently groups that are differently situated in terms of their access to power. Historians of women have often commented on how adding women to history can dramatically shift perspectives on the past, the structure of the narrative, and the conclusions reached about social, political, and economic change. In short, using oral histories as first-person accounts can reveal the sometimes awkward fit between women's history and the periodization found in textbooks. Oral histories with women provide entrée into the variant patterns, undercurrents, and contradictory impulses at work in the past. In this respect, what students take away from doing oral histories with women can provide important insights about the messiness, complexity, and incommensurability of different groups' historical experiences, thus providing important insights into the power of social location in history.

Doing Oral History

Oral history is, in the end, more art than science. Anyone interested in using oral history to do women's history will quickly conclude from published and online materials that the technical aspects of the process do not present formidable barriers to initiating student projects. Contemporary writing about oral history emphasizes the notion that "there is no single 'right way' to do an interview."[6]

That said, other hurdles may present themselves, nonetheless, the most obvious of which may be related to finding appropriate subjects for a project. Keeping in mind the availability or lack thereof of informants related to certain topics and questions is an important consideration with which to start planning the project. Equipment is another issue, although finding reasonably priced tape recorders is not too much of a problem these days. Related to this is the decision of whether to go digital or video. Helping students find appropriate background material to frame their understanding of a period—especially when investigating local or state history topics—can be challenging. Crafting good questions and training students to be good listeners (plenty of counterexamples of poor listening can be found on television talk shows) may, in some cases, require a good deal of in-class time. Transcribing interviews can also be an extremely time-consuming task; instructors need to make some decisions ahead of time about protocols concerning such matters.

Once the process begins, the identity of the subject and interviewer may play a role in the outcome. Linda Shopes writes about an oral history conducted as part of the Federal Writers' Project interviews with former slaves. Two interviews with the same subject are presented, one done by an African American interviewer and the other by a white interviewer. The point Shopes wishes to make here is the critical role played by the social location of the interviewer in relation to that of the subject. As she concludes in the section on interpreting oral histories, the genre is inherently subjective, situated, and contingent.[7] Keeping these factors in mind will help students make sense of their own experiences of reading, interpreting, and doing oral histories.

In terms of interpreting oral history, complicated issues of memory, interpretation, and historical representation present themselves in oral history. Discussion of such issues lies beyond the scope of this chapter but can be pursued in the myriad publications now devoted to the subject.[8] For historians, these issues are not terribly dissimilar to the problems of interpretation that must be confronted in assessing other historical sources. For feminist historians, the questions that must be asked of the transcripts of an oral history interview echo those that would be directed toward any documentary source: What is the context in which this document was created? Who is the speaker? What does the speaker's social identity suggest about her perspective on this subject? If the interview concerns a life history, then in what way might the narrator be shaping the story retrospectively to add coherence and purpose to the story? What other evidence confirms or contradicts the narrator's story? Looking back on the interview, how well considered were the questions asked, the topics broached? What subjects were not addressed, and how might these lacunae have influenced what was said? What relationship did the interviewer have with the interviewee, and how might that have influenced the narration? Did the twists and turns from the intended questions signal the interviewees' efforts to avoid particular topics?

Understanding Women's Suffrage through Oral History

The tale of women's suffrage told in most American history textbooks typically follows the contours of other political narratives, most notably emancipation of the slaves and passage of the Thirteenth, Fourteenth, and Fifteenth Amendments. Quite commonly, textbook authors structure such stories around the themes of expanding freedom and citizenship. Eventual success—in this case, passage of the Nineteenth Amendment in 1920—came about as the result of a long struggle led by several visionary but effective leaders. Along the way, various groups of men and women offered resistance, yet, the textbook narrative goes, the indefatigable suffragists conquered hurdle after hurdle, ultimately securing victory.

Over the last twenty years, historians have contributed numerous accounts of state-by-state efforts to pass suffrage amendments, rounding out knowledge about regional variations in this campaign.[9] Recently, scholars have also paid attention to the comparative aspects of the suffrage movement, particularly English-U.S. connections. Feminist historians have argued that passage of the Nineteenth Amendment must be seen as the result of a collective effort, of collaborations occasionally along lines of class and race, often working across national boundaries, and not simply the achievement of a few heroic leaders. But even as the story of women's suffrage has gained space in textbooks and revisionist interpretations continue to refine the narrative, little attention has been given to what happened "after suffrage."[10] Passage of the Nineteenth Amendment provides a climax to the story, and the structure of textbooks rarely allows much room for denouement.

Nevertheless, a few scholars have investigated how women used the vote in the 1920s and 1930s, seeking to determine when a "women's vote" emerged.[11] Creation of the League of Women Voters, the advent of the flapper and the "new woman," and appointment of women such as Frances Perkins to the highest ranks of the federal government are standard fare in treatments of women during these decades. However, one issue generally left unexplored is the question of political socialization for women, specifically, how changes occurred in their political and social identity as a result of winning the franchise. Most women coming of age in 1920 had presumably not been raised to see themselves as political actors with direct responsibility for making choices among candidates. Stepping into the ballot box meant taking on a new role, one that not all women may have immediately felt comfortable adopting. What was it like? How easy was it for nonvoting women to become voters? How might answering such questions provide insights into the intersection of gender roles and political processes in the American past?

Finding answers was the goal of an oral history research project undertaken by the Alice Paul Centennial Foundation in 1995 to commemorate the seventy-fifth anniversary of passage of the Nineteenth Amendment. Funded by the New Jersey Historical Commission, the project identified nine New Jersey women who had voted in 1920. Under the auspices of the Columbia University Oral History Research Office, interviewers received training in oral history. They then prepared an oral history guide, outlining a set of topics to be used for each interview. At the same time, interviewers were encouraged to respect the notion that each interview was a unique exchange, capitalizing on interesting yet unanticipated subject matter as it emerged. The guide provided a set of topics but not a script. The results of this oral history project offer fascinating insights into the experiences of the first cadre of New Jersey women to exercise the franchise in national elections.

I describe this project to demonstrate the contributions oral history can make to teaching women's history, whether as a primary source that brings history alive or as an individual or class project in which students engage in doing history. Although many authors have advocated for the insights afforded by oral history[12] and others for the unique intersection of gender and memory,[13] I focus here on how oral history complicates women's history, just as women's history complicates American history. This is not just a matter of teaching multiple perspectives of the national story but also of the ways in which studying women tends to confound many of the fundamental aspects of the themes, narratives, and chronologies built from conclusions about evidence limited by the contours of men's experiences.[14]

The history of marginalized groups helps to guard against overgeneralization, reductionism, or determinism in teaching about the past. Oral history as a vehicle used in reclaiming such histories also provides alternative perspectives on how women (and men) shape their lives through choices made within social, political, familial, economic, personal, and historical contexts. Folding women's recollections of voting in 1920 into the political narrative around the Nineteenth Amendment demonstrates that history is as much about the effects of everyday women's choices—writ large—as it is about decisions made by powerful men.

The New Jersey Story

In the months after ratification of the suffrage amendment, the *Newark Evening News* reported regularly about New Jersey women's involvement in voter registration, their consideration of candidates, and impending participation in the elections on November 2, 1920. In late August, the Morris County Clerk announced that he would request that women vote in the larger towns between 10 A.M. and 4 P.M., promising that "every possible effort will be made to handle the increased vote without annoyance or embarrassment to the voters."[15] One hundred and ten women (of 175 individuals in all) attempted to register to vote in Essex County in early September.[16] As the elections approached, the paper reported that the presence of many women as candidates for office nationwide made the election notable.[17] And on November 3, 1920, the paper noted that a ninety-six-year-old woman from Orange, a hotbed of woman suffrage and club movement activity in the state, cast her very first ballot for a Republican candidate.[18] The paper also commented that women's suffrage had created "unprecedented conditions" in the election.[19]

One might assume that such coverage signaled that the vast majority of eligible female voters cast their ballots in the November elections. Research conducted by historians and political scientists about women's voting patterns nationwide during those early years indicates that this was hardly the case. The proportion of women who turned out to vote during the 1920s and 1930s was significantly lower than the proportion of men.[20] Nevertheless, one historian who has written about the situation in New Jersey "after winning" (the vote) has found that suffragists did not retire from their energetic engagement with politics in the decades after 1920.[21] Although women failed to gain equal rights after they won suffrage, they did take on expanded roles as "moral prodders," operating increasingly outside the political system through reformist, nonpartisan groups organized on the basis of women's special interests and purported moral qualities.[22]

To get a more specific sense of what that first election experience was like for women, we interviewed nine individuals between the ages of 95 and 100. Most were lifelong residents of New Jersey, although a few had been born or lived elsewhere. On several occasions, the interviews were conducted with the help of a close family member who assisted in bringing recollections to mind. In speaking with these women, we developed an understanding about why more women did not vote immediately after passage of the Nineteenth Amendment. For example, one woman voted in a cigar store. She told us that she felt uncomfortable voting in a space that was essentially off-limits to women at other times. Another told us she voted in opposition to the wishes of her father. When she came home from voting, her father became very angry with her because "he was of the old school and didn't really think women should have the right to vote."[23] On the one hand, Edna Schaefer Barnard spoke of being challenged at the polls as to whether she was of the required age to vote. On the other hand, Helen Garvey Hauerstein remembers voting with her father and her seventy-seven-year-old grandmother.[24]

Glenna Murphy, who was teaching in South Orange in the northeastern part of the state, traveled almost an hour by train to Dover in northwestern New Jersey, and then by trolley to her family's home in Succasunna, so she could vote.[25] She told the interviewer that she presumed her father had voted in favor of giving women the vote in the statewide referendum on suffrage in New Jersey in 1915, the year similar referenda went down to defeat in Pennsylvania, Massachusetts, and New York, as well as New Jersey. She said he was adamantly in favor of women's suffrage. She describes her parents as Democrats who probably voted for James Cox in the presidential election. Despite her respect for her parents, she voted Republican, for Warren G. Harding. She told us she felt it was important to make up her own mind about such matters.

Another woman from a prominent family in Englewood, Janet Van Alstyne, attended Vassar College between 1918 and 1922. She was president of the student government organization there and remembers Inez Milholland, a Vassar student who was suspended for organizing a suffrage rally in a cemetery. Overall, she doesn't recall much discussion of politics at Vassar during those days. Nevertheless, she said that when news of the ratification of the Nineteenth Amendment reached the college, the students "thought it was marvelous."[26] Her mother served as program chair and then president of the Englewood Women's Club. As president, she invited Carrie Chapman Catt, leader of the National American Woman Suffrage Association, to speak to the club. Van Alstyne remembered meeting Catt when Catt came to the family's house to change clothes before the speech.

Van Alstyne also remembered voting for Cox, the Democratic candidate, because her father voted for him. After she got married in 1923, Van Alstyne "followed [her husband's] advice because he knew what he was talking about."[27] Her husband, a lifelong Republican, served as town councilman, state assemblyman, and state senator. Although she herself was not actively involved in politics, she lauded the contributions of the suffragists, calling them special people "who felt that liberating woman was a cause."[28]

Our subjects commented repeatedly that they recognized how important their act of voting was for the country and its women; indeed, most of them had been voting regularly for seventy-five years at the time of these interviews. One woman, Ruth Churchill from Chatham, said that when the Nineteenth Amendment passed, she, her mother, and her grandmother were thrilled with the opportunity. Her aging grandmother remarked, according to her recollections of her youth, that even "if they had to take [her] by ambulance," she was going to vote.[29]

Three of the nine women interviewed were teachers; one was a lawyer. Four were involved in local politics. Some were Republicans; others, Democrats. All were voting about the time they completed their schooling or began their first jobs. Our interviewees were quite aware of how long it had taken women to gain the right to vote. A few had joined the local parades and festivities in celebration of suffrage. They also reflected on the widespread public discussion, some of it quite negative, about women's voting in the months leading up to the election. According to Edna Rickard, some men complained that women were too emotional to make sound judgments in voting and shouldn't even be allowed to drive cars.[30] Although almost all our subjects' mothers supported women's voting, not all their fathers had. Several, including the lawyer Ann Schmerling Salzberg, remained involved in politics throughout their lives. Yet Salzberg was frustrated with women's progress since suffrage, remarking, "You know we women are our worst enemies."[31] She felt women were too timid in demanding their rights and pushing for social change.

One interesting theme across these interviews was the secrecy that surrounded one's voting. Repeatedly, our subjects stated that their friends refrained from talking about politics; sometimes they didn't divulge their choices to family members. The subjects seemed consistently surprised by questions concerning how other family members had voted, seeing it as violating the secrecy voting demanded, even from siblings and parents. Most knew their parents' party affiliations and assumed they voted the party line, but rarely did these women pose the question of personal choice directly.

In her interview, one African American woman, Edith McCleary, passionately described her strong commitment to voting.[32] She always voted until she entered a nursing home in her nineties. Her parents both supported women's suffrage and spent considerable time discussing politics within the family. She recalls first voting Republican—for Harding, Coolidge, and Hoover—and then switching to the Democrats with Franklin Delano Roosevelt. McCleary also said that numerous groups, including African American women's clubs, the American Legion, and the League of Women Voters, all tried to induct women into the voting process by sponsoring forums about the elections. She, too, noted that many men were upset with women's voting because they did not believe it appropriate for women to be involved in politics.

These stories add texture and detail to the newspaper accounts of the day, providing what might be called the human interest factor. Several key understandings emerge. First, the women recalled that many women did not register or vote in 1920. By contrast, the newspapers consistently emphasized the large numbers of new voters being registered in the months up to the November elections of 1920. Subsequent political science research indicates that less than 50 percent of eligible female voters exercised their right to vote during the 1920s.[33] Second, these women believed strongly that their voting was socially, historically, and politically significant, even though none described herself as a suffragist. They agreed that women deserved the vote and disagreed with the antisuffragists, a vocal and active group in New Jersey at this time.

New Jersey's newspapers made much of the antisuffragist efforts of the liquor interests, who believed women's suffrage would bring prohibition of alcohol. State temperance groups had been staunch advocates of women's suffrage since the late nineteenth century. Oral history, like history in general, focuses on those individuals whose lives appear to have contributed to "progress" as defined by later generations. Many textbooks scarcely mention the widespread, organized opposition to suffrage among men *and* women in the years before the amendment.

What emerges from these interviews are insights, albeit fragmentary ones, reaped from a very small sample of women of very advanced years, into what the process of voting meant to women in 1920. What did we learn? The knowledge gained from these exchanges goes beyond refinement of the standard narratives concerning the suffrage struggle. Reflecting on these women's experiences as voters in 1920 provides a different understanding of the meaning of this chapter in American history, as well as a better grasp of what it means to do history, including recognition of the imperfect nature of historical evidence, the imaginative as well as analytical processes that are demanded in writing history, and the partial, tentative, and contingent nature of the resultant narrative.

What did we learn that we would not have learned from textbooks or conventional primary sources? One lesson was surely the degree to which the act of voting pressed women to operate within masculine-identified buildings. Such circumstances undoubtedly made some women reluctant to "transgress" gender-differentiated spaces to exercise their newfound right. We also were reminded of how little talk of politics went on in some families and social circles. The secret ballot was a relatively new innovation in New Jersey at this time; this may have meant keeping confidential one's choices, even from family and friends. Likewise, we learned that some women needed to overcome their socialization and their fathers' disapprobation in order to vote. This reminds us that old attitudes die hard and new attitudes are not necessarily universally held, even when majorities support political or social change.

We also encountered reminders of the strong negative views certain individuals held about women's entrance into active citizenship. Elizabeth Jessup remembered a story about her father, who was serving on the school board with a woman at that time:

> Somehow a woman got on the school board; I don't know how it happened.... It was a terrible thing to have a woman on the school board is how people felt in those days. Women shouldn't go into public office... I was raised so strongly that way that I still feel that men should be in the high offices—governor on up. I like to look up to a man. I think that women have gone entirely too far. I don't say that they're not capable. I don't mean it in that light. But I don't know why men vote for women. I don't.[34]

This quotation is a potent reminder that we must not romanticize women's history. Elizabeth Jessup exercised her right to vote, but she clearly had strong reservations about women's running for office—even if it was only the local school board. Individual women define their interests in very different ways; our students need to be open to the notion that while we do "women's history," there are many "women's histories." Doing oral history offers a unique opportunity to encounter that diversity up close and learn about women whose stories may be inspiring or demoralizing, provocative or pedestrian, enlightening or frustrating—in short, much the same as women's lives. We should not anticipate that all oral histories our students do with women will put them in touch with women they want to emulate.[35] We make plaster saints of women at the risk of historical verisimilitude. Through oral history, students will surely come to understand how much more complicated and interesting women's history can be than the tidy accounts offered in most textbooks.

Getting Started

Numerous practical resources about oral history are available.[36] One place instructors might consider starting is the Web site for the Oral History Association (OHA) (http://www.dickinson.edu/oha). This organization publishes a journal, the *Oral History Review*, and holds annual conferences drawing individuals with a variety of backgrounds to discuss their experiences with oral history. Some excellent resources are included here throughout the footnotes.

Instructors interested in using oral histories produced by others may want to start at the Web site http://www.inthefirstperson.com, which provides an index to thousands of diary entries, letters, and oral histories. Likewise, abundant materials are available in more focused collections, such as those provided at the end of this chapter. Several Web sites address the how-to of:

interviewing (http://bancroft.berkeley.edu/ROHO/resources/1minute. html);
transcribing (http://www3.baylor.edu/Oral_History/Styleguiderev.htm);
indexing (http://www.loc.gov/vets/transcribe.html);
organizing projects (http://www.dohistory.org/on_your_own/toolkit/ oralHistory.html);
writing with oral histories (http://www.unc.edu/depts/wcweb/handouts/ oral_history.html).

The most important idea to emphasize is how unimportant fidelity to such technicalities is in the end. What is important is the potential of oral history for providing powerful insights into how women have lived their lives—insights that will capture student interest in unique and lasting ways.

Recommended Oral History Web Sites

- The oldest oral history project in the United States is located at Columbia University (http://www.columbia.edu/cu/lweb/indiv/oral/ about.html) and contains nearly 8,000 taped memoirs.

- Another early project is the Black Women's Oral History Project undertaken by the Schlesinger Library of Radcliffe College in 1976 and available as part of the Sophia Smith Collection at Smith College (http://www.smith.edu/libraries/libs/ssc/ohlist.html).
- Also begun in the 1970s, at the University of California at Berkeley the Suffragists Oral History Project (http://bancroft.berkeley.edu/ROHO/projects/suffragist/) features seven lengthy interviews with women involved in the women's suffrage movement, most notably Alice Paul and Jeannette Rankin.
- At California State University, Long Beach, the Virtual Oral/Aural Archive (http://www.csulb.edu/voaha) interviews begun in the 1970s include suffragists and other reformers, women in the military and on the home front during World War II, and more contemporary Chicana and Asian American women activists. For Chicana women, also see the New Mexico State University Oral History Project (http://archives.nmsu.edu/rghc/index/Women.html).
- Two collections containing oral histories of recent immigrant women are the Tamiment Library and Robert F. Wagner Labor Archives at New York University (http://www.nyu.edu/library/bobst/research/tam/) and the Mujeres Latina Digital Collection at Iowa State University (http://cdm.lib.uiowa.edu/cdm4/index_latinas.php?CISOROOT=/latinas).
- The Activist Women's Voices: Oral History Project (http://web.gc.cuny.edu/Womenstudies/activism.html) includes a number of oral histories of Puerto Rican women.
- The Rutgers Oral History Archives of World War II, the Korean, Vietnam, and Cold Wars can be found at (http://oralhistory.rutgers.edu). In a few cases, scholars have developed documentary film projects from the oral histories. See, for example, *Good Work Sister! Women Shipyard Workers of World War II: An Oral History*, a result of the collaborative effort known as the Northwest Women's History Project (http://www.goodworksister.org/GWS.1.html).

NOTES

1. Susan Armitage makes this point in "Here's to the Women: Western Women Speak Up," *Journal of American History* 83, no. 2 (September 1996), 551–559.

2. Ronald J. Grele, "Directions for Oral History," in David K. Dunaway and Willa K. Baum, eds., *Oral History: An Interdisciplinary Anthology* (Walnut Creek, CA: Alta Mira, 1996), 63.

3. For more information on these projects, see http://www.columbia.edu/cu/lweb/news/libraries/2004/2004-06-09.ohro_chinatown.html.

4. See Roger Clark, Jeffrey Allard, and Timothy Mahoney, "How Much of the Sky? Women in American High School History Textbooks from the 1960s, 1980s, and 1990s," *Social Education* 68 (January–February 2004), 57–61.

5. I develop this point in my article, "Putting the Actors Back on Stage: Oral History in the Secondary Classroom," *Social Studies* 89 (January–February 1998), 19–24.

6. Alistair Thomson, "Fifty Years On: An International Perspective on Oral History," *Journal of American History* 85, no. 2 (September 1998), 582. Shopes is quite clear on this point in her article about oral history at the History Matters Web site (http://www.historymatters.gmu.edu/mse/oral/).

7. Shopes, "Making Sense of Oral History: Who Is the Interviewer?" (http://www.historymatters.gmu.edu/mse/oral/question2.html).

8. The *Journal of American History* has published essays on oral history annually each September since 1987. Consulting *JAH* as well as the *Oral History Review* will bring readers of this chapter up to date on the issues confronting the field.

9. The classic work on the suffrage struggle is Eleanor Flexner and Ellen Fitzpatrick, *Century of Struggle: The Woman's Rights Movement in the United States*, 2nd ed. (Cambridge, MA: Belknap Harvard, 1996). Sherna Berger Gluck edited a set of oral histories with suffragists, published as *From Parlor to Prison: Five Suffragists Talk about Their Lives* (New York: Monthly Review Press, 1976/1985).

10. Kristi Anderson, *After Suffrage: Women in Partisan and Electoral Politics before the New Deal* (Chicago: University of Chicago Press, 1996).

11. Some examples include Margaret Smith Crocco and Della Barr Brooks, "The Nineteenth Amendment: Reform or Revolution?" *Social Education* 59, no. 5 (September 1995), 279–284; Paul Kleppner, *Who Voted? The Dynamics of Electoral Turnout, 1870–1980* (New York: Praeger, 1982); and Ethel Klein, *Gender Politics* (Cambridge: Harvard University Press, 1984).

12. See, for example, Michael Frisch, *A Shared Authority: Essays on the Craft and Meaning of Oral History and Public History* (Albany: State University of New York Press, 1990); Ronald J. Grele, *Envelopes of Sound: Six Practitioners Discuss the Method, Theory, and Practice of Oral History and Oral Testimony*, 2nd ed. (New York: Praeger, 1991); Alessandro Portelli, *The Death of Luigi Trastulli, and Other Stories: Form and Meaning in Oral History* (Albany: State University of New York Press, 1991); Paul Thompson, *The Voice of the Past: Oral History*, 2nd ed. (New York: Oxford University Press, 1988); and Robert Perks and Alistair Thomson, eds., *The Oral History Reader* (New York: Routledge, 1998).

13. Selma Leydesdorff, Luisa Passerini, and Paul Thompson, eds., *Gender and Memory* (New Brunswick, NJ: Transaction, 2005); Sherna Berger Gluck and Daphne Patai, eds., *Women's Words: The Feminist Practice of Oral History* (New York: Routledge, 1991).

14. One of the first essays to raise these questions was Joan Kelly's "Did Women Have a Renaissance?" in *Women, History, and Theory: The Essays of Joan Kelly* (Chicago: University of Chicago Press, 1984).

15. *Newark Evening News*, August 21, 1920.

16. *Newark Evening News*, September 8, 1920, 14.

17. *Newark Evening News*, October 30, 1920, 3.

18. *Newark Evening News*, November 3, 1920.

19. Ibid.

20. William Chafe, *The American Woman: Her Changing Social, Economic and Political Roles, 1920–1970* (New York: Oxford University Press, 1972), 29.

21. Felice Gordon, *After Winning: The Legacy of the New Jersey Suffragists, 1920–1947* (New Brunswick, NJ: Rutgers University Press, 1986).

22. Ibid, 4.

23. Interview with Edna Schaefer Barnard by Jennifer Yerex-Pozo and Susan Butterfield, August 12, 1996, Mendham, New Jersey. This interview and others cited in this chapter are housed at the Alice Paul Institute, Mt. Laurel, New Jersey.

24. Interview of Helen Grace Hauerstein by Larry Hauerstein, September 10, 1996.

25. Interview of Glenna Murphy by Margaret Crocco, July 29, 1996.

26. Interview with Mrs. David (Janet) Van Alstyne by Delight Dodyk, August 5, 1996.

27. Ibid.

28. Ibid.

29. Interview of Ruth Churchill by Margaret S. Crocco, August 6, 1996.

30. Interview of Edna A. Rickard with Margaret S. Crocco, September 1, 1997.

31. Interview of Ann Schmerling Salzberg with Barbara Irvine, August 1, 1996.

32. Interview of Edith Gregory McCleary with Janet Jones, July 11, 1997.

33. Chafe, *The American Woman*, 29; see also Anderson's discussion of the changes women's voting made in *After Suffrage*, 5–19.

34. Interview of Elizabeth Jessup by Barbara Irvine, August 1, 1996.

35. See, for example, Kathleen Blee's *Women of the Klan: Racism and Gender in the 1920s* (Berkeley: University of California Press, 1991).

36. A sample of useful books available about oral history includes Donald A. Ritchie's *Doing Oral History: A Practical Guide*, 2nd ed. (New York: Oxford University Press, 2003); Barry Lanman and Laura Wendling, eds., *Preparing the Next Generation of Oral Historians: An Anthology of Oral History Education* (Lanham, MD: Alta Mira, 2006); Eva M. McMahan and Kim Lacy Rogers, eds., *Interactive Oral History Interviewing* (Hillsdale, NJ: Erlbaum, 1994); James Hoopes, *Oral History: An Introduction for Students* (Chapel Hill: University of North Carolina Press, 1979); Glenn Whitman, *Dialogue with the Past* (Lanham, MD: Alta Mira, 2004); and Valerie Raleigh Yow, *Recording Oral History: A Practical Guide for Social Scientists* (Thousand Oaks, CA: Sage, 1994). See also Linda Shopes, "Making Sense of Oral History," in *History Matters: The U.S. Survey Course on the Web*, at http://historymatters.gmu.edu/mse/oral, February 2002; Judith Moyer's "The Step-by-Step Guide to Oral History," at http://www.dohistory.org/on_your_own/toolkit/oralHistory.html; the Indiana University Center for the Study of History and Memory's Guide to Oral History Techniques, at http://www.indiana.edu/~cshm/techniques.html; and the Bancroft Library at Berkeley's *One Minute Guide to Oral History*, at http://bancroft.berkeley.edu/ROHO/resources/1minute.html.

17

Who is Teaching Women's History? "Insight," "Objectivity," and Identity

Nicholas L. Syrett

I teach U.S. women's history. As an undergraduate, I majored in women's and gender studies and was often asked, particularly by those outside academia, why on earth I had chosen my major. I felt quite sure that my friends majoring in architecture and biology were not asked the same question. The question seemed to arise from a notion that only women ought to be interested in women's history or gender studies. Men remained genderless in this analysis, in the same way that white people often remain "raceless." Some people assumed that I had chosen my major because I was interested in gay and lesbian studies, since women's studies was the academic home for most of the courses offered in that area at my college. While I am gay and did take one class in queer theory, this was not actually the case.

Behind the question of why a man would take a course in or teach women's history lies the assumption that those who study the history, sociology, or theory of a group must be, in essence, studying themselves. Why else would anyone bother?[1] Of course, most historians are clearly not studying themselves—medievalists are not living in the Middle Ages; Napoleonic scholars are not nineteenth-century Frenchmen. Yet the assumption is that even when a twenty-first-century woman historian studies the role of women in medieval France, she is really just reading and writing about herself. The result is a number of different expectations and assumptions on the part of our students that affect how they perceive our place in the classroom and the knowledge we attempt to share with them.

My perceived lack of identification with or personal investment in studying women leads some students to believe that they are receiving a more objective treatment of the material than they might receive from a female professor. Students also seem to believe that a female professor is both more personally invested in the material and more in touch with the subject matter. Both of these assumptions may work, in different ways, to a professor's advantage, but neither is without significant problems.

This chapter explores the role of sex[2] (and, to a lesser degree, race and sexual orientation, as they are perceived by students) in the women's history classroom. It attempts to elucidate the expectations students bring to such courses. It also examines the ways that we, as men and women, queers and straights, people of varied races and ethnicities, might think about addressing our (perceived) identities in the classroom. I do not pretend to have identified the solution to the problems of our students' expectations of us as teachers as they relate to our identities, but I do hope to raise a number of issues related to this question. This discussion reveals how our identities are at work in the classroom, often without our actively thinking about it.

Let me say at the outset that it is my firm belief that anyone trained in a field and committed to being a good teacher should have the right to teach it. I teach both women's history and queer history; I am very much identified with queer history in ways I am not when I walk into a women's history classroom. But that I am *qualified* to do either has nothing to do with being a gay white man and everything do with the fact that I was trained to teach both and that I keep up to date in the recent scholarship of both. To insist that one be in some way "related to" or a "part of" the people one teaches or studies creates an absurd burden—and places it only on certain practitioners of history.

In the best of all possible worlds, our students understand this, but they also bring a number of other expectations to the classroom, especially the women's history classroom. My realization that I was accorded a special privilege in teaching about women was first driven home to me when in graduate school I was a teaching assistant (TA) in an "Introduction to Women's Studies" class at the University of Michigan. The 250-person class was taught by a professor of English and women's studies who was assisted by a group of five doctoral candidates from a variety of disciplines: English, psychology, history, American studies, and social work, in the two semesters that I taught it. Both times I was the only man. The class included a unit on the history of feminism in the

United States, and it became clear fairly quickly that I was having a much easier time talking about the second wave of the women's movement than my female fellow TAs. Why? Because I was perceived as an objective voice on the question of women's anger toward men. While my colleagues were meeting resistance from their (primarily female) students, I was a man who validated women's anger toward men and a patriarchal society. I was at least partially able to counteract the stereotypes students had about feminists and make them seem the rational historical actors that they were. To them, I was not "invested"; thus I enjoyed certain unearned advantages. I had achieved my pedagogical goals, but I had done so through the very structures of privilege that those of us teaching the class—and, indeed, the very people we were studying at the time—were attempting to undermine. And I wasn't really sure how to get around it.

I now teach classes on the history of women, gender, and sexuality throughout U.S. history at a mid-size university in northern Colorado.[3] Slightly more than 86 percent of the students here are white.[4] Most, but not all, history majors are jointly registered in a dual-degree program to teach high school history when they graduate. My university enrolls about 60 percent women and 40 percent men and, as the original teachers' college in Colorado, has a long history of sex imbalance.[5] Classes in women's history are predominantly taken by women, though this probably has little to do with the university sex imbalance and much more to do with the subject matter; certainly, there are other classes where men predominate. Many students in the women's history classes are neither history majors nor minors; they are taking the class for credit in women's studies or simply because they are interested in the subject matter.

In my class on women in the United States since 1877, I gave my students a survey. The goal was to have a better understanding of how they felt about a male professor teaching such a course. Amateur sociologist that I was becoming, I gave the same survey to another class of mine on the history of sex and sexuality in America to 1920 and to classes of four different colleagues: a white woman teaching a class on women in Europe to 1700; a white man teaching "The Age of Jackson"; a white woman teaching "The American West, 1850–Present"; and a white woman teaching a class on the Great War and its aftermath.[6]

I asked students whether (and how) they believed the sex of the professor had an impact on the way that he or she taught and whether the sex of the professor affected how the student experienced the class. Many students realized that they were being set up. In their answers, they declared that, although sex might have an influence on either teaching or the students' experience, so, too, did myriad other things, not least of which was the personality of the individual professor. Others declared vehemently that they believed sex irrelevant to teaching and learning. For them, the knowledge and training of the professor were of paramount importance.[7] Still others, primarily women being taught by women, explained that they were pleased to have women professors because they found women more approachable and, as women themselves, found it inspiring to be taught by an accomplished female professor. I should also say that not one student, either in the surveys or in class itself, has challenged my ability to teach the class or the suitability of having a man do so in the first place.[8]

I recognize the unscientific nature of this informal polling. Readers can take it for what it's worth. Yet I am intrigued by the ways in which many students did believe the professor's sex had an impact on his or her treatment of the materials and/or the way the students experienced the class. My female colleague teaching women's history had the highest percentage of students who believed that her sex influenced both her teaching (74 percent) and the experience of the class (70 percent). My own numbers in women's history were 40 percent and 63 percent, respectively, and in the class on sexuality, 36 percent and 56 percent. My male colleague teaching "The Age of Jackson" received the lowest percentages of students who saw his sex as influencing his teaching, at 17 percent and 33 percent, respectively. Two other female colleagues fell in between these numbers (40 percent/25 percent for the Great War; 42 percent/13 percent for the American West).

If these findings were to hold true across the board, then the results may suggest that students believe being a woman influences how a female professor teaches more than that being a man influences the way a male professor teaches. They also believe that the sex of a professor has a real effect—even if inadvertent and unintended—on the experience students have in the classroom. To some students, then, sex matters, for women when they teach, and for students in classes taught by men or women that focus on women and sex.

The written responses are much more instructive than the raw numbers. Of the three classes outside women's history, students expressed a number of beliefs about the influence of sex on teaching. In the class on the Great War, for instance, one student noted that she believed sex accounted for why my female colleague concentrated more on "individuals' experience with the war than on battles," despite the fact that my colleague tells me she does not give the battles short shrift. Another claimed that her inclusion of women in the lectures was due to her sex and that she tended to "explain things more" than a man would. Quite a few of my U.S. Western historian colleague's students noted that she spent more time talking about issues of race and gender than would a male professor. Most of those who made these observations were pleased with this addition, although one believed that the professor had consequently "left out a lot of important parts of the U.S. West to talk more fondly of what women were doing." What is worth noting is that almost half of the students in this class made note of this emphasis on race and gender. In the case of my male colleague, only a quarter of his students commented on his inclusion of these issues. In fact, both professors teach extensively about race and gender.

My own students in the women's history course articulated three basic themes: First, some believed that, predictably and erroneously, I was more objective than a woman would be. One noted that I covered topics "with less bias than other female instructors I've had in the past." Another said that my being a man "helped to keep the class more objective without personal stories." Second, others said that it somehow meant more to them to be taught women's history by a man. They felt they might have been able to dismiss the material more easily if taught by a woman. Third, many students noted that for them it was refreshing to see that a man could be a feminist. Either they found this encouraging themselves, or they believed that it was so for the male students in the class. They also believed having a male professor made it either easier or more necessary for the male students to take the material seriously.

The class on the history of sexuality gave surprisingly different responses, some of them no less problematic. Students tended to disagree about the degree to which my being a man made me more or less sympathetic to the plight of women throughout history. Some noted that a woman "would have been more prone to go overboard discussing how 'wronged' women were in history and how *unfair* it was to women, rather than just acknowledging that fact, [and] moving on." Conversely, another claimed that "he sympathizes with women in all circumstances. The condemnation of men throughout the course tends to make it seem as though he is simply attempting to pacify the women in some way rather than present any dignified picture of men." What differed most substantially in this set of surveys was the degree to which many students appreciated having a "male point of view" or "man's perspective" on the matters at hand. This is disturbing on a number of levels, not least of which is that it seems clear that even after covering approximately 300 years of history, they are still convinced such a singular thing exists. A number of them tied this male perspective to a greater ease in discussing sex in a classroom, and others simply believed that a woman would have been "more preachy" than I had been. I feel like I am plenty preachy about women's sufferings, yet they experience what I say as filtered through the lens of who I am, at least in terms of my sex.

A couple of students from both classes took the time to comment on their perception of my sexual orientation, noting in more or less explicit ways that they understood me to be gay. They believed this had an effect on my teaching and/or the experience of the class. One student noted, "He's definitely not your average macho guy and seems to very much understand what it[']s like to be different and persecuted for that difference." Another student, also in the women's history class, put it this way: "I assumed after meeting him he was gay. So the way I see it is that he is for both sides of the spectrum." Perhaps my favorite comment came from a student in the class on the history of sexuality, who answered in the affirmative when asked if my sex had an impact on how I teach: "Yes, had a strong insi[gh]t on the subject. Also, appears to be 'gay', so a very credible source."

Of those women's history students who believed that my female medievalist colleague's sex had an impact on her teaching, it was in terms of her purported "personal insight." Though a number of students sidestepped the questions, believing them to be the trap that they in some sense were, many believed that "it is easier for a female to relate to woman's history." Another affirmed the difference that her sex makes in her teaching and wrote specifically about an article they had read on gossip: "when she discusses topics like gossip, she can relate to it + therefore relate it to the class in an easier-to-understand way." Not only did they believe that my colleague could relate to the material better than a man could but also that she taught from a "woman's perspective," and that this allowed for a better understanding and presentation of the materials. Despite the fact that both she and I teach about gender as a historical construct subject to myriad other influences that at times make men's and women's roles in the past seem almost unrecognizable to us today, many of our students' attitudes can be summed up in the following comment on my colleague's teaching: "She is a woman, and so her view of the way women were treated in the middle ages is very different than a man who was teaching the class."

Of the students who bothered to give positive or negative evaluations of the courses, the professors, or the influence of our sexes on our teaching and/or their experiences, the overwhelming majority of the comments were positive. This may simply be because they like us (and we're grading them). As noted earlier, a sizable number of students also made a point of declaring that they either did not believe the sex of the professor made a difference or that while it certainly made a difference, so, too, did many other factors (like experience, education, and personality). Yet what seems clear is that many students believe a woman's sex is a factor in her teaching, one that has consequences for the content and their experience of the class. This is worthy of note, particularly so because none of us makes a point of talking about "being a man" or teaching "as a woman." For these students, sex (and sometimes sexual orientation) trumps training, particularly for women.

The survey results and my experience lead me to the conclusion that men are believed to be more objective about gender history than are women, but that women are believed to be able to use their "female traits" to be better teachers.

Although both of these notions are problematic, men seem to benefit more from these students' inferences. To investigate whether these beliefs held true at other colleges and with other teachers, I sought out other men who taught women's history and asked them about their experiences.[9] I also asked these men to talk about the ways that they address the fact of their maleness in the classroom, if they do so at all.

Most of what my respondents said supports the impressions given by the student surveys; only one claimed that being a man had no effect whatsoever on the classroom. Most believed that their students understood them to be more objective than female professors teaching the same subjects, and almost all identified this as unfortunate. A number of them either asked students explicitly in class about the issue or had asked them in previous student evaluations about this matter. Their impressions were borne out by those responses. Students claimed that male professors were less invested in or identified with the material, and that they were less biased and more objective. They also believed that it was significant to have a man teaching women's history because it showed that the materials were as important as any other part of history. In other words, having a man care enough about women's history to teach it demonstrated that it was worthy of study in the first place. Some also indicated, like my students, that they were surprised and pleased that men could be feminists and that they found this encouraging. They, too, appreciated having "a man's perspective" on the issues, though they did not elaborate on what that might mean.

All of this leaves us, then, with the understanding—not exactly earth-shattering—that students filter what we tell them through their perceptions of our subject positions and that, for men teaching women's history, this works largely to our advantage. However, the assumptions undergirding such advantages are erroneous. Given that we are unable (or, as the case may be, unwilling) to change our sex, race, or sexual orientation for the purposes of teaching, what can teachers of women's history (or any history, for that matter) do about the ways in which our identities work for and against us in the classroom? The debate on this issue seems to revolve around either acknowledging one's subject position and having a conversation about it and its implications for the classroom, or refusing to do so. I will use myself as an example and begin with the latter, in part because it is the most straightforward; it is also what I have done up until this point, though I believe writing this chapter has changed my mind.

The logic behind not discussing one's subject position is compelling. A majority of the men who responded to my query said that they do not discuss the fact of their being male, at least not explicitly at the beginning of the class, because they want to demonstrate to the class that they are there to impart knowledge about something worth studying and that their sex is irrelevant to their ability to do so. In one sense, this works to alleviate the stress that might be associated with students' perception that men might be unqualified to teach about women; in this strategy, it is simply not up for discussion. In its very omission of such a discussion, it insists that the class is what it is and that the professor is qualified to teach it because the department has hired him to do so. Further, it is appealing to historians who do believe that training is the ultimate qualifier for teaching. It abides by our standards of legitimacy.

But as I have demonstrated, students approach these issues somewhat differently than historians do. In refusing to acknowledge the fact of maleness in the classroom, men perpetuate the very privilege that this subject position grants us. We continue to seem objective and unbiased, and our female colleagues continue to seem implicated and invested (in both the positive and negative senses). Of course, all teachers want to seem objective to their students, or at the very least, they want to seem authoritative on a subject. But this perceived objectivity is an unearned advantage that women teaching women's history do not always have. Would it not be beneficial to discuss one's subject position, as it relates to the material and the classroom, in order to open up a dialogue about the construction of history itself and about the very real effects of gender? Although I encourage dissent in my classes, the last thing I want to do is encourage my students to be able to dismiss what they have learned in the class because they believe my ideological position on gender makes all my choices suspect. To be sure, all of my choices—from class format to choice of papers to readings assigned—are subject to bias. History itself is far from objective, as its constant rewriting amply demonstrates. It is created by real live actors with different experiences and opinions. But to what degree do I want to open up all of my choices for discussion, particularly in an area of study that is already perceived as being so politically and ideologically loaded? Am I not already laboring under an arduous burden in attempting to convince my students—even the women students—of the import and significance of gender? These are reasonable concerns, and I return to them later.

Talking about my position as a man also gives me pause because I am resolutely opposed to talking about another facet of my identity in the classroom, my sexual orientation. While I am well aware that many of my students perceive me as gay—as do most people I encounter in the world; at least this is my impression—I do not discuss the issue in class. I do this for a number of reasons. First, in most senses, I think it is irrelevant, and here I speak defensively as someone in a nondominant group. Second, I don't want them to believe they have a right of access to my personal life; by discussing my sexual orientation in class, I believe I would be implicitly saying that they have a *right to know* and perhaps a right to an opinion. They do not. Third, queer people are already in the awkward position of being understood as being more sexual than straight people because it is precisely through our sexuality that we are understood as "other." In this formulation, I become marked and categorized by my desire and sexual practices in a way that straight people simply are not. I do not wish to reify this. While I recognize, and to a certain degree agree with, the arguments made by others about the importance of coming out as a symbol of change, acceptance, and inspiration, particularly for queer or questioning students, I am made profoundly uncomfortable by the prospect of coming out in the classroom, and so I do not.[10] I do not pass, and I am perfectly comfortable allowing my gendered self-presentation to be read as queer, but I will not make it a subject of conversation, at least not in the classroom itself.

But discussing my position as a man teaching women's history is different in a number of significant ways, not least of which is that it is not a decision to reveal something that the students cannot help but apprehend from the moment they enter the classroom. It is also different in kind because my maleness (and my whiteness) puts me in the dominant group (twice over), and my sexual orientation does not. By discussing the fact of my maleness, I would be acknowledging the privilege that I am generally accorded, not an inappropriate way to begin a semester-long conversation about the way that gender has historically structured knowledge, power, and experience. There is no question that this would, in some ways, undermine the authority that many of us hope to achieve in the classroom, particularly on the very first day of school. It might, however, be a productive way to encourage students to question how gender and power operate in all of their pedagogical relationships and in everyday life as well. Having such a conversation would necessitate a discussion about essentialism; I do not want students to assume that I have a "man's perspective" or that I will be teaching them "as a man." Although both of these are true to a certain extent, I am keenly interested in avoiding the idea—as we explore throughout any class in women's history— that men or women can ever be reduced to a singular perspective or experience.[11]

The decision to discuss one's subject position explicitly is one that must take into account the can of worms being opened and that also allows enough time to discuss all the issues thoroughly. What recommends it, however, is the fact that many of our students do think it matters that we are men and women (of varying races and sexual orientations); we can either address these beliefs or ignore them. This is no more or less true for male or female teachers. Ignoring them may well mean perpetuating them.

My hesitant conclusion, in working on this chapter, is that it is simply more incumbent on those of us who are members of at least one dominant group (male, white, heterosexual, perhaps others) to discuss that aspect of our identities in teaching women's history, or any other history, for that matter. After conducting this research, I feel compelled to discuss the fact of being a man, and yet I am still convinced that it is perfectly appropriate to decline to discuss my sexual orientation. That is, conversation about unearned "objectivity" is essential to a critical pedagogy, but discussion of the nondominant aspects of one's identity, while potentially beneficial, does not seem to be as necessary. It would also go some way toward encouraging students to think about the ways that they are unconsciously understanding their female teachers who teach them about women or their black professors who teach them African American history. It would, in essence, contribute what little I am able to leveling the playing field.

NOTES

My thanks to Margaret Crocco, Barbara Winslow, and particularly Carol Berkin, for inviting me to participate in this collection. I also thank the students who answered my surveys, the men who responded to my query on H-WOMEN, Erika Gasser for a last-minute fax from the library, and my colleagues Joan Clinefelter, Linda English, Erin L. Jordan, and Brian Luskey for allowing me to give surveys in their classes. Finally, thanks to Erin L. Jordan, Ann M. Little, and Brian Luskey for reading and commenting on a draft of this essay.

1. For more on this set of assumptions, see Katherine J. Mayberry, ed., *Teaching What You're Not: Identity Politics in Higher Education* (New York: New York University Press, 1996).

2. Throughout this chapter, I deliberately use *sex* instead of *gender* to note a difference between male people and female people, men and women. To me, *gender* is the constellation of characteristics that make up masculinity and femininity, as well as the ways in which society is organized along different lines with different expectations for women and men (gender roles). This is not to say that gender is not relevant to the discussion as well; I think that the fact of my being a not particularly masculine man has an impact on my classes. And certainly students' expectations about the way men and women ought to behave and what they think men and women believe are a part of their perceptions of gender. This, however, is much more difficult to measure with any degree of consistency. I am also convinced that the fact of my being a man (as opposed to being a woman) has, at least in some cases, *more* consequence than does the *kind* of gendered man I happen to be. Despite the fact that I also recognize the constructedness of the category of sex itself, pace Judith Butler, this is why I insist on using *sex* instead of *gender*.

3. In the fall of 2006, the University of Northern Colorado enrolled 10,799 undergraduates and 2,182 graduate students (http://www.unco.edu/about_unc/, accessed January 24, 2008). Although the school Web site explains that forty-nine

states are represented at UNC, students from outside the state of Colorado are in a distinct minority.

4. See http://www.unco.edu/acctservices/instanalysis/pdf/enrlrpts/ FiscalYr0506_Final.pdf, 2, accessed May 15, 2007.

5. See http://www.unco.edu/acctservices/instanalysis/pdf/factbooks/f05fctbk. pdf, 7, accessed May 15, 2007.

6. All surveys were administered during the final three weeks of classes and were given in the manner of student evaluations. The professors gave the same instructions to each class (which said nothing about the purpose of the survey, apart from the fact they were giving it for a colleague who was going to write an article based on the responses). They then asked for a volunteer to return them to my office and left the students alone to answer them. The surveys for all six classes were identical and were as follows:

> What is your sex?
> What is your major?
> Before taking this class, did you happen to know the sex of the professor?
> If you did NOT, can you remember expecting it to be a woman or a man? If so, which?
> Why did you have that expectation?
> Do you think the sex of the professor has had an impact on how he or she has taught the class? How so? Be as specific as you would like to be.
> Do you think the sex of the professor has had an impact on the experience of the students or for you in particular as a student? How so? Be as specific as you would like to be.
> Feel free to continue writing on the other side of the page.

7. If nothing else, these students believe that they are *supposed* to think that sex is irrelevant to teaching, even though some of them might well unconsciously filter their impressions through the prism of the professor's sex.

8. This is particularly interesting, given the resistance met by some white teachers of African American history, for instance, or straight teachers of queer history. While it would be beyond the scope of this article to fully explore why this discrepancy exists, my suspicion is that it has to do with the type of institution and the makeup of the student body in the school and the specific class, as well as in the very different histories and contemporary realities of race, sex, and sexual orientation in today's society. On this issue, see Vince Nobile, "White Professors, Black History: Forays into the Multicultural Classroom"; Leon Litwack, "The Two-Edged Suspicion," both in *Perspectives* 31, no. 6 (September 1993), 1, 7–11, 13–14; Nancy Sorkin Rabinowitz, "Queer Theory and Feminist Pedagogy," in Amie A. MacDonald and Susan Sánchez-Casal, eds., *Twenty-First Century Feminist Classrooms: Pedagogies of Identity and Difference* (New York: Palgrave Macmillan, 2002), esp. 176–180; Nancy C. Unger, "Teaching 'Straight' Gay and Lesbian History," *Journal of American History* 93, no. 4 (March 2007), 1195.

9. I sent a query to the electronic Listserv H-WOMEN and sent the same questions to one other historian who I knew had extensive experience teaching U.S. women's history. Thirteen men responded either to me or to the list as a whole about

their experiences. Two women also responded (one to me, one to the list) with observations on the questions. In addition, two men responded to me with an interest in the subject, but I did not hear from either of them again with answers to my questions. The original e-mail is as follows:

> I am interested in hearing from men who teach (or have taught) women's history (especially of the U.S.) for an article about the pedagogical implications (or strategies) of being male and teaching this subject. I'm particularly interested in hearing answers to the following two questions:
>
> 1. In what ways has your being male had an impact upon the class, either in terms of your teaching or the ways that your students (in your impression) react to you and/or experience the class?
>
> 2. Do you address the fact of your identity in teaching a class in women's history? If so, how? If not, do you have particular reasons for not doing so?
>
> I have tried to leave the questions somewhat open-ended in order to encourage whatever thoughts/answers/impressions respondents might have.
>
> While I recognize that many men probably also teach classes in the history of sexuality, queer history, or the history of men and masculinity (and that the subjects all certainly overlap), for the purposes of this essay, I am only interested in those who teach students who have signed up for classes that are explicitly labeled "Women's History" or "Women's and Gender History" of some variety.
>
> Please feel free to forward this e-mail to anyone you know who might fit the bill.

10. On coming out in the classroom, see, among many other publications, Michele J. Eliason, "Out in the Heartland: Lesbians, Academics, and Iowa," in Beth Mintz and Esther Rothblum, eds., *Lesbians in Academia: Degrees of Freedom* (New York: Routledge, 1997), 43–50; Charlotte L. Goedsche, "Out on a Small Southern Campus," in ibid., esp. 76–77; and Nancy Goldstein, "The Making of a Lesbian Academic, 1974–1995," also in ibid., 81–88.

11. On essentialism and gender difference, see Diana Fuss, *Essentially Speaking: Feminism, Nature, and Difference* (New York: Routledge, 1990); and Judith Butler, *Gender Trouble: Feminism and the Subversion of Identity* (New York: Routledge, 1990).

PART IV

What We Know (and Don't Know) about Teaching Women's History

18

What Educational Research Says about Teaching and Learning Women's History

Linda Levstik

No one is ever satisfied with history education. In 1898, the authors of the American Historical Association's (AHA) *The Study of History in Schools* complained that there was no "recognized consensus of opinion in the country at large, not one generally accepted judgment, not even one well-known point of agreement, which would serve as a beginning for a consideration of the place of history in the high-school curriculum."[1] Although opinions about the goals and standards for history education probably vary at least as much now as they did at the turn of the twentieth century, history educators today have an important advantage over their predecessors: a substantial body of empirical research concerning children's and adolescents' historical thinking.[2] Current research may not answer all questions about teaching women's history, but it does suggest possibilities instructors can test in classrooms, as well as some pitfalls worth avoiding.

Intellectual Tools and Historical Thinking

Perspective and Agency

It would be difficult to conceive of historical thinking separate from some understanding of perspective. How can anyone possibly make sense of ideas and events in the past if they fail to recognize how differently others might imagine their world? Left to sift through more or less fragmentary evidence, negotiate shifts in language, look to historical context, and try to account for their own perceptions, historical inquirers struggle to make sense of past perspectives. Some researchers posit hierarchies of perspective recognition based on studies of students' explanations of past perspectives. Students begin by seeing the past as largely unintelligible and populated by people too stupid to make better choices, move toward an understanding that people in the past might have different worldviews than people in the present, and finally come to recognize broader historical contexts and conditions that frame different perspectives.[3]

An alternative approach suggests that perspective recognition may better be understood as a set of related elements whose development may or may not be particularly linear. Elements of perspective recognition might include a sense of "otherness," shared "normalcy," historical contextualization, differentiation of perspectives, and contextualization of the present.[4] While the sense that others are different than ourselves is normally well developed by age four, recognizing that different perspectives make good sense to the people holding them, and are not evidence of ignorance or stupidity, develops more slowly and with some difficulty.[5] Sometimes comparisons between now and then reinforce student misperceptions by emphasizing what the past lacked relative to the present rather than relative to earlier times. In these instances, emphasizing what was normal at a particular moment in time without making the present comparison might help students better normalize the past.[6]

In cases where instruction points out similarities in perspectives between past and present, however, students may more easily recognize the likelihood that people living in the same time hold multiple perspectives. A study of eighth graders examining the U.S. antebellum period provides one example in this regard. As students began their study, they did just what the research would suggest, describing people's attitudes in the past as ignorant and incomprehensible. As they encountered evidence of different perspectives, however, students were better able to contextualize those perspectives and explain how they affected people's behavior. In fact, after their instructor introduced the concept of perspective, students used it to remind each other that people's attitudes and expectations were different in the past and that it took quite some time for ideas to change. They regularly referenced perspectives held by relatives and public figures that paralleled those they encountered in nineteenth-century sources. Students sometimes slipped into overgeneralization (all women or all men thought similarly) or assumptions of stupidity (ignorance led people to deny women access to higher education) but usually caught themselves or each other, often drawing on historical documentation to explain why a correction was necessary.[7]

If even young children recognize that different people hold a variety of perspectives, students' difficulty in recognizing multiple historical perspectives may be largely an artifact of instruction. Given access to various perspectives and instruction that encouraged them to account for different perspectives, students in the antebellum study not only recognized perspectives but also looked for them. In contrast, curricular materials or instruction employing broad-brush generalizations that ignore, say, antislavery Southerners, slave-owning Northerners, draft resisters prior to Vietnam, people who opposed Japanese relocation, and women who worked against suffrage signal that students should ignore their own experience of diverse perspectives and apply a majoritarian perspective to the past. Further, instruction that enjoins students from making moral judgments about past perspectives because "that's just how people thought back then" further limits students' understanding of how multiple perspectives operate in history: Not all people "back then" thought alike or accepted existing social, cultural, or political conditions any more than people do now. Assuming otherwise not only misrepresents the past but also suggests that current differences are abnormal or irrelevant and should be discouraged.[8]

Sometimes, too, broad cultural forces encourage overgeneralization and simplification of different perspectives, especially in regard to controversial issues. Asked whether their male and female peers might view the significance of women's history differently from men's history, for instance, students in one study in the United States argued for gender-based differences based on stereotyped notions of how opposite-sex peers would think.[9] While these stereotypes did not go unchallenged, the majority of students maintained a dichotomous view of male-female perspectives. As the study of antebellum America suggests, however, instruction can challenge these assumptions. Given historical questions that encourage perspective recognition and a wider array of historical sources, students question stereotyped assumptions. In the antebellum study, for instance, they wondered whether "women inside the reform movement all had the same opinions," whether some were "moderate or right wing within the reform," how women in the movement felt about women who were not, what percent of the population of women were involved in reform, what "sacrifices [were] made in order to achieve reform," and if a pattern of "disrespect for women" marked other countries. Perhaps, a student argued, "differences are something that a culture has to learn to adapt to and to live with and to adjust to and to respect."[10]

In the context of analyzing multiple perspectives, students also described women's historical experiences in terms of agency that varied by race, class, religion, and region. Women might not vote, they argued, but some petitioned for social change, joined social and political interest groups, or controlled their own resources. Further, they noted that chattel slavery or indentured servitude limited agency for other women. When one student presented historical evidence that differences existed even within categories—within families, for instance—students modified their initial generalizations to account for family and personal inclinations as well as race, class, ethnicity, and region. Their final project displayed a multiplicity of perspectives within and across these categories. As these students' responses suggest, specific attention to perspective, opportunities to discuss differences, and the progressive introduction of sources that challenged students' initial conceptions supported more sophisticated historical thinking than might be predicted on the basis of standardized test performance.[11]

That students can recognize and analyze past perspectives is certainly important to historical understanding. However, perhaps the most challenging element of perspective recognition—and the least researched—relates to contextualization of the present. How do we come to recognize that our own perspectives exist in historical context? When asked what current ideas people in the future might find strange, for instance, students in one study struggled to think of any examples, usually resorting to mentioning outmoded technologies. Only occasionally did they identify contemporary perspectives that might be regarded as strange or difficult to understand by people in the future, arguing that people would think current attitudes about sexual orientation were foolish or that religious views would change.[12]

Other aspects of contextualizing one's own perspectives also challenge students. Students may, for instance, claim that history taught them to respect differences and avoid discrimination on the basis of race, class, or gender so long as differences exist at a distance. Once those differences are up close—a local problem, for instance—historical perspective may be replaced by local prejudices.[13] Discomfort also accompanies challenges to current perspectives. In the antebellum study, for instance, some students expressed concern about framing their study with women's perspectives. They worried that this wasn't "normal" history, that instruction might be "missing something," "going too far," or being "against men," even though men's perspectives appeared in the unit of study. When asked if they had felt the same concerns about "missing something" when the curriculum focused on men, the uniform response was that, though they now considered women's history important, they had never wondered about the absence of women in previous coursework.[14]

Sometimes, too, imagined connections to groups or individuals in the past make students reluctant to examine some perspectives. In a study of secondary girls' responses to a women's history course in the Netherlands, ten Dam and Rijkschroeff found that girls distanced themselves from women they perceived as "lagging behind." The researchers argue that students' reluctance to contextualize women's history or their own current experience developed in response to instruction emphasizing women as victims of history rather than its agents. As have others, ten Dam and Rijkschroeff argue that a narrative primarily built on oppression misrepresents women's and men's experiences while reinforcing misperceptions regarding individual, group, and institutional agency.[15]

Very little research deals directly with agency—the means by which groups, individuals, and institutions act—as an element of inquiry in history education, though it has long been a feature of professional history discourse. At present, we generally glimpse agency in passing in studies of other aspects of historical thinking, but only rarely as the focus of scholarly attention. In one study, instruction directed explicit attention to agency in the history under study while in others the researcher raised questions about the lack of transfer between studying historical agency and applying the concept to local issues.[16]

Narrative

Unlike agency, narrative has been the subject of considerable attention among educational researchers in history, as well as literacy education. In fact, few other historical tools receive quite so much attention and are so regularly and uncritically suggested for instructional use as narrative. At the risk of oversimplifying a complex concept, I use *narrative* to describe constructed sequences of events (an author selects and orders information) that are causally and chronologically related.[17]

Historians have long used narrative to order and assign cause and effect and explain perspective, motivation, and agency related to experiences in the past. Students, too, have experience with narrative. Even the youngest children internalize story structures or schemata and rely on them as one important way to organize experience.[18] Narrative helps students remember and make sense of certain features of the past by suggesting an underlying logic to events and a "moral to the story." This feature is quite clear in studies of readers' response to historical narratives. Children and adolescents tend, for instance, to understand historical fiction, biography, and autobiography as operating "as if it were a person," inviting readers to imagine themselves in the past and to have some moral response to the issues raised in the narrative.[19] Narratives enlist the readers' identification with or repugnance toward the protagonist(s), while suggesting that other (antagonistic, often) perspectives are possible, though not necessarily desirable. Students reading a biography of Jane Addams, for instance, might recognize the perspectives held by different historical actors operating in her life and explain some of the bases for their positions, but they will tend to view them through Addams's (or the author's) eyes. Similarly, they are likely to learn something about urban problems as Addams understood them and, again assuming a positive portrayal of Addams, to view the cultural tools she brought to bear in tackling problems as appropriate choices. Similarly, a novel about Japanese American internment during World War II may introduce differing perspectives and types of agency employed within and between interned Japanese Americans, the American Indians on whose land some internees were held, the European Americans organizing removal and administering the camps, and communities outside the camps, but those perspectives are filtered through a moral lens. Historical narratives, especially those written for children and adolescents, generally call for some sort of moral response—they were written expressly to elicit this kind of reaction. Readers may be intended to recognize the complexity of immigration and urbanization in Jane Addams's Chicago or to understand how the U.S. government came to confine its own citizens in internment camps, but they are also expected to view the conditions in Chicago and in the internment camps as fundamentally wrong—an abrogation of human rights that should never happen again and a violation of basic American principles.[20]

Historical narratives also show institutional agency (governmental expressions of power and control), group agency (groups organizing for survival, resistance, social control), and individual agency (persuasion, reaching across boundaries, maintaining personal values or habits, individual resistance, making the best of bad circumstances). The challenge lies in balancing the kinds of agency offered in historical narratives. Historical fiction, for instance, tends to emphasize individual agency, but historical monographs might focus more on group or institutional agency. Overbalancing in either direction misinforms students regarding the power of individuals relative to group and institutional power.

Finally, curricula that frustrate narrative-born expectations (that history will involve multiple perspectives, human motivation, agency, and moral dilemmas, for instance) may generate boredom and outright resistance. As one student explained, her textbook description of the American Revolution "just says Americans were right, not why they were right, or why the British fought." She viewed the historical narratives she read as better explaining people's perspectives, motivations, and agency than did the textbook's more distanced, less personal voice.[21]

Overall, current research suggests that well-crafted narrative motivates interest and highlights important elements of historical thinking, including perspective recognition and agency. At the same time, the power of narrative sometimes works against critical analysis. If, for instance, a narrative is well written and intuitively "right," neither the accuracy of its underlying historical interpretation nor its moral stance is likely to be challenged. Not only do people have difficulty recalling stories when expected elements of story schemata are missing but also children and adolescents tend to omit or conflate information and sometimes invent "fanciful elaborations" based on their ideas about human behavior in order to maintain story logic.[22]

The affordances and constraints of narrative just described refer to narratives crafted by someone other than students. Research on student-generated historical narratives is thin, perhaps because once students move beyond elementary or middle school, they so rarely generate narratives in history classes. And even at earlier grade levels, reports on student-created historical narratives are largely anecdotal. A primary conclusion derived from this literature is that scaffolding—instructional support—matters. Students who receive some degree of instructor or peer feedback prior to a final draft tend to write stronger, more coherent narratives, for instance. While the optimal frequency of feedback remains unclear, research in literacy education suggests that feedback should concentrate on one or two medium components (structure, mechanics) and one or two message components (strength of idea or argument, felicity of language) at a time. Audience also matters. Overall, students' writing improves when they perceive their writing as purposeful communication with real audiences.[23]

Narrative is a common feature of our experience as consumers of history, but narrative is also an element of historical inquiry. First, narratives can be sources themselves, analyzed as one would any other historical evidence. Instructors call attention to how these narratives are structured, how evidence supports or fails to support alternate interpretations, and how the narratives themselves represent a moment in time and perspectives extant at that time. Second, narratives can be the product of investigation—a student-generated interpretation in the form of written, recorded, or performed narratives. As students develop their own interpretations, they call on prior experience with narrative sources and model their own work in concert with or in opposition to the narrative templates.

Overall, students benefit from reading, watching, and listening to multiple genres of historical narratives, as well as from writing or producing historical narratives. Limiting their experience to other people's narratives means that they miss an important component of historical inquiry—an opportunity to construct an evidence-based historical interpretation for an interested audience.[24]

Evidence

An odd thing happens to evidence in the history classroom: It is too often separated from historical inquiry. Instead, students engage in exercises in "sourcing"—evaluating a document or set of documents separate from a larger inquiry that might motivate interest or provide a reason for analyzing sources. The "Who Fired the First Shot at Lexington Green" exercise, for instance, involves evaluating the trustworthiness of a variety of primary sources related to the Battle of Lexington Green. Determining that available evidence exists to settle this question isn't intended to help students understand the American Revolution so much as it is to learn something about the nature of historical sources. This may be justified as an introduction to historical evidence, but investigations of sourcing exercises such as this generally conclude that student performance is contradictory: Overall, students recognize that historical sources can be biased or incomplete, but they have difficulty understanding how such incomplete information can be used to produce useful historical accounts. Too often students are left wondering how to choose between one biased account and another and what difference there might be between their own ideas about what could have happened and historians' conclusions.[25]

Part of the problem for students may be that sourcing is meaningless by itself. It is, after all, only one piece of the more complex intellectual tool of inquiry. Without some background information and context, there can hardly be a meaningful historical question, and without a worthwhile question, a source cannot be considered "evidence" of much of anything. Indeed, recent online history programs often begin with powerful questions that better frame the selection, evaluation, and use of historical sources.[26] Trying to solve the Lexington Green question or similar tasks is more problematic because this isn't a question that arises among historians, in public debate, or in discussion. Rather, it is a question largely confined to classrooms. Were the task framed as a question about the political implications of determining who fired the first shot or the effectiveness of either side in exploiting this incident, it might be more interesting, more significant, and more likely to facilitate students' understanding of historical evidence. Such a question at least establishes a context that might justify the instructional effort required for inquiry.[27]

Inquiry

To some extent, perspective, agency, narrative, and evidence can be understood separate from student engagement with inquiry. Students can recognize perspective and agency in historical narratives, evaluate the evidence used to support narratives, and debate the merits of various historians' interpretations. But this is only one part of historical thinking. If we acknowledge that people are active constructors of meaning, limiting students to learning how others make meaning cannot be justified. As should be clear by now, elements of inquiry are well within the reach of even relatively young students. Putting those elements together may be challenging, but a variety of studies demonstrate that with attention to question selection, support in selecting and analyzing evidence, and explicit attention to perspective, agency, and narrative, even elementary-age children can engage in historical inquiry. Contrary to persistent claims that only content matters, however, context matters, and research increasingly attends to the intersection of content, context, and historical thinking.

Context Matters

I was forcefully reminded of the power of instructional contexts several years ago when I was interviewing fifth graders following instruction on archaeology. When asked to consider the relationship between history and archaeology, students described archaeology as open-ended and investigatory, and history as closed and a product of someone else's research.[28] Their response was not surprising, given the nature of instruction in each subject. Their archaeological study exposed them to the processes of archaeology (stratigraphy as evidence of chronology) and engaged them in some of the processes of archaeologists (excavation and classification). In contrast, their experience with history consisted almost entirely of listening to stories about "famous" people, explanations of cause and effect, founding narratives, and the like, and then answering questions based on the stories. In contrast, students engaged in historical inquiry describe history very differently—as multiperspectival, interpretive, and relevant to their lives.[29]

Not everyone is equally interested in this kind of history, of course. Some students resist challenging approaches, preferring the safety of traditional forms they have already mastered. Some policy makers feel more comfortable with traditional forms as well, especially if history instruction sticks to national narratives of progress and exceptionality. When the Florida legislature decided that history could not be interpretive—only the facts!—they reflected fears about the consequences of introducing students to histories that might not reify the existing social order.[30] Their response highlights the influence of sociocultural contexts beyond (but extending into) the classroom.

In some instances, vernacular histories developed within various racial, ethnic, religious, and regional groups to counter school histories. Simone Schweber's work is particularly interesting here. In studies of history instruction in two "fundamentalist" schools—one Christian, one Jewish—Schweber notes the impact of a historical narrative in which God/Yahweh is the primary historical agent and students understand historical agency as enacting divine purpose. In this instructional context, a religious narrative frames students' conceptions of perspective, agency, evidence, and historical inquiry. In consequence, students in these settings tend to dismiss narratives that do not take divine will into account.[31]

Similarly, students in other school settings may dismiss or resist instruction that ignores or misrepresents the vernacular histories they understand as their own.[32] Consider, for instance, how "westward expansion" in the United States might be understood by children of Mexican, Apache, Chinese, or Anglo ancestry; how differently Maori or European-descent students might understand British settlement in New Zealand; how Taiwanese and Chinese students understand the creation of the Republic of China; and so on. Developing history instruction sensitive to these differences is an ongoing challenge, and attempts at offering a more pluralist history often meet considerable resistance.[33]

Broad national patterns also influence historical thinking. In the United States, students generally describe history, vernacular or otherwise, as explaining "who we are and how we got here" and identify progress and freedom as important themes in their country's history. In Northern Ireland, where "who we are" is tied to sectarian divisions, instruction emphasizes the lifeways of people in the past, and students tend to explain history as the study of past lives. In New Zealand, where history traditionally emphasized connections to Britain and the former Commonwealth, students described their own country's history as a potential source of good ideas from which other people might draw inspiration but express more interest in the histories of people in distant places.

Similar cross-national diversity marks students' thinking in regard to the significance of women's history. In investigations outside the United States, for instance, female students ascribe more significance than do male students to issues of social justice or the history of everyday life, where women might figure more prominently than in political history. In New Zealand, male and female students ascribe significance to women's history more consistently than in the United States, arguing that New Zealand historically relied on the labor of men *and* women, especially in times of war and economic depression, and therefore, women's history is as significant as men's. They also note that because gender inequities continue, studying women in different roles not only provides important role models for girls and women but also offers evidence that women perform as well as men in these roles. Similar patterns appeared among Ghanaian students. Interestingly, New Zealand's prime minister at the time of the study there was a woman, as was her leading opponent. In Ghana, too, women hold traditional leadership positions (Asantewaa or Queen Mother, for instance). No woman has held similar office in the United States, although parallels to the Asantewaa can be found in some American Indian societies. It would certainly be interesting to know more about these cross-national differences (and similarities), but at this point, few researchers focus on historical thinking and its relationship to women's history.[34]

Given such different instructional and cultural influences, it is inappropriate to ascribe invariant or age-related stages to historical understanding. Rather, conceptual understandings appear to develop at different times, depending on the intersection of students' prior experiences with cultural and instructional contexts. As instructors, we cannot change what happened before students enter our classes or, often, what goes on around our schools, but we can create classroom environments that support historical thinking. Without instructional support, however, students will continue to struggle to make sense of the past, retaining no more than the broadest outlines of mainstream or vernacular narratives.

Perhaps we can draw at least one compelling conclusion regarding these issues: The volatility of history points to its importance. If historical interpretations had no cultural import, no one would argue about them. To the extent that history influences how individuals, groups, and nations understand themselves and their relationships with others, it remains controversial. Instruction that pretends otherwise misrepresents history and leaves students at a loss in understanding history's power in their lives.

If we seriously expect students to think historically in regard to women's history, they need opportunities for all three kinds of historical experience: in-depth, purposeful inquiry into worthwhile questions about women's historical experiences supported by careful teacher mediation and constructive feedback, discussion and analysis of a variety of women's history genres, and finally, consideration of how women's history might inform students' own historical agency. And for this, we need a deeper, richer research base.

Historical Thinking in the Context of Women's History

After more than two decades of research on teaching and learning history, only a small number of studies include gender in their analyses, and few note any substantial differences in male and female performance.[35] In my own experience as a researcher, few students report more than passing attention to women in their history classes. As one middle school student told me, "I don't remember anything about women or women's rights coming up until like now."[36] The research on the development of students' historical thinking suggests that this need not be the case. Given the variety and depth of women's histories, new technologies for accessing historical sources, and information on students' developing historical thinking, instructors can more confidently engage students in inquiry that takes women's historical agency and multiple perspectives seriously, that uses narrative as source as well as interpretive tool, and that offers students the opportunity to consider patterns of human behavior and their contemporary manifestations.

NOTES

1. American Historical Association, *The Study of History in Schools: A Report to the American Historical Association from the Committee of Seven, 1898* (accessed 7 May 2007). Available at http://www.historians.org/pubs/archives/CommitteeofSeven/index.cfm.

2. For a fuller discussion of "tool use" in relation to historical thinking, see James Wertsch, *Mind as Action* (New York: Oxford University Press, 1998); and Keith Barton and Linda Levstik, *Teaching History for the Common Good* (Mahwah, NJ: Erlbaum, 2004).

3. Peter Lee and Rosalyn Ashby, "Empathy, Perspective Taking, and Rational Understanding," in *Historical Empathy and Perspective Taking in the Social Studies*, ed. O. L. Davis Jr., Elizabeth Anne Yeager, and Stuart J. Foster (Lanham, MD: Rowman and Littlefield, 2001), 23.

4. Barton and Levstik, *Teaching History for the Common Good.*

5. Judy Dunn, *The Beginnings of Social Understanding* (Cambridge: Harvard University Press, 1988), 173–74, 211; Samuel S. Wineburg, *Historical Thinking and Other Unnatural Acts* (Philadelphia: Temple University Press, 2001).

6. Lee and Ashby, "Empathy, Perspective Taking, and Rational Understanding," 21–50.

7. Linda S. Levstik and Jeanette Groth, "Scary Thing Being an Eighth Grader: Exploring Gender and Sexuality in a Middle School U.S. History Unit," *Theory and Research in Social Education* 30 (Spring 2002), 233–54.

8. Betty Bardige, "Things So Finely Human: Moral Sensibilities at Risk in Adolescence," in *Mapping the Moral Domain*, ed. Carol Gilligan, Janie Victoria Ward, and Jill McLean Taylor (Cambridge: Harvard University Press, 1988), 108.

9. Linda S. Levstik, "The Boys We Know; the Girls in Our School': Early Adolescents' Understanding of Women's Historical Significance," *International Journal of Social Studies* 12 (1999), 19–34.

10. Levstik and Groth, "Gender and Sexuality," 242.

11. Ibid., 248–51.

12. Linda S. Levstik and Keith C. Barton, "'They Still Use Some of Their Past': Historical Salience in Elementary Children's Chronological Thinking," *Journal of Curriculum Studies* 28 (1996): 531–76.

13. Linda S. Levstik, "Crossing the Empty Spaces: New Zealand Adolescents' Conceptions of Perspective-Taking and Historical Significance," in *Historical Empathy*

and *Perspective Taking in the Social Studies*, ed. O. L. Davis, Elizabeth A. Yeager, and Stuart J. Foster (Boston: Rowman and Littlefield, 2001), 69–96.

14. Levstik and Groth, "Gender and Sexuality," 233–54.

15. Geert ten Dam and Rikki Rijkschroeff, "Teaching Women's History in Secondary Education: Constructing Gender Identity," *Theory and Research in Social Education* 24 (1996), 71–88.

16. Linda S. Levstik and Kathi Kern, "Teachers Engaged in Historical Interpretation," paper presented at the annual meeting of the National Council for the Social Studies (November 2006); Kent den Heyer, "Historical Agency and Social Change: Something More than 'Symbolic' Empowerment," in *Curriculum and Pedagogy for Peace and Sustainability*, ed. Louise Allen, Donna Breault, Danny Cartner, Bryan Setser, Michael Hayes, Ruben Gaztambide-Fernandez, and Karen Krasny (Troy, NY: Educator's International Press, 2003); Kent den Heyer, "Between Every 'Now' and 'Then': A Role for the Study of Historical Agency in History and Citizenship Education," *Theory and Research in Social Education* 31 (2003), 411–34; Simone A. Schweber and R. Irwin, "'Especially Special': Learning about Jews in a Fundamentalist Christian School," *Teachers College Record* 105 (2003), 1693–1719; and Simone A. Schweber, "'Breaking Down Barriers' or 'Building Strong Christians': Reflexive Affirmation and the Abnegation of History," *Theory and Research in Social Education* 34 (2006), 9–33.

17. See Grant Bage, *Narrative Matters: Teaching and Learning History through Story* (London: Falmer, 1999); Tom Holt, *Thinking Historically: Narrative, Imagination, and Understanding* (New York: College Board, 1995); Louis O. Mink, "Narrative Form as a Cognitive Instrument," in *The Writing of History: Literary Form and Historical Understanding*, ed. Robert H. Canary and Henry Kozick (Madison: University of Wisconsin Press, 1978), 129–49; and Hayden White, "The Value of Narrativity in the Representation of Reality," in *The Content of the Form: Narrative Discourse and Historical Representation* (Baltimore: Johns Hopkins University Press, 1987), 1–25.

For more general treatment of the connections between narrative and thinking, see Barbara Hardy, "Narrative as a Primary Act of Mind," in *The Cool Web: The Pattern of Children's Reading*, ed. Margaret Meek, Aiden Warlow, and Griselda Barton (London: Bodley Head, 1977); Gordon Wells, *The Meaning Makers* (London: Hodder and Stoughton, 1986).

For a working definition of narrative, see Barton and Levstik, "Teaching History for the Common Good."

18. Jean Matter Mandler, *Stories, Scripts, and Scenes: Aspects of Schema Theory* (Hillsdale, NJ: Erlbaum, 1984), 31–73.

19. Linda S. Levstik, "Narrative Constructions: Cultural Frames for History," *Social Studies* 88 (1995), 113–16.

20. Ibid.

21. Terrie L. Epstein, "Adolescents' Perspectives on Racial Diversity in U.S. History: Case Studies from an Urban Classroom," *American Educational Research Journal* 37 (2000): 185–214; Peter Seixas, "Mapping the Terrain of Historical Significance," *Social Education* 61 (January 1997), 22–27; Levstik, "Narrative Constructions," 115.

22. Bruce VanSledright and Jere Brophy, "Storytelling, Imagination, and Fanciful Elaboration in Children's Historical Reconstructions," *American Educational Research Journal* 29 (1992): 850.

23. Christine Pappas, Barbara Kiefer, and Linda Levstik, *An Integrated Language Perspective in the Elementary School: An Action Approach,* 4th ed. (New York: Addison-Wesley, Longman, 2006); Nancy Atwell, *In the Middle: Writing, Reading, and Learning with Adolescents* (Portsmouth, NH: Boynton/Cook, 1987).

24. Barton and Levstik, "Teaching History for the Common Good."

25. Peter Seixas, "The Community of Inquiry as a Basis for Knowledge and Learning: The Case of History," *American Educational Research Journal* 30 (Summer 1993), 310, 314–15; Tom Holt, *Thinking Historically;* Linda S. Levstik and Keith C. Barton, *Doing History: Investigating with Children in Elementary and Middle Schools,* 3rd ed. (Mahwah, NJ: Erlbaum, 2005).

26. John Saye and Tom Brush, "Student Engagement with Social Issues in a Multimedia Supported Learning Environment," *Theory and Research in Social Education* 27 (1999), 472–504; John Saye and Tom Brush, "Comparing Teachers' Strategies for Supporting Student Inquiry in a Problem-Based Multimedia-Enhanced History Unit," *Theory and Research in Social Education* 34 (2006), 183–212.

27. Keith C. Barton. "Teaching History: Primary Sources in History—Breaking through the Myths," *Phi Delta Kappan* 86 (June 2005): 745; Linda S. Levstik and Dehea B. Smith, "I've Never Done This Before: Building a Community of Inquiry in a Third-Grade Classroom," in *Advances in Research on Teaching,* Vol. 6, ed. Jere Brophy (Greenwich, CT: JAI, 1996); Levstik and Groth, "Exploring Gender and Sexuality," 233–54. For research in Britain, where work with historical sources has been a prominent part of history curricula, see Rosalyn Ashby and Peter J. Lee, "Information, Opinion, and Beyond," paper presented at the annual meeting of the American Educational Research Association (April 1998); Peter Lee and Rosalyn Ashby, "Progression in Historical Understanding among Students Ages 7–14," in *Knowing, Teaching, and Learning History: National and International Perspectives,* ed. Peter N. Stearns, Peter Seixas, and Sam Wineburg (New York: New York University Press, 2000), 199–222; Peter Lee and Rosalyn Ashby "History in an Information Culture: Project Chata," *International Journal of Historical Learning, Teaching and Research* 1 (June 2001), 75–98; Christine Counsell, "Historical Knowledge and Historical Skills: A Distracting Dichotomy," in *Issues in History Teaching,* ed. James Arthur and Robert Phillips (London: Routledge, 2000), 58–59; and Chris Husbands, Alison Kitson, and Anna Pendry, *Understanding History Teaching: Teaching and Learning about the Past in Secondary Schools* (Philadelphia: Open University Press, 2003), 70.

28. Linda S. Levstik, A. Gwynn Henderson, and Jennie Schlarb, "Digging for Clues: An Archaeological Exploration of Historical Cognition," in *The International Review of History Education,* 4, ed. Peter Lee (London: Taylor and Francis, 2005).

29. Levstik and Groth, "Gender and Sexuality," 233–54; Denis Shemilt, *Evaluation Study: Schools Council History 13-16 Project* (Edinburgh: Holmes McDougall, 1980).

30. Bruce Craig, "New Florida Law Tightens Control over History in Schools," *History News Network* (cited 7 May 2007). Available at http://hnn.us/roundup/entries/26016.html.

31. Simone A. Schweber and R. Irwin, "'Especially Special': Learning about Jews in a Fundamentalist Christian School," *Teachers College Record* 105 (2003), 1693–1719; Simone A. Schweber, *Making Sense of the Holocaust: Lessons from Classroom Practice* (New York: Teachers College Press, 2004).

32. For a discussion of vernacular history, see John Bodnar, *Remaking America: Public Memory, Commemoration, and Patriotism in the Twentieth Century* (Princeton, NJ: Princeton University Press, 1994); for the impact of vernacular histories on students' response to school history, see Terrie Epstein, "Deconstructing Differences in African American and European-American Adolescents' Perspectives on U.S. History," *Curriculum Inquiry* 28 (October 1998), 397–423.

33. In the United States, see Gary Nash, Charlotte Crabtree, and Ross Dunn, *History on Trial: Culture Wars and the Teaching of the Past* (New York: Knopf, 1997).

34. For further discussion of cross-national findings, see Barton and Levstik, *Teaching History for the Common Good*; Levstik, "Adolescent New Zealanders' Conceptions of Historical Significance and National Identity"; Linda S. Levstik and Jeanette Groth, "'Ruled by Our Own People': Ghanaian Adolescents' Conceptions of Citizenship," *Teachers College Record* (2003) (April 2005), 563–586; Keith C. Barton, "'Best Not to Forget Them': Adolescents' Judgments of Historical Significance in Northern Ireland," *Theory and Research in Social Education* 33 (2005), 9–44; and Keith C. Barton and Alan W. McCully, "History, Identity, and the School Curriculum in Northern Ireland: An Empirical Study of Secondary Students' Ideas and Perspectives," *Journal of Curriculum Studies* 37 (2005), 85–116.

35. See Stephen J. Thornton, "From Content to Subject Matter," *Social Studies* 92 (2001), 237–42; Linda S. Levstik, "NCSS and the Teaching of History," in O. L. Davis, ed., *NCSS in Retrospect* (Washington, DC: NCSS, 1996).

36. See Levstik and Groth, "Exploring Gender and Sexuality," 246.

Additional Resources

BOOKS

Abelson, Elaine. *When Ladies Go A-Thieving: Middle Class Shoplifters in the Victorian Department Store*. New York: Oxford University Press, 1989.

Allgor, Catherine. *A Perfect Union: Dolley Madison and the Creation of the American Nation*. New York: Henry Holt, 2006.

Armitage, Susan, and Elizabeth Jameson, eds. *The Women's West*. Norman: University of Oklahoma Press, 1987.

Attie, Jeanie. *Patriotic Toil: Northern Women and the American Civil War*. Ithaca, NY: Cornell University Press, 1994.

Bailey, Beth. *Sex in the Heartland*. Cambridge: Harvard University Press, 1999.

Bartlett, Elizabeth Ann. *Liberty, Equality, Sorority. The Origins and Interpretation of American Feminist Thought: Frances Wright, Sarah Grimké, and Margaret Fuller*. Brooklyn, NY: Carlson, 1994.

Bataille, Gretchen M., and Kathleen Mullen Sands. *American Indian Women Telling Their Lives*. Lincoln: University of Nebraska Press, 1994.

Berkin, Carol. *First Generations: Women in Colonial America*. New York: Hill and Wang, 1996.

Blanton, DeAnne, and Lauren M. Cook. *They Fought Like Demons: Women Soldiers in the Civil War*. Baton Rouge: Louisiana State University Press, 2002.

Boydston, Jeanne. *Home and Work: Housework, Wages, and the Ideology of Labor in the Early Republic*. New York: Oxford University Press, 1990.

Brown, Dorothy M., and Elizabeth McKeown. *The Poor Belong to Us: Catholic Charities and American Welfare*. Cambridge: Harvard University Press, 1997.

Carson, Mina. *Settlement Folk: The Evolution of Social Welfare Ideology in the American Settlement Movement, 1883–1930.* Chicago: University of Chicago Press, 1990.

Casey, Kathleen. *I Answer with My Life: Life Histories of Women Teachers Working for Social Change.* New York: Routledge, 1993.

Chmielewski, Wendy E., Louis J. Kern, and Marilyn Klee-Hartzell, eds. *Women in Spiritual and Communitarian Societies in the United States.* Syracuse, NY: Syracuse University Press, 1993.

Clinton, Catherine. *Fanny Kemble's Journals.* Cambridge: Harvard University Press, 2000.

———. *The Plantation Mistress: Woman's World in the Old South.* New York: Pantheon, 1982.

Clinton, Catherine, and Christine Lunardini. *Columbia Guide to American Women in the Nineteenth Century.* New York: Columbia University Press, 2000.

Clinton, Catherine, and Nina Silber, eds. *Divided Houses: Gender and the Civil War.* New York: Oxford University Press, 1992.

———. *Battle Scars: Gender and Sexuality in the American Civil War.* New York: Oxford University Press, 2006.

Cobble, Dorothy Sue. *The Other Women's Movement: Workplace Justice and Social Rights in Modern America.* Princeton, NJ: Princeton University Press, 2004.

Cohen, Lizabeth. *A Consumers' Republic: The Politics of Mass Consumption in Postwar America.* New York: Knopf, 2003.

Cohen, Miriam. *Workshop to Office: Two Generations of Italian Women in New York City, 1900–1950.* Ithaca, NY: Cornell University Press, 1993.

Cohen, Patricia C. *The Murder of Helen Jewett.* New York: Vintage, 1998.

Cott, Nancy. *The Bonds of Womanhood.* New Haven: Yale University Press, 1977.

———. *The Grounding of Modern Feminism.* New Haven: Yale University Press, 1987.

———. *Public Vows: A History of Marriage and the Nation.* Cambridge, MA: Harvard University Press, 2000.

Daley, Caroline, and Melanie Nolan, eds. *Suffrage and Beyond: International Feminist Perspectives.* New York: New York University Press, 1994.

Dayton, Cornelia. *Women before the Bar: Gender, Law and Society in Connecticut, 1639–1789.* Chapel Hill: University of North Carolina, 1995.

Des Jardins, Julie. *Women and the Historical Enterprise in America: Gender, Race, and the Politics of Memory 1880–1945.* Chapel Hill: University of North Carolina, 2003.

Deutsch, Sarah. *No Separate Refuge: Culture, Class, and Gender on an Anglo Hispanic Frontier in the American Southwest, 1880–1940.* New York: Oxford University Press, 1987.

Diner, Hasia. *Erin's Daughters in America: Irish Immigrant Women in the Nineteenth Century.* Baltimore: Johns Hopkins University Press, 1983.

Dorsey, Bruce. *Reforming Men and Women: Gender in the Antebellum City.* Ithaca, NY: Cornell University Press, 2002.

Drachman, Virginia D. *Sisters in Law: Women Lawyers in Modern American History.* Cambridge: Cambridge University Press, 1998.

Dublin, Thomas. *Women at Work: The Transformation of Work and Community in Lowell, Massachusetts, 1826–1860*. New York: Columbia University Press, 1979.

DuBois, Ellen, and Vicki L. Ruiz. *Unequal Sisters: A Multicultural Reader in U.S. Women's History*, 3rd ed. New York: Routledge, 2000.

DuBois, Ellen *Feminism and Suffrage: The Emergence of an Independent Women's Movement in America*. Ithaca, NY: Cornell University Press, 1999.

DuBois, Ellen , ed. *Elizabeth Cady Stanton-Susan B. Anthony: Correspondence, Writings, Speeches*. New York: Schocken Books, 1981.

DuBois, Ellen, and Lynn Dumenil. *Through Women's Eyes: An American History with Documents*. Boston: Bedford St. Martin's, 2005.

Dudden, Faye. *Serving Women: Household Service in Nineteenth Century America*. Middletown, CT: Wesleyan University Press, 1983.

Edwards, Laura F. *Scarlett Doesn't Live Here Anymore: Southern Women in the Civil War Era*. Urbana: University of Illinois Press, 2000.

Enstad, Nan. *Ladies of Labor, Girls of Adventure: Working Women, Popular Culture, and Labor Politics at the Turn of the Twentieth Century*. New York: Columbia University Press, 1999.

Evans, Sara. *Born for Liberty: A History of Women in America*. New York: Free Press, 1989.

Faragher, John Mack. *Women and Men on the Overland Trail*. New Haven: Yale University Press, 1979.

Farnham, Christie Anne, ed. *Women of the American South: A Multicultural Reader*. New York: New York University Press, 1997.

Faust, Drew G. *Mothers of Invention: Women of the Slaveholding South in the American Civil War*. New York: Vintage, 1997.

Finnegan, Mary Margaret. *Selling Suffrage: Consumer Culture and Votes for Women*. New York: Columbia University Press, 1999.

Forbes, Ella. *African American Women during the Civil War*. New York: Garland, 2000.

Fox-Genovese, Elizabeth. *Within the Plantation Household: Black and White Women of the Old South*. Chapel Hill: University of North Carolina Press, 1988.

Freedmen, Estelle B. *No Turning Back: The History of Feminism and the Future of Women*. New York: Ballantine, 2002.

———. *The Essential Feminist Reader*. New York: Modern Library, 2007.

Gabaccia, Donna. *From the Other Side: Women, Gender, and Immigrant Life in the United States, 1820–1990*. Bloomington: University of Indiana Press, 1994.

Gilfoyle, Timothy. *City of Eros: New York City, Prostitution, and the Commercialization of Sex, 1790–1920*. New York: W. W. Norton, 1992.

Gilmore, Glenda Elizabeth. *Gender and Jim Crow: Women and the Politics of White Supremacy in North Carolina, 1896–1920*. Chapel Hill: University of North Carolina, 1996.

Ginzberg, Lori D. *Women and the Work of Benevolence: Morality, Politics, and Class in the 19th-Century United States*. New Haven: Yale University Press, 1990.

Ginzberg, Lori D. *Women in Antebellum Reform*. Wheeling, IL: Harlan Davidson, 2000.

Glenn, Evelyn Nakano. *Unequal Freedom: How Race and Gender Shaped American Citizenship.* Cambridge: Harvard University Press, 2002.

Glenn, Susan A. *Daughters of the Shtetl: Life and Labor in the Immigrant Generation.* Ithaca, NY: Cornell University Press, 1990.

Green, Elna. *Southern Strategies: Southern Women and the Woman Suffrage Question.* Chapel Hill: University of North Carolina Press, 1997.

Hendricks, Wanda A. *Gender, Race, and Politics in the Midwest: Black Clubwomen in Illinois.* Bloomington: University of Indiana Press, 1998.

Hewitt, Nancy A., ed. *A Companion to American Women's History.* Malden, MA: Blackwell, 2004.

Higginbotham, Evelyn Brooks. *Righteous Discontent: The Women's Movement in the Black Baptist Church, 1880–1920.* Cambridge: Harvard University Press, 1993.

Hine, Darlene Clark. *Shining Thread of Hope: The History of Black Women in America.* New York: Broadway, 1998.

Hoffert, Sylvia D. *When Hens Crow: The Women's Rights Movement in Antebellum America.* Bloomington: University of Indiana Press, 1995.

Horowitz, Helen Lefkowitz. *Alma Mater: Design and Experience in the Women's Colleges from Their Nineteenth-Century Beginnings to the 1930s.* New York: Knopf, 1984.

Hune, Shirley, and Gail Nomura, eds. *Asian/Pacific Islander American Women: An Historical Anthology.* New York: New York University Press, 2003.

Hunter, Tera. *To 'Joy My Freedom: Southern Black Women's Lives and Labor after the Civil War.* Cambridge: Harvard University Press, 1997.

Isenberg, Nancy. *Sex and Citizenship in Antebellum America.* Chapel Hill: University of North Carolina Press, 1998.

Jameson, Elizabeth, and Susan Armitage, eds. *Writing the Range: Race, Class, and Culture in the Women's West.* Norman: University of Oklahoma Press, 1997.

Jeffrey, Julie Roy. *Frontier Women: "Civilizing the West?" 1840–1880*, rev. ed. New York: Hill & Wang, 1998.

———. *The Great Silent Army of Abolitionism: Ordinary Women in the Antislavery Movement.* Chapel Hill: University of North Carolina Press, 1998.

Jensen, Joan M. *Loosening the Bonds: Mid-Atlantic Farm Women 1750–1850* (New Haven: Yale University Press, 1986).

Johnson, David K. *The Lavender Scare: The Cold War Persecution of Gays and Lesbians in the Federal Government.* Chicago: University of Chicago Press, 2004.

Jones, Jacqueline. *Labor of Love, Labor of Sorrow: Black Women, Work and the Family from Slavery to the Present.* New York: Basic Books, 1985.

Karlsen, Carol. *The Devil in the Shape of a Woman: Witchcraft in Colonial New England.* New York: Vintage, 1987.

Kerber, Linda. *Women of the Republic: Intellect and Ideology in Revolutionary America.* Chapel Hill: University of North Carolina, 1980.

Kerber, Linda K., and Jane Sherron DeHart, eds. *Women's America: Refocusing the Past.* New York: Oxford University Press, 1991.

Kessler-Harris, Alice. *Out to Work: A History of Wage-Earning Women in the United States.* New York: Oxford University Press, 1982.

————. *In Pursuit of Equity: Women, Men and the Quest for Economic Citizenship in 20th-Century America*. New York: Oxford University Press, 2001.

————. *Gendering Labor History*. Urbana: University of Illinois Press, 2007.

Klein, Laura F., and Lillian Ackerman, eds. *Women and Power in Native North America*. Norman: University of Oklahoma Press, 1995.

Knupfer, Anne Meis. *Toward a Tenderer Humanity and a Nobler Womanhood: African American Women's Clubs of the South and the Advancement of the Race, 1895–1925*. New York: New York University Press, 1996.

Kupperman, Karen. *Indians and English Facing Off in Early America*. Ithaca. NY: Cornell University Press, 2000.

Lasch-Quinn, Elizabeth. *Black Neighbors: Race and the Limits of Reform in the American Settlement House Movement, 1890–1945*. Chapel Hill: University of North Carolina Press, 1993.

Leonard, Elizabeth D. *Yankee Women: Gender Battles in the Civil War*. New York: W. W. Norton, 1994.

————. *All the Daring of the Soldier: Women of the Civil War Armies*. New York: W. W. Norton, 1999.

Lerner, Gerda. *The Majority Finds Its Past: Placing Women in History*. Chapel Hill: University of North Carolina Press, 2005.

Lovett, Laura. *Conceiving the Future: Pronatalism, Reproduction, and the Family in the United States, 1890–1938*. Chapel Hill: University of North Carolina Press, 2007.

Matthews, Glenna. *American Women's History: A Student Companion*. New York: Oxford University Press, 2000.

Matthews, Jean. *Women's Struggle for Equality: The First Phase, 1828–1876*. Chicago: University of Chicago Press, 1997.

McBride, Genevieve. *On Wisconsin Women: Working for Their Rights from Settlement to Suffrage*. Madison: University of Wisconsin Press, 1993.

McCurry, Stephanie. *Masters of Small Worlds: Yeoman Households, Gender Relations, and the Political Culture of the South Carolina Low Country*. New York: Oxford University Press, 1995.

Mead, Rebecca J. *How the Vote Was Won: Woman Suffrage in the Western United States*. New York: New York University Press, 2004.

Meyerowitz, Joanne. *Women Adrift: Independent Wage Earners in Chicago, 1880–1920*. Chicago: University of Chicago Press, 1988.

————. *How Sex Changed: A History of Trans-Sexuality in the United States*. Cambridge: Harvard University Press, 2002.

Morantz-Sanchez, Regina Markell. *Sympathy and Science: Women Physicians in American Medicine*. New York: Oxford University Press, 1985.

Morgan, Jennifer L. *Laboring Women: Reproduction and Gender in New World Slavery*. Philadelphia: University of Pennsylvania Press, 2004.

Morton, Marian J. *Emma Goldman and the American Left: "Nowhere at Home."* New York: Twayne, 1992.

Norton, Mary Beth. *Liberty's Daughters: The Revolutionary Experience of American Women*. Boston: Little Brown, 1980.

Painter, Nell Irvin. *Sojourner Truth: A Life, a Symbol.* New York: W. W. Norton, 1996.

Peiss, Kathy. *Hope in a Jar: The Making of America's Beauty Culture.* New York: Metropolitan, 1998.

———. *Cheap Amusements: Working Women and Leisure in Turn-of-the-Century New York.* Philadelphia: Temple University Press, 1999.

Perdue, Theda, ed. *Sifters: Native American Women's Lives.* New York: Oxford University Press, 2001.

Pfeffer, George Anthony. *If They Don't Bring Their Women Here: Chinese Female Immigration before Exclusion.* Urbana: University of Illinois Press, 1999.

Plane, Ann. *Colonial Intimacies: Indian Marriage in Early New England.* Ithaca, NY: Cornell University Press, 2000.

Ransby, Barbara. *Ella Baker and the Black Freedom Movement.* Chapel Hill: University of North Carolina Press, 2003.

Rosen, Ruth. *The World Split Open: How the Modern Women's Movement Changed America.* New York: Penguin, 2001.

Rosenberg, Rosalind. *Beyond Separate Spheres: Intellectual Roots of Modern Feminism.* New Haven: Yale University Press, 1982.

———. *Divided Lives: American Women in the Twentieth Century,* rev. ed. New York: Hill and Wang, 2008.

Ruether, Rosemary Radford, and Rosemary Skinner Keller, eds. *Women and Religion in America.* 3 vols. San Francisco: Harper and Row, 1981–1986.

Ruiz, Vicki L. *Cannery Women, Cannery Lives: Mexican Women, Unionization, and the California Food Processing Industry, 1930–1950.* Albuquerque: University of New Mexico Press, 1987.

Ruiz, Vicki L., and Ellen Carol DuBois, eds. *Unequal Sisters: A Multicultural Reader in U.S. Women's History,* 3d ed. New York: Routledge, 1999.

Ruiz, Vicki L., and Virginia Sanchez-Korrol, eds. *Latina Legacies: Identity, Biography and Community.* New York: Oxford University Press, 2005.

Rupp, Leila. *Worlds of Women: The Making of an International Women's Movement.* Princeton, NJ: Princeton University Press, 1997.

Ryan, Mary. *Women in Public: Between Banners and Ballots, 1825–1880.* Baltimore: Johns Hopkins University Press, 1990.

Schlissel, Lillan, Byrd Gibbens, and Elizabeth Hampsten. *Far from Home: Families of the Westward Journey.* New York: Schocken, 1989.

Schlissel, Lillian, Vicki L. Ruiz, and Janice Monk, eds. *Western Women. Their Land, Their Lives.* Albuquerque: University of New Mexico Press, 1988.

Schultz, Jane E. *Women at the Front: Hospital Workers in Civil War America.* Chapel Hill: University of North Carolina Press, 2004.

Scott, Ann Firor. *Natural Allies: Women's Associations in American History.* Urbana: University of Illinois Press, 1991.

Shaw, Stephanie G. *What a Woman Ought to Be and Do: Black Professional Women Workers during the Jim Crow Era.* Chicago: University of Chicago Press, 1996.

Sherr, Lynn, and Jurate Kazickas. *Susan B. Anthony Slept Here: A Guide to American Women's Landmarks.* New York: Times, 1994.

Shoemaker, Nancy, ed. *Negotiators of Change: Historical Perspectives on Native American Women*. New York: Routledge, 1995.

Sinha, Mrinalini Sinha, Donna Guy, and Angela Woollacott. *Feminisms and Internationalism*. Oxford: Blackwell, 1999.

Smith, Barbara, et al., eds. *The Reader's Companion to US Women's History*. Boston: Houghton Mifflin, 1998.

Smith, Bonnie G., ed. *Global Feminisms since 1945*. London: Routledge, 2000.

———. *Women's History in Global Perspective, Vols. 1–3*. Urbana: University of Illinois Press, 2004, 2005.

Sneider, Allison L. *Suffragists in an Imperial Age: U.S. Expansion and the Woman Question 1870–1929*. New York: Oxford University Press, 2008.

Solinger, Rickie. *Wake Up Little Susie: Single Pregnancy and Race before Roe v. Wade*. New York: Routledge, 1992.

Solomon, Barbara Miller. *In the Company of Educated Women: A History of Women and Higher Education in America*. New Haven: Yale University Press, 1985.

Stansell, Christine. *City of Women: Sex and Class in New York, 1789–1860*. Urbana: University of Illinois Press, 1986.

Stevenson, Brenda. *Life in Black and White: Family and Community in the Slave South*. New York: Oxford University Press, 1996.

Szczygiel, Bonj, Josephine Carubia, and Lorraine Dowler, eds. *Gender Landscapes: An Interdisciplinary Exploration of Past Space and Place*. University Park: Pennsylvania State University Press, 2000.

Terborg-Penn, Rosalyn. *African American Women in the Struggle for the Vote, 1850–1920*. Bloomington: University of Indiana Press, 1998.

Tong, Benson. *Unsubmissive Women: Chinese Prostitutes in Nineteenth-Century San Francisco*. Norman: University of Oklahoma Press, 1994.

Ulrich, Laurel Thatcher. *Good Wives: Image and Reality in the Lives of Women in Northern New England, 1650–1750*. New York: Oxford University Press, 1982.

———. *A Midwife's Tale: The Life of Martha Ballard, Based on Her Diary, 1785–1812*. New York: Vintage, 1991.

Van Burkleo, Sandra. *"Belonging to the World": Women's Rights and American Constitutional Culture*. New York: Oxford University Press, 2001.

Walters, Ronald G. *American Reformers: 1815–1860*, rev. ed. New York: Hill and Wang, 1978/1997.

Washington, Margaret, ed. *A Narrative of Sojourner Truth*. New York: Vintage, 1993.

Weiner, Lynn Y. *From Working Girl to Working Mother: The Female Labor Force in the United States, 1820–1980*. Chapel Hill: University of North Carolina Press, 1985.

Weisenfeld, Judith. *African-American Women and Christian Activism: New York's Black YWCA, 1905–1945*. Cambridge: Harvard University Press, 1997.

Wheeler, Marjorie Spruill, ed. *Votes for Women! The Woman Suffrage Movement in Tennessee, the South, and the Nation*. Knoxville: University of Tennessee Press, 1995.

White, Deborah Gray. *Ar'n't I a Woman? Female Slaves in the Plantation South*, rev. ed. New York: W. W. Norton, 1999.

Wolfe, Margaret Ripley. *Daughters of Canaan: A Saga of Southern Women.* Lexington: University Press of Kentucky, 1995.

Woloch, Nancy. *Women and the American Experience,* 6th ed. Boston: McGraw-Hill, 2006.

Yee, Shirley. *Black Women Abolitionists: A Study in Activism, 1828–1860.* Knoxville: University of Tennessee Press, 1992.

Yellin, Jean Fagan. *Women and Sisters: Antislavery Feminists in American Culture.* New Haven: Yale University Press, 1990.

Yellin, Jean Fagan, and John C. Van Horne, eds. *The Abolitionist Sisterhood: Women's Political Culture in Antebellum America.* Ithaca, NY: Cornell University Press, 1994.

Yung, Judy. *Unbound Feet: A Social History of Chinese Women in San Francisco.* Berkeley: University of California Press, 1995.

BOOK CHAPTERS AND ARTICLES

Alonso, Harriet Hyman. "Jane Addams: Thinking and Acting Locally and Globally." *Journal of Women's History* 16.1 (2004): 148–164.

Bederman, Gail. " 'The Women Have Had Charge of the Church Work Long Enough': The Men and Religion Forward Movement of 1911–1912 and the Masculinization of Middle-Class Protestantism." *American Quarterly* 41.3 (September 1989): 432–465.

Frederickson, Mary. "Surveying Gender: Another Look at the Way We Teach United States History." *History Teacher* (August 2004): 476–483.

Hill, Patricia R. "Rethinking New Thought." *Reviews in American History* 29.1 (March 2001): 85–92.

Kerber, Linda K. "The Meanings of Citizenship." *Journal of American History* 84 (December 1997): 833–854.

Leach, William. "Transformations in a Culture of Consumption: Women and Department Stores, 1890–1925." *Journal of American History* 71.2 (September 1984): 319–342.

Scott, Joan W. "Gender: A Useful Category of Historical Analysis." *American Historical Review* 91.5 (December 1986): 1053–1075.

Smith, Rogers M. " 'One United People' Second-Class Female Citizenship and the American Quest for Community." *Yale Journal of Law & the Humanities* 1 (May 1989): 229–293.

The Queer Issue: New Visions of America's Lesbian and Gay Past. *Radical History Review* 62 (Spring 1995).

WEBSITES

American Memory Project. "African-American Odyssey." Library of Congress. http://memory.loc.gov/ammem/aaohtml.

———. "Prairie Settlement: Nebraska Photographs and Family Letters." Library of Congress. http://memory.loc.gov/ammem/award98/nbhihtml/pshome.html.

American Social History Project. "History Matters: The U.S. Survey Course on the Web." Center for Media and Learning, Graduate Center, CUNY, and Center for History and News Media, George Mason University. http://historymatters.gmu.edu.

American Women: A Gateway to Library of Congress Resources for the Study of Women's History and Culture in the United States. Library of Congress. http://memory.loc.gov/ammem/awhhtml/awgateway.html.

"American Women's History: A Research Guide." Middleton, Ken. Middle Tennessee State University Library. http://www.mtsu.edu/~kmiddlet/history/women.html.

"Captivity Narrative of Mary Rowlandson": http://womenshistory.about.com/gi/dynamic/offsite.htm?site=http://digital.library.upenn.edu/webbin/gutbook/lookup?num=851.

"Do History." Harvard University. http://www.dohistory.org.

EDSITEment: "The Best of the Humanities on the Web." National Endowment for the Humanities. www.edsitement.neh.gov.

"The Emma Goldman Papers." Candice Falk. University of California, Berkeley. http://sunsite.berkeley.edu/Goldman/.

"Feminist Perspectives on the Self." Meyers, Diana. *Stanford Encyclopedia of Philosophy*. Stanford University Press, 2004. http://plato.stanford.edu/entries/feminism-self.

"First-Person Narratives of the American South." University of North Carolina, Chapel Hill, NC. http://docsouth.unc.edu/fpn/. Also available at: http://memory.loc.gov/ammem/award97/ncuhtml/fpnashome.html.

H-Women Board of Editors. "H-Women Discussion Network." H-Net: Humanities and Social Sciences Online. http://www.h-net.org/~women.

National Women's History Project. http://www.nwhp.org.

Salem Witchcraft Trials Documents: http://etext.lib.virginia.edu/salem/witchcraft/.

Sarah Osborn Recollects Her Experiences in the Revolutionary War, 1837: http://historymatters.gmu.edu/d/5833/.

Selected Women and Gender Resources on the World Wide Web. Weisband, Phyllis Holman. University of Wisconsin Libraries. http://www.library.wisc.edu/libraries/womensstudies/others.htm.

"The Triangle Factory Fire." Cornell University's School of Industrial and Labor Relations. http://www.ilr.cornell.edu/trianglefire/.

The United Nations Commission on the Status of Women: 60 Years of Work for Equality, Development and Peace. http://www.un.org/womenwatch/daw/CSW60YRS/index.htm.

"Using Online Resources to Re-Center the U.S. History Survey: Women's History as a Case Study." Lindenmeyer, Kriste. *Journal of American History* 89, no. 4 (2003): 1483–1844. http://www.historycooperative.org/.

"The Valley of the Shadow." University of Virginia http://jefferson.village.virginia.edu/vshadow2.

"WestWeb: Making It on Their Own: Women in the West." Catherine Lavendar, College of Staten Island Library. http://www.library.csi.cuny.edu/westweb/pages/women.html.

Women of South Carolina in the American Revolution: http://sciway3.net/clark/
    revolutionarywar/womenofrevolution.html.
Women's Bibliographic Resource List II. National Archives and Records
    Administration Archives Library Information Center (ALIC). http://www
    .archives.gov/research/alic/reference/women-supplemental.html.

Index

CPSIA information can be obtained
at www.ICGtesting.com
Printed in the USA
LVOW12s0538110917
548235LV00002B/8/P